ARTICLES
OF WAR

The Spectator Book of
World War II

Companion Volume

Views from Abroad: The Spectator *Book of Travel Writing*
Edited by Philip Marsden-Smedley and Jeffrey Klinke

ARTICLES OF WAR

The Spectator Book of World War II

*Edited by Fiona Glass
and Philip Marsden-Smedley*

Foreword by Ludovic Kennedy

GRAFTON BOOKS
A Division of the Collins Publishing Group

LONDON GLASGOW
TORONTO SYDNEY AUCKLAND

Grafton Books
A Division of the Collins Publishing Group
8 Grafton Street, London W1X 3LA

Published by Grafton Books 1989

British Library Cataloguing in Publication Data
Articles of war: the Spectator book of
World War II
1. World War 2 — Biographies — Collections
I. Marsden-Smedley, Philip.
II. Glass, Fiona   III. The Spectator
940.54′8

ISBN 0-246-13394-5

Typeset by Ace Filmsetting Ltd, Frome, Somerset
Printed in Great Britain by
William Collins Sons & Co. Ltd, Glasgow

CONTENTS

Part Six 1944

FOREWORD

by Ludovic Kennedy

This collection of articles, diary notes and poems from *The Spectator* covers the years 1938–45 (though pieces about the war that appeared later have also sensibly been included); and those of us who remember the period will find the changes in attitude and language that have taken place in the half century since particularly striking.

The death of the essay, for instance. Who today, writing about the likelihood of imminent war, would dream of opening, as 'Strategicus' did in June 1939: 'For a fortnight or more we have been enjoying to a degree rare in this capricious climate the unclouded glories of an English summer.'

Then there was the *de haut en bas* attitude, now thankfully obsolete, from which few leader-writers were immune and which found expression in pieties like this, written soon after war had broken out: 'All classes, it is earnestly to be hoped, will from the first cultivate a rigid simplicity of life, both for its moral value and as a means of avoiding unnecessary expenditure – particularly on such things as alcohol, tobacco and cosmetics.'

Other things strike one: the custom of referring to the Führer as *Herr* Hitler (rather than Chancellor Hitler), presumably to belittle him; the extraordinary certainty of victory from quite early on, first voiced by Osbert Sitwell in November 1939 and reiterated in a leader soon after Dunkirk: 'We see no possibility of Germany defeating us'; and then, only two years later and before the tide had begun to turn, the publication of the Beveridge Report with its promise of a National Health service and old-age pensions 'after the war' – a phrase that crops up time and again.

One notices too the high moral tone. The German bombing of the suburbs of Paris in June 1940 was 'a wanton violation of the rules of war': our lads would never bomb anything but military targets and, when they couldn't find any, would bring their bombs back. By war's end we had razed Hamburg, Dresden and most of Berlin to the ground, with – to our surprise – hardly a dent in German morale or war production. But self-delusion was often the order of the day. After Russia had become Britain's ally, Sir Bernard Pares could write of Stalin as a statesman who after the war would protect the rights of small nations such as Poland and Czechoslovakia.

Running like a thread throughout the book and giving it a unity it might otherwise lack are selections from Harold Nicolson's weekly column, at first called 'People and Things', later 'Marginal Comment'. His urbane reflections on the war and wartime life nicely mirrored the times. One week he would relate how more than 65,000 children evacuated from London were found to be verminous and that many had never had a hot meal or seen a vegetable in their lives; the next he would sum up the significance of General de Gaulle or describe how the cinema had removed the barriers between the known and the unknown, thus impoverishing the imaginations of the young. In one 'Marginal Comment' which I recall causing a stir at the time, he declared that works of art were more important than human lives and that he would not hesitate to sacrifice his sons if by doing so St Mark's could be saved. In *The Spectator* fifteen years later his son Nigel recorded that he had received this news 'with mixed feelings', as well he might.

Among the rest are many riches: Robert Byron's absorbing account of visiting Munich in 1938 with Unity Mitford and the Redesdales; Robert Kee's acute assessment of Richard Hillary; Mavis Tate on Buchenwald; Leonard Cheshire, VC, OM (the only man ever to hold both decorations) on the preparations for dropping the bomb on Nagasaki; General von Schweppenburg and Colin Welch on different aspects of the Normandy campaign; Graham Greene on the falsity and fatuity of newsreel commentaries; and a war poem by Joe Ackerley which, if not quite in the class of Owen and Sassoon, is certainly not far from it. All in all, a most entertaining and informative collection.

EDITORS' PREFACE

At the outbreak of war, the then Editor of *The Spectator*, H. Wilson Harris, was faced with 'loss of staff, loss of contributors, loss of advertisements, loss of revenue, loss of circulation, [and] a severe rationing of paper' ('*The Spectator* in Wartime', 11 October 1940). In spite of these difficulties the thinner *Spectator*, twenty-four pages as compared with forty-eight pre-war, increased in circulation. The Editor writes buoyantly of finding one day at the offices in Gower Street that 'nothing more was wrong than shattered windows, blown-in doors, and no gas'; and concludes that 'any moment may bring a new crisis, but there will always be some way round it'.

The wartime *Spectator* did not attempt to bring its readers up-to-the-minute despatches from the Front. There was a weekly article by 'Strategicus' (H.C. O'Neill) which summarised and analysed the military situation. 'News of the Week' dealt with recent foreign and domestic developments, and Harold Nicolson provided his unfailingly thoughtful and elegantly written 'People and Things', which later became 'Marginal Comment'. In addition there was a leading article, four middle articles, letters and reviews, and 'Country Life' by H.E. Bates.

In editing this selection, we felt that where *The Spectator* really shone was in conveying the experiences and feelings of those who were living through the war at home. Since military histories are available we have only included Strategicus' articles on moments of immense national importance. For the post-war generation, the war is slipping into history. Our parents knew what it was like, but we don't. We have tried to concentrate on those pieces, or letters, or poems, which give a strong sense of personal experience. H.E. Bates discovered that the war had 'smashed the silence of the English railway carriage' ('Fellow Passengers', 18 October 1940). Julian Huxley found himself pursuing a Grevy zebra around Regent's Park after an air-raid had released it ('Air-Raids and the Zoo', 1 November 1940). Rose Macaulay writes poignantly of what it is like to lose all one's books (and one's home) in an air-raid, and have to make 'a list of books I had had; that is the saddest list' ('Losing One's Books', 7 November 1941). We have also tried to show what else was occupying people's minds. From as early as 1942 onwards there was increasing interest in planning for a post-war Britain, in health, housing, education, and town-planning. Some writers, like Hamilton Kerr in 'London 1970' (21 July 1944), saw great opportunities for rebuilding a better city after the bombing – some, alas, still waiting to be grasped.

Several contributors are well known, but this was not a criterion for our choice, and many famous people wrote dull pieces which we did not include. We left out many wonderful articles which had nothing to do with the war – notably Graham Greene's film reviews – with great reluctance.

We have divided the material chronologically, to give a sense of the progress of the war and people's changing attitudes, and to follow a limited number of themes. Apart from the Prelude, the sections cover each year of the war, until the last one which contains portraits of leading wartime figures. Post-war reminiscences have been put in where they fit chronologically, to give a better flow to the book.

Fiona Glass
Philip Marsden-Smedley
October 1988

Part One
1938–1939
PRELUDE TO WAR

NUREMBERG, 1938: THE FINAL RALLY

Robert Byron

In September 1938, at the height of the Czechoslovak crisis, the travel writer and journalist Robert Byron attended the Nazis' last Party Day rally at Nuremberg with Hitler's friend Unity Mitford. He had long realised the danger to peace of the Nazi ideology, and from March 1938 was engaged in voluntary preparation of war propaganda for the Director Designate of the future Ministry of Information. By persuading Unity Mitford to include him as a guest at the 1938 rally he hoped to observe the impact of the Nazis on parade.

On his return from this visit Byron wrote: 'There can be no compromise with these people – there is no room in the world for them and me, and one has got to go. I trust it may be them.' He did not live to see them go. While on an intelligence mission he was lost at sea by enemy action on his way back to Meshed, Iran, early in 1941.

As German pressure mounted on Prague for political self-determination for three million Sudeten Germans resident in Czechoslovakia, Byron went first to Munich to meet Unity and the Mitford parents, Lord and Lady Redesdale.

Monday 29 August 1938
While I was lunching at Arthur's [club] with Tom [Mitford], worm Halifax [Foreign Secretary], worm [Sir John] Simon [Chancellor of the Exchequer] and worm [Sir Nevile] Henderson [British Ambassador in Berlin] all came and sat down at the next table looking very contented. I could hardly go on with my food.

Meanwhile, with Franco's reply and proposal for withdrawal of troops and consequent evaporation of the Anglo-Italian 'agreement'[1], worm [Neville] Chamberlain's policy of 'appeasement' has vanished into a wisp of fog; it has not only failed and in the process accelerated the prospect of war; it has vanished altogether, leaving us rudderless as before but now in much narrower waters.

Now I am on my way to the *Parteitag* at Nürnberg to see if I can find

[1]Signed in April 1938, conditional on the withdrawal of Italian troops from Spain.

some evidence to modify the above opinions. I was to have gone straight out with Tom, but at the last moment he could not get away, owing to the Advocate General [Sir Henry MacGeagh] being ill, and rather than arrive at Nürnberg alone, I have come on in advance to join Unity and the Redesdales in Munich. Whether I shall be welcome at Nürnberg or even find a bed, I don't know. Both at the Embassy in London and at the Amt für Ehrengäste in Berlin I am on the list of *Ehrengäste* [honoured guests]. But I have had no invitation. On the other hand neither has Tom.

The stations along the line are all decorated against the festival. But in general I seem to observe a shabbiness and deterioration very different from the Germany of 12 years ago. (I was last in Bavaria in 1926.) Some say this is my imagination. The total absence of colour in the landscape strikes me again vividly.

3 September

Sitting in a train between Ansbach and Munich, in the heart of the enemy country so to speak, I recall the unfolding of the danger to me personally. I am not talking of philosophical considerations – a prescient man might have foretold the present situation when Mussolini bombarded Corfu ('23) and the Nazis came to power in '33. These were the concrete stages as I felt them:

1. *1929–35.* Another war 'impossible'.
2. *Summer 1935.* Another war 'possible'.
3. *Autumn 1935.* War with Italy likely.
4. *Autumn 1936* (on my return from China). Ashamed of my country and worried that she should have thrown away her moral strength. Felt, as a person of military age, that I should now be called on to fight, not for any apprehensible purpose, but because Baldwin, [Samuel] Hoare, Eden had made a muddle.
5. *February 1938.* Eden's resignation robs our foreign policy of last vestige of direction. Wonder if it is possible to bring the Government to its senses by organising boycott of state services on part of all people under 40 (not a practical idea, but that is what I thought).
6. *March 1938.* The rape of Austria. Too late. War now inevitable. But pray I may be wrong and Chamberlain's policy of appeasement may work out.
7. *May 21, 1938.* Ray of hope. HMG (accidentally I believe owing to the train-myth and Ribbentrop's [German foreign secretary] skill in antagonising Sir Nevile Henderson) warns Germany not to expect English neutrality if she invades Czechoslovakia. A salutary effect on German public opinion. (I am in Berlin for Whitsun.)

8. *August 1938.* Vast German manoeuvres, interpreted as prelude to invasion of Czechoslovakia.

9. *August 22, 1938.* The worm Simon in a speech at Lanark reminds Germany of England's inability to be neutral, though in as minor and unconvincing a key as possible. But snarls of rage from Berlin press show that this was more effective than I expected.

5 September

Reached Regina Palast 1.40. Bobo [Unity Mitford] had gone to the station to meet me, but was soon back. Found Redesdales lunching at Haus der Deutschen Kunst, one of the Führer's new buildings. Very plain classical, but I can't make out about the stone – whether it is of the stone here, a porous flaky stuff like compressed white gravel, that marks very uglily – or of concrete.

Then motored out to Nymphenburg to see the Amalienburg; the blue and silver room and the yellow and silver one adjoining are *masterpieces.* Dined, with our food on our knees, at the Platzl – fearful crowd – Lord Redesdale and Bobo had to go on an hour in advance to claim the table, or rather four places at it, that they had ordered the day before. Bobo said the only time she had ever been comfortable there was when she was with [Julius] Streicher [mayor of Nuremberg]. Very amusing performance, yodellers, playlets etc. Very Bavarian, the whole playlet making fun of Prussian visitors and jokes at the régime, but impossible to understand, being in such broad dialect, a song ending up with the word *gouffa* – meaning drunk, at which everyone linked arms and rocked. Then looked in at the gigantic Hofbräu opposite, where everyone was a good deal drunker (it was Saturday evening), scene of the Party's early exploits, and so to bed. I spent an hour in the Regina bar watching the *jeunesse dorée* sipping sweet cocktails through straws.

In the afternoon we looked into an Altdorfer exhibition of appallingly bad paintings – either forgeries or he was an appallingly bad painter, but the ugliness and cruelty of German painting of that period, when not redeemed by *art*, is horrible – and explains much. Yesterday, Sunday, I was out early and went a round of the churches, the Frauenkirche very fine – vast Gothic – in every one sermons going on, or rather announcements from the pulpits in which I heard frequent references to schools – churches all *packed*, gigantic as they are.

Back to hotel to find all English papers confiscated. Bobo drove me to Pinakothek. But first we made a detour to see if the Führer is back. No – she can tell by there being no one outside the very unpretentious building in which his flat is situated. Then to gallery. A lot of familiar Rapha-

els – acres of gigantic Rubens – fine Filippo Lippi and an unattractive
Botticelli pietà. A fine El Greco 'Divestment', smaller than the Toledo
one and less colour – fine Titians of woman and Charles V in a chair –
lovely Tiepolo. But all in bad condition, varnish dull and spotty, colours
obscured.

To lunch at the Osteria [Bavaria], a little *bürgerlich* restaurant which
the Führer got into the habit of using when the Party headquarters were
nearby and where Bobo first met him by staring (story of hat peg not true).
Bobo took her seat in the Führer's place. Otherwise ordinary middle-class
families having their midday lunch.

Bobo said [Dr Ernst] Hanfstaengl's [formerly in charge of foreign Press
relations] escapade was due to her. He was always such a bore saying he
had a much more dangerous time in the war by staying in America, where
people threw bricks through his window, that sitting in the
Reichskanzlei in Berlin one day she suggested to the Führer to send him
to Spain. So he was popped into an aeroplane as a practical joke and they
landed at Leipzig – but he got it into his head that they were trying to
murder him, rushed back here, tried to get hold of his sister, failed and
fled to Zurich.

Lord and Lady Redesdale came in and found us, she saying she had
been to church. Bobo disgusted – but confident she will not behave in
such a way after the *Parteitag*.

Delicious sweet wine *en carafe* – lunch off blue trout – Redesdales drive
off to Nürnberg. Bobo and I go for walk in English Gardens and have tea
in the Chinese Tower. I start on Foreign Policy, saying that it is up to Germany to obey the principles of *Mein Kampf*, one of which is to keep England sweet while expanding in East. On this view, German diplomacy
very poor. Bobo takes the view, it is all England's fault. I say it may be, but
that is not the point – conditions are deteriorating. She says she is confident there will be no general war, because it would be the ruin of the Führer's whole life and policy – if one of his new buildings was bombed, it
would nearly kill him. War hate in England due entirely to the fact that
England (and the rest of the world for that matter) is the wholesale victim
of propaganda, and this run by Jews who have every reason for wanting to
make war on Germany. Also partly fault of Conservative Party who had
to create a war feeling in order to get re-armament. We agree (though for
different reasons) on subject of present government: though whereas I
say I should be glad to press a button and feel they had vanished, but not
actually shoot them myself, Bobo wants to shoot them personally. She
now has a gun which she keeps by her bed loaded and when she was in
hospital the other day, they were all frightened lest she should get delirious and fire it off – she *wants* to shoot a man. I said I thought she should

shoot a woman first, so as not to be accused of being a feminist – then she said she would be accused of being a lesbian.

I said that though Eden may have been the greater enemy of Germany, I thought from the German point of view his resignation a pity, because he was the only person who rendered English policy slightly calculable. I did not blame Germans for not knowing what English policy is, because no one ever takes the trouble to explain it to them – all they hear is Lord Londonderry [Minister for Air 1931–1935]. Bobo hates him, so agreed. I said I thought relations would be better if they could calculate what they were dealing with and read her the preliminary passages of Sir Eyre Crowe.[2] She was impressed by this last but still said it was all our fault for rejecting overtures and offers of German alliance. She says Führer may be risking a few years' temporary estrangement with England by doing what he knows to be *right* over Austria and Czechoslovakia, but alliance will come in the end, the whole racial doctrine postulates it, and anyhow Germany will now be so powerful that England will sue for an alliance. She admitted Führer had made one mistake by sending Ribbentrop to England [as ambassador] – she said that, though she was certain there would be no war, it wouldn't matter to her (as a German) if it did, because she knew Germany was 'destined' to win. 'All writers since [Houston Stewart] Chamberlain'[3] had said so and felt this: didn't I feel the same? I said 'What about the last war?' She said, that was just a tempering. Now, within lifetime of Führer, they were destined to become top nation and poor old England (she was sorry to say, being fond of the place) would become a second-rate power unless it saved itself by proffered alliance. Finally she would not admit and could not even begin to see that a diplomacy which in two or three years has raised up the whole world in potential coalition against Germany is from the German point of view faulty. I called her view short term, accusing her of thinking only of Austria, Rhineland etc. She called mine short term, because in a few years the estrangement would be over and the Anglo-German alliance to dominate the world would be either a reality or England would go under. Of course what England was really waiting for was a man with a brain – though she admitted it might take 100 years to find one. Diana [Unity's sister, wife of Sir Oswald Mosley], she said in passing, has staked her life on being linked with the dictator of England. If he fails to attain dictatorship, she will commit suicide.

[2]1907 *Memorandum on the present state of British relations with France and Germany*, exposing German ambitions to make Britain a subordinate ally to Germany, and estrange her from France.

[3]Author of the pan-German, anti-semitic *The Foundations of the Nineteenth Century*.

When we got back to the car, there was an anonymous note in it saying it made a decent Englishman feel positively unwell to see two Hakenkreuz [swastika] flags in an English car. Then we drove off to the Führer's flat and seeing a drove of cars outside it, unloading luggage, knew him to be there. So we dined at the Hotel and then went to the Osteria in the hope of finding him, but he didn't come. The Redesdales telephoned from Nürnberg they had been given a sitting-room in the *gasthaus* and were comfortable.

6 September
Saw the Glyptothek, a wonderful collection of sculpture including the new marble of the Discus-thrower which must be one of the finest in existence. Bobo says the Führer was overcome with the buildings in Rome and regretted he didn't have time to see them properly. He said to her two or three days ago, '[Konrad] Henlein [leader of the Sudeten German party] wants to come and see me, I can't imagine what about.'

She and I left about 12 in her car and striking the *autobahn* were in Nürnberg about 2 or 2.30. The *autobahn* looked very fine in rolling country – fits the landscape so well. Bavarian pastoral country is charming – I don't care for the forests – no colour – the same petunias everywhere, but the old arms of light blue lozenges has largely disappeared. On arriving here, Bobo told the hotel commandant that the Führer had told her she could invite five people (actually it was five members of her family) so I was able to have Tom's room, a great blessing, as otherwise I should never have got in and should have had to go off and sleep in a train. The English consist of Redesdales, Bobo, self, Clive, [Lord] Brocket, Ward Price [of the *Daily Mail*] (other journalists in a train), Lord Stamp [member of Young Committee for German reparations], Lord McGowan [chairman of ICI]. We walked out and saw the Führer in his diarrhoea-coloured uniform standing up in a black car on his way to the Rathaus. Nürnberg very prettily decorated – municipal banners, green wreaths tied with gold – but the swastika, black and white on a lot of scarlet everywhere, rather monotonous.

I went to an organ recital in the church of St Lawrence and it came to me, perhaps for the first time, how very deeply our civilisation is bound up with Christianity, how it is Christian and how valuable are the principles with which Christianity has infused it. They are life, the others death.

We didn't get tickets for the *Meistersinger* (they always open proceedings with this). Bobo was ill when the application should have gone in. We were sitting in the hall before dinner, when suddenly Lord Redesdale appeared among the surging mob of Fascists, Phalangists in red berets,

Germans in every kind of uniform, all covered with orders and medals and badges, with his head bowed, walking slowly this way and that. He was looking for a needle Lady Redesdale had dropped from her tatting.

I went on a *bräu* crawl after dinner – first struck up with two Hanoverian SA men who grew quite maudlin over Waterloo and my race cousinship and were genuinely horrified at any prospect of war between the two countries, a prospect which honestly did not seem to have occurred to them until I mentioned it. We parted on terms of warmest friendship. Then I found an obscure *bräu* in a passage full of SA men with their arms round the barmaid and one of them thumping on a piano – a real Teniers scene – then another big *bräu* where I talked to an airman, local, who thought any possibility of war was entirely due to the Jews and could hardly be persuaded that Eden wasn't of that race. To bed at two.

This morning in a bus to the Luitpoldhalle, a vast hangar or similar building all draped for the opening ceremony. Vast band and choir. The Führer and all the familiar faces walk in, tear up the main aisle to the sound of 'Heils', then the standards to a march – the *Rienzi* overture, which sounded curiously unsuitable and intellectual, then a hymn about God. Then the deathroll of the old fighters, including [Horst] Wessel and Planetta – the Führer looked as if he really felt this. Then greetings. Then Streicher made a speech. Then the Führer's speech was read by [Rudolph] Hess [Deputy Führer]. Points which scored most applause: 'The Führer is always right.' 'What he does is always necessary.'

He read in an English paper that he was going to make a pact with the major powers as he couldn't face the Congress without. Instead of any pact, he faces them with nine new *gaus* (districts). He leaves unemployment to the democracies. A good many jokes. Bobo says 'he has a charming sense of humour' – he nearly died of laughing when Lord Redesdale told him he didn't care for Berlin because he couldn't get any skating.

All was well managed, and should have been impressive. I was waiting and expecting to be impressed but wasn't. Artistically the endless scarlet with black and white circles on it, combined with hordes of diarrhoea uniforms, ugly. But one has a feeling of death – of the absence of the vital spark. I don't mean of anti-mind, or anti-freedom, but something even more negative. Quite different from Russia in this respect – there the effort is intelligible, the emotions vivid or even sharable. Here one feels this can't last because there is nothing to make it last, a perfect vacuum of ideas. I don't say this is true, but it is what I felt. Looking at Göring, Ribbentrop, Goebbels (who is a dwarf), Streicher, was like looking at so many automata, in whom the attributes that define a human being have been lost. The Führer did not give one that impression – nor Himmler.

His proclamation didn't mention Czechoslovakia, or even touch on it indirectly. Even with my little knowledge of German I could distinguish the quality of his speech from the others. It wasn't *all* clichés. The others teemed with things we have been hearing for years – how people can go on listening to them is extraordinary.

I didn't think the enthusiasm remarkable, though the general theme of Gross Deutschland (i.e. Austria) obviously had everyone's approval.

The poverty of women's clothes *most* noticeable. The general crowd in this town is uglier than anything I have ever seen, even in Russia. It makes Altdorfer, Bosch and Breughel seem quite photographic. Everyone stares with horror, envy and resentment at Bobo's really very mildly painted face.

This morning's ceremony has left me with the impression of a people doomed on earth and in heaven. I never got that feeling in Russia. I expected to get the impression of a vigorous evil which must be destroyed at all costs – and perhaps I do. But that is subordinated to the negativeness and vacuity of it all. It is not so much intellectual poison as intellectual and spiritual death – a greater death than physical death – the death of Byron's 'Darkness' (look this up). I wonder if I am right, or if not, what has given me this impression.

I am now going for a walk with the Redesdales.

7 *September*
The Reichsarbeitsdienst [Reich labour service] parade – in the stadium – a much finer building of granite, marble stairways, mosaic ceilings, lack of refinement – but *good*. We had five places on the middle tribune just behind the Führer, Göring etc. Sir Nevile Henderson spent most of the morning in conversation with Göring. [André] François-Poncet [French ambassador] with Ribbentrop.

Forty thousand men on parade – with spades – and 2,000 women. Former took an hour parading past the Führer standing in his motorcar – they were divided into 10 lots – goosestepping, which when really finely done by a bandleader is akin to ballet dancing. The essential is to keep the body rigid and point the toes and seem to spring from the toes. After marching past they all ran about a mile and reappeared at the end of a gigantic vista. Finally about 2,000 naked men (it was very cold and wet) came to the front. Then songs as per programme – a sort of religious service – with intonations from different parts of the field.

I found it uncomfortable to see human beings thus volatised and in a purely civil matter. But the whole proceedings were far more intelligible than yesterday's. A lot of cant and clichés etc., but a sense of the land, *die Deutsche Erde*:

Mögen Wasser, Moor und Bruch, mag der Sturm auch schnauben,
Unser Junges Werk gelingt, weil wir daran glauben.
[Let the waters, marsh and fen in the tempest toss and turn,
Our young men their work complete, our creed to work and learn.]

First line has genuine ring, second awful. But what really rang true was: *'Wir sind die Fahnenträger der neuen Zeit'* ['We are the standard-bearers of the new age'] as the standards at either corner of the field were waved the while. One could see what Christopher Sykes has often told me, but what is hard for anyone that did not know Germany in the Twenties to realise, into what fearful confusion and mental anarchy the ideas of that period must have thrown Germany and how natural and spontaneous is the present reaction against them. Bobo was greeted by Goebbels and Streicher on the way out.

Party now increased by Lord and Lady Hollenden, Thelma Cazalet [MP for East Islington]. Last night Bobo talking to a serious young MP called [Norman] Hulbert called him a Marxist liberal. It is amusing to see people take her so seriously.

It is also curious that Houston Chamberlain should have been translated by Lord Redesdale's father. Lord Redesdale said as a boy he couldn't bear the word *'Grundlagen . . .'* (*Foundations of 19th Century*). Now he has just brought the damned book for his library.

No mention of Czechoslovakia, unless the following verse:

Mauern und Grenzen von Menschen erdacht
Können das Reich nicht zerstören.
Blut ist stärker, als feindliche Macht,
Und was Deutsch sein will, muss Deutschland gehören.
[Stone walls and frontiers invented by men
Cannot destroy our glorious Reich.
Blood is stronger than enemy Might,
What Germans desire is Germany's right.]

Sung with great fervour.

Of course German diplomats see our attitude as merely strengthening the Czechs to resist. To read the English papers one would suppose war due any hour now, French reservists called up etc.

My bedroom has a boot-jack.

Spent a charming evening yesterday walking about with Lady Redesdale before dinner – drank beer and ate sausages up at the castle, overlooking the town and all its lovely steep old tiled roofs as lights came

out. Saw exquisite baroque interior, very sane and non-florid, the
Aegidien Kirche.

Ward Price gloomy about war at lunch. How one could ever get out of
this place I don't know. Not much chance of a train with 600,000 extra
people here.

8 September

Spent last evening going round town with Virginia Cowles [of the *Sunday Times*] and Herr von Luft, joined James Holburn [*Times* correspon-
dent] later. Perpetually being called up from London. *Times* published
leader [7 September] saying Czechs better divest themselves of the
Sudeten territory before it is too late. This leader got in by some intrigue
(presumably by Astor [proprietor of the *Times*]). FO yesterday issued a
denial of this being their view. At the same time 82 Sudetens [arrested for
gun-running] were being violently maltreated in Mähreich (verify name)
[Mährisch Ostrau]. Henlein [leader of the Sudeten German Party] was
here in the Grand Hotel. Categorical reports:

    a. that he has seen the Führer.
    b. that he hasn't.
    c. that he has left for the scene of outrage and will report on Friday.
    d. that he has not left.

Meanwhile the *Times* has been ringing up Holburn every few minutes
to give him the latest from Prague. Sudetens had broken off negotiations
with Czech government, but Runciman [leader of independent British
peace mission in Prague] obliged them to go and see Hodza [Prime Minister of Czechoslovakia]. They were with him at 1 a.m. when we left. Spent
rest of evening with an absurd British Fascist who comes here to wear his
absurd full dress uniform.

This morning all papers full of the outrage. I feel extremely depressed.
Virginia saw Henderson and François-Poncet yesterday. Latter gloomy,
former full of feeble optimism.

8 September. Evening

Went to the Congress this morning. Bobo sat us in the front row. Having
been informed by representative of German FO that foreigners aren't
expected to make the Nazi salute I was unwilling to do so; but having sat
by Bobo in this position and having no hat to remove, and having
resolved, in addition, to submit to any humiliation rather than restrict
such insight as this week will give into the 'movement', I stuck out my
arm and when the party leader, walking at a great pace, suddenly swept
round the corner, my fingers were nearly bitten off by the Führer and I
half withdrew my arm, thus assuming a position of grotesque flabbiness

– altogether I felt embarrassed. Whenever I raised my eyes I met those of Goebbels or Himmler or the Führer. Bobo could tell by the look he cast her that the Führer was not in a good mood – but he seemed to warm up later, casting smiles at her when the Burgenland [an Austrian district where Unity often stayed] was mentioned – and he emitted a most amiable smile when he went out. The standards at close quarters, to that wonderful tune, were terrific – particularly the ones borne by motor cycle riders in black crash helmets with silver badges.

Music is indeed incorporated in the state procedure here (cf. Annunzio in Trieste).[4] Before the Congress opened, a piece of Beethoven played.

[Hans] Frank [Minister of Justice] spoke first on justice – a snarling evil speech full of German rancour and bitterness against the democracies. He foresees that Schuschnigg [Austrian Chancellor deposed at the *Anschluss*, March 1938] will be found guilty of treason. He maintained that whereas crime in the last two or three years has increased 100 per cent in the democracies, in Germany it has *decreased* by 100 per cent. But though he quoted German figures, he did not quote English or American. Followed Dr Todt who has built the *Autobahnen* – lots of figures – an agreeable speech.

Followed [Dr Otto] Dietrich, the press minister, an endless catalogue, textual, of lies in the foreign press – but very good humoured. Even the SS men in front had difficulty in keeping a straight face when they heard that German men were forbidden to shave more than four times a month. Abused Mme Tabouis [French journalist], Pertinax [André Geraud], the *Week* (a 'cheese wrapper', *Käseblatt*), the *News Chronicle* for General Reichenau's putative outline of world domination[5], Poliakov . . . a witty speech. But he asked in the end, quoting some English idiotic statesman who said the press was a great danger in international relations, why the democratic governments didn't do something about it!

Lessons:
1. How weak the Germans must feel themselves to bother about the foreign press (reference to the fact that their defeat in 1914–1918 was due to *Lüge* [lies]).
2. Dietrich dealt with none of the serious accusations: no mention of the *Times* leader on 'the Rape of Austria' [15 March 1938] or 'Homage to

[4]Gabriele D'Annunzio made music a state institution in the city state of Fiume, Dalmatia, which he seized and held 1919–20.

[5]On 12 July the British press had carried accounts of a speech given by General Walther von Reichenau on German ambitions in Spain and Portugal.

Murderers'. This speech was circulated textually to correspondents. I fear they may distort how amusing and good tempered it really was, apparently it doesn't quite read so.

Journalists who have been in Germany some time comment on the extraordinary amiability of the proceedings so far. Perhaps this misguided people has begun to realise that it may not be quite wise to antagonise the whole world.

Faces:

Ribbentrop a very distinguished female novelist.

Goebbels more amiable than in photographs.

Himmler terrifying, he sucks his teeth and keeps them bared.

The Führer is peculiar for the pink and white podginess of his face. The lines under his eyes go very far out and splay out at the end – eyes like peas, but a good-humoured face obviously very moved by music.

I sat next to Colonel Bolitho, Lord Lieutenant of Cornwall, at dinner. He as much as expressed his opinion, and his gratitude, that the British ships sunk in the Mediterranean were sunk by the British Navy out of Franco sympathies.[6] I said, 'Could I have dreamed 10 years ago, that I should ever hear an Englishman talk like that, I should have become a Swiss or an Icelander.' Holburn this evening says all is quiet and conciliatory in Prague.

9 September

This morning to the Congress – thank God we were spared the first row and sat in the third. First speech on *Arbeitsdienst* [labour service] – the remark that got the most clapping was the hope that one day all the European races might work together. The usual comparisons with foreign countries, lists of those who have introduced *Arbeitsdienst* and in what degree. Bulgaria somehow came in very prominently but I didn't quite understand how. Second on food production – all statistics of course had gone up. Great enthusiasm for statement that it would now be guaranteed to keep the *Deutsche Volk* in bread (and I think sugar) for two years. Third speech on press – but in abstract, no reference (that I could hear) to foreign press.

So far I have got two definite impressions of government policy (though I don't say they are of unique importance):

1. Push the people into a fool's paradise re war supplies.

2. To stir up and disintegrate the forces that brought Germany to her last pass.

[6]Between April and August 1938, 14 British merchant ships were sunk or badly damaged by Italian planes while supplying Republican-held ports on the east coast of Spain. On 26 July the *Dellwyn* had been sunk in Gandía harbour in sight of HMS *Hero*.

In the afternoon Lady Redesdale and I went off for a drive round the camps. The Führer caused consternation to 25,000 women including Miss [Thelma] Cazalet [MP for East Islington], by not appearing at their parade. Journalists in depths of pessimism. French Government said to have sent angry note threatening complete mobilisation. Henderson told Ward Price there was much more tension here behind the scenes than appears. François-Poncet [French ambassador in Berlin] has left.

Tea with Duke of Coburg – an amiable old gentleman with pleasant conversation. Then in the evening the Government *Appell der politischen Leiter* [roll-call of political leaders] – a wonderful sight – 34 lots of scarlet flags and in between them 33 bright blue searchlights going straight up into the sky but appearing to meet at a point and form a dance. There were 100,000 men in the arena. Then 25,000 flags entered in one main stream and 14 little ones on either side, all shivering and twinkling scarlet and gold. The great tribune had its bowls of torchlights and all the flags lit up between its pillars. The Führer made a speech saying he saw clouds on the horizon and hoped he could call on all of them.

10 September
I was half asleep when I wrote last night. Now we have just got up early and been to the parade of the Hitler *Jugend* in a smaller arena. One ingenious piece of showmanship: two ranks of flags, one black, the other red, entered the arena from different sides and when they met under the tribunal marched through one another. Baldur von Schirach [Reich youth leader] spoke, a neat-looking man. Enthusiasm more spontaneous than at other parades – I have not noticed the *frenzied* enthusiasm (it is a peculiar note) I expected, but this may be due to the orderliness of the German character.

One reflects: this is undoubtedly democracy. But it is one which postulates, not the rational human being judging questions for himself, but the emotional creature subordinating his judgment to the mass instinct. Both are true, but this system puts humanity on a much lower plane. Thus, this morning, when a section of the *Jugend* suddenly divested itself of some white clothing so as to form two vast initials A.H. I had a feeling of disgust – that *men* should be used for such a purpose.

What we are seeing here, I suppose, is the annual Witenagemot. The whole ceremonial is of a remarkable kind. It is certainly that of a democracy rather than of a tyranny – there's no cringing or bowing and a general ease pervades the Führer's entourage. And it is new in that it incorporates, indeed is based on, the last resources of the age – floodlighting, relaying, motorcars – and does them without being shoddy, because these devices are the essence of it. I haven't seen a horse – not one. Is this to be explained by the fact that the Führer doesn't ride?

Bobo says the Führer is very easily bored – lives on excitement and only really looks well at such times. She said to him after he dismissed the generals in February: 'Well, you have caused a fuss this time.' He replied: 'One must do something. Life becomes too boring otherwise.' Not that I should take this literally, but it indicates a certain temperament. He hates exercise, only taking very short walks, but likes tearing about in a car. He sometimes reads, but only late at night. When, as sometimes happens, she spends whole days with him in Munich he is always restlessly planning things to do and then not doing them because they aren't exciting enough.

11 September
I lunched yesterday after writing the above with Virginia Cowles [of the *Sunday Times*] at the Württembergerhof. At 20 to three the correspondents came back literally fainting with the violence of Göring's speech, which we had missed, arriving too late. He had called the Czechs 'cultureless hogs'.

Ribbentrop [German foreign minister] gave a tea at which the Führer was present. The Redesdales and Bobo spent an hour with the Führer after it. He seemed not in the least worried about anything and talked mainly of the weather and the *Arbeitsdienst* [labour service].

There was a conference in the evening. I could follow a good deal of Goebbels, who has most singular pansy gestures. He set out to compare *National Sozialismus, Bolschewismus* and *Demokratie*, the second is the bastard son of the last, though *Demokratie* makes a pretence of not recognising this fact. All Democracy dates from the French Revolution. That ushered in an age. That age is now ended.

Half the speech was taken up with quotations from the foreign press. That *ghastly* German sarcasm, the honeyed serpent lumbering with elephant's feet. But oddly enough, no great response. In his most contemptuous vein he quoted several foreign papers as calling Czechoslovakia 'an oasis' in Central Europe. Waited for laugh. None came. Again he got shouts of derision for quotations that culture was dead in Germany. Like Dietrich, he avoided any of the really important attacks. Said that the Germans hadn't started the blackguarding match. The democracies started it. The Germans wanted true friends. They had found some and would find others. Evidently the foreign press is a *mania*. Any reproof to their press by foreign governments is given headlines in the newspapers.

A party at the SS Bivouac in the evening. Himmler received the guests. He has a very small hand, a sort of doll's hand. I sat next to an old soldier who may have been [Hermann] Kriebel. He said he had been Chiang Kai-

Shek's military adviser for years and had only just returned. Oddly enough he was also besieged as a lieutenant in the Boxer Rising. He says result of war unpredictable but China has become a nation. He obviously couldn't say what he wanted to. He referred to the Führer as 'Hitler' – in connection with the *Badenweiler* march which the Führer has annexed as his own. He said that march, or rather its refrain, opened the battle in 1914 – without orders. He was a member of the armistice commission at Spa, a genial old boy. The Redesdales had Ribbentrop, but he didn't mention the war. A present – white vase with sweets in it.

Later I joined [Jules] Sauerwein [of *Paris Soir*], Dr [Karl] Silex [of *Deutsche Allgemeine Zeitung*], Virginia and Ward Price [of the *Daily Mail*] – the aristocracy of the Press. Sauerwein became apocalyptic. Wagging a finger at Silex, he said: 'If you wait, you can get what you want. But if you make a war, you will have the whole world against you.'

Silex: 'We know what that's like.'

Sauerwein: 'The whole world. You don't know how you are hated.'

Silex: 'Yes we do.'

Sauerwein: 'I say, if you make a war, Germany is doomed, *doomed*.'

Silex (in effect): 'We can't help that.'

Sauerwein then explained in my ear what he meant by doomed. He said that after another war, Germany would be literally depopulated – the Germans would have to be exported from Europe and divided. He wondered if the inhabitants of New Zealand would care to exchange their islands for Germany.

Silex argued that the present quarrel was one for Germany and Czechoslovakia to settle alone [in his column of 9 September he said British promotion of settlement in the Sudetenland had failed]. The old general at supper had said the same: 'If there is a war, this time England will be the criminal.' I tried in both cases, but with singular lack of success, to explain that English foreign policy was not merely a thing of the moment but a line we have pursued for 200 years. It seemed to me that Germany was always led to disaster by her diplomats.

Silex: 'Diplomats count for nothing.'

R.B.: 'Well, the people who conduct relations between nations, whoever they are. They are not informed of what English foreign policy is – they therefore cannot calculate for it properly' and so on.

Sauerwein said in my ear, he was an old man, though he had been a journalist for many years, and had met a number of important people, he trusted he attached no undue importance to himself. But tomorrow he was lunching with the Führer, who he used to know well – and if he got a chance, he would say the same to him as he had said to Silex: 'If you make war now, Germany is doomed.'

Ward Price earlier had been whispering in Bobo's ear that the only way to save the world was for him to have an interview with the Führer. She was not responsive. He is a very amiable man, courteous, amusing and always out to help anyone.

It is funny to be introduced, not as a Byzantinist, or a traveller or an oil magnate or an architectural critic, but as an occasional contributor to the *Times* – funny, but remarkably effective!

Got to bed at 4.30, and was called, O God, at six, to see the dedication of the new SA and SS standards. A new stadium. A new and equally effective ritual. A new speech of the Führer! But I began to feel I couldn't bear much more of it. Now they are marching through the town, five hours of them – to the old market place, now called Adolf Hitler Platz.

When we got back at 10.30 Lord Redesdale had just been rung up by the Oxford Group [for moral rearmament] at Interlaken saying they wanted to 'change' the Führer and if he would show the Führer a letter they had written in the *Times* of the 9th this would undoubtedly be effective. Lord Redesdale replied he hadn't got and couldn't get a copy of the *Times* of the 9th, also that he was unlikely to see the Führer again. Bobo said they rang her up every morning from London for three weeks offering to send someone out to do the changing – by aeroplane. But, as she said, she doesn't want the Führer changed. Lord Redesdale: 'No, damn it, I like the fellow as he is.'

I wonder at moments whether the whole thing is really the nightmare I feel or a scene from the Palladium. Bobo said to Lord Redesdale: 'As there isn't going to be a war, now you'll get the credit for having stopped it.'

Himmler apparently dotes on the Oxford Group and writes to its English members discussing their troubles with them. Frau Himmler has a twitch of the face.

I have been reading *Crome Yellow* [by Aldous Huxley] – bought it as embodying the age that is past – as indeed it does. But Mr Scrogan gives a singularly accurate forecast of this present German state (1921) except that the guiding intelligences are *not* rational – or are they? I take off my hat to Huxley.

I must note the extraordinary similarities with Russia.

1. Proclamation of a belief in a new age.

2. A new hagiography.

3. A new ideography (the Führer's successors will find it difficult to remove the swastika – it is on every bridge, every doorhandle, interlaced in every mosaic, etc.).

4. Revolutionary shrines, the Brown house etc.

5. Leader passion.

6. Unimportance of Foreign Minister (Rib's star is sinking).

7. Celebration of Revolutionary festivals – here November 9th is the chief one, I suppose that is the Munich *Putsch*. The *älte Kämpfer* [old guard] do the same march through Munich, and halt at the place where they were killed.

8. Elevation of gangsters into heroes.

Have just seen Ward Price, who has come back from lunching at the Burg with the Führer. Sauerwein had no opportunity to say anything. The Führer in a very genial mood, talking about the weather, 'Good for the potatoes, bad for the *Parteitag*.' Ward Price thinks this augurs well for the speech tomorrow night. I found the letter in the *Times* and attach it – a lot of tripe. Had Lord Redesdale shewn it to the Führer, it would have been equivalent to asking him to believe in God! The people who want 'morally rearming' are the people who sign such a letter [Lord Baldwin of Bewdley, Lord Salisbury, Lord Trenchard] – the English upper classes. But we are entering a harder age – in which we shall need a far sterner defence than Buchman [founder of Oxford Group].

13 September

Somewhere near Cologne. We got up early, as I think I have described, on Sunday the 11th – to the dedication of the SA and SS flags. The rest of the day was spent meandering through the town – I slept in the evening. Virginia and I walked to the old town and ate hot sausages at the little restaurant below the grill. A pleasant scene and to us it seemed one of the last of such evenings. We resolved, whatever else we accomplished, to see that the blood of this generation, should it be shed, should be on the heads of the Appeasers. Then we dined with Ward Price and Sauerwein, while at dinner Ward Price wanted on telephone to be told that the Prime Appeaser [Neville Chamberlain] had sent for the Press and told them that England would fight. Virginia detected the influence of [Sir Robert] Vansittart [diplomatic adviser to the government] and of her private communication on him. Said in March this might have saved us all. Said now, at the end of such a week as this, Chamberlain could and has only made things worse.

Stayed up late talking to Clive and Lord McGowan [chairman of ICI]. Woke up yesterday with a sore throat and the jitters and ordered a car for 11 p.m. to take me to Frankfurt. Saw the *Wehrmacht* display – aeroplanes that landed in 20 yards, gliders ditto, anti-aircraft guns and so on, a musical ride – then to Congress Hall where Hitler made the speech [saying Germany would help the Sudeten German inhabitants of Czechoslovakia to self-determination] that now all the world knows of (there was nothing about PM's pronouncement in the German papers). As his fury mounted, and his hair grew untidy, the nightmare of the whole week came to its climax (though I scarcely understood any of what he was saying) – as one finally realised that it was a nightmare from which one might never wake up. I noticed, despite the terrific enthusiasm of the audience, that many German women and some of the soldiers were realising this too.

Back to dinner. Bobo's confidence all gone – for the first time, she admitted the possibility, indeed the probability of war – and wondered what to do with herself – she can't come back to England, yet would be an enemy alien in Germany. She sent her love to her family, and seems to contemplate a time of unhappiness, though bravely keeping up her spirits by saying she would be in Prague for the *Einmarsch* [marching in].

At 11.30 I asked Clive if he would care to come in the car. Instead he saddled me with a mysterious colonel of dandyish appearance named Rocke who lives in Rome and was so anxious to get to London that he left all his luggage in Bamberg for Clive to pick up.

We left at 1 a.m., ran into fog and got to Frankfurt at six – whence the Colonel took an aeroplane. I was assured I could get to London tonight, but my train was late and I don't think I shall make connection with any Ostend boat. I may fly. There seems so little time left that even the first sight of this hideous grey Rhine lacks interest. I want to be home.

Or shall we wake up one day?

© *Lucy Butler*   *22 and 29 August 1987*

BYRONIC ROMANCE

Diana Mosley

SIR: I have not seen your issue containing Robert Byron's diary (22 August), but should like to comment upon words concerning myself, apparently quoted in it. It is inconceivable that my sister Unity, who knew me and my opinions so well, could have talked the rubbish Byron pretends she did. The mother of four little children (even if, unlike me, she were brave enough) could never contemplate suicide. Tragic though I thought England's declaration of war against Germany to be, when no British interest was involved, and tragic though its consequences have been for England, Europe and the world, my husband and children were my first concern.

As to dictatorship, this is a fantasy, a question too long to discuss in a letter.

My old friend Robert Byron was an intelligent man, but spies, as we know from experience, even though they may be called 'intelligence agents', are prone to every sort of lie, as Malcolm Muggeridge observes in his memoirs. Their imagination runs away with them.

Politics were not his forte, and my only quarrel with Byron was an aesthetic one. I never could take very seriously a man who announced that the Parthenon was like a row of herring bones. He was violently anti-classic, and hence perhaps exaggeratedly romantic. He is romancing in his diary. DIANA MOSLEY

Temple de la Gloire, 91400 Orsay, France   *5 September 1987*

MOSLEY CONTRA MUNDUM

A.L. Rowse

SIR: In the war against the criminal Nazi regime, 'no British interest was involved'! (Diana Mosley, Letters, 5 September.) Only a fool or a Nazi fanatic could think such rubbish.

As a German-Swiss professor, observing their criminal record, said to me: 'Europe cannot live with a united Germany.'

That is the fundamental fact. If we had submitted to Hitler controlling the whole of central and eastern Europe, Britain would have been at his mercy. We know what that was from the unspeakably criminal record against Jews and Slavs and all over Europe. And not only these, but against the finest of their own Germans, like my friends Adam von Trott and Helmuth von Moltke.

We are grateful to you for publishing heroic Robert Byron's diary: he understood the issue and foresaw what Hitler's appeasers would bring down on us.

We do not want history re-written by a friend of these criminals, ignorant of history and of no political judgment, whom a sense of shame, if not common sense, should tell to shut up. A.L. ROWSE

St Austell, Cornwall   *26 September 1987*

MISTAKEN WAR

Diana Mosley

SIR: With reference to Mr Rowse's furious letter (26 September) the truth is that Britain gave a guarantee to Poland in 1939, a blank cheque which bounced. It was in no position to help Poland then, any more than it is now.

Despite the criminal neglect of its armaments by Tory and Labour governments in the Thirties, Britain declared war on Germany, and sent an army to France with what arms there were. Eight months later Germany defeated France and most of our army escaped from Dunkirk, leaving its armaments behind. Surely this was the moment of our maximum weakness, and Hitler's maximum strength? The Channel ports were in German hands. He made no attempt to invade, but turned east and lost the war in Russia, like Napoleon before him.

The war was bound to have one of two results: either we should have lost – a disaster; or Germany would lose, ensuring the triumph of communism, another disaster. Rather than declaring war, it would have been wiser to build up our arms, not throw them away in France, and use them if we, or any of our possessions, were attacked. The war was disastrous for England, which lost its world position and was reduced to its present little measure. Russia has swallowed up half of Europe, and with its massive armaments poses a threat to the remainder. It has hitherto been kept in check by huge American armies stationed in Europe, and American nuclear power. Europe has been an armed camp ever since the 'end' of the war. However grateful Mr Rowse and I may be to America, I at least regret the time when we were masters of our own fate, a great power, and a civilising influence in the world. England, having made itself powerless, can no longer play balance of power politics, but within united Europe it still has a vital role.

I am sorry to write such obvious facts, but I suppose Mr Rowse's diatribe has to be answered. The world is full of cruel atrocities, but war is not the way to eliminate them; they proliferate in time of war. In itself, and in its results, it is the greatest atrocity of all. DIANA MOSLEY

Temple de la Gloire, 91400 Orsay, France   *10 October 1987*

I WAS A BLACKSHIRT MENACE

Ronald W. Jones

The only Labour speaker I heard at any length during the election campaign warned that Mrs Thatcher's followers were hellbent on installing a right-wing dictatorship in Britain. 'You don't have to go far back,' he illustrated, 'to recall Oswald Mosley – rich, landowning, privileged, Tory MP for Harrow – and remember how he realised the dreams of these people when he had his blackshirted, jackbooted legions marching through the streets of Britain.'

There seemed little point in fudging a jolly exposition with facts – Mosley's last major political post was that of Chancellor of the Duchy of Lancaster in a Labour administration – but as I wandered out into wet Wiltshire, I found myself wondering if people really do believe that Fascism in Britain ever constituted an important political factor; nasty nuisance, perhaps, but important? Ummm.

You see, without great effort of memory, I can recall being a member of Mosley's fascist legions, tramping through London's streets and, although we hadn't got jackboots and black shirts were banned, I was obviously part of this hideous threat to Britain's democratic wellbeing.

I joined the extreme political Right at the time of the Munich Crisis in 1938. At a street corner meeting near Earls Court station a stocky man with an unlovely rasping voice and a strange habit of enunciating on occasion as though he was regurgitating, was speaking on behalf of the 'British Council Against European Commitments'. Frankly, as an excessively randy and equally repressed teenager, I was not unduly interested in the fate of Sudetenland, but I was smitten into trembling worship by the lovely blonde girl who stood beside William Joyce's platform handing out leaflets. I took a leaflet and read it under the street light; I had to find words for conversation with the goddess.

They were a well-connected lot, this British Council – Viscount Lymington, an admiral, a major-general, plus a few captains. Apparently, William Joyce, believing that national danger was no time for political bickering, had generously thrown into the fray his National Socialist League on the side of the Viscount for the duration of the crisis. The entire membership, I was later to discover when my own name had been included, was William Joyce, John McNab, Quentin Joyce, Frank Joyce, Margaret Joyce, a lunatic drunken Irishman who was taken off to a mental home, and a man named Price.

There were also two or three Roman Catholic priests from the Victoria area who, mindful of the Spanish civil war, believed that Joyce and his stalwarts might intercede at some future date on behalf of nuns facing violation; they were not actually members of Joyce's party but gave guidance to their flocks and came to indoor meetings, lending an aura of benign respectability. Of course, I was not to know that the blonde goddess, and sundry of her Irish sisters from Victoria, had been bidden by their parish priests to attend Joyce's meetings but were totally a-political.

Thus, on that first night and all subsequent occasions, the blonde girl was unable to answer my searching questions of the policy of the British Council. However, my obsessive courtship meant that I spent every night over the next months with William Joyce and his tiny entourage. With the dismemberment of Czechoslovakia, the British Council Against European Commitments was wound up – Britain had not been committed to the defence of the fledgling democracy – and William Joyce and his National Socialist League (now plus me) were thrown back on their own paltry resources, which meant they were evicted from one office in Wilton Road for non-payment of rent, took a basement office in Vauxhall Bridge Road, where there always seemed to be a shortage of cash to feed the electric light meter. If Adolf was paymaster, he was damned stingy.

But all this while I was determined to prove my valour in the eyes of the blonde. I carried the platform for Joyce to meetings, dished out leaflets and listened for long hours to the sad little thwarted man. He so wanted to be completely British and accepted as such, but his view of the British was romantic: dashing, fine, chivalrous gentry and decent, hard-working peasants. Although American-born (the only American hanged for treason to Britain) he had lied about his age and managed to join up in the first war, and in the trenches he had found the Britain of his romantic dreams. He forced himself to master a true, uppercrust English accent and only succeeded in producing a parody.

If the dream became flawed it had to be the fault of the circumstances and not the chimera. The counterfeit penny dropped as early as the middle Twenties – it was 'alien forces' besmirching his idealised England of Kipling, Kitchener and King. And the most easily identifiable alien forces were the Jews. After that, it was only a short step to the Joyce of the immediate pre-war days.

Brave? Oh yes, he was brave all right. I can so well remember plunging behind him into the heart of a mob literally howling (mobs do and it's frightening) with fury. Me, carrying the collapsible platform, my bladder wanting to empty from fear, and this terrible little man forging on determined to hold his meeting and, to this day, I believe that the only reason we did not finish up in hospital or the morgue was the fact that sheer weight of bodies pressed us down and we finished up flat on our faces beneath dozens of winded howlers.

Alas, none of this impressed the blonde girl. After an incident when we sat together in the darkened Cameo news cinema, Victoria, she went to the 'Ladies' and did not return.

With the blonde vanished, my interest in the National Socialist League waned and, overnight, I ceased dropping in every evening at the basement. After a week of so, postcards and then letters from William Joyce arrived, first wondering about my absence, then demanding my presence and, finally (I think very sadly, but he had lost one-eighth of his membership) lamenting my departure.

But for months every free hour of mine had had a purpose and now I was abruptly thrown back on my non-existent resources for amusement and interest – the Left long ago appreciated the vacuum faced on resignation and this is why it takes a Hungary to get any of them to resign.

It was thus predictable that a week or so later I should be found doing a Bisto-kid thing outside the British Union (the 'Fascist' had been dropped from the title of Mosley's movement by that date) bookshop near Chelsea football ground; the aroma was promising, with an array of books, pamphlets and other publications indicating that this rather seedy-looking shop was a stronghold of Britain truly on the march, with Union flags a-plenty and the monarch's picture having its proudful place.

Slightly off-putting, the middle-aged man in baggy grey trousers and crumpled sports coat, pottering around fussily arranging piles of Action inside, did not appear to be one of life's great marchers. Even with the glasses, Mr Hutton – if he had a Christian name, nobody knew it – was myopic. He peered at me, furrowed his forehead and considered my expressed desire to join in the rebirth of Britain. 'I suppose you'd better come along tonight,' he suggested. 'They'll all be in.'

That evening I met the entire active branch of the Kensington Branch of the British Union – Ernie Matthews, the District Leader, aged around 26, an electrician, something imprecise in the Electrical Trades Union, with a physical – and particularly facial – appearance that a malicious antisemitic cartoonist would have used as a model for his reviled Jew. Ernie was probably the most Jewish-looking man I have ever met. Not, I rush to add, that he was an unattractive man; on the contrary, with his great beak of a nose, mobile but so expressive huge brown eyes, and zany sense of humour, Ernie was very likeable.

However, if there was any marching to be done, Ernie was physically equipped to do it, but the citadels of International Jewish finance would hardly be stormed by a Nordic type.

For marching, the rest of the branch appeared ill-equipped. There was a 21-year-old grocer's son, horribly overweight and admitting to a 'bad heart'. Movement of any type did not appeal to him. Then there was Dubois, a projectionist at a Walham Green (since inexplicably changed by Labourites to 'Fulham Broadway') cinema. Slim, very dark of complexion and totally taciturn, he spent that first evening and every succeeding evening that I saw him, sitting in a corner fingering a rather long knife. It was said that he worked as a projectionist because he had bad feet – I did not attempt to unravel that.

Then there was an old (around 60) couple named Mr and Mrs Thomas. She bulgingly untidy of appearance, always carrying a shopping bag, suffered with her 'insides', and he, silvery-haired, raw-faced, voice reduced to a harsh grate from a million outdoor meetings, suffered with his 'chest'. Both had been members of the Communist Party and had made the transition from extreme Left to extreme Right with all the ease of Nazi Party officials in East Germany after 1946 – sorry, in reverse.

Barrett was a tall, loose-limbed to the point of near disconnection, adolescent who spoke but rarely. However, he could march. So could Betty, a Portuguese girl working as a maid in South Kensington, who had been steered by Salazar's embassy to the correct political party in Britain. Then we had Molly (masculine) and Betty (feminine), the two lesbians, except that, the *Guardian* Woman's Page not having been invented, nobody referred to them as such; they simply lived together and slept together but they didn't march because Molly would not allow Betty to be put at risk. Additionally, and also not for marching, a number of 'captains' dropped in on occasion; one gathered they were not actually members – not quite the thing, perhaps. They tended to be smallish 40-year-olds, with badly-cut, flattened down yellowish hair and brisk moustaches, and belted light-brown raincoats that they wore all the time. I got the impression that these gentlemen were not well-to-do.

What did we do to storm the ramparts of reaction? We sold *Action* outside South Kensington and Earls Court stations, where on one occasion William Joyce (he had broken with Mosley some years earlier) saw me and expressed his sorrow that I had joined the 'Jew fascists'. We carted the collapsible soapbox around and held meetings opposite Earls Court station, in Sloane Square and at a corner off Kensington High Street.

Because Ernie, our District Leader, was often away on mysterious business with the ETU, I became a speaker (I was just 16 masquerading as 21) and, according to the police, the best speaker they had known the movement possess in that area. Modesty compels me to admit that, although I was obviously a naturally talented speaker, my success accrued largely from the fact that I spoke only from the published policy of the movement, which contained nothing anti-Jewish, pro-German or pro-Italian . . . just rather old-fashioned naked patriotism.

Incidentally, it has been alleged that the police were rather in favour of us. This I doubt. They frequently affirmed that we were all – fascists, communists, greenshirts, all the fringe – bloody nuisances. Marginally, they preferred us to the communists because we did not indulge the Red tactic of rolling ball-bearings in the path of police horses. But I can well recall not moving when ordered to do so and three tall, craggy policemen sorting us out with the heavy rolled capes they carried in those days. They had not drawn truncheons, of course, but scarcely needed to with the impact of those damned capes.

But what had happened to the blackshirted legions I had seen pictured marching to Olympia and into the East End a few years earlier? I asked around and I studied the file copies of *Action* and the answer was revealing for the insight it provided upon an innate quality of the mass of the British people. Undoubtedly in the early Thirties there had been a mass surge towards the patriotism espoused by Mosley's BUF on the part of rather hearty men and women. These people did regard communism as an unpleasant, alien force and they liked nothing better than the opportunity to make Red noses bloody. But these people lacked the gutter instincts of the Stormtrooper or the Squadristi – a bloody good punch-up and then ten pints of beer, yes, but gangs setting upon people and beating them up was not their line. And then Mosley (he always afterwards denied this, but his memory must have been at fault or he simply lied) allowed the antisemites to take over. Over a matter of months the massed membership of the hearty types simply dissolved.

And so, by 1938-9 when a march was ordered by national headquarters, our pitiful little bunch of five or six would make our way to the Embankment starting point. From all over the Home Counties – a huge area of population – similar straggling groups would arrive and when we set off on our march we might have nearly 2,000 marchers – 2,000 out of 15 million. When Mosley in 1939 held his 'national' meeting in the Empress Hall, Earls Court (capacity under 30,000), there were vast areas of embarrassingly empty seats. Doesn't say much for the Blackshirt menace, does it?

Why, then, was the myth fostered and why is it still maintained? Is it not just possible that if you want people to fight off a fascist menace, you must have some semblance of such a menace or you'll have to invent one?

Consider this: we held undisturbed meetings at three venues in the Kensington area, but on one occasion, with Barrett and Portuguese Betty obediently following, I took the platform to a new position, on the corner of a side-street off Fulham Road, near the hospitals. The meeting went famously, until two taxis arrived and eight or more rather tough gentlemen emerged. They said nothing. I was knocked off the platform, which was stamped into firewood, and all our copies of *Action* and other literature were dispersed to the winds. We were not badly bruised.

Why this clinical destruction of a peaceful meeting? From a police inspector who judiciously arrived a little later – 'They were the Walham Green boys. They do the strong-arm stuff for the local Commies. Seems they don't want you to hold meetings here, sonny.'

But, as the same gentry could have smashed every other of our meetings, it would seem probable that they had drawn up their guidelines for the Blackshirt menace, which had to be seen by the populace to be believed, but not permitted to step out of line.

I agree that the East End posed some problems, but by 1938 membership of Blackshirt branches was numbered in scores and not hundreds. Perhaps the most vital indication of the impotence of the movement in those days lay in the fact that you did not wear a 'Flash and Circle' armband in, for instance, Balls Pond Road – you wouldn't dare.

6 August 1983

Mr Jones joined up in 1939, and served in North Africa, Italy and North Europe – in the British Army.

A YOUNGER POINT OF VIEW

Christopher Hobhouse

In the present crisis, we have heard much of the views of those who fought in the last war, and still more of the views of the mothers and grandmothers of every nationality. But scarcely an echo has been heard of the views of those to whom *The Spectator* has lent special prominence – the Englishmen of under thirty. If there is a war, they get the worst of it:

if there is peace, they enjoy it the longest. Above all, if peace is purchased at a price, it is they who have ultimately to pay that price.

A man of sixty-nine, however high his standards of sincerity may be, can hardly find it in his power to take so long a view as those of us who are still under thirty. Peace in his time means one thing, peace in our time another. However thankful we may be for his experience and his sincerity, we cannot but fear a tendency on his part to think in months instead of years.

Up to the very day of Mr Chamberlain's departure, there was to be felt in the massing of public opinion a single-mindedness unknown since 1931. Like the components of a letter lock, the various sections of the nation, from left to right, had clicked into sudden alignment. A few days have sufficed to destroy this unity of resolution. Just then, we were sarcastic about the cocksure attitude of Herr von Ribbentrop. But now the reaction upon us which he calculated has set in; and a refuge has been found in specious talk about peaceable settlements and in cowardly criticisms of the Czechs.

There is no need to stress the immense strength of the position that we held ten days ago. The whole world stood beside us. Germany's pledged friends were wavering in their decision. In Germany itself the common people showed with what terror they looked forward to the outcome of a war. If at a time when such a huge preponderance of power lay in our hands, the resolution of our leaders has faltered, it can only be because they have decided that victory itself would cost too dear. I am sure that this belief is not shared by the generation to which I belong.

Even a victorious war would mean, most obviously, a heavy cost in life. 'Thanks to Mr Chamberlain,' writes Lord Castlerosse, 'millions of young men will live. I shall live!' He puts it with a nice impartiality, but with some exaggeration. Perhaps a million of young men may be reprieved for yet another year or two; but they themselves are the last to suppose that the payment of Danegeld is going to do more than to put off the catastrophe. There are higher motives than self-preservation: and rather than that all of us should live to be blackmailed, insulted and despised, I conceive that quite a few of my generation would face the grimmest sacrifice, as other generations have done before them.

A war, even a victorious war, would cause immense material damage, and at home. In imagination this is perhaps the most vivid of its terrors. It may seem preposterous that those of us who are prepared to undertake tireless agitations to prevent the demolition of a single house, who will go to law to stop the felling of a tree, should yet be ready to embrace the risk of seeing whole acres of our cities, and of London in particular, reduced to dust. London is good to look at, and good to live in: but heaven forbid that its wealth and beauty should outlive its position as the capital of a great and trusted Power. Our trappings are not so precious that we cannot face the weather in them: and if those who get the best of modern life can feel this way, how much more gladly will the inhabitants of tenements and alleys sacrifice their material surroundings in a cause where the honour and interest of a whole Empire are combined.

Besides the dread of personal loss and of material damage there lurks another apprehension, not to be uttered save discreetly and in the most private circles. It is the fear that even a victorious war would cause a further shifting in the relations between one class and another. That the mere fact of fighting in alliance with the USSR is likely to infect the people of this country with Bolshevism is a thesis that requires too much swallowing. Rather it is insinuated that the last war brought about as much in the way of social change as was good for the working classes: so what is to be looked for at the end of another? This loathsome whisper finds no listeners among the younger generation: and indeed it is hard to credit that there are men whose class-consciousness is such that they put their rents and dividends above the independence of their country.

It is too late now to talk of a victorious war. All our advantages have dropped away from us, and we face the menaces of the future alone against an adversary whom we have ourselves exalted to the skies. But there is one form of consolation in which the elderly have taken refuge, which is really too nauseating for the consciences of those of us who are going to have to pay the price in humiliation and surrender all our lives. It is the consolation of abusing the Czechs, and minimising the value of the sacrifice we force upon them. We are told that we had no legal obligations to fulfil, that there was much to be said on both sides. Why this odious hypocrisy should only show itself after our resolution had been fully considered, declared, and then abandoned, it is sufficiently easy to perceive.

Let nobody suppose that the ordinary citizen, whose voice will soon be heard, feels any special interest in the Czechs as a people, or as a democratic State. He does not care whether the Government of Prague is a band of brigands, or their rule a systematic oppression. What he understands perfectly is the consistent march of German policy. *Parcere superbis et debellare subjectos* is the motto of the Third Reich: and it is the urgent anxiety of the younger generation that they should be allowed some share in deciding in which category they are to take their place.

23 September 1938

NATIONAL UNITY AND THE NATIONAL GOVERNMENT

J. Grimond

To the Editor of THE SPECTATOR

SIR: You have expressed the feelings of many who felt that the Agreement at Munich was a shameful necessity. You express their feelings again when you call for a new resolve and national unity.

But is it to be national unity behind Mr Chamberlain, Sir Samual Hoare and Sir John Simon?

The present Government was elected in 1935 upon its promise to support the League of Nations. Sir John Simon had already been forced to resign the Foreign Secretaryship owing to distrust of his sincerity, but at the election the Government reiterated their loyalty to the League and its ideals. Mr Chamberlain said 'that the National Government put support of the League in the forefront of its policy'. Again in December 1935 he said: 'The League of Nations is the keystone of our foreign policy.' In November 1935 Sir Samuel Hoare was 'deeply anxious to make collective action successful'. He was rash enough to assert that 'our policy has not changed since my speech at Geneva, nor will it change after the election'. He described the Government's policy as 'simple and straightforward to the utmost degree', and remarked that 'it was fortunate for him that British traditions remained constant in foreign affairs'. Meanwhile the thought came to Mr Chamberlain 'that if we were to have a change of Government . . . [foreign countries] would feel that our lead was weakened and they would not know if in future they could rely on the British Empire or not'. Sir Samuel Hoare again dismissed any suggestion that 'they were going to let down the League in future' as 'electioneering claptrap'.

Within a month we had the Hoare-Laval plan.

Since then the Government, and especially the Inner Cabinet, has referred less and less to the League or the ideals they boasted at the election. They have abandoned the policy they were elected to pursue. Their alternative policy has failed to enforce non-intervention. They have failed to reach agreement with Italy or, on the other hand, to defend British ships in Spanish waters. They made no attempt to use the League or collective action either to satisfy Germany's legitimate claims or as a defence against aggression. In the end they were forced to choose between the Munich agreement and a war against a strengthened Germany with insufficient arms. Mr Chamberlain, acting with courage, avoided war: but it may be asked why if the agreement at Munich was honourable were we to endure the horrors of war rather than accept the terms demanded at Godesberg?

As for rearmament, the necessity of it was insisted upon at the last election. 'It is a duty we owe to the people of this country that our shores shall be as secure as human effort can make them.' (Sir Samuel Hoare, November 1935.) Mr Chamberlain in October 1935 is reported to have said that 'there is not one of the small countries in Europe which knowing the present state of our defences has not breathed a sigh of relief when they heard that at last we were going to put ourselves in a position to defend ourselves if necessary and to fulfil our obligations under the covenant'. The estimates for the fighting services for 1935, 1936 and 1937 total something like £476,000,000. The total amount spent on rearmament and defensive measures is greater. In September of this year we found ourselves with a hundred anti-aircraft guns to defend London.

It may be said that this is bringing up past history and old grievances. But to decide upon the ability of our present leaders we must look at their record. Can the country unite behind an inner cabinet of four which contains two discredited foreign secretaries, and whose performance is so far from its promises? If the Government desire unity and co-operation, if they desire to be trusted, should they have answered so evasively the questions put them in Parliament by their own supporters and the Opposition on rearmament or our policy in Spain?

At the end of seven years of National Government we have been led to the brink of war without armaments. If we are to have new resolve, new hope and great sacrifices must we not have new Ministers worthy of this awakening – leaders who can inspire confidence that we shall be rearmed and whose deeds are more like their words? – Yours faithfully, J. GRIMOND

40 Gloucester Square, W.2   *28 October 1938*

THE BLIND EYE

Graham Greene

I left Vera Cruz on April 30th in the German liner *Orinoco*, travelling third class. The shadow of the Spanish war stretches across the South Atlantic and the Gulf: one couldn't expect to escape it in a German ship calling at Lisbon.

My cabin held six, but at first there were only five of us: an old man who never spoke a word, a fat Mexican who spat all night upon the floor and said *'No puede dormir'* because he couldn't sleep, and a young Spaniard with a hard handsome idealist's face and his small son whom he disciplined like a drill-sergeant. There was no doubt at all where *he* was going, and, when I returned to my cabin just before we sailed, I found a stranger wearing a beret and an old suit which didn't look natural: you felt he was used to a better cut. There were others in the cabin, too: they blocked the door after I got in: they wore their berets like a uniform and each had a little gold chain round his neck with a holy medal dangling under the shirt. At first I couldn't understand their Castilian – they seemed perturbed, they wanted to know who I was. The word 'Ingles' didn't reassure them, but when I said 'Catolico' and showed *my* lucky charm, they looked a little easier. The stranger was a stowaway, he was going to 'pay the Reds'; I must promise to tell no one, they said, blocking the door, till we had left Havana. As we sailed out of Vera Cruz that night we passed a Spanish ship which had been impounded since the war started and the third-class emptied on to the deck and gave the dark and silent boat a noisy farewell: 'Arriba España,' 'Viva Franco.' The stewards smiled gently, bringing round the salad, hearing nothing.

After Havana the volunteers began to disclose themselves, more than two dozen of them. Many of them had their wives and children with them, they wore their uniforms quite openly when we were once at sea, black forage caps and Sam Browne belts, blue shirts with the Falangist fasces embroidered on the pocket. They were very noisy and carefree – without bravado: you felt that going to war was one of the natural functions of man. There was something agreeably amateur too about their Fascism – I think the Germans looked a little askance when the arms went up in salute – for nothing at all, for a silly old man, for a joke. Arriba

Españas and Viva Francos burst boisterously out for no reason on the hot unshaded deck, with a hint of mockery. Killing the Reds – that was a man's occupation, but all this dressing up to do it, that was a joke, a game. They enjoyed it, but not in the serious German way. O the consultations on deck, the handing out of envelopes, the open conspiracies. There was one printed form which aroused my curiosity: instructions from Burgos? I learned what it was when Sunday came.

The blind non-intervention eye was very blind indeed, and the German ear was very deaf. On Sunday there was a church parade: the volunteers marched up to Mass in the first class: twenty-five of them lined the wall in uniform, one man stood at attention on each side of the altar: it was impressive, as a funeral is. A monk preached (I had seen him playing chess, cheery and unshaven in an old striped shirt and no tie). He preached on suffering and sacrifice and offering up your agony to God. After the Mass was over, before the priest had time to leave the altar, the volunteers broke into the Falangist hymn – that was what they had been learning all the week from the printed forms. And then, inevitably, the Fascist salute: Arriba España, Viva Franco: every arm went up but mine, yet no one minded at all. These were Spaniards, not Germans.

It was odd comparing them with their German allies: the young German farmer, for instance, from Chiapas, who joined heartily in the right cries and hated Christianity. I tried to involve him in argument in front of the volunteers – 'this,' I wanted to indicate, 'is your ally.' They stood listening with mild astonishment, the holy medals dangling round their necks, while he plunged bull-like at Christianity.

'But you must admit that – so far – nationalism hasn't produced any art, literature, philosophy to compare with the Christian?'

'I see you do not know the works of Ludendorff. Listen to me. The Christians have only winned because they have killed all not Christian. Once we had nothing to give people, only Religion. Now we give the Nation. But we are not atheists like the Reds. We have a God, one God.'

'The old Jewish Jehovah?'

'No, no. A Force. We do not pretend to know what he is. A Principle.'

The volunteers listened politely to the new Germany, but one of the cooks jumped overboard: he hadn't been home for ten years; perhaps he couldn't stand the prospect.

The day before Lisbon silence came down on the third class. There were no Arriba Españas all the afternoon. The stern father walked up and down, up and down, his child hanging to his arm, up and down, drowned, you could tell, in a sea of unreality: here, for ten days, he had been on a pleasure cruise, there the train for Salamanca left at nine. There was a farewell dinner – perhaps the last good meal before the trenches: 'Auf

Wiedersehen' inside a little scarlet heart on the menus, and then a speech – about 'our great Ally' and Austria – and sacrifice. It wasn't only the Germans who had been turning blind eyes all these days: but the blind eyes of the Spanish volunteers were now beginning to open – like those of new-born children opening on the awful lunar landscape of the human struggle.

1 July 1938

WHAT WE SHOULD FIGHT FOR

W.J. Cooksey

To the Editor of THE SPECTATOR

SIR: I am an ordinary working man, which in my part of Great Britain means an unemployed man. I fought in the Great War, and I suppose I shall fight in the war that is expected now, if it comes. So I think your readers may be interested to know what I and many others of my sort are thinking.

We are thinking that at Munich we were finally and definitely let down.

I love my wife and children, and I would give my life to save them, and so I am sure would Mr Neville Chamberlain. But the other day he didn't give his life or mine, he gave other people's lives, to save Mrs Chamberlain and their children and grandchildren and mine. He sacrificed Mr and Mrs Schmidt and *their* children and grandchildren, when he handed over the Socialists, Jews, Christians and Pacifists, in the Sudetenland, to their persecutors. His excuse was that they were people we 'knew so little about'. But we knew enough about them to admit Czechoslovakia to our 'International Club for mutual protection against gangsters', and while he was a member of that club he played the game in a most sporting manner. When gangsters came along and demanded his person he said, 'Look here, you fellows! I don't want to make trouble. I'll hand over every penny I've got so long as I'm left my liberty.' While he was getting out his purse, we had a whispered colloquy with the gangsters, and next moment we had pushed him out, and locked the door on him.

I say 'we' because it was my country, along with France, that did this dirty, mean, contemptible trick, a trick that earns the hatred of every true-hearted man and woman. Two years earlier we had played the same dirty trick on Abyssinia, a dark-skinned member of our Club, whom we had admitted to membership after much deliberation. When the gangsters came demanding his person we made a show of rallying to his defence, but we left the side door open so that they could snatch him. We are shortly to be asked to count him for dead as from November 15th, though every time we go to the back door we hear him screaming.

The effect of these ruthless betrayals on the ordinary plain man like me, is to make him hate and despise their perpetrators. It is useless to ask for a united country to face the Hitler-menace, while to those who will do the fighting, Hitler stands not only for himself and Mussolini, but also for Chamberlain and Halifax and Simon and Hoare. I am ready to offer my life again for the cause for which I fought in the Great War, but it will be to fight against Hitler and Mussolini and against this crew of slimy hypocrites (for so they seem to me), these callous selfish holders-on to privilege, who are ready to betray me and mine (and already *have* betrayed us) because we too are people they 'know so little about'.

I will fight under any leader who may arise in any country who will lead his armies to restore international decency, and what goes along with it, justice as between man and man at home – the right to lead a happy and useful life and to earn my bread in the sweat of my brow, and not any longer to be compelled to rot inactive, half starved and always grumbling, like a poor relation. – Yours, &c., W.J. COOKSEY.

28 October 1938

SPLITTING OF THE ATOM

The splitting of a uranium atom, announced from Columbia University last Tuesday, marks an important step forward. The breaking up of atomic nuclei by bombardment with various particles is now a commonplace of physics, but this experiment differs from all others in that a large atom was split into two atoms of more or less equal size. Previous attempts at atom-splitting had resulted, so to speak, rather in knocking chips off the atoms than in dividing them into two. There has always been a hope that some such process would make available the vast stores of atomic energy which make every handful of dirt a potential source of true wealth. In the Columbia experiments it was found that the uranium atom, when split, gave out six thousand million times as much energy as was needed to split it. If this process could be performed on the large scale, a wholly new source of power would be made available; but, in fact, our present methods of atom-splitting can only break up infinitesimal quantities of matter. Such experiments as these, though of the greatest scientific interest, are but finger-posts on the road to that Golconda of power which is locked in the heart of the atom.

3 February 1939

NEWS OF THE WEEK

The first indirect effect of the annexation of Czecho-Slovakia is a final demonstration of the impossibility of conducting any normal negotiations in the future with a Germany dominated by Herr Hitler. All negotiations are based on some principles, and Herr Hitler acknowledges none but the hegemony of his country. In the interests of that he will lie, deceive, threaten and rape. The outstanding fact about the invasion of Czecho-Slovakia is the report, apparently authentic, that the President, M. Hacha, whom Herr Hitler had summoned to his presence, as he summoned Dr Schuschnigg a year ago, was told that unless he submitted to the invasion, and indeed actually invited it, Prague would be blown into the air. That is the situation that exists. It reveals in its true light the sincerity of the pretension that what concerned Herr Hitler six months ago was the grievances of the Sudetendeutsch. They served their turn as excuse for the seizure of the great line of the frontier fortresses of Czecho-Slovakia. Now no excuse is needed. Covetousness and ambition can be displayed in all their nakedness, without even an affectation of draping them decently. The final fate of what was Czecho-Slovakia is not yet clear. Hungary, as a vassal of Germany, may be allowed to have Ruthenia, and her common frontier with Poland. Slovakia, utterly incapable of standing by itself, may be permitted the fiction of independence. Moravia and Bohemia certainly will not. They are temporarily under military administration, and the administration may find the Czechs are of different fibre from the Austrians.

The Death of Czecho-Slovakia

It was Tuesday that saw the final downfall of the Czecho-Slovak Republic. Last week the Federal President, Dr Hacha, made a last attempt to save the unity of the Republic by dismissing the Slovak Prime Minister, Father Tiso, and installing Dr Sidor as his successor. An appeal by Father Tiso, on Monday, to Herr Hitler produced a demand from Berlin to Prague for the immediate summoning of the Slovak Diet, which on Tuesday, with Father Tiso reinstalled as Prime Minister, proclaimed the independence of Slovakia, and asked for the protection of the Reich. In Carpatho-Ukraine the Prime Minister, Father Voloshin, appealed to Herr Hitler and Signor Mussolini, but neither made any attempt to hinder the advance of Hungarian troops, which are making slow progress towards the Polish frontier. On the afternoon of the same day President Hacha visited Berlin, where on Wednesday morning it was announced that Germany had assumed 'protection' of the Czech people; during the day German troops invaded Bohemia and Slovakia and entered Prague. Herr Hitler has once again applied the principle of self-determination, with the result that the Czechs and the Slovaks will be governed from Berlin and the Ruthenians from Budapest.

17 March 1939

PEOPLE AND THINGS

Harold Nicolson

I ask my German friends when they come to London to tell me how many of their compatriots listen in to our broadcasts in the German language. The replies which I receive are contradictory. I have seen seven Germans in the last three weeks. Two asserted that they had never heard that any such service existed. The other five assured me that the British news bulletin was the great event of the day. One of them (a young engineer whom I had known in Munich) was more explicit. He told me that he had a friend who lived in the flat opposite. They took turns to listen in to London. In the tram next morning the one who had listened would inform the one whose night off it was of what had been said. They had evolved a formula under the cover of which this information could be exchanged. 'Did you hear,' the listener would begin, 'those filthy lies which they put out from London last night?' 'No,' the other would answer, 'I was attending a group meeting.' 'Well,' his friend would continue, 'they had the impudence to say . . .' And the colloquy would end with a joint chorus of 'Lies, lies, lies.' The other occupants of the tram would be entranced by this dialogue. A few furtive winks would be exchanged.

I myself listen fairly regularly to the news bulletin in German. I do not see how it could be improved. Those of us who heard the shrieks of Marshal Goering on Sunday night, who heard the steam-saw of 'Sieg-Heil!' grating upon the wireless will understand how effective are the sedative tones of the announcer from London. That surely is the correct method of propaganda. The nerves of the German people are becoming frayed by hysterics. How effective for them must be the still small voice of reason. I was told by one of my more intelligent German friends that at first the contrast between the dynamics of German broadcasts and the sedatives of our own persuasion caused a giggle among German listeners. When you are accustomed to swashbuckling, the civilian walk seems a gigolo slouch. Yet this was but a momentary impression. The Germans are becoming bored by their own hysteria; the gentle voice from London is welcomed as a calmative. I cannot praise the BBC too highly for their intelligence in thus modulating these talks.

24 March 1939

CONVERSATION IN CAROLINA

George Edinger

'England's a pretty good country, ain't it?' asked the surveyor *à propos* of nothing in particular.

'What's that? Oh, England,' said the traveller in fertilisers. He felt, as the only one present who had been there, that the remark was probably addressed to him.

'Sure England's all right. It's all them wild-cat countries next door that's been her trouble. Kinda difficult.'

'She otta done somethin', though,' insisted the bank manager.

'Sure she otta done somethin',' the traveller leant forward, 'that's what I said to 'em, England otta done somethin'.'

'Way I see it,' the bank manager announced, 'is this: England's got a fine soil, raise most anythin', if the people could only get a hold of it. But it all belongs to those Lords they got over there. Now these Lords,' he looked around at the assembled company, 'they're frightened as hell they'll lose it all, once you get democracy on top in Europe, what *we* call Democracy I mean, so they just won't have the Dictators beat over in Europe, not anywhere they won't. It's a kinda insurance for them.'

The traveller, who had been there, shook his head. 'That ain't quite right, Joe,' he said.

'Well, it's the way most of us figger it out around here,' insisted the surveyor.

'Sure,' said the insurance broker, 'wasn't that the gang that outed Edward the Eighth, 'count of his having said the miners got a raw deal?'

'It wasn't that,' protested the traveller, 'it was cos of *her*.'

'Aw, shucks. I believed all that boloney till they went an' outed Anthony Eden.'

'That's the man I always *did* like,' the innkeeper mused, 'Anthony Eden.'

'Not I, I didn't,' the editor of the local paper interposed, 'they'd ha' got us right over onto England's side with that man, and I wouldn't see these United States in a war for England again. No, Sir, we been had for suckers once, and they ain't paid us back the money they hired.'

'What d'ya mean, would a got us onto England's side? Ain't we on England's side?' the surveyor wanted to know.

'Sure we're on England's side, same as England was on Abyssinia's side,' said the newspaperman impatiently, 'but that's not what I meant. I meant fighting.'

'They otta paid back,' the traveller admitted, 'they certainly otta paid back.'

The bank manager saw his chance. 'They'd ha' paid, if the people could only get a hold o' their own country and make it raise crops, 'stead o' them Lords keeping it all for themselves.'

'Hear they're talkin' about another token payment,' commented the innkeeper after a short pause.

'If I was the President,' announced the man who was only the bank manager, 'I'd say to 'em, "Well, send along your token payment and maybe we'll let you have a coupla fellers for a token army." '

' 'Cording to the English,' began the traveller apologetically, 'they paid us back some, paid back the whole capital, they say.'

'That can't be right,' said the innkeeper.

'Did you ever hear, it wasn't for themselves they hired the money, that they was guaranteeing the French and the rest so's they could fight Germany,' the traveller wondered.

'No, I never heard that,' said the surveyor.

'Well, anyhow,' the bank manager summed up, 'we gotta keep out o' Europe. 'Taint none of our quarrel and we gotta keep out. For what should we get by coming in, I wanta know that. We came in last time and got called a whole lotta names, lotta Shylocks they called us, that's all we got fer coming in last time.'

'I been up over the State line,' said the surveyor, meditatively, 'they seem to think we couldna very well keep out, in Roanoke.'

'O, so that's what they think in Roanoke.'

'Yes, Sir, that's what they think in Roanoke.'

'Aw, where's the sense?' said the banker, disgusted.

'It weren't none of England's business,' said the traveller suddenly.

'What wasn't England's business?'

'That trouble they got into in Spain, nor Czecho-Slovakia.'

'They gotta alliance with Czecho-Slovakia,' insisted the bank manager.

'No, Sir, *they* ain't got no alliance with Czecho-Slovakia.'

'Well, no more had we got a alliance with England in 1917. But we come in. We come in for Democracy and we come in for Liberty, though we got no alliance. And they called us a lot o' Shylocks, and then they went and sold China and Abyssinia and Czecho-Slovakia and Spain and got rid o' Edward the Eighth.'

'And Anthony Eden,' insisted the innkeeper.

'That was a awful cruel thing they did to Edward the Eighth, turn a man out o' his own country like that; they're awful vindictive the English,' the bank manager went on.

'Sure, they sold the Chinese and the Abyssinians and the Czechs and they sold Spain and you'll see they'll sell the Jews, sell the lot down the river, and they had us for a lot o' suckers with all their boloney 'bout democracy,' the newspaper man summed up.

'Well, we ain't all that noble,' insisted the man who'd been to England.

'What's that?'

'I said we ain't all that noble. We sold them out 'fore they sold us; over the League of Nations we sold 'em, time we sold our own President.

'... And the way I see it,' he went on, 'it don't help none to bring all that up. Maybe if we'd kinda said more they might ha' kinda done more.'

'Sure Edward might ha' done more and Anthony Eden might, but not this lot, they'd never ha' done anything,' the innkeeper persisted.

'Well, maybe they'd ha' had another lot then,' he said irritably. 'Anyhow, there's a hell uv a lot that's wrong with England, and there's a hell uv a lot that's not too good right here in these United States, and I always did wanta know who made all the dough outta that deal over the State Capitol. But there's one thing they got in England that we got right here in these United States, that's the way we're talking today; and we don't need to worry none about who's listening, and that's what we don't wanta lose.'

'Yea, that's right.'

'Sure it's right. And if ever some of them wild-cat leaders they got over there was to wipe the floor with England and we got Japan kicking up rough, well, maybe then we might lose it. And that's why I say if England's in, we just *gotta* come in.'

'Yea, that's OK if they'd ha' had Edward VIII and Anthony Eden, but I don't see why we wanta help those Lords keep all that land ...'

I was feeling tired, and I moved away to my room, preserving the secret of my nationality till morning, because I was too weary to argue.

But the negro boy who showed me the room had already guessed. Or maybe he had been reading the luggage labels.

'Law Suh, you sho doan wanna worry what they done said,' he assured me, 'you doan wanna worry. Dere's just one thing counts a mighty lot. We speak da same language.'

31 March 1939

A SPECTATOR'S NOTEBOOK

Janus (H. Wilson Harris)

Recruits, I read, are flocking to the colours. In fact the flocking season has begun. This is how one of them flocked, thirty-six hours after the announcement about doubling the Territorials was made. Having a free afternoon (X tells me), I made my way to the nearest Territorial headquarters and inquired for the recruiting office. Actually there wasn't any

recruiting office, but I succeeded in interviewing two military gentlemen, who unfortunately could do nothing for me; but if I could go to the
regiment's drill hall at Shepherd's Bush that evening, I might have better
luck. I was unfortunately engaged that evening; but, undeterred, I took a
'bus to another barracks in a different part of London. Here a cloistral
calm prevailed in the deserted halls; I waited a few moments, penetrated
into various empty rooms, and at length found another military gentleman, wearing the same fair moustache and check suit which appears to
be the uniform of the officers of the British Army. 'Could I enlist in the
Territorials?' I asked with some diffidence. 'Well – ah – you see, there's
nobody here now, you know. Could you wait a couple of hours? Sure to be
someone here then.' Unfortunately I couldn't wait. Finally a sergeant was
discovered. 'Well, we can't do anything at the moment. Could you come
back tomorrow morning?' On the following morning, conscious of being
a bore and a nuisance, I re-presented myself. 'Well, you see, we can't do
anything till after Easter, but you'll certainly get a letter from us then.'
What is recruiting like in ordinary quiet times?

7 April 1939

POEM

Geoffrey Grigson

In this quiet room, at this quiet time
In anxious Europe, things come casually
To our sensation. The innocent light hangs
Over the roadway, still the hedge fulfils
Its civil job, the tree sounds slightly
Like the sea, and the accepted rain is slight.

Stand at the window. The cigarette
Is warm, your clock ticks calmly.
This seems the quiet of our two neighbours,
And the moral law, in which the normal
Nights and weeks go by, things are themselves
And seldom metaphors or noticed, and the symbols
From the rain and blackness do not,
As now, so actively engage us.   *5 May 1939*

'TILL SEPTEMBER'

(A Leading Article)

For a fortnight or more we have been enjoying to a degree rare in this capricious climate the unclouded glories of an English summer. Sunlight, foliage, flowers, the songs of birds, have made all who are fortunate enough to have access to the country realise what life is and how it should be lived – till the drone of an aeroplane overhead, or some memory from the morning paper, brings its chill reminder of an overshadowing menace. The very peace and lavishness of Nature may foster perilous illusions. The situation that has produced recurrent crises and perpetual apprehension since the Munich talks has not in any essential element improved. Certain reassuring signs can be discerned, and in their aggregate they amount to something not insubstantial, but the approach to anything resembling settled peace is inappreciable. A new crisis may be precipitated at any moment, but there is some basis for the prediction that, since nations which live on their own crops must get their harvest in, the present lull is likely to continue till September, or, at any rate, till August.

Let us assume the lengthier reprieve, and take it that till September – when the Nuremberg Conference falls due – there will not be a major crisis in Europe. Such optimism may be baseless. War may be upon us at any moment. But it is worth while postulating the respite in order to consider how, if we get it, it can be employed. There is too prevalent a tendency to await September, or whatever the critical month may be, with an inert and passive fatalism, to take for granted that though there may be a temporary lull, September or August must inevitably bring crisis, and very probably war. That is a disastrous frame of mind. The fact to emphasise untiringly is that the postponement of crisis, if postponement there be, is of value supremely as an opportunity for making war less likely. No statesmen worthy of the name, no citizens capable of intelligent exercise of the functions of citizenship, could be content to drift blind and helpless towards whatever abyss may lie before them. Events in the affairs of States do not happen without human volition. There will only be war because the political leaders in one or more countries desire it. And it may be averted either by depriving such leaders of the motive that impels them to war, or by convincing them that war, if they attempt it, will not achieve their ends. It is to this twofold task that we must apply ourselves with all intensity of effort between now and the actual or symbolic September.

The first business of the democracies is to deter the dictatorships from war. That policy is being pursued with some success. The Peace *Bloc* is genuinely and undeniably a peace *bloc*. Not only is all idea of aggression foreign to it; it is in no way hostile to the principle of peaceful change; what it is pledged to resist is change by force of arms. The nucleus of the *bloc* – Britain, France, Poland and Turkey – is a formidable coalition. When the negotiations with Moscow are concluded it will be an act of desperation on Germany's part to make a move that would precipitate war. The delay in reaching a final agreement with Russia is unfortunate, but the difficulty about the Baltic States is not fictitious. Russia's attitude regarding it is reasonable and intelligible; so equally is ours. Reconciliation of the two views may not be easy. But the main principle, of mutual defence against aggression, is unequivocally accepted by both sides, and anyone who believes that failure to complete the agreement as speedily as had been expected means that either party would stand aside in the event of German aggression will be laying himself open to very sharp disillusion.

Unfortunately, persistent self-deception is prevalent in certain quarters in Germany. Herr von Ribbentrop, who has misunderstood this country more comprehensively than any other German diplomat ever accredited to the Court of St James's, appears still to have the ear of Herr Hitler (who can read no English papers, and is dependent on other people's selections from them), and to be able to convince him still that a crime like the rape of Czecho-Slovakia can be repeated with impunity. That is where the capital danger lies. And that is why the question whether a stable peace can ever be achieved while the present *régime* in Germany survives assumes dominating importance. The seizure of Czecho-Slovakia has proved the utter hollowness of Herr Hitler's earlier declarations that he desired to bring no one under the aegis of the Reich but Germans; his own record in the matter of broken pledges demonstrates the futility of signing any agreement with him; while the erection of the suppression or falsification of news (as, most recently, in the case of the Germans in Spain) into a major instrument of State policy, has the deplorable effect of duping ordinary peaceable German citizens into the sincere belief that acts of patent aggression are acts of self-defence by which an unoffending nation must seek to break through encirclement.

The problem created by those facts is grave – but not necessarily insoluble. All Germans are not Nazis; and many Nazis, who are in the party because they cannot afford not to be, are as ready to listen to reason as men like themselves in Britain and France. Between Britain and Germany, or Germany and Poland, there is no disputed question which reasonable men could not settle in a week. Danzig is the most obvious example. The situation there is admittedly anomalous, for the Allies at the Peace Conference thought it better to create an anomalous situation than to carry out their first intention, and hand over the city in fee simple to Poland. If a better *modus vivendi* at Danzig is sought it can be reached without difficulty between a peaceful Germany and a peaceful Poland; but not between a peaceful Poland and a Germany bent on a new domination, and treating Danzig as merely the first step towards the next objective. It is hard to believe that Herr Hitler thinks of it as anything but that.

But moderate men among leading Germans are not entirely silent, though they speak most clearly when furthest from Berlin. In Colombo, on Monday, Dr Schacht said, 'Give us a real League of Nations, where every Power is included, and not one group,' and he added that all Germany needed was raw materials, and he believed that would be peaceably settled in the near future. That is language we can understand, and it is calculated to win immediate response. We shall not stop to point out whose action it was that reduced the League to what Dr Schacht calls a single group; if he speaks for his countrymen in calling for a new and all-inclusive League of Nations, he will nowhere find stronger support than in Great Britain; and if Germany's one need is for raw materials we will be the first to concert means of giving her access to them – if only we can be convinced that it is with a peaceful, not an aggressive, Germany that we are co-operating.

That is the opportunity that offers between now and September, hard though it is to make concessions to a *régime* which interprets all concession as weakness, and so misrepresents it to the people through all the vast propaganda machine which it directs. The nature of the *régime* in Germany can be determined by no one but Germans, but the existence and policy of the present *régime* gravely accentuate international tension, yet between British citizens and German citizens a full and friendly understanding is still possible. If obstacles to understanding do exist we are ready even for some sacrifices to remove them – but only if we are dealing with a people prepared, as Germany's present leaders are not, to observe the ordinary standards of international intercourse, and to meet friendly advances as friends.

9 June 1939

PEOPLE AND THINGS

Harold Nicolson

During the past week I have met three elderly and experienced Europeans. The first was the son of one of Franz Joseph's Ministers and has since childhood been a student of international affairs. The second was a refugee German journalist who served the Weimar Republic with distinction and who still retains his old contacts with German life. The third was an Italian exile. With each of these three observers I discussed at length the question of the inevitability of a second German war.

On four main points my friends were agreed. They agreed, in the first place, that Herr Hitler did not desire a major war, still less a war upon two fronts. His astrologers had assured him that the star of his destiny was in opposition to Mars and that a successful war did not figure among the rewards which were so lavishly provided by his horoscope. On the other hand, Herr Hitler was convinced that destiny would not accord him many more months of active life, and he was determined, before retiring to Valhalla, to accomplish his mission by leaving Germany dominant in Europe, the Mediterranean and the Middle East. Nor should we forget that the Nazi system is a hoop which topples over if it stops.

In the second place my Austrian, my German and my Italian were in accord in believing that Herr von Ribbentrop had now succeeded in convincing the Führer that he had nothing to fear from the present British Government. The British people, according to Herr Hitler's former Ambassador, had even now not realised the implications of 'broadened strategy' or the White War. They had failed to detect any menace to their own interests in German rearmament, in the occupation of the Rhineland, in the seizure of Austria, Bohemia and Albania, or in Spanish non-intervention. Similarly they would not be prepared to resist broadened strategy when applied to Danzig, Budapest, Belgrade, Sofia or Rumania. It thus appeared almost certain to my three friends that Herr von Ribbentrop would now advise his master to organise a self-determination *putsch* in Danzig, to deal Poland a rapid and perhaps overwhelming blow, and at the same moment to lull British opinion by an offer of a 'general settlement' as an alternative to aerial bombardment. They were of the opinion that in the event of our concluding an agreement with

Russia within the next few weeks this *Kraftprobe* would be launched immediately. Should the Moscow negotiations break down or be suspended, then the attack upon Poland might be postponed until after the harvest . . .

30 June 1939

PEOPLE AND THINGS

Harold Nicolson

'The English winter,' wrote Lord Byron, 'ends in July in order to begin again in August.' The truth of this apophthegm was abundantly proved during the course of last Sunday. The gale from the south-west had about it that peculiar and snow-laden bite which one associates with a February north-easter. The rain alternated between a Scotch mist and an Icelandic downpour. The yachts of the rich shuddered at their moorings in Southampton Water. It was the boats of the poor that ventured out into the turmoil of the Solent.

Having endured five hours of howling wind and rain, I put in to the comparative calm of Lymington. I shed my oilskins for a mackintosh. I went (accompanied by Dr Malcolm Burr's truly admirable book on insects) to the local pub; and there, to my joy, I met a fellow politician. He was in some distress. Being interested in the defence of his country he had arranged to visit a signalling section of the territorial army which (unwisely perhaps) had selected Lymington for a Saturday to Monday camp; he had been unable, however, such had been the force of wind and tide, to get beyond Calshot spit and had returned to the Hamble River; from there he had taken a car to Lymington in order to rescue that signal section. We found it. It was as drenched as the sheets of last week's newspaper floating sodden down the Thames. Night was already approaching. He agreed to take seven of them back to the Hamble River. I agreed that two of them should sleep upon my yawl. They would at least be dry. In the comparative warmth of the cabin we discussed the Danzig situation.

The elder of my two unexpected but most welcome guests was employed in a wholesale business. His hours were 9.0 to 5.30, he was allowed Saturday afternoon free, and was given three weeks' holiday a year. Four nights a week were spent in his regimental drill-hall perfecting his signalling with lamp and buzzer and flag. Practically every week-end was also absorbed by the territorial army and of his three weeks' holiday he spent a fortnight every year in camp. He had disliked it at first but now he loved it. His regiment had become part of himself.

My second signaller, when disguised as a civilian, was employed in a well-known London club. His hours alternated between 7.30 to 5.0 one day, and 12.30 to midnight the next. He was accorded only every other Sunday and that was always absorbed by territorial work. The Club authorities did not, it appears, allow him more than a fortnight's holiday in the year. That fortnight was spent in camp. Thus year in and year out he never obtained a free day to himself. He did not resent this unduly. He doubted whether any holiday he could himself devise would be as gay or varied as the training camps which he attended. His was a blithe and manly soul.

So we discussed the Danzig situation.

I explained to them at length, and with precision, the actual import of Articles 102–105 of the Treaty of Versailles. The City of Danzig, I explained, although inhabited by a majority of German Nationals, was so situated as to be able to bar Poland's access to the sea. That access, as they would remember, had been guaranteed by Point Thirteen of the Fourteen Points enunciated by President Wilson on January 8th, 1918, and accepted by the German Government as one of the conditions of their surrender. My two guests were not in the least interested in President Wilson. I therefore returned to the Treaty of Versailles. By Article 102, I explained, Danzig had been created a Free City under the protection of the League of Nations. By Article 104 this Free City was included within the Polish Custom frontier and Poland was guaranteed the control and administration of the Vistula and the right to develop railways and harbour works. No discrimination was to be exercised within the area of the Free City against persons of Polish origin or language.

My discourse, I observed, was not making its mark. They gazed up at the sky-light with polite and patient eyes. It became apparent to me that they were not interested in the juridical status of Danzig and that what they wanted was, not the facts, but the ideas behind the facts. I therefore embarked with fervour and not without eloquence, upon the theme of democracy. That did not go down at all; an expression of agonised resignation settled upon their features. I changed the theme. I spoke to them of the British Empire; of Gibraltar, Malta, Aden and Hong-kong; of all that the White Ensign meant to us and ours; of the vulnerability of our long lines of communication; of the ancient principles of policy handed down to us by our ancestors; of the dangers to which our liberties, nay our very independence would be exposed were any single Power (or group of Powers) to achieve supremacy in Eastern Europe or the Mediterranean. They acquiesced. I realised all too well that these bastions of Empire, these once resounding names, these once reverberating phrases, had stirred them no more than I should be stirred were someone to mention Thurloe Square.

A change of method was evidently essential. I adopted the Socratic method. 'So you are not prepared,' I asked them, 'to fight for Democracy?' 'You bet we're not,' they answered. 'Then surely,' I suggested winningly, 'you must agree that it is illogical to spend so many of your spare hours training to be soldiers if you are not prepared to fight when the moment comes?' 'But who said,' they protested, 'that we are not prepared to fight? We're mad keen to fight.' 'But what do you want to fight for?' I asked them. 'We don't want to fight *for* anything in particular; we want to fight Hitler.'

This reply is not one which is provided for in the admirable *Notes for Speakers* issued from time to time by the Central Office of the Conservative Party. I was disconcerted. 'But *why* do you want to fight Hitler?' I asked them. 'Well, he's treated us like a piece of dirt. He let us down after Munich; he broke his word. That's why we want to get at him.'

'And what about Italy?' I asked them, feeling entranced.

'Oh, Italy,' they answered, 'one does not count Italy either way.'

'Oh, but one should,' I warned them, 'one really should.' They smiled.

'And if war comes,' I continued, 'you would be prepared to serve overseas?' 'Yes, we should like that.' 'But where particularly? Egypt, India, Africa?' They thought for a moment. 'I know where *I* should like to fight,' the younger one said suddenly, 'I should like to fight in Germany.'

I lay there, afterwards, listening to the sharp lap of Lymington water against the hull. It had been an exhausting day. Wind and rain and the howl of angry waters. Behind it all had ached our incessant unhappiness, that constant churning in one's mind of fears and facts, of statistics and anxieties. Everything was quiet now. My two territorials were fast asleep. I went on deck. The little boats around me lay silent at their moorings with a single light at their mast heads. A single light. A riding light. I climbed into my bunk feeling happier than I have felt for many months.

14 July 1939

THE OTHER DAY

Jan Masaryk

The other day an Englishman said to me at luncheon: 'I know how you must feel, but believe me when I tell you that the occupation of Bohemia and Moravia or a similarly drastic action was essentially necessary to make a real impression on the lethargic public opinion of this country and to make us wake up to the facts of the situation. Your country has rendered us a great service.' *Sur ce* I had another helping of raspberries (home-grown).

The other day I met a German friend who is supposed to be very well informed indeed. Said he: 'If I did believe in reincarnation, I certainly would know that the Führer is the reincarnation of Frederick the Great. He is the greatest soldier-diplomat we have had since Frederick the Great. It is miraculous how quickly he mastered the art of soldiery and strategy. The occupation of Bohemia and Moravia was a strategic necessity, long ago decided upon by the Führer. At least 40 divisions would have been necessary to deal with Czecho-Slovakia, and 20 even after the Sudetenland had been cut off. Moravia and Slovakia are essential as a stepping-off place against Poland. Of course Munich was just a subterfuge.' (My friend used the expression '*Augenauswischerei*'). 'Nothing ever did and never will interfere with the Führer's military plans once he makes up his mind. Naturally we must have Danzig and the Corridor and Upper Silesia, and we shall. We also must have an absolutely free hand in Central Europe and the Balkans. Italy on the other hand will be given a free hand in Africa to compensate her for the German drive to the Mediterranean. If your people (meaning Czechs) ever try any funny business it will be suppressed with utmost ruthlessness – that I know for a fact.' Refreshed and enlightened I proceeded on my way.

The other day I met an old Hungarian friend and asked him whether Hungary was not looking at what is left of Slovakia as the next addition to the lands of the Crown of Saint Stephen. Said he: 'Not for a long time. We want the Slovaks to have a good dose of the Germans first. Before long the Germans will succeed (as only they know how) in making themselves thoroughly hated, and some day our chance will come. You (meaning the Czechs) have done more for Slovakia and Sub-Carpathia (where my informant has been recently) than Hungary would have done in a century – so why should we hurry?' Having delivered himself of these words of wisdom my friend left me to my own thoughts. (I am a Slovak on my father's side.)

The other day, walking down Piccadilly, I recognised a familiar figure – a friend from Prague whom I have known for many, many years. I rushed up to him and touched his shoulder. He looked at me, turned white and said: 'For God's sake go away, I have reason to believe that I am being watched by the Germans.' I walked up Half Moon Street wondering what next.

These are experiences of the past two weeks.

In Prague, while everything is being stolen that the gangsters, calling themselves Protectors, can lay their hands on (they are even trying to steal the soul of my people, in which they are having no success whatever, thank God), a week of German culture was held. Hacha and the rest of the poor Czech dignitaries had to attend. Mozart and Schubert was played to SS and SA in uniform – our people have no uniform, it has been stolen by the Germans.

Himmler has recently visited Prague and the terror has increased to a still less human pitch. Himmler is treading where good King Wenceslaus once did. European moral and ethical gilt-edged securities have reached an unprecedentedly low level.

4 August 1939

PRIMROSE HILL

Louis MacNeice

They cut the trees away:
By day the lean guns leer
Across their concrete walls;
The evening falls
On four guns tucked in bed.

The top of the hill is bare,
But the trees beneath it stretch

Through Regent's Park and reach
A rim of jewelled lights –
The music of the fair.

And the wind gets up and blows
The lamps between the trees
And all the leaves are waves
And the top of Primrose Hill
A raft on stormy seas.

Some night the raft will lift
Upon a larger swell,
And the evil sirens call
And the searchlights quest and shift,
And out of the Milky Way
The impartial bombs will fall.

25 August 1939

NEWS OF THE WEEK

The war has been slow in gathering momentum in the West. When people went to church on Sunday morning, if they did, we were at peace; when they came out the country was at war. But apart from the incidence of necessary regulations the first few days have been a time of expectation. Through Sunday, Monday and Tuesday nothing seriously disturbed the tenor of life at home, for while there were air-raid alarms there were in those days, so far as is known, no raids, though there could obviously not be long to wait for them. But the news of the sinking of the *Athenia* was a tragic reminder of what was in store, and the successful RAF raid on German ports on Monday was inevitably accompanied by some casualties. Movement on the western front too has been slow to develop, and meanwhile the full brunt of the German attack has fallen on Poland. The problem before France and Britain is how best and most rapidly to relieve the pressure there. With regard to that General Gamelin and Lord Gort have no doubt matured their plans. At home there will be a wholly different way of life to settle down to. Evacuation has considerably changed the distribution of the population; the movement of vehicles after dark will be so difficult that the streets will be almost empty; the decentralisation of business has begun on a large scale and will continue. All classes, it is earnestly to be hoped, will from the first cultivate a rigid simplicity of life, both for its moral value and as means of avoiding unnecessary expenditure – particularly on such things as alcohol, tobacco and cosmetics.

8 September 1939

ENTERTAINMENT IN WARTIME

The closing of all theatres and other places of public entertainment at the beginning of the war was perhaps a necessary precautionary measure, and in London and other evacuation areas it was obviously wise at the first stage of the emergency. But it is as clear as can be that such a ban on entertainment could not possibly remain general without an incalculable loss to the good spirits and morale of the nation. In the last war in areas not far behind the Front Line and not free from danger of shells and bombs the troops were allowed to congregate for concert-parties and similar amusements. Such relief was invaluable to their spirits. It would be a grave mistake not to make all the use we can of actors, variety artists and musicians who have the will and the skill to take our minds off the pressing disquietudes of the war. In reception areas at least there should be no hesitation in providing facilities for such recreation. 'Equity' has for some time been organising its members with a view to the provision of repertory companies, etc., for the provinces or wherever they may be needed. Mr Basil Dean has made the excellent suggestion that an entertaining authority (possibly under the chairmanship of Lord Esher) should be set up as part of the Civil Defence Administration.

8 September 1939

BOMBING-RAID

Graham Greene

I had been reading Halévy's Epilogue to his *History of the English People* on the way to the aerodrome, bumping through the flat salty eastern county when the first labourers were going to work; yesterday's posters still up outside the little newsagent's which sold odd antique highly-coloured sweets; the squat churches surrounded by the graves of those who had had placid deaths. Halévy is depressing reading – 1895–1905; the old power politics which have returned today: secret arrangements between politicians: words astutely spoken at social gatherings: agreements which were anything but gentlemen's: the sense of middle-aged men with big ideas in a shady racket. One always prefers the ruled to the rulers, and the servants of a policy to its dictators: this hardbitten unbeautiful countryside, this aerodrome – belonging to Eastland – where none of the officers flying the huge camouflaged Wellington bombers was over twenty-three.

Presumably the war between Eastland and Westland had the same political background one found in Halévy – human nature doesn't change; but the war was on and nothing mattered except careful navigation, so that you descended from the clouds on the right target, and a delicate hand and eye, so that you didn't crash while hedge-hopping half a dozen counties at 200 miles an hour. You could even enjoy yourself now that war was on. At tea-time a bomber zoomed down and up, almost brushing (so it seemed to the inaccurate eye) the mess room window, making everybody jump – you could shoot the mess up without a court-martial because it gave practice to the machine gunners round the aero-drome in sighting an enemy target.

I hadn't realised the amount of clothes one had to wear; one felt like a deep-sea diver, in overalls, with the heavy shoulder-straps and steel clamps of the parachute equipment and the inflated waistcoat for saving one's life at sea, the helmet with the padded ear-pieces and the micro-phone attachment dangling by the mouth with a long flex to be attached to a point near one's chair. But then this is not the kind of war which entails much walking: it is a sitting war from which it is impossible to run. Nor, knowing only passenger planes, had I realised the fragile look of

the huge bombers inside, all glass and aluminium, tubes coiling everywhere, a long empty tunnel like a half-built Underground leading to the
rear gun; a little cramped space in front behind the cockpit for the navigator at his table and the wireless operator. In the cockpit you feel raised
over the whole world, even over your plane: space between your legs and
glass under your feet and glass all round, enclosed in something like the
transparent bullet-nose of a chlorotone capsule.

Under the feet at first there was water as we drove for half an hour out
over the North Sea, climbing to 12,000 feet, hands and toes chilling. We
were the leading plane of four, and it was odd up there in the huge din
(the Wellington is the noisiest bomber these pilots have handled), in the
immense waste of air, to see the pilot use the same trivial gestures
through a side window as a man might make signalling to a car behind.
Then as an indication to the other pilots that he needed room, he wob-
bled his plane and the whole squadron turned, a lovely movement in the
cold clear high altitude light: the great green-brown planes sweeping
round in formation towards Westland and the distant inland target.

Then the Blackwater: Gravesend – with the oil tanks like white counters on the Tilbury side. Cloud obscured everything, and afterwards it
seemed no time at all before the engines were shut off and each plane in
turn dived steeply down, cutting through the great summer castles of
cloud, and it was Hampshire below. So far no fighter squadron had intercepted us: whether we had been a mark for anti-aircraft guns we couldn't
tell, but they had had their last chance. It was low flying from now on to
the target in Berkshire – a maximum height of about 200 feet at 200
m.p.h., too low for gunfire; nor could any fighter squadron in the upper
air observe us as we bumped just above the hills and woods the same colour as ourselves. Once, miles away, little black flies at perhaps 8,000 feet,
three fighters patrolled a parallel track and slowly dropped behind: we
were unspotted. One felt a momentary horror at the exposure of a whole
quiet landscape to machine-gun fire – this was an area for evacuation, of
small villages and farms where children's camps might possibly be built,
and it was completely open to the four aircraft which swept undetected
from behind the trees and between the hills. There was room for a hundred English Guernicas.

In an airliner one doesn't recognise speed – a Hercules seems slower
than a cross-country train, objects below move so slowly across the window pane at three thousand feet; but at 200, and we were often at 100 and
sometimes as low as 50, the world does really flash – county giving place
to county, one style of scenery to another, almost as quickly as you would
turn the pages of an atlas. We were out of Hampshire, climbing down
so close to the turf that it was like combing a head, up the forehead and

over, into Berkshire, above our target, wheeling round, one great wing revolving like the sail of a windmill against the bright summer sky, off again, and five minutes later cutting across a fighter aerodrome, with the planes lined up and the men idling and no chance of taking off before we were away, driving a long route home along the Thames, above the film studios of North London and back into the flat Dane-drenched eastern counties. It must be the most exciting sport in the world, low flying, but the bumps are hard on the stomach and I wasn't the only one sick – the second pilot was sick, too, and the navigator passed me an encouraging note – 'Not feeling too good myself.'

Over the coast at 100 feet, the popular resort, people resting on the beach after boarding-house luncheon or taking reluctant exercise on the pier, and out to sea again, climbing into the comfortable smooth upper air: then the last turn, the pilot signalling to his squadron, and the four planes closing up – the sense of racing home. Everybody began to smile, the navigator packed up his maps and instruments and drawing pins in a big green canvas bag, and the Wellingtons drove back in close formation at 260 miles an hour. It had been a good day: even if the war had been a real one, it would still have been a good day – the six-hour flight over, sweeping along to the buttered toast and the egg with the tea and the radio playing in the mess. Whatever causes a future Halévy might unearth of the war between Westland and Eastland, these men would not be responsible – action has a moral simplicity which thought lacks.

18 August 1939

PEOPLE AND THINGS

Harold Nicolson

Some amusement (and we are in need of amusement) has been caused during the last days by the Ministry of Information. It is not in any sense malicious amusement, since most sensible people realise that the Ministry contains men of first-rate ability who will soon be doing useful and efficient work. But for the moment the cumbersome movements of this gigantic bulk raise a smile in the darkness. It is as if a Judge, an ex-Ambassador, a Treasury Official, an Indian Civil Servant, plus the whole

Chatham House set, were suddenly placed in charge of the *Queen Mary* and told to take her rapidly out to sea. Round and round she circles in majestic trepidation, while the military on the banks tell her to turn to the left, while the naval authorities yell at her to veer to starboard, and while the air-folk circle over her advising her not to budge an inch. In a few days now the rudder will be righted, the charts will be spread out in the chart-room, the navigators will take control, and this fine vessel will sweep out confidently beyond the Needles. Everybody will settle down to a particular job. The Ministry will become one of the most efficient and vital Departments of State. It will hum happily like a hive.

It is a hive, I notice, into which countless bees, and some drones, are most anxious to enter. I have received many letters this week from the distant cousins of distant acquaintances telling me that they know French quite well, 'could easily learn Spanish in a short time', and feel that the Ministry of Information is their spiritual home. I reply that I am not an official of the Ministry and cannot help them. A distinguished friend of mine, who also is supposed to be (but is not) in the Ministry of Information, has received so many letters asking for his influence and assistance that he has prepared a printed form. This form runs as follows: 'I am not in the Ministry of Information. If you get there before I do, I hope you will get me in. If I get there before you do, I shall try to get you in.' Although we may be amused and slightly irritated, by this scramble for positions, yet in fact a raging appetite to do something is a healthy sign. I have been much struck by the fact that none of the letters I have received comes from people whose age, health, or capacity would fit them for military service. Many of the applicants have suddenly found themselves deprived of their own livelihood and are naturally anxious to obtain some other form of employment. And in nearly every letter I get there occurs the phrase 'I simply cannot stand hanging about doing nothing.' That assuredly is an admirable spirit.

22 September 1939

THE CINEMA: NEWS REELS.
At various cinemas

Graham Greene

War always seems to surprise somebody; a year after Munich trenches which were begun that autumn are still being dug on the common outside; even the news-reel companies have been caught unprepared. They must have expected the temporary closing of the cinemas; they must have been prepared for censorship, and yet, like the newspapers, they have to rely on Germany as their chief source of supply – an admirable picture of the siege of the Westerplatte, and another of the war in Poland. What have they got ready for us from the home front, and how have their commentators risen to the great occasion? One remembers what Hemingway did for *Spanish Earth*, and one hopes . . . Even a war of nerves has its heroic angle.

As we fumble for our seats the too familiar voice, edgeless and French-polished, is announcing: 'The Queen has never looked prettier.' Royalty is inspecting something or other: 'Royal interest inspires them to redoubled efforts.' Women 'bus conductors climb aboard: 'For men passengers it will make going to work almost a pleasure'; they wave holiday girl hands. Mr and Mrs Chamberlain walk in the Park; complete strangers take off their hats – an odd custom. The Duchess of Kent, instead of going to Australia, makes splints: 'We never thought we would live to be grateful to Hitler.' Very slowly we approach the violent reality; the Expeditionary Force marches to the coast, whippet tanks move through the woodlands, and the voice remarks something about 'shoulder to shoulder in this death struggle for liberty.' Surely by now we should realise that art has a place in propaganda; the flat and worthy sentiment will always sound hypocritical to neutral ears beside the sharp and vivid statement. There was much that Hemingway had to slur over in his commentary: his cause was far more dubious than ours, but the language was much more effective. Let us hope that Germany is not employing a commentator of his standard, for I cannot believe that neutral opinion – or home opinion if it comes to that – will be impressed by the kind of words we listen to – shoulder to shoulder, liberty, baby-killers . . .

The siege of the Westerplatte provides the best few minutes in any news cinema. It would have been interesting to hear the German commentary, for the picture seems to make the same odd psychological mistake as the Italian film of the Abyssinian War. The emphasis is all on power directed towards an insignificant object – we cut from the belching guns of the Schleswig-Holstein to the huge bombers taking off, from the calm complacent face on the captain's bridge to the pilot's face at the wheel, sweating, shadowy, intent: it is all smoke, flame, blast, inevitability. Nobody, we feel, can stand against this for an hour, and the mind answers quickly back that two hundred men stood it for a week. It was an astute move to show this film in England.

From Poland come some pathetic scenes of mob enthusiasm. Col. Beck and the British Ambassador bow from a balcony: the faces of the crowd are excited, enthusiastic, happy . . . The German film of the advance into Poland is beautifully shot and well staged – so well staged (the cavalry cantering in broken sunlight through the woods, the machine-guns rushed to the edge of the meadow grass) that one suspects old sequences of manoeuvres turned and mounted at leisure. Only the huge smashed bridges – like back-broken worms writhing in water – carry the stamp of real war. The same effect is given by the French films cleverly cut in with shots from the pre-war German film of the Siegfried line: the balloon falling in flames is too tidy.

None the less, fake or not, these war pictures from the East and West are impressive, well directed, and edited with imagination, and there is no reason why pictures from the defence front should not be equally effective. A different conception of news is needed – shadows of gold keys and cut ribbons and beauty queens linger. But news no longer means leading figures; we want the technique Anstey used in *Housing Problems*; America is more likely to listen with sympathy to the rough unprepared words of a Mrs Jarvis, of Penge, faced with evacuation, black-outs, a broken home, than to the smooth handled phrases of personalities. Above all, we don't want the old commentators, with their timid patronising jokes; this is a people's war.

29 September 1939

PUBLISHING AND THE WAR

Geoffrey Faber

Few of those who carried on as publishers during the last war are still alive and publishing; and it is strange how little they have to tell their fellow-publishers about the conditions which lie ahead of us today. If these conditions resembled the conditions which developed between 1914 and 1918, then the publishing world would have reason to expect, after the first stage of readjustment, something in the nature of a boom – an experience which it has not enjoyed for years. War encourages reading. Both to the fighting forces and to civilians it brings long hours of boredom and anxiety, which books alleviate as nothing else can. It intensifies emotions, makes men more receptive to the things of the mind, more willing to think and to feel, at the same time as it puts them in greater need of distraction and amusement. It is safe to say that in 1939 these factors will not be less powerful than in 1914; on the contrary, restrictions placed upon public entertainments and public movement must enormously strengthen them.

But there are other factors – partly known, mainly unknown – which may make it difficult for publishers to make the most of the great opportunity which confronts them. The most obvious of these comes under the label of 'distribution'. Huge readjustments of population are bound, at least for a time, to upset the normal channels of supply. Perhaps the effect will be less than might be expected, because a very large proportion of the evacuated population is not much given to reading. Yet some effect there must be. Moreover, the shift from the evacuated to the neutral and receiving areas must put a continuing strain upon the whole transport-system of the country; which must be largely reorganised for the distribution of vital necessities. All this will, no doubt, clear itself up in no very long time, provided that transport is not progressively restricted, and not hindered by the effects of aerial bombardment. Damage to the railways and to the main roads might very easily make the distribution of books extremely difficult. By far the greater part of book-buying, as between the bookselling and the publishing halves of the book trade, is done in London, and must, almost certainly, continue to be done in London. The problem of distribution is, therefore, a problem of first importance.

Next comes the question of manufacture. This, for publishers, depends mainly on their ability to obtain paper, on the ability of printing houses up and down the country to staff their machines, on the ability of bookbinders up and down the country to obtain cloth and boards, and on the maintenance of communication by road and rail between papermills, printers, binders, and publishers. A paper control has already been set up by the Ministry of Supply, and the most urgent representations have been made to the authorities on behalf of the Publishers' Association to safeguard as far as possible the supplies of paper for books. There are good grounds for hoping that the paramount importance, for the public morale, of maintaining an adequate flow of new books, including fiction, is understood in official quarters.

To the technical problems of distribution and manufacture must be added others of a less immediately obvious kind. The first of these concerns the great difficulties which many, if not all, publishing-houses will experience in keeping a sufficient and sufficiently experienced staff. Book-publishing is a far more exacting business than most people realise. Every book needs meticulous and intelligent attention at each stage of its development from manuscript to volume form. Apart from this, it has often to be edited at one end, always to be publicised at the other. Again, the mere business of keeping, handling, packing and despatching a multiform and continuously changing stock, in a publishing house of any size, calls for a considerable and experienced staff. If anything like an adequate output of books is to be maintained, an adequate staff is essential.

The other 'less obvious' consideration is one impossible to assess. Paper, print and publishers are all useless, if the books are not written. For the last year shrewd observers on the backstairs of the book world have been noting a progressive decline in the quantity and quality of worthwhile manuscripts. The reason is easy to see. Ever since Munich the atmosphere of Europe has grown more and more unfavourable to creative literary work. A time of recurring crises, with intervals of heightening tension and a growing fear lest civilisation may have been fatally betrayed by the democracies – such a time dries up the wells of imaginative thought. 'How can I write with the world in this state?' is a cry I have heard more than once in the last few months.

Now that the decision has been taken to fight, and the nation has resolved to end the new barbarism in Europe, there should be a lifting of this deadweight from the minds of writers. But other influences may take its place. The effects of ARP are depressing enough to ordinary people; to many authors they will be disastrous, unless they live in the less vulnerable parts of the country. And there is a more insidious danger than this.

The type of mind which expresses itself in literature is apt to be more than ordinarily conscious of the pressure of events and opinion. It is also apt, at times, to despise its own nature, to crave for the plain job of the plain man. In a prolonged modern war, with the whole community tightly organised for a collective struggle, a writer will need an uncommon resolution, and an uncommon conviction that authorship is his proper and most valuable form of service, if he is to prevent himself from being used by the unintelligent will of the herd, or of the bureaucracy, for tasks better performed by others.

To readers of *The Spectator* it is needless for me to defend the values of literature. Those values rise to their highest point in a war undertaken in order to save the world from barbarism. The function of the author, at such a time, becomes infinitely more important than at any other. That is not to say that literature, in war, should consist of nothing but noble sentiments. Literature – as I have argued before, in resisting the demand for a censorship – has to be taken as a whole, as the one means which the nation or the race has of 'thinking aloud'. It must express all moods, and appeal to all needs. It lives by freedom – by the very freedom for which we are now to fight. May some such conception as this unite our writers and give them, each in his own particular kind, the courage and the gaiety which the country will look to them to exhibit.

I have said little about the plans which publishers have made, for there is little to be said. Some offices have moved, in whole or in part, from London, but there has been no general migration. It would seem that, for the present at least and so long as possible, the publishing trade will remain concentrated in or close to London. It will continue to operate to the maximum of its capacity. So far as the autumn season is concerned, there will be no shortage of new books, though there will naturally be a considerable reduction of output. To look further ahead is difficult; but most publishers are no doubt doing as my own firm is doing – planning to maintain as nearly as possible a normal output. It is too early yet to say whether costs will rise to such a height that the prices of books will have to be increased. I trust not. It is the policy of the Government to prevent a rise in prices; though the high cost of compulsory insurance of saleable goods against war risks, if it is applied to books, can only be met by a surcharge related to published prices.

As for the type of new book which is most likely to be in demand, and therefore most likely to be published, I do not myself anticipate any very startling changes. It would not surprise me if the demand for crime stories decreased; imaginary violence loses its attraction in the presence of real violence. Books about the war, and the future reconstruction of the world, are likely to have a vogue. Poetry may receive a new stimulus.

Fiction of all kinds should begin to see better days. I should expect that any book which is born of honest and serious thinking will be more willingly read than in peace-time. And there is certainly a huge public waiting for the first new writer who can catch the note of humour, which is the natural reaction of our race to danger.

15 September 1939

A SPECTATOR'S NOTEBOOK

Janus (H. Wilson Harris)

What, by the way, is the BBC coming to? Twice on Wednesday (very likely there were other opportunities of which I failed to take advantage) news about Moscow, Berlin, Rome, the Western Front, sinkings of neutral ships, was followed by the singular observation that 'A walk in the country is urged by the Ramblers' Association as . . . ,' if I remember, specially beneficial for nerves, limbs and other organs or fibres; farmers, therefore, ought not to be allowed to plough up footpaths. The Ramblers' Association is no doubt an admirable body. So, to take a random example, is the Governesses' Benevolent Institution – and ex-governesses are likely to have a particularly bad time during war. Will the BBC give them a show? If not, why not? If so, what other estimable organisations may apply?

Every notable method of war-winning deserves publicity and praise. Here is one, in the form of an official notice – roneoed.

'To . . .
I notice that there is a practice of wearing somewhat unorthodox clothes by the women members of this staff.
I should be glad if you will discontinue this habit as I prefer that the women members will come on duty in what can be regarded as normal women's clothing.

[Signature illegible]
Air Raid Precautions Controller.'

The abnormal women's clothing in question was, I understand, slacks – in which no war could be won.

6 October 1939

CLERIHEW COMPETITION

First Prizes

Ribbentrop
'S buying ersatz ginger-pop,
Which he sells again
As champagne.

When appeased, Adolf's figure
Swells and grows bigger and bigger.
Oppose him, and Hitler
Grows littler.

Belisha
Rigs out his militia
In headgear more suited to deacons,
Or beacons.

W.E. GREEN

Mr Churchill
Cannot read Virgil:
Biographers with a little Latin
Will always put that in.

WILLIAM STEWART

10 November 1939

PEOPLE AND THINGS

Harold Nicolson

I flew to France the other day in a mood of melancholy. It was a wet and wind-swept morning and the wide wings of the aeroplane glistened with scudding rain. Below them, through the sleet, slid the orange woods of England, and thereafter an iron-coloured sea was streaked with bars of foam. As we approached the French coast the sky lightened; a pale gleam of sunshine touched the cabin windows with a wet finger; and then suddenly we swung into a lake of blue sky and below us shone a little Norman harbour which I have known and loved for many years.

My melancholy did not leave me. The past loomed as an aching memory, and the future as an aching apprehension. I looked down sadly upon the coloured forests, upon the clear straight roads, upon the towns and villages clustering round their mairie and their church. 'In every one of those houses,' I thought, 'is some heart torn with anxiety or weighed down by depression.'

It seemed intolerable to me that for the third time in living memory this gentle and pacific people should be exposed to outrage by the barbarians of the east. It seemed intolerable that a civilisation so ancient and yet so progressive, so intricate and yet so simple, so diverse and yet so balanced, should once again be molested by the rude hands of the *'ivrogne tudesque'*. It seemed intolerable that this France (the elder sister of all reasonable men) should once again be assaulted by the cancer of a total war. My heart was wrung with pity for a people who have assuredly not merited the sufferings to which, generation after generation, they have been exposed. And as I thought these things the great wing of the aeroplane swung upwards and with a wide sweep we slid down to earth. A number of French Deputies and journalists had come to meet us. They greeted us with exuberant delight. In the warmth of their gaiety, in the sunshine of their confidence, the mists of melancholy were soon dispersed.

10 November 1939

A WAR TO END CLASS WAR

Osbert Sitwell

Often in the past the slow, robust good humour of my countrymen has angered me, but never again shall I allow myself this mood of irritation, for now I realise fully, in spite of the thousand very minor cruelties with which it is encrusted, the wisdom that such laughter conceals. Thus, in a time when good fortune – except for the profiteer, whose days are in any case numbered – can scarcely be said to exist, it is at least fortunate for the nerves and minds of each of us that no one, whether journalist or politician, dares to produce a new claptrap slogan. 'British grit' and 'Keeping our chins up' are alas! still allowed, because traditional; as soon have a harlequinade without a red hot poker or a red nose, as a war without them. But even our tolerance of them is only good-humoured, while should anyone ever again be insensitive enough to talk of a War to End War, or of Making the World Safe for Democracy, a strong tide of furious laughter would soon drown his brazen voice. For, though the last war failed to end wars, it did at least end our patience with slogans that provoke, and because of the hatred they beget, prolong them, and their evil after them.

The present and abiding mood of the British people, then, will tolerate neither catchwords nor white feathers, and has no need of hatred upon which to maintain its spirit. We recognise now, too late, that over-hatred and over-kindness combined to lose us the last peace, and it is essential for our well-being at the end of this war that none of us should have been worked up to that hysterical state of hatred in which clear thinking becomes impossible; for we must regard Germany coolly, objectively, and keep our aims in view. We have got to rid a powerful nation of the leaders who by their bigotry and madness condemn their people to destruction, and we have, which is more difficult, to rid that people of the germ, latent in the blood, which makes so great a country recurrently liable to such brutal and senseless leadership.

Since, as a race, we are given to acting rather than thinking, and to relying upon instinct rather than upon any process of ratiocination, we must plan very clearly the aims to be realised, and the means by which to realise them. We must attempt to allow ourselves, within the framework of necessary regulations, the fullest liberty of thought and action; above all, we must repel the advances of bureaucracy, and give battle to it where we see it. And, when peace comes, we must allow other nations to think differently from us, and propose no British model for the government of other States. Parliament, for example, is only suitable to people who *like* freedom and are used to it, and to countries where Everyman is born a politician rather than a soldier. We must remember that in spite of their loud voices and over-insistence on their virility, the Germans are a sentimental and very feminine people, impressed by the 'sheik-stuff' handed to them by Hitler and his gang of toughs. These qualities, the liking of being hypnotised, the wish to be prostrate and, at the same time to bully and cringe, will, alas, continue long after Hitler, Goebbels and Co. are dead: so, also, will their good qualities, now foully exploited, German, courage, and loyalty, German patience and love of organisation.

Certain things in the German character are, perhaps, difficult for us to understand; but we must make the effort, and we must find a way of harnessing German energy to the general benefit . . . Thus the eighteenth century found a method of keeping the German love of battle within bounds. The more civilised Powers used German troops as mercenaries, and thus ensured that those who most loved fighting were killed off at regular intervals and *in defence* of civilisation. (Nineteenth-century opinion, it is true, was shocked by this: but for a time, at any rate, it settled the eternal German problem: and if the salient characteristic of the members of a race is the wish to be killed – and, of course, to get others killed as well – who are we to gainsay their desires?) Duelling, again, is salutary for the more backward spirits, and should never be discouraged. But, on the other hand, is it not possible once more to utilise these qualities in the service of all mankind? Just as the termites have developed a special type of warrior-ant, could not German forces, instead of being forbidden altogether as after the last war, be used for guaranteeing International Law, rather than destroying it? Their loyalty, if they could be persuaded to undertake such work, could be relied upon and they could defend dangerous frontiers and serve as part of the forces at the disposal of the coming International Order.

Even at the moment, the British can reply to Germany with other means, in addition to fighting. No one can tell when an air-raid will occur: but in consequence, the public is keyed up, and at the same time unable to find a use for its leisure. But even in such hours, an effective response is possible. Thus, the Nazis enjoy burning books: well, instead of deploring this habit, let us read the books they burn. We shall gain by that amount of learning. Let us remember, too, that the Nazi *régime* was built up on the cult of physical fitness, and that, while such a cult is all very well in its way, and as part of a larger conception, no equivalent stress was ever laid by Nazis upon *mental* fitness; only upon a fitness which enabled its victims to obey to their own doom. The great benefactors of mankind have not been instructors in 'physical jerks', but poets and scientists, thinkers and musicians. Einstein, the most eminent German of today, is noted less for his aptitude for long or high jump, for the ability to touch his toes or for chest expansion, than for his mathematics and his love of the violin.

It would be well, therefore, to reply to Nazi Germany by inculcating in British schools, with equal force, a love of intelligence and an understanding of higher things, and by a deliberate cultivation of the individual powers of thinking along unorthodox and un-old-school-tie lines: for let us make no mistake, our own fault has been mental laziness, and a refusal to respect intelligence except in its most practical forms. Joy through bodily health has been emphasised in Germany, and to a lesser degree here. Let us now advocate a Joy Through Intelligence Movement.

But perhaps in these matters I tend to be extreme. And extremes must be eschewed, for they are what we are fighting against. Thus, each of us, whatever his political tendencies, now sees most clearly the end to which fanaticism in himself or others leads, so that, if a catchword were needed, one might be found ready in a War to End Class War. We have no use for extreme ways of thinking, and recognise at last that the traditional English love of compromise is more than a way of living; it is an aim in itself, the golden middle road which avoids the lies and bloodshed and torture on each side. Even our most fanatical politicians must be by now disillusioned equally with Moscow and Berlin, those two ugly masks to the same face. There is little to choose, except in daring, between thug and vulture, and we are fighting for a way of life in which thugs and vultures will no longer dare to attempt control of the fates of other beings.

17 November 1939

TRIBUNAL DAY

Cynthia Saunders

The KC laid his black hat and coat on a red leather chair underneath the trellised window overlooking the High Street, rubbed his hands and said, 'A cold morning, Sergeant.' 'Yes, Sir, very cold,' the policeman answered. It was ten o'clock. The door opened and the interpreter came in, shook hands with the KC and the Sergeant, and said cheerfully, 'Let's turn them all down this morning and get to lunch early.'

'I'm sorry you're feeling so bloodthirsty, Miss Simmons,' the Sergeant said, 'make them think we're in Germany, eh?'

At 10.15 enter the first alien. It was quite a way from the door to the two chairs placed at a discreet distance from the little table behind which the Judge sat. On his left was the Sergeant, acting as secretary, taking down everything that was said; on his right the interpreter.

'Are you Grete Schmidt?'

'Yes,' a large, homely woman replied.

'When were you born?'

'Eighteen, six, ninety-three,' came the answer in Teuton fashion, meaning June 18th, 1893.

'And when did you come to England?'

'One, five, thirty-five.'

'Are you Jewish?'

'No.'

'What is your religion?'

The buxom cook spread herself. She had wanted to say so much, but the questions came a little too fast.

'Me? I believe in the Lord, and He made the world a very big place and I don't understand why people should always be being told they must go home.'

The interpreter smiled, the Sergeant smiled and the Judge passed his hand over his mouth.

'Nevertheless, Miss Schmidt, why are you in England now?'

'Because I like England. I don't like Austria with Hitler there.'

'Have you any money over here?'

'O yes, Sir, I save.'

'In a bank, Miss Schmidt?'

'No, Sir – one's pocket is one's best friend,' and she drew out a little leather satchel with pound notes.

Miss Schmidt had excellent references and 'her lady' was outside. Exempted from internment until further notice.

Next, an elderly Jewish couple. The man limped badly, walking with a stick. He sat down with some difficulty. 'Excuse me, I am lame – the Nazis,' he said. 'I am sixty-five today, my birthday.' The Sergeant leant across and shook hands with him. 'Congratulations.' Then the old Jew broke down for a few seconds. So did his wife. Miss Simmons looked away to the window and the Judge waited patiently.

The questions began. When it came to his former profession he had a rare one. He had made the printed silk ribbons often used on wreaths. 'Hitler took my business, my grandfather founded it, you see in the concentration camp they broke my leg . . . and in the High Street my wife knows . . . but you see I have come here . . .' He was dithering helplessly. Shades of former cross-examinations.

Miss Simmons translated, adding that it would be kinder to serve, and de-restrict.

The Judge thought so, too, and asked her to translate how he hoped they would both have a peaceful time in England. They tottered out, their registration books endorsed: 'Victims of Nazi Oppression, exempt from Internment and from all restrictions applicable to enemy aliens.' A little shred of happiness for past miseries. The Tribunal had been sitting for three weeks, but it took a few seconds to recover from this.

'Next, please.'

The door opened and a very beautiful youngish German woman tripped across the floor up to the two chairs, of which she took one and lifted it firmly to the table, sitting down immediately opposite the Judge (a thing he could not bear). Miss Simmons caught the Sergeant's eye and the Judge's, but not the beautiful woman's, who was out by every means in her power to win or die. She wheedled and charmed the KC in vain. It only got her case postponed for Home Office and other files to be sent down from London.

'Only she is too like a copy-book spy to be real,' the Judge observed to Miss Simmons at luncheon.

'Next, please.'

This was an Austrian boy of 19, parlourman in the house of a Staff Captain. Yes, he waited at table (and overheard everything), no, he wasn't a refugee (and so had deliberately become Stateless), but Austria under Hitler, &c. Rather a tall story. Anyway unsuitable for employment in Staff Captain's house. Tribunal had no power to make him leave or be dismissed; only power to intern or exempt from internment with or without travelling restrictions. Interned.

Then four refugees, then luncheon, and another half-dozen, all straightforward cases.

Finally, about 4.15, the last for the day.

She spoke very little English, and answered every question in monosyllables. She was not a refugee. She had had two sisters over here in service, like herself, who had gone back to Germany shortly before the war started. Why had she stayed? No answer. Had she deliberately stayed? Yes. Would she like to go back now? No. Was she a member of the *Arbeitsfront*? No. Had she voted when the German ship came? No? Why not? No answer. It was getting late and the Tribunal was getting no further. A shame that the last case should be so tedious. It was no use starting all over again. Suddenly Miss Simmons had an idea. Had the young woman any special friend in England? Yes. Who?

'My employer—'

'Are you engaged?'

'He's the father of my child.'

That, too, may be the price of refuge.

17 November 1939

THE LATEST ANTI-JEWISH HORROR

Oswald Garrison Villard

Mr Villard, who had just returned from a tour in Germany, was editor and proprietor of the New York NATION from 1918 to 1932, and was one of the best-known editorial writers in the United States.

What may prove to be the final act of the incredibly brutal and cruel tragedy which Adolf Hitler has inflicted on the Jews in his power is now going on, and without receiving the attention of the world as it should because of the pressure of war news. With practically no publication of the plan in the German newspapers, Adolf Hitler is going ahead with the creation of a so-called Jewish State, located in Poland, near Nisko, on the San, south-west of Lublin. A stretch of land, about 50 by 60 miles in area, has been set aside. It is enclosed by a barbed-wire fence, and only Jews will be allowed to live therein. Into this small territory are to be crammed no fewer than 1,945,000 Jews. What is to become of the Poles who have inhabited this region is not stated, but it is said in various quarters that the land is exceptionally poor. Whether it is poor or rich, this mass-migration by force has been begun now, in the dead of winter, and in a manner that cannot be interpreted as anything else than a determination to create, not a Jewish State, but a most horrible concentration camp, which can certainly become nothing else than a habitation of death.

For these unfortunate people are forbidden to leave with more than 300 marks. They are permitted to take with them only such hand-bags as they can carry. All the rest of their belongings, the furniture in their apartments, the rest of their means, their jewels – everything is stolen from them in the usual custom of the men who declare that they belong to the purest and noblest strain of humanity the world has yet seen. No preparations are made for their reception; they are simply to be dumped in and left to shift for themselves. If they cannot find shelter in the deserted homes of the evacuated Polish peasantry, why, they can freeze to death, or build new homes, without means, without materials, without tools, without anything. How they are to subsist when they get there no one knows. How those who survive until the spring will obtain seeds and farming tools and cattle and horses no one can imagine. It is impossible to conceive of any more barbarous cruelty – and it is deliberately calculated. Behind the barbed-wire fence the Jews are to live or die in circumstances which would not be permitted in any civilised country if the victims were dogs or cattle.

Not only are 1,500,000 Polish Jews to be confined there, but to them are to be added 150,000 from the Czech Protectorate, 65,000 Viennese, 30,000 from Posen and West Prussia, and 200,000 from the rest of the Reich. This means that every remaining Jew in Berlin and elsewhere will be forcibly interned. People of the greatest refinement and culture are to meet the same fate as the Polish Jewish peasants. Perhaps these figures for the Reich are a little too high, for according to the latest report of the Reich Association of German Jews, as published in the *Rotterdamsche Courant*, the number of Jews in Germany has fallen from 500,000 in 1933 to 185,000 on October 1st, 1939. Of these, some 77,000 are men, and 108,000 women, of whom no fewer than 95,000 reside in Berlin. A majority of the whole number is totally without means, and subsists on the capital remaining to those who were well-to-do or wealthy. No one is allowed to work except some able-bodied men who have gone to labour on farms; they report, by the way, that they are kindly received and humanely treated by the farmers. Otherwise not a penny of earned income comes to these people. There they sit, forbidden to be in the

streets after eight o'clock at night under penalty of arrest, without anything to do, with only two repaired synagogues available in Berlin for religious services, and with practically no places of entertainment open to
them. Day after day they sit at home, and every time the door-bell rings
expect that the order has come to prepare for immediate departure for
Poland, and what they consider certain death.

The forced migrations began on October 17th. The first to go were
those from the Protectorate, the second from Austria, the third group
from Posen and West Prussia, and the last from the Reich, the movement
being in charge of the Gestapo. There are being taken out of Vienna every
week some two thousand men, women and children, but at the end of
October one such transport comprised only fourteen hundred persons,
according to information given to the *Allgemeen Handelsblad* of The
Hague, because so many had sought to escape this fate through suicide or
flight. 'In the last fourteen days,' its Berlin correspondent reported on
November 10th, 'in Vienna alone 82 Jews have committed suicide, of
whom 36 were women.' Nowhere were the deportations pushed more
vigorously than in Moravian Ostrava, where already many Jewish-owned
houses are standing empty. What this actual evacuation means in terms
of human suffering I learned from a letter sent to an American official by
an Aryan German residing in a certain town. Writing to this official, this
German asked whether the United States could not be induced to protest
against the horrible cruelty of this transportation. He stated that a
trainload of cattle-trucks containing these unfortunates had stood for
twelve hours in the station of the town in which he resided, that they
were without food or conveniences of any kind, and had no heat. He
declared that the moans and groans of these desperately wretched suffer-
ers could be heard a long distance from the station. He declared that he
was a loyal German, but that he could not keep silence in the face of such
horrible wickedness. Not one word of this, of course, can appear in a
German newspaper. The public is, therefore, utterly unaware of what is
being done, and individuals will not believe the truth when it is told to
them.

What adds to the general confusion of these strange migrations is that
Russia and Germany have just signed an agreement for the repatriation
of German citizens in Soviet-occupied Poland and Soviet citizens in the
German-occupied section, and that at least 500,000 Jewish refugees, of
whom 350,000 have received Soviet citizenship, are now reported to be in
Lemberg, the chief town of the Soviet-occupied Polish Ukraine. Hitler is
currently reported to be migration-mad; ever since he hit upon the idea
last winter of moving the Germans out of the Italian Tyrol his mind has
occupied itself with the shifting of minorities out of the regions in which

they are to be found, and reuniting them with people of their own race. But with the Jews the motive is to get rid of them without loss of time, and, as has been said, without the slightest regard for what may become of them after they have reached their destination. It goes without saying that Hitler would not thus treat cattle on the railroads, for such cruelty to them is forbidden by strict laws.

I suspect that there is an ulterior motive behind all this. It is altogether probable that one reason why these poor people are stripped of almost everything before being thrust into this charnel-house is that Hitler may point to them when they die off of hunger and cold and say: 'See, I told you these were a parasite people who could only live by battening on Gentiles. I gave them territory on which to build their own State, and see how utterly they have failed.' I did not dare, for their sake, to call on more than a very few Jews while I was in Germany, lest I injure them. But I found that they were entirely aware of what transfer to this 'State' meant. Their one request of me was that I make known to the English and American Jewry just what this proposal signifies, and beg them not to be misled. They pointed out that even if this 'State' were adequately prepared for the migration, it still could have no economic future, since it will be surrounded on all sides by hostile communities, who will doubtless not be permitted to do business with those surviving unfortunates within the barbed-wire. I have no hesitation in saying to German friends that if the Hitler Government were in every other respect a model one, I should still consider it utterly damnable because of what it has done to Jews who felt the power of this despot.

1 December 1939

Part Two
1940

With best wishes from Mrs. Smith

Every scrap of **METAL** is wanted—
for guns and tanks and ships.

Every scrap of **BONE** is wanted—
for planes, explosives and fertilisers.

Every scrap of **PAPER** is wanted—
for ammunition and many other things.

By carefully putting out every bit of scrap
metal in her house, every bone and every
scrap of paper, Mrs. Smith has given the
Government valuable defence material. She
has rendered her country a very real service.

HELP TO WIN THE BATTLE OF BRITAIN AT YOUR OWN BACK-DOOR

"UP HOUSEWIVES AND AT 'EM!"

RIGHT BEHIND THE GESTAPO

Hans Hohkum

An extract from the sensational book published this – or next – week by the Phony Press.

I got my position in the first instance through denouncing my parents. My father was old and unemployed, my mother was bedridden. I was working in a sausage factory. We lived together in a humble flat in the Goebbelstrasse. One evening I came home from work to find them listening to a foreign broadcast and reading the Jew journal *Spectator*. It was no moment for half-measures. Primed with my telephonic description of the treacherous scene, the Gestapo were round before bedtime. My parents went to a concentration camp where, their enfeebled constitutions proving unequal to the conditions, they were dead within a week. I got the flat to myself. Previously I had always felt that it was crowded.

For getting rid of these enemies of the State, I was given a minor post in the Gestapo. I rapidly made my mark. I was fortunate in having numerous family connexions and an extensive acquaintance. Within a month I had compromised the lot. A few, whom I managed to inveigle into the company of Jews, were executed; the rest were sent to Buchenwald. When they were disposed of, I started to work backwards through my career – my last employers (and fellow-employees) first, and so on back to the family of the nurse who had tended me in my cradle. Finally, it could be said that I had not a relation, a friend, or a former colleague still at liberty.

This was the signal for promotion. One day Himmler sent for me. He wanted someone to watch Ribbentrop, who had stood in his way by appropriating an actress who had been under Himmler's personal protection. I saw that this was my chance. Within a week, Ribbentrop, noticing my surveillance, had sent me a note (and a case of – somewhat indifferent – champagne) suggesting an interview. He wanted someone to watch Goering, whom he suspected of conspiring against his position. I took on the job on a half-time basis. Concealing myself in Goering's shadow, I stalked him for three days. At the end of them he summoned me. He had lost some medals; Goebbels (who had not any, except the regulation Iron Cross) was suspected. Would I watch him? Thus I found myself serving three masters, determined that soon all three should be my servants.

I had not long to wait. I shadowed Goebbels (suffering from the usual black eye) for a day. At cocktail-time he surrendered. Asking me in to his house, ostensibly to inspect a new collection of indelicate pictures, he mentioned the name of Hitler. There were doubts of the Führer's loyalty to the Reich. Would I care to undertake an examination? The pay was not bad; I took on the job.

Hitler, who seemed less observant than the others, permitted me to follow him for a whole week before issuing a summons. Here I feel bound to correct some misapprehensions. The Führer is not, at heart, a politician. He received me in his music-room, where on a bullet-proof piano he was tracing out with one finger *Siegfried's Journey to the Rhine*. I attracted his attention by spitting into a cuspidor, maintained – I suppose – for the benefit of the American Ambassador.

'My achievement is less great than that of Strauss,' he began

'Of Wagner, Mein Führer,' I corrected him.

Hitler rose in a rage. 'That democrat, Anglophile and Jew!' he fumed.

'He was the composer of *The Ring*,' I reminded him.

Hitler sank into a chair. 'I became confused,' he said, with simple humility.

For half an hour we talked as one man to another. At the end of it I knew him as no one else. His tragedy was that he was a man of simple ambition, elevated to the heights by the remorseless destiny of the German nation. He wanted to compose an opera, he wanted to build a public lavatory in every city of the Reich, he wanted to write a novel. 'My publishers tell me,' he said with an innocent smile, 'that *Mein Kampf* shows that I have a decided talent for fiction.' The eagerness of the craftsman was on his face. 'But these fellows,' he pathetically complained, 'make me always wear a military uniform, deliver speeches, invade countries, and threaten a European war. I will tolerate these injustices no longer. I want to be a simple man with an umbrella and a bowler hat, just like the English Chamberlain, even if he is a Jew.'

It was impossible not to be touched by such a speech. And, fortunately, I at once saw the way in which I could make my genuine sympathy serve my ambitions.

'How would it be, Mein Führer,' I exclaimed, 'if you were to allow some of your irksome duties to devolve upon others? How would it be to make someone else do the routine work – the making of speeches, the checking-up on Ribbentrop, Goebbels, and so on – thus leaving yourself free to do the things that really interest you?'

'But who?' he queried.

This was my chance. 'Mein Führer, I myself will assist you,' I answered.

Thus it was arranged. We spent the rest of the evening making-up. Aided by a feminine friend of the Führer's, who has a talent for theatricals, I truncated my moustache, plucked my scalp, and gummed my features into a scowl. I was fortunately of the same build and colouring as the Führer. After two hours' work it was difficult to distinguish between us – as was proved when a servant entered and (the Führer having retired for a moment) addressed me with correct servility.

Cast your minds back to the Führer's public appearances since July, 1936. You will agree that they are infinitely numerous, but half of their number refer not to the Führer himself but to me! It was not the Führer but I who rode in triumph into Vienna; it was not the Führer but I who settled the Jew Chamberlain at Munich; it was not the Führer – for he was faithful to one woman – but I who entertained various actresses who performed in Strauss in Munich and elsewhere. It was not the Führer but I – but why go on? At least half of the Führer's public appearances since 1936 were made, as I have explained, not by him but by me. While I was reprimanding Goebbels for involving himself in scandal, decorating Goering for gallantry in Austria, or propelling Ribbentrop (whom I never liked) towards another diplomatic gaffe, the Führer was resting quietly in the seclusion of Berchtesgaden, playing the piano (with one finger), designing imaginary buildings, drinking milk, and eating little cakes . . .

I had, of course, for one must live, kept on my other jobs. I had the best of opportunities for watching Ribbentrop (in the interests of Himmler), Goering (in the interests of Ribbentrop), Goebbels (in the interests of Goering), the Führer (in the interests of Goebbels), and – to square the circle – Himmler (in the interests of everyone). It can be seen that I was the real power behind the Party, the Army, the Foreign Office, the Propaganda Ministry, and, of course, the Gestapo. It was arduous work, but the total pay – Rm. 10,000,000 – was good, and I felt that I was really serving the State. Between July, 1936, and August, 1939, I was the instrument of no fewer than 234 traitors and Jews being executed, and no fewer than 1,837 Jews, saboteurs and race-defilers being sent to concentration camps – which gives me an average substantially better than Bradman's. I should have been content to remain indefinitely at my post.

It was, however, not to be. On August 20th, 1939, there was a Cabinet meeting attended by the Führer, Goering (in the uniform of an Admiral of the Fleet), Ribbentrop (in rat-catcher), Goebbels (in mufti) and others. I intended to announce a *coup*, which would confirm my position as second only to the Führer. Waiting until they were assembled, I entered the room.

'Mein Führer,' I exclaimed, 'I have positive evidence that Ribbentrop, Goebbels, and – to a lesser extent – Goering have been conspiring against the State. They have been exploring the possibilities of an alliance with Bolshevik Russia.'

I shall never forget the look on the Führer's face. It was that of a man dragged into politics against his will, and made moreover publicly to endorse policies which he knew to be ruinous. He threw me an intimate, sorrowful and appealing look.

'I know,' he said. 'It is too late to turn back. The treaty will be announced tomorrow.

Bowing, I withdrew. You can imagine what thoughts raged within my breast. I knew that there was no time to be lost. As soon as the Council Room was shut, I took to my heels. One of the office Mercédès was in the Wilhelmstrasse. I requisitioned it, and – stopping only at the office of a rich industrialist, whom I compelled to hand over an enormous sum – drove rapidly to the airport. I flew the Gestapo plane at full speed to the friendly soil of a neutral country.   D.V.

16 February 1940

ROUND EUROPE WITH MR WELLES

Mallory Browne

As European Editorial Manager of THE CHRISTIAN SCIENCE MONITOR, *Mallory Browne was one of three American journalists to accompany the US Under-Secretary of State Sumner Welles to Rome, Berlin, Paris and London.*

When Mr Sumner Welles arrived in Naples, less than three weeks ago, to begin his European tour, a heavy veil of silver mist obscured, but could not completely conceal, the smoking volcano in the background. Only a dim outline of its towering, haze-enshrouded bulk could be discerned far across the placid blue waters. Yet even that vague shape of Vesuvius, with its shadowy plume, was imposing enough to dominate the whole sparkling harbour and tranquil bay. There was something in the scene symbolical of Mr Welles' entire round of 'fact-finding' visits. They, too, have been veiled in a thick mist of persistent silence from beginning to end. But one felt, somehow, that Mr Welles' general impressions were not far different from those of us who were his constant fellow travellers. What, then, were these impressions?

First of all, that the main conclusion which must be drawn from Sumner Welles' tour is that no visible basis exists for any compromise peace settlement between the Allies and Germany, either now or in the near future. To the extent, therefore, that the Under-Secretary of State was sent over to Europe in the hope, however slender, of finding such a basis for peace, he has failed. But in so far as his mission was the avowed one of gathering full and first-hand facts about the European situation, he has been thoroughly successful. When Welles has delivered his report in Washington, President Roosevelt will be in possession of an unrivalled store of information about the war outlook and peace prospects, information which is bound to strengthen his hand immeasurably for whatever game he chooses to play in the approaching presidential elections.

In Rome, Welles undoubtedly found Mussolini ready to share in any peace efforts, though not anxious to take the initiative. That Italy as a whole generally wants to keep out of war was apparent during the visit there. The boastfully aggressive attitude and martial spirit which one felt in the Italian atmosphere two or three years ago was conspicuously absent this time. One heard anti-war, and especially anti-German, feelings expressed freely and most emphatically by many Italian people. Officially, however, the key-note sounded during Welles' visit was pro-Axis; every effort was made to emphasise that Italy was not neutral, but 'non-belligerent'.

Would the Duce, in any circumstances, lead Italy into war on the side of Germany and against Britain and France? The impression in Rome is that he is himself still undecided. Mussolini must be very sure of himself before he takes any drastic action these days. He cannot act inconsiderately and alone – not any more. The army, the Vatican, the Royal Family, even public opinion, all have to be reckoned with in Italy today. This new restraining factor may quite possibly prove to be a vital element in the development of the situation.

From the Berlin visit three main impressions stand out. First, the German people ardently wish for peace. The first question I was asked by the first German to whom I talked after crossing the border was: 'Has Mr Welles brought us peace?' Again and again in Germany we were asked this anxious question – just as we were asked it, for that matter, in Italy, Switzerland, France and England. But that definitely does not mean that the people in the Reich are not determined to win the war, and confident that they *will* win it. On the contrary, the Germans have probably never been as solidly united behind Hitler and the Nazi *régime* as they appear to be today in support of the war. It is perfectly true the ordinary people in Germany are suffering from the food shortage, the restrictions, the rationing. They submit to privations far beyond anything yet approached

in Britain or France. Bread is abundant and not bad; potatoes are plenti-
ful. But the average German family is lucky if it can have meat once a
week, vegetables occasionally, an egg or two once a month, a meagre
ration of butter and virtually no other fat, almost no coffee (and what
there is poor in quality), and very little tea. Yet there is no slightest sign of
any tendency to revolt at these and many other restrictive conditions. On
the contrary, as one very mild-mannered German lady said to me: 'We
endure it all gladly if it helps us to smash England.'

There is no doubt of the complete success, within Germany, of
Goebbels' hate-campaign against England. The whole force of this hypnotic propaganda is directed toward the British and their Empire. France
is hardly ever mentioned, but the hope of driving a wedge between the
Allies seems to have been abandoned, at least momentarily.

Viewed from Berlin, in the midst of this hermetically sealed atmosphere of mesmeric thought, the effort of Britain and France to shake the
German people's loyalty to Hitler, and wean them away from their Nazi
régime by dropping tracts and leaflets, seems pitifully unavailing. Welles
and his party were in Berlin the weekend when the British Government
announced a whole series of particularly successful RAF flights over Berlin, yet neither I nor any member of the mission, nor so far as we could
ascertain any American journalist in Berlin, saw or heard anything of any
such flights, nor encountered anyone who had seen any trace of either
the planes or the flares and leaflets stated to have been dropped.

The second major impression from Berlin was that not merely the German people – as is natural and obvious – are confident of victory, but the
Nazi chiefs themselves, including Hitler, are genuinely convinced that
they have at least a good chance of winning the war. Of course, they proclaim their complete certainty of overwhelming victory. But when allowance has been made for a large dose of bluff and propaganda, there still
remains a fairly solid core of apparently sincere conviction on the part of
those Nazi leaders who are in a position to know what is going on that the
Reich can and will win. There seem to be several reasons for this firm
belief. One is their confidence in what the Nazis insist is the overwhelming superiority of the German air force. Another is the pact with Soviet
Russia.

A third reason given in Berlin for the Nazis' confidence in a German
victory is that this time a Greater Germany of 90,000,000 is fighting only
two enemies, Britain and France, whereas in the last war there were, not
just two, but two or three dozen, Allies. Furthermore, great emphasis is
laid on the fact that now Italy and Japan, both on the Allied side last time,
are now 'very friendly' to Germany.

This leads to the third main conclusion – that Germany is above all anxious to keep America out of this war. Britain and France alone the Nazis are confident they can defeat – or at least that they can avoid being defeated by these Allies. But the entrance of the United States into the war on the Allied side would be bound to destroy all hope of a German victory. There was apparently much talk with Welles of Germany's desire for peace, and also of Germany's readiness to re-establish a nominally 'independent' Poland and a 'guaranteed' Czechoslovakia, as well as protestations of Hitler's willingness to disarm whenever the Allies did. It was evident, however, that neither the Nazis themselves nor Mr Welles ever entertained the slightest illusion about such alleged peace terms as these. All knew there was not the remotest chance of the Allies accepting or even considering them.

Furthermore, in Berlin, Nazi officials talked openly and aggressively of the 'spring offensive', which they loudly proclaimed would begin soon in the form of intensified attacks on British shipping both by submarines and bombers. There was also talk of aeroplane attacks on harbours and ports, although this was much less precise. The official thesis put out by the Wilhelmstrasse during Mr Welles' visit was that the war would shortly begin in earnest in the west, and that there were 'numerous unpleasant surprises' in store for the Allies.

Outwardly, the feature of his Berlin visit which affected Mr Welles most was the black-out – the first Mr Roosevelt's envoy had experienced. Although still not quite so complete as London's, the black-out in Berlin has been tightened up lately. In addition, the effect of the German blackout seems to be heightened and intensified by the feeling of mental darkness, the sense of being completely shut off from all light from the outside world.

Paris formed a perfect contrast to this totalitarian darkness. In the French capital there is, properly speaking, no black-out, but merely a dimming and hooding of lights. A more apt symbol of the difference that strikes one so forcibly when coming from Nazi Germany back to democratic France and Britain would be hard to find. Democracy on this side of the fence may have had to be *mise en veilleuse*, as the French say – that is, the lamp of liberty may momentarily be turned down a bit low, but one feels both here and in Paris that this is plainly but an emergency measure to help it last through the night of war.

As if to emphasise this contrast, Mr Welles very pointedly went to visit the principal Opposition leader in Paris, the French Socialist chief, Léon Blum. It can be stated definitely that M. Blum, like Premier Daladier himself – and for that matter like the Opposition leaders and the Government heads in London as well – made it perfectly clear to Mr Sumner Welles that there can be no compromise between this light of liberty and the darkness of totalitarian aggression; and that the Allies are unwaveringly united in their determination not to lay down arms until a lasting victory – not merely a patched-up truce – for freedom and peace has been assured.

15 March 1940

THE LAST SHOOT

Peter Hill

We are not, as a general rule, invited to shoot with our local aristocracy. Whether it is something thought to be lacking in our antecedents or our address, whether it is that we do not bring to the ritual of shooting the correct formality of manner, or whether it is because we refuse to sell the modest property in which we spend our weekends, and which forms a solitary enclave in the vast tract maintained by a sporting peer, the fact remains that we are not customarily invited to assist in massacring the pheasants which, in their sleek and domesticated thousands, overrun the countryside in which we live. Our contacts with these noble birds are normally restricted to casual encounters in the fields or on the roads – where, when we meet them in large and well drilled detachments, we try either to avoid them or to run them down, according as to whether we think there is anyone that matters likely to be watching or not.

War, the Great Leveller, however, changed all that in the closing days of February. A month of snow and frost had produced a situation for which there was no precedent. The birds were massed about the fields in numbers almost large enough to challenge the attention of the police; of the guns normally available to decimate them, a large proportion had been diverted to targets of greater national importance. It was a moment for a big decision, and our sporting peer took one. He sent to us (and to others not normally thus dignified) an invitation to shoot.

It was a delightful morning, though it gave a slight impression of being liable to revert to the icier conditions of a fortnight before. There were some twenty guns; a detachment of the peasantry, about two platoons strong, had been enlisted to act as beaters. We took up our positions outside the first covert with feelings of the keenest anticipation.

From the further limits of the wood came the croaks and hisses which the peasantry emit on such occasions. The wood was reputed to be a good one; we expected it at any moment to release a cloud of birds. For some five minutes nothing happened. Then, with a tremendous noise, two woodpigeons flew out. It was not the kind of shoot at which anyone would pay attention to such humble fowl. The croaks and hisses of the peasantry continued and grew louder. Finally, after five more minutes of blandishments and threats, the red faces of the honest men emerged from among the trees. Our host moved apologetically down the line, explaining that there was no previous instance in recorded history of that wood proving barren. We set off to trudge the half-mile to the next covert on the list.

Outside that covert we stood (or sat, if we rose to shooting-sticks) for some twenty minutes. No pheasants emerged. A third similarly declined to yield a solitary bird. At a quarter past twelve – the beaters looking woe-begone, the gentry beginning to Permit Themselves a Smile – we were herded into cars and driven away to luncheon. During the meal we discussed, with infinite deliberation, the War.

Afterwards, we were driven a couple of miles in a different direction, our host remarking through his teeth that this would have to be considered the real beginning of the shoot. The beaters were instructed to scrutinise every square foot of the enormous wood into which they were introduced. Judging by the time they took to reach the other side, this injunction was obeyed. By the time their puzzled faces were visible among the trees, it was three o'clock.

We formed a disconsolate procession as we walked in the direction of the last covert. Our host strode silently in front, flanked by two keepers whose faces were pale with mortification. The guns, murmuring fitfully, followed. The detachment of beaters, silent and morose, brought up the rear.

Halfway towards our objective we came up to four enormous stacks of hay and straw. Between them – beautifully sheltered from the wind, and enjoying the declining sun – a horde of plump and comatose birds encrusted the ground. There seemed to be about a thousand of them.

Our approach caused them not the slightest alarm. A few, mildly curious, raised their heads to watch us, the majority continued an unhurried pursuit of food. One, recognising in a keeper a familiar friend, strutted confidently towards him, as if demanding to be fed.

Suddenly from our host came the bellow of a soul tormented beyond endurance. The birds visibly recoiled. The bellow, swiftly modulating into articulate abuse, was repeated, and the affronted birds rose in a tawny cloud and swept away to a plantation half a mile distant. No one fired a shot . . . It was, as I have said, the last shoot of the year.

29 March 1940

PEOPLE AND THINGS

Harold Nicolson

[I was thinking] of other men over in the United States who are not Americans. I thought of W.H. Auden and Christopher Isherwood; I thought of older men who also had retired within the ivory tower. I thought of Aldous Huxley and of Gerald Heard. These men have been my friends. For nearly a quarter of a century I have admired Aldous Huxley as one of the most intelligent of our authors and as a man who possesses a brilliant, inquisitive and enfranchised mind. I have looked on Gerald Heard as the most delightful of companions and as one of the most saintly men that I have known. I have seen Wystan Auden playing upon the Malvern Hills, and Christopher Isherwood shyly and slyly observing human behaviour from a retired seat in a Berlin café. Huxley has exercised, and still exercises, a great influence upon my own and the succeeding generation; Heard has brought the novelties of science within the scope of the ordinary man; W.H. Auden is rightly regarded as among the most gifted of our younger poets; and with Isherwood rests, to my mind, the future of the English novel. Why should these four eminent Georgians have flown? Mr Stephen Spender remains; yet I fear that the siren calls which reach him from America may induce even that great bird to wing silently away.

It is not so much that the absence of these four men from Europe will cause us to lose the Second German War. It is that their presence in the United States may lead American opinion, which is all too prone to doubt the righteousness of our cause, to find comfort in their company. For if indeed four of our most acute and sensitive writers demonstrate by their exile that they wish to have no part in the blood-stained anarchy of Europe, then surely the ordinary American is ten times more justified in remaining aloof from so inhuman a business and in proclaiming that isolationism is not only comfortable and convenient, but righteous and intelligent as well? How can we proclaim over there that we are fighting for the liberated mind, when four of our most liberated intellectuals refuse to identify themselves either with those who fight or with those who oppose the battle? For in truth the Americans well know that this is

no ordinary case of petty shirking. It should matter little were a handful
of interior decorators or dress designers to remain in, or to escape to, the
United States and thereby to evade the anxieties and deprivations of
their friends. The only feeling which that type of *embusqué* could rouse
among the Americans would be a feeling of contempt. But these four
exiles are striking figures; they are men of high intelligence, honour and
courage; and if they, at such a moment, deny Europe, then the Americans
will feel, with a relief of uneasy conscience, that Europe is in fact something which a man of integrity, strength and education has the right to
deny.

Let it not be supposed that I am suggesting that Aldous Huxley, Gerald
Heard, Isherwood or Auden should return to Great Britain and immediately engage in mortal combat. Mr Huxley, at least, has always been a
convinced pacifist, and I do not for one instant criticise the sincerity of
his convictions. Far from it I am well aware that (but for a strain of obstinacy in my own character plus thirty years spent in studying German
psychology and the nature of Germany's ambitions) I might be myself a
member of the Peace Pledge Union. But of this I am certain, that if I were
a pacifist I should be a militant pacifist, and that in times of stress and
danger I should not desire to remain outside the conflict. Mr Huxley was
prominent, while still living in this country, as a member of the Peace
Pledge Union; in fact it was he who wrote the drill-book of the
organisation. I cannot but feel that if I, by using brilliant powers of dialec-
tic and persuasion, had induced many worthy people to adhere to a cause
which is now none too popular in this country I should be anxious, when
the moment of acute controversy arose, to be present with my flock.

Here, essentially, is my quarrel with these Four Horsemen of the Apoca-
lypse who have now dismounted and led their horses back into the distant Hollywood stable. I have small criticism to make of the ivory tower
so long as one remains in it. My criticism is against those who leave their
tower when the sun of June is upon the meadows and then retreat to it
when the winds of autumn begin to howl. 'Pacifism,' wrote Mr Aldous
Huxley, 'is the application of the principles of individual morality to the
problems of politics and economics.' I entirely agree with him, and if my
family were in grave difficulties I should consider it incumbent upon me,
on the grounds of individual morality, to come to their assistance. 'War,'
writes Mr Huxley again, 'is justified when it is waged in defence of the
vital interests of the community. But the nature of modern war is such
that the vital interests of the community cannot be defended by it.' It is
with this axiom that he preaches the doctrine of non-resistance. I wonder

whether, if Mr Huxley were a Dane of equal intellectual independence, he would today agree with his own axiom.

I doubt whether he would seek today to defend his attitude and that of his companions upon such grounds. It is easier, when Western civilisation is bursting into flames and thunder, to retreat into the gentler solitudes of the Wisdom of the East. Mr Huxley strives, by practising 'detachment', by refusing to concern himself with what is terrible or wicked, to find 'illumination'. I do not imagine for one moment that so fine a soul as his can find detachment easy or illumination rapid. There must be moments, even for him, even in Hollywood, of doubt whether the Higher Wisdom can best be defended at a distance of three thousand miles. There must be moments when he must ask himself whether it is not conceivable that he is being guilty of spiritual arrogance.

19 April 1940

ABSENT INTELLECTUALS
Stephen Spender

SIR: In your issue of April 19th Mr Nicolson makes some very acute comments on the departure of Auden, Isherwood, Gerald Heard and Aldous Huxley to the USA. In the course of these remarks he says: 'Mr Stephen Spender remains; yet I fear that the siren calls which reach him from America may induce even that great bird to wing silently away.'

May I reassure Mr Nicolson? This great bird has every intention of remaining where he is put, and of helping, to the best of his ability, and until he is called up, Mr Cyril Connolly with the editing of *Horizon*.

A good many remarks have been made about the voluntary exile of Auden and Isherwood. I think that most of this criticism misses the point, because the arguments which apply to political actions do not apply to artists. Considered as a political gesture, Gauguin's renunciation of Western civilisation and departure for the South Seas was impractical and irresponsible. Everyone would find it absurd if Monsieur Blum, for example, did it. However, in the history of painting it had enough significance to be justified. Similarly, if Auden and Isherwood say that they have left Europe because 'our civilisation is done for' so that 'our culture must emigrate', they are being silly, because culture is not something you can pack up in a bag and take away when a continent is at war. What does matter, however, is their writing. And if they succeed in writing better in America than they have done here they will be justified, in spite of the very sensible objections raised by Mr Nicolson.

Aldous Huxley and Gerald Heard are in a different boat, as they are to some extent political thinkers, claiming to have practical programmes for saving the world. Mr Huxley wrote an ambitious book claiming that if violence is countered with violence, even in a defensive war, you will create in yourself the very evil which you are fighting against when it comes from the outside. He said that this was a matter of observation and not just theory. It surprised me that during the Spanish War, when the opportunity was offered, no pacifist observers were sent on both sides to check up on the theory of how ends were affecting means. No one would expect Mr Huxley and Mr Heard to stand between the Siegfried and Maginot lines, as he seemed to suggest was practical in part of his book, but a good many of their followers must be disappointed that they are not here observing conditions and sympathising passively with other pacifists.

Meanwhile Mr Gerald Heard is learning about Yoga in Hollywood, and he has written a book outlining the steps by which a new form of society can be made to save civilisation from the dangers which surround it. This is a poetic book, based on false analogies between psychology and physiology, but nevertheless the arguments are moving and interesting. As Mr Nicolson observes, Mr Heard is a man of saintly character, and when his disciples unwrap his bulky books, the manuscripts of which have been safely convoyed across the Atlantic, they must feel such admiration tinged with misgiving as the earliest Christians might have felt, supposing Christ had retired to a pleasant suburb of Rome, dictated the Gospels to a chosen disciple, and then mailed them back to Jerusalem. However, this method might have had some advantages. There would have been no need to argue about the accuracy of the texts, Christianity would have had an amiable air of detachment and remoteness, so that probably there would have been no religious wars. – Yours, &c., STEPHEN SPENDER

26 April 1940

THE SUPREME CONFLICT

(A Leading Article)

This country is bracing itself to meet new perils under new leadership. The imminence of the peril and the change of Government are not unconnected. There seems every reason to believe that Herr Hitler, misreading utterly the effect of a political crisis on the national effort, chose this moment to launch his offensive in the West. And that attack in itself was undoubtedly responsible for the swift and smooth transition from Mr Chamberlain's leadership to Mr Churchill's. That is already a matter of history. Mr Chamberlain is serving loyally under Mr Churchill as Mr Churchill had served loyally under him, and to the sum of their differing but necessary qualities is joined still the wise judgement, the calm resolution and the high integrity of Lord Halifax. On them pre-eminently the Government rests. Mr Attlee and Mr Greenwood, while in many respects not the outstanding figures in the Labour Party, represent in the War Cabinet the unwavering support of that Party as a whole, and, together with the appointment of Sir Archibald Sinclair to the Air Ministry, make the new administration representative as no Government in the last war was of the country as an undivided whole. That is an immense advantage, and it is all the greater for the inclusion in the Government of men like Mr Bevin, who come from the industrial rather than the political wing of the Labour movement.

There is no profit in discussing Mr Churchill's administration man by man. Not all the new Ministers are improvements on the old, and one or two who well may be have yet to demonstrate it. Of those who believe there are two men indispensable in the present crisis some would have preferred to see Lord Halifax the head of the Government, and some Mr Churchill. Those, and there are avowedly many such in the Labour Party, who would have preferred that Mr Chamberlain should retire, not merely from the Premiership, but from the Cabinet, do well to recognise that it is at the express desire of Mr Churchill, who has worked daily with him for eight months, that he remains, and that the new Prime Minister would certainly not offer any place in his restricted Cabinet at this crisis from dictates of mere chivalry. Apart from his personal qualities, to which his Cabinet colleagues have borne frequent testimony, Mr Cham-

berlain is the titular and the accepted leader of the Conservative Party.
He is more a party man than either Mr Churchill or Lord Halifax, and his
presence in the Cabinet has the same importance – apart from other
grounds – as Mr Attlee's. Now the Cabinet is formed. The other
Ministries are filled. Some of the best of Mr Chamberlain's appointments
are continued. The new Prime Minster, by the vigour of his personality,
will inspire the country to new efforts, and charge it with new confidence. The only concern is lest in his zeal he should overtax his strength.
The dual office of Prime Minister and Minister of Defence is a heavy
charge. It is essential that he should school himself to devolve.

Thus captained the nation faces an ordeal sterner than any other in its
history. The prostitution of the air in the service of war, and Germany's
present preponderance of strength in that element, means, among many
things, that foreign troops may reach English soil, and have to be dealt
with there, for the first time since the bow-and-arrow war of the Norman
Conquest. They are likely to be few. The Navy is a surer shield than ever
so far as invasion by sea is concerned, and the Royal Air Force has already
demonstrated its unquestioned superiority, machine for machine, and
pilot for pilot, over the enemy. But the immensity of Germany's air force
constitutes a peril it would be folly to underrate, even though her pilots
may deteriorate in quality as the front-rank fighters meet their fate.
Except in rare cases the chivalry of the air is unknown in Germany. Civilians in Belgium and Holland are being ruthlessly machine-gunned and
bombed. There will be no greater mercy for our own if the opportunity
for ruthlessness offers here. Meanwhile Herr Hitler has added two more
felonies to his black and lengthening list. So far from giving the smallest
excuse for his attack on them, Holland and Belgium, like Norway, have
done themselves grave injury by the very rigour of their neutrality, since
it forbade them from so much as discussing with France and Britain the
contingency of an attack by Germany. In every detail the history of
twenty-five years ago repeats itself. Less than a week before war broke
out then the German Minister in Brussels assured the Belgians that they
had no need for anxiety. Then, as now, the false and hollow pretext of an
impending attack on Belgium by French and British troops was adduced.
Then, indeed, a twelve-hour ultimatum was presented. This time Belgium was invaded before she had even received the invader's demands.
The fate of Holland was the same, but her preparations were less adequate and the capitulation of her army after five days' fighting is a grave
blow, though one that was not entirely unforeseen. An unchanged Germany has fallen upon an unchanged Belgium. King Albert, when the
blow fell, immediately put himself at the head of his country's troops.
King Leopold, who, as a boy of thirteen, donned a private's uniform in the

trenches on the Yser in 1915, has done the same today. The victory which ultimately crowned the father's arms is of good omen for the son's.

But the struggle that must come first will be more bitter, more deadly, and more searching than the four-years' war. It will come far nearer to our doors. It will call for courage and discipline and endurance such as was demanded of the Belgians then, but not of the civilian population of this country. The character of the war is already being revealed and could always have been predicted. Victory will be ours if we can withstand the blows that Hitler will rain on us with concentrated force till the inevitable strain on his supplies first slows his aggression down, and then brings it to a halt. Defensive measures that ought to have been taken long since must be taken without a day's delay. Anti-air-raid precautions of all kinds must be intensified. Life may be saved and morale preserved by them. Measures for coping with an incursion of German troops by air must be improvised forthwith. The offer of the services of the British Legion, made by the Legion's President, Sir Frederick Maurice, on Sunday, should be accepted at once. There is the nucleus there of an organisation covering the whole kingdom; the Local Volunteer Defence Force whose creation Mr Eden, as Secretary for War, announced on Tuesday will need leadership and training. The Legion should be able to supply both. In searching out possible traitors within our frontiers effective action must take precedence over abstract justice. The internment plan put in operation on Sunday, and the wider plan announced on Monday, will fall hardly on thousands of completely innocent men and women. It must be so. No risks can be taken now. And most of those interned will soon be able to dispel suspicion and regain their liberty.

Not only the British Army, but the British people, is going into battle. Before those whose part in the war lies at home plain duties lie. They must cultivate a calm courage, checking irresponsible rumour and denouncing defeatist talk. They must work as they have never worked before at any task which furthers the national effort in any sphere. They must let no disaster daunt them, at home or in the field. It was after four years of disaster – the retreat to the Marne in 1914, the Gallipoli failure in 1915, the slaughter of Verdun and the Somme in 1916, Passchendaele and the deadly peak of the submarine peril in 1917, the all-but-successful German drive in the spring of 1918 – that the Allied armies collected their strength for the series of strokes that gave them victory before that year was out. It seems impossible that we have before us a four-years' war today. There is every sign that Germany will stake everything – is staking everything – on a concentrated assault. It will be terrific in its impact, and much ground may have to be yielded for a time. It is a contest of endurance against momentum, and morally and materially we have a power of endurance that the Germans lack. We shall need it all.

17 May 1940

PEOPLE AND THINGS

Harold Nicolson

One of the strangest incidents in Monday's memorable debate in the House of Commons was the reception accorded to Mr Neville Chamberlain. Mr Churchill, on entering, had been greeted from all parts of the House with what can correctly be described as 'sympathetic' cheers, since there was not a member who did not desire to demonstrate the sympathy felt for a man shouldering so great a burden at so sad a time. But when Mr Chamberlain stalked in from behind the Speaker's chair he was greeted with an ovation verging upon a demonstration. He seemed startled for a moment by the virulent enthusiasm of his friends; he hesitated, smiled, and made a stiff and bashful inclination of the head. The friends continued to roar applause; one of the stoutest of his supporters, Mr Walter Liddall, the Scunthorpe stalwart, actually yelled; and Mr Beverley Baxter rose in his seat and waved a little scrap of paper aloft.

What was the meaning of this demonstration? The whole House would have joined in a reverent and respectful requiem in honour of a man who has borne great sorrows, made tremendous mistakes, but carried himself throughout with high moral dignity. Even the most ardent of Mr Chamberlain's critics joined in the applause as a tribute to a fine action finely undertaken. His resolute and unselfish broadcast address of Friday night was still resonant in our ears. But why this unusual ovation? Mr Chamberlain, in all certainty, 'has his friends'. I have for long been puzzled by the devotion which he arouses in his followers. His intimates assure me that never has there been a man who so successfully conceals his charm or whose character is so lucid and serene. Those who have worked closely with him during these nine months of war have all testified to the toughness of his fibre and the speed and decision of his mind. But why should his back-bench followers feel such personal emotion for a man who has never encouraged intimacy, and whose shyness lurks like the primrose under a dark stone of reserve?

Mr Chamberlain has never been a good mixer. On the one or two occasions when he has visited the smoking-room a hush of awkward awe has descended upon that gay tap-room as when the headmaster, with unconvincing conviviality, looms in upon the sixth-form tea. Mr Churchill, on the other hand, alternates between aloof preoccupation (during which mood he is oblivious of all around hm) and the utmost friendliness. At the very summit of last week's crisis he could have been observed sitting in the smoking-room, waving a gigantic cigar, sipping his ginger ale, and reducing two Labour back-benchers to delighted paroxysms of laughter. His wit on such occasions rises high in the air like some strong fountain, flashing in every sunbeam, and renewing itself with ever increasing jets and gusts of image and association. Not so Mr Chamberlain. His jokes are few and far between, and have their cumbrous side.

The true nature of the devotion which he inspires in so many of his followers is something which ought to be analysed and examined by those who are interested in the condition and future of the Conservative Party. It is not the descendants of the old governing classes who display the greatest enthusiasm for their leader; it is rather the descendants of the industrial revolution. Mr Chamberlain is the idol of the business men; they feel that he understands their perplexities, their ignorance, their sad little optimisms, their harmless ambitions; they have during all these years identified themselves with this representative of the backbone of England, and any decline in his prestige is a decline in their own. They do not have the same personal feelings for Mr Churchill. They do not feel that Mr Churchill understands that their desire for distinctions is no mere social greed but a quite respectable wish to separate themselves from the mediocrity by which they are surrounded. There are awful moments when they feel that Mr Churchill does not find them interesting.

The Prime Minister himself appeared totally unaware of these currents of feeling. There is a certain naïveté about Mr Churchill as about all truly great men. He sat there, hunched like a surly bulldog, with Mr Attlee peeping out behind his left shoulder. He is a great-spirited man and therefore generous, nor has he ever allowed rancour to infect his lavish zest or to check the rush and thunder of his adventure. A great Elizabethan sat there hunched between a great Victorian and the agreeable, able, admirable representative of the shape of things to come.

Yet for him, at that moment, there must have been one thought which recurred in a spasm of unutterable regret. Since even if he were able to summon around him the whole choir of angels and archangels, he could not at once retrieve those years which the locusts have eaten. He told us, in Garibaldian language, that he had 'nothing to offer but blood, toil, tears and sweat'. Yet even his buoyant energy, even his incandescent faith, even his faculty of inspiring the dull with vision and the lazy with speed, will not immediately suffice to exorcise the quick demon by whom we are today confronted. Ultimate success is certain, now that he is at the helm. Immediate success is a boon which may come to us with good fortune, but which no wise man can expect.

I returned to my rooms, and as a distraction from my bitterness I read some of the speeches which Winston Churchill has delivered since 1932. Again and again did he warn us that Germany was aiming at the mastery of the air, and that without one instant's delay we should prepare our jigs and tools. The locusts, all those years, had nibbled at the leaves of time; and today the very man who warned them, who denounced their silly optimism, who castigated their blindness, who begged them in fervent words to see clearly and strongly, is the man upon whom the fierce burden of their errors has descended with terrific might. He must indeed be a great man who is able to dismiss such frustrations from his mind. He sat there, resolute and unperturbed, listening to the speeches which followed; obviously moved by the affectionate and vivid tribute paid to him by Mr Lloyd George. There we had 1918 greeting 1941. It was a memorable sight. What memories of escapade and combat, of triumph and defeat, of loyalties and betrayals, of deep friendships and fierce animosities, must have passed during those minutes through his mind. In his veins flow two hundred and thirty years of English history, and the destiny of his country, which he worships with so deep a passion, is now entrusted to his hands.

Often have I sought to discover the essential quality of this most remarkable man. Is it his abundant energy, his Elizabethan zest of life, his almost fifteenth-century *virtù*? Is it his versatility and the rapid variety of his many gifts? Is it a combination of will-power and imagination, of vision and tenacity? Or is the quality which has given such consistency and pattern to his adventurous life the simple quality of profound patriotism? I turned to a speech which he had made in April 1933:

> We ought, as a nation and Empire, to weather any storm that
> blows at least as well as any other system of human government.
> We are at once more experienced and more truly united than any
> people in the world. It may well be that the most glorious
> chapters of our history have yet to be written. Indeed, the very
> problems and dangers that encompass us and our country ought
> to make English men and women of this generation glad to be
> here at such a time. We ought to rejoice at the responsibilities
> with which destiny has honoured us, and be proud that we are
> guardians of our country in an age when her life is at stake.

It is indeed a privilege to fight under such leadership and in such a cause.

17 May 1940

DEATH OF A TOWN

Martin Lindsay

For a week we had been disembarking troops and unloading stores at
Namsos. The work was all done at night, and at daybreak the ships had
moved out of the fjord. Everything was hidden away, and the gang planks
and other harbour tackle were replaced precisely as before. But we
thought that it was only a matter of time before the continual air
reconnaissances would discover our existence and our base would be
bombed. For this reason most sensible people were living on the outskirts
of the town, though some were still staying at the so-called Grand Hotel,
which was but fifty yards - in fact, just a bomb's miss - from the jetty.

Whenever aircraft was seen the church bells were rung. They were
rung as usual at 9 a.m. on April 20th, but, except that those who were in
the streets went indoors, nobody took any notice, so accustomed were we
to air reconnaissance. Breakfast at the Grand Hotel was suddenly
interrupted by the deafening explosion of a bomb bursting close outside
it; the whole house shook, and several windows splintered. There was a
rapid consultation as to the best course of action. Some were for running
out of the town, and others for going down into the cellar. An officer

looked down the steps leading to it, and said not for him at any price. Meanwhile bombs fell, one or two every minute, but though they were obviously fairly near it was impossible to tell in which direction they were bursting. For half an hour people stood in the hall or sat on the stairs, still discussing where to go. By this time the bombardment was getting so hot that something more than debate was clearly called for. A naval officer went down into the cellar and was killed when the hotel received a direct hit a few minutes later. The others ran out and succeeded in getting clear of the town by stages. A friend of mine was dodging up the main street when he saw a Heinkel in front of him release four bombs simultaneously, all falling in his direction. He crouched in a doorway as they burst one block behind him. At this time we had no anti-aircraft guns, so the enemy were able to fly as low, as slow, and wherever they liked. Low planes machine-gunned people as they ran up the streets and made their way out to the woods.

It is difficult to assess the casualties. The main attack in the morning was upon the railway station and quay, and most people undoubtedly got clear of the town, though no doubt a number were trapped in buildings and cellars. Most of us have come to the conclusion that cellars should be avoided at all costs if the enemy are bombing, though they provide good shelter from machine-gunning. All are agreed that a wood is the ideal form of cover; at the very worst you must have at least a rabbit's chance. Machine-gunning from the air is disconcerting, but very seldom seems to have any other appreciable effect. I myself was fired at five or six times in a fortnight, but I believe they missed by at least fifty yards on each occasion. No form of marksmanship can be more difficult than shooting from a moving aeroplane at a usually moving target. It is often hard to know at what a plane, however low, is firing. A good soldier once told me that the great thing in war is to get rid of one's conceit, and that once one has realised that the enemy is probably firing at somebody else, one's offensive power is enormously increased.

The bombing continued intermittently throughout the morning at the rate of about fifty bombs an hour, the enemy coming over in waves. Sometimes there was a lull of fifteen or twenty minutes. There was also a longish break when they returned to Trondheim for lunch. In the afternoon, satisfied with the damage to the station and harbour, they attacked the remainder of the town in earnest. A large number of incendiary bombs were dropped, and as most of the houses and shops were made of wood huge fires were soon blazing everywhere. One has heard many stories of the quiet heroism, tragedy, and even comedy that took place during this awful day. Four Frenchmen, because they had been told to do so, manned the fire station throughout the bombardment; two of them were killed or injured. Two others, official photographers, remained in the church tower all morning, taking a film. A friend of mine heard that some suspected Nazi sympathisers were still in the gaol. An inner door barred his way to the cells. In the best cinema tradition he fired his revolver at the lock, but the bullet only ricocheted round the room, nearly hitting him in the back. Just then a man ran in to say that the prisoners had all been evacuated, and that the roof was falling in. In the middle of the fiery furnace one man took shelter in a refrigerator and froze to death. Another hid all day in three feet of water in an open grave in the churchyard. Most people huddled under trees and rocks just outside the town, crouching under any cover available, holding their breath during the whistle of each falling bomb, and shuddering as it detonated; several grazed their faces trying to get closer into the rocks in their anxiety to avoid that rain of death. To add to their misery it was bitterly cold and damp.

About six o'clock a snowstorm put an end to the bombing, and a few people began to trickle slowly back to see what had happened to their property. The fires raged all that night and next day, and when they burnt out the centre of the town had been, quite literally, razed to the ground, and now looks like the pictures one has seen of Ypres after the two years' shelling. You can stand in what was formerly the High Street and look all round for two hundred yards or so, and see scarcely a ruin above waist-level, so flattened out is everything. After the crackle of burning timber, which sounded like odd rifle shots, had died out, one heard for a day or two the most extraordinary metallic banging and hammering sounds from pieces of scrap iron and steel that had been left partially suspended, not yet having come finally to rest. It sounded as if the dead were trying to force their way up through the ruins. The burning town made a tragic yet amazingly beautiful spectacle on that clear, cold night. The roads leading from it were thronged with men and women, some carrying in rucksacks what little they had been able to save, and pathetic elderly people huddled together in lorries. Outlying farms did noble relief work providing food and accommodation for the homeless.

In eight hours' bombardment a number of people had been killed, and more injured. Two thousand others had lost everything they possessed except the clothing in which they stood. A town representing man's effort and achievement over a hundred years and more had been destroyed in one day. Such is war.

24 May 1940

RETURN TO NAMSOS

Peter Fleming

'Purpose of Visit . . .' The last question on the hotel registration form was not easy to answer. In a civilised country like Norway it didn't really matter what one put down, but I felt an odd reluctance to prevaricate, to evade the issue. I was certainly not on business. 'Tourism' is an abject formula, indispensable behind the Iron Curtain but unfit for use elsewhere. 'Research' would have given my motives too intellectual, and 'Sentiment' too emotional, a gloss. In the end I wrote 'Curiosity'.

The friendly girl behind the desk took the form without looking at it. 'You notice some changes in Namsos, perhaps?' she asked. It was clear that she knew who I was.

Thirty years earlier almost to the day – on 14 April 1940, to be exact – I had had my first sight of Namsos, a little wooden town tucked under beetling outcrops of rock at the head of a thirteen-mile-long fjord. In the previous week the Germans, in a series of daring operations, had seized all the principal Norwegian ports; the Allies, with a recklessness to which the frustrations of the phoney war and the bellicosity of Winston Churchill may have made contributions of roughly equal importance, resolved to challenge the invaders on Norwegian soil; and amid barely describable confusion three separate expeditionary forces were directed on Narvik, Namsos and Aandalsnes.

In London, however, there was some uncertainty (that is to say, nobody had the slightest idea) whether Namsos was or was not in German hands, and it was prudently decided that a reconnaissance of this obscure little port – only 125 miles by road north of Trondheim, where the enemy had been installed for a week – should be carried out before an attempt was made to land there. Less prudently, it was also decided that I should carry it out.

As the Sunderland droned towards the Norwegian coast my last-minute orders from the cruiser *Glasgow* ended: *'Essential observe complete secrecy.'* But it is hardly possible to dissemble a four-engined flying-boat, and after circling low over Namsos for ten minutes without seeing – except for some herring gulls – any sign of life, we had no more idea than Mr Neville Chamberlain whether the Germans were in the town or not.

So we veered off southwards, landed in an arm of the fjord at a little place called Bangsund and, after being assured by a Norwegian in a rowing boat that the Germans had not yet arrived, sent an officer ashore to ring up the Namsos telephone exchange and tell them to stop all outgoing calls. Then we took off again, touched down off Namsos and taxied up to the wooden quay, now peopled by an apprehensive crowd. We landed, I made some sort of speech and we tried, unsuccessfully, to contact the Navy on our portable wireless sets.

Today, thirty years later, these events are vividly remembered by the senior citizens: as is the controversy – only resolved by the appearance that evening of four Tribal class destroyers – as to whether or not I was a German officer in disguise. But it was what happened six days later that made the deepest impression.

In the intervening nights, which gave us only about four hours of darkness, a British territorial brigade, cumbered with enormous fur coats but short of transport and totally devoid of any supporting arms, had somehow got ashore and been deployed southwards towards Trondheim without being observed by the Luftwaffe's thrice-daily reconnaissances. On the night of the 19th three battalions of Chasseurs Alpins, less their indispensable mules, were landed; but nobody had told the French that we were playing hide-and-seek, and when the Luftwaffe arrived, bang on time, for their pre-breakfast inspection the Chasseurs engaged them, ineffectively, with machine-guns. By noon the little wooden town was a holocaust; by dusk two-thirds of it had been destroyed. Astonishingly, there were only six fatal casualties – two Norwegian civilians and four French soldiers. I was reported killed, and several American papers published trite but kindly obituaries.

The Allied Force Commander was that legendary, admirable character, Adrian Carton de Wiart, VC. He flew out in a Sunderland which came under air attack while rendezvousing with a destroyer, and his only staff officer was wounded: so for some days I found myself acting as his batman, driver, chief of staff and (mercifully on rare occasions) cook.

The Luftwaffe, unopposed save – towards the end – by a very few AA guns, continued to pound Namsos whenever weather permitted. Standing the other day outside the little wooden house which the General and I had shared, high up under the rock-face which dominates the town, I remembered the morning when I had to tell him that Fanny, the beautiful Norwegian girl who did for us, had departed to safer quarters in the countryside.

'Don't blame her,' said the General, accepting a mug of melted snow to shave in; the supply of water, as of electricity, no longer existed. 'I'll go and scrounge some of those French rations while you do the breakfast.'

Shovelling more snow into the saucepan (it takes an awful lot of snow to produce a very little water), I watched him saunter down the steep hill towards the quay as the church-bells rang and the first air-raid of the day was unleashed. A conspicuous figure in his red hat (Carton de Wiart refused to wear a steel helmet), he maintained an even pace down the centre of the gutted street. Machine-guns chattered; smoke drifted from burning buildings; the Heinkels were flying so low that the bombs had no time to whistle before they burst. Carton de Wiart paid not the slightest attention. From safe bivouacs in the wooded heights around Namsos hundreds of men were watching him – French infantry, British base personnel, all in some degree shaken by their recent ordeals, all (at a guess) becoming a little more war-worthy as they followed his lackadaisical progress.

The Luftwaffe went home with empty bomb-racks. The General returned with some delicious sardines. His single eye surveyed my preparations for breakfast. Devastation was all around us. 'Better get rid of those egg-shells somewhere,' he said. 'Don't want the place in a mess.'

The Allied plans for a pincer movement on Trondheim from Aandalsnes and Namsos were, after much shilly-shallying, abandoned; German air supremacy decisively cancelled what had never been much more than a pipe-dream. On the short night of 2 May the Royal Navy, with some help from the French, extricated us from Namsos, a sour, charred, flat mass of rubble, eerily and dangerously illumined by a huge dump of inextinguishably burning coal.

Today these frightful scars have healed. A new, pleasant, unpretentious town has risen on the ruins of thirty years ago. Only one of the massive German barracks still stands, and there is no longer any trace of what the Norwegians called 'the English Channel'. This was an enormous anti-tank ditch, built right across the middle of Namsos by Russian and Yugoslav prisoners of war, who were treated with extreme inhumanity. A main theme of the Allied deception plans in the last war was the simulation of a threat to Norway, and the construction of this obstacle, at the head of a long, narrow fjord lavishly protected by minefields and coastal artillery, is one of the many proofs offered by the Norwegian coast-line that Hitler's intelligence was successfully deluded. It was called 'the English Channel' because the citizens felt that, if the Allies could get across the Atlantic, and across the North Sea, and all the way up the fjord, they would probably manage, somehow, to get across the big ditch in the High Street.

I was surprised, as well as touched, by the warmth of my welcome. I had, after all, been the harbinger of doom and disaster; I had aroused in stout hearts and bewildered minds hopes which were soon proved cru-

elly false; no single action of mine had done anybody in Namsos any
good, indeed I cannot remember one which failed to inconvenience the
population and endanger the town. 'It is 126 years,' I had often, and sometimes querulously, been reminded in 1940, 'since Norway was involved
in war.' Now people who had been children then, apprised by the local
paper of my presence, stopped me in the street and said how glad they
were that I had come back. I suppose the truth is that in a small place the
past, however unpalatable, is converted quite quickly into legend; and
legend, especially in a small place, is something to cherish in all its
aspects.

Fanny, for a short spell the Force-Commander's elfin cook-house-
keeper, now a handsome lady with five children, apologised for deserting
our quarters and seemed not to blame us at all for deserting her country.
Other old acquaintances took the same line: so did the man I had come to
see, though he had suffered worse than any of the survivors of 1940.

Henrik Andersen was then harbourmaster of Namsos, and the Allies
owed a great deal to him. It was he who, on the day I landed and while I
was still under a cloud as a putative impersonator, persuaded the four
pilots whom the Navy needed to go out and guide the destroyers in. In the
crucial following nights the small harbour was regularly overcrowded
with ships, all anxious to get away before the quick dawn came. When
the troops disembarked, they found none of the normal apparatus of a
base – no Embarkation Staff Officers, no Military Police, no signs directing traffic, nothing – except Henrik Andersen, and Martin Lindsay, and
me; and it was up to us, with such volunteer help as we could scrounge, to
restore the *status quo* – to put the gangways and the coils of rope and all
the other stage-properties back where they had been the day before, so
that the Luftwaffe's first, early-morning emissary would take back to
Trondheim the same *mise en scène* that his cameras had recorded yesterday.

It was mainly thanks to Andersen that this *trompe l'oeil* succeeded, for
five nights, in its purpose, that we won the game of hide-and-seek. When
we left I handed over to him what was left of the thick wad of Norwegian
bank-notes with which, by courtesy of the Bank of England, my theoreti-
cally clandestine mission had been provided.

Carton de Wiart took a poor view of the senior naval officer in charge
of the arrangements for our evacuation. 'I don't know much about
butterflies, but I've heard of a Red Admiral. Never realised there was a
yellow variety.' When the last destroyer to leave Namsos had embarked
the rearguard and the stragglers, she was ordered to open fire on the
assorted vehicles which, now massed on the quay, had made possible our

withdrawal. 'I only hope,' the Force-Commander wrote, sub-acidly, in his official dispatch, 'that no Norwegians were killed.'

I asked Andersen if any had been killed. 'No,' he said, 'but a shell came through the harbourmaster's office and I felt most lonely. You had all gone. Nothing was left of Namsos, nobody there. Only me. And now this shell in my office. Lonely, that was how I felt.'

We were talking in a sort of private reception-room in the new hospital; Andersen, now in his late seventies, has to go there for monthly blood-transfusions. In the long years after the Allies left he worked for the Resistance: was betrayed: and fell into the hands of Rinnan, a young sadist quisling working for the Gestapo who was executed, with six of his associates, after the war. Andersen was atrociously tortured and condemned to be shot. An elderly German, who had nominally taken over his duties as harbourmaster, interceded for him. Andersen was reprieved; he would be transported to a concentration camp in Germany. But the ship which was to transport him was sunk by the RAF and Andersen survived the war.

From his son's letters I had expected to meet a ghost, a man wandering in his mind, inarticulate, moribund. Not a bit of it. Reprieved from a formal execution, he has because of what was done to him lived under the shadow of death for more than a quarter of a century; only constant blood transfusions kept him alive. Yet nobody could have been jollier, more perceptive, less self-pitying, more grateful for being made by King George VI a member of the order to which, at the time of writing, a majority of the Beatles still belong.

He remembered Carton de Wiart as 'a lovely man'. The Allied Force-Commander was not given to hyperbole, but I think he might have returned the compliment, suitably modified.

16 May 1970

NEWS OF THE WEEK

The minds and thoughts of the whole of the British Commonwealth – and the United States – are centred on a few square miles of ground on the Belgian frontier where the British Expeditionary Force, its left flank exposed by the surrender of the Belgian Army, is fighting a desperate rearguard action in its endeavour to reach the coast. Its morale is unbroken, its cohesion intact. The objective, presumably, is Dunkirk, which has been converted by the French into an entrenched camp, and is said to be firmly held. Supplies are still going in there, and there is reasonable hope that a large part of the BEF may get away by sea. But there must be a rearguard for which that will be beyond all hope. The French fleet and the RAF are effectively co-operating, and as the battle gets nearer to the coast the naval guns will be able to fire over the retiring Allies on the pursuing Germans. Never, probably, in military history has a British Army borne itself more magnificently in the face of overwhelming odds. The fate of the French Army fighting shoulder to shoulder with it cannot be predicted, for the time has passed when there can be any hope of a counter-attack by General Weygand. He is fully occupied, and occupied effectively, in consolidating the new Allied defensive line on the Aisne and Somme. In Flanders, as elsewhere, the RAF has achieved the impossible. Numerically the tide in that sphere has begun to turn. Not only have the actual losses on both sides in the past month been such as to reduce the great disparity in numbers between the opposing forces, but there is reason to believe that the Allies are now receiving more machines a month than the Germans, and that the rate of output will henceforward rapidly increase. Germany, moreover, is being driven more and more to rely on inexperienced pilots.

31 May 1940

NEWS OF THE WEEK

The Germans have entered with unexpected speed on the second stage of their war of annihilation. The launching of the great 120-mile offensive on the Somme on Wednesday morning may have been due to a desire to strike before General Weygand had time to perfect his defences, or to Hitler's own necessity to pursue a lightning war before his own resources are exhausted, or, more probably, to both. There are grounds for both apprehension and confidence. It is clear that again the Germans are throwing their full strength into the assault and showing characteristic disregard for the sacrifice of their infantry. The danger of a break-through by their mechanised forces is considerable, but the French will have learned their lesson and realised the imperative necessity of closing immediately any gaps so made, and leaving the tanks that have broken through to be cleaned up in the back-areas. This is the first time General Weygand has had a free hand, for he took supreme command too late to have any real chance of restoring the situation in Flanders. He has fresh armies to rely on, and even the first reports of the battle now developing show that new devices for checking tank-attack are proving successful. If the Germans can be held approximately on the present line the tide will already have begun to turn against them, for the one thing Herr Hitler cannot do is to stand still. But the inferiority of the Allies in men and material is a grave disability. The hard-tried divisions back from Dunkirk will have to take their places in the line as soon as equipment is available for them, and the Military Service Act will be producing a steady flow of reinforcements as long as they may be needed. But guns and tanks and aeroplanes are the determining factors. The decision of the United States Government to release 2,000 field-guns with ammunition is of equal moral and material importance. For the rest the fate of the British Army, as Lord Beaverbrook said on Wednesday, is in the hands of British factories and munition-works.

British and German Losses

In stating that 335,000 men, British and French, had been withdrawn from Dunkirk, the Prime Minister added that the losses to the BEF in killed, wounded and missing (which includes prisoners) were 30,000. Grievous as this loss is, it is a small total when we consider the severity of the fighting and the circumstances of the withdrawal. There are obviously no completely reliable figures on which to base an estimate of German losses in the battle against Dutch, Belgians, French and British. Conservative French estimates suggest 500,000, and the number according to some authorities is much higher. At different stages of the three weeks' battle the relative proportions of the losses varied much. During the lightning advance of the mechanised German units from the Meuse to Boulogne it is probable that the attackers lost fewer men than the attacked. But at all points where the German infantry were engaged and held they suffered far more than the Allies. The German figure of 61,238 killed, wounded and missing may have been arrived at by the simple process of dividing by ten. In regard to material, Mr Churchill says that we have lost nearly 1,000 guns and all our transport and armoured vehicles with the Army in the north. Against this it is fair to set the fact that Ger-

man losses in aeroplanes from British action alone have been at least four
to one. Also a considerable proportion of the whole German tank force is
out of action.

Bombs on Paris

Early this week German aeroplanes have twice bombed the town and district of Le Havre, and on Monday afternoon large numbers of bombers
dropped more than 1,000 high explosive or incendiary bombs on suburbs
of Paris. The figures of casualties suffered were 254 killed and 652
wounded, of whom the great majority were civilians. The German communiqué claims that the bombs were dropped on aerodromes and industrial plant of the French Air Force, but in fact they fell far from military
objectives. Flying at over 30,000 feet, it was impossible for the aeroplanes
to aim effectively at specific targets, and in fact the attack amounted to
an indiscriminate bombardment of an open city, and was a wanton violation of the rules of war. The use of the new syren bombs was an indication of the fact that terror was part of their purpose – a form of assault
only effective in lowering civilian morale. Retaliation has been instant.
French machines attacked the vicinity of Munich and Frankfurt, but
military objectives only, and British aeroplanes bombed munition-
factories and refineries in the Ruhr. On such occasions the British fly low
to make sure of their objectives. The Nazis would do well to remember
that every blow on Allied open cities is likely to recoil upon themselves.
Le Havre, with its docks, it is fair to say, was a legitimate target.

7 June 1940

COUNTRY LIFE

H.E. Bates

Pigs and Pig Clubs

With a flourish of leaflets, the Minister for Agriculture urges us to revive
the times when every cottager kept a pig. He recalls the enthusiastic days
when there were not only pig clubs but also, I believe, gooseberry clubs.
Since that time the word pig has lost none of its meaning, though the
raspberry has largely replaced the gooseberry as a symbol, and I do not
know whether the Small Pig Keepers' Council is quite tactful in suppos-

ing that the pig is likely to be an asset 'to the social life of the countryside'. Years of bureaucratic muddling have made the cottager and the
allotment holder very wary of the pig. It will need all the resources of
Ministerial propaganda to bring back into rural life that annual ceremony of pig-killing so vividly described in *Jude the Obscure*. Until
recently a man who kept a pig could not regard a single chitterling of it as
his own. This absurd situation is now ended – 'the small pig-keeper may
kill and cure his pig for his own family's consumption, provided he has
had it for at least two months for fattening and he obtains a licence to
slaughter, either directly or through his pig club, from the local Food
Control Committee'. He may also sell to a local retail butcher, in the market or to a bacon factory. A good deal of information, more especially on
pig clubs, may be obtained from the Small Pig Keepers' Council, Victoria
House, Southampton Row, WC1, and it is well to remember that in one
year of the last war 400 pig clubs produced something like 4,000,000 lbs
of meat.

Local Defence

In country districts the response for Defence Volunteers has been excellent. Gamekeepers, farmers, farm labourers, lorry drivers, fruit growers,
ex service men of all kinds have been formed into village units. In the
way typical of countrymen they show independence and sturdiness
rather than enthusiasm. They dislike the outside control which consigns
them to positions of defence which they regard as absurd, and which
makes little or no use of their knowledge of local territory. That knowledge, it seems to me, may be of the very greatest importance. The position of a forty-acre field, the class of road leading to a remote railway
bridge, the judgement of distances – always difficult – across country
intersected by hedges; all these are things of which the countryman's
knowledge is invaluable and are services which he can readily supply, if
asked, in addition to his time. He is very much aware, too, of certain
aspects of the parachute menace for which he feels there is not yet any
adequate protection. In two months' time the standing corn crops will be
targets for incendiarism. Nor does a farmer feel that his services are being
well used when he is asked to leave a hundred and fifty head of cattle for a
solitary post, without telephone, four miles away. The gap between the
mind of Whitehall and the mind of the countryman is very large. The
defences of the countryside will be all the better when it is lessened and
the services of countrymen are intelligently and fully used.

Pests and Crops

When I asked the seed-merchant for a remedy for cabbage root-grub –

dustings of lime or calomel are said to be effective – and remarked that it seemed an extraordinary year for pests, he replied with that sepulchral fatalism which countrymen seem to enjoy exhibiting: 'Yes, but there's a war on, and you *will* get pests. Always notice you get everything in the way o' pest when there's a war.' Certainly, against all expectations, spring crops have been seriously threatened, both on farms and in gardens, by plagues of leather-jacket, flea-beetle, wire-worm, root-grub and caterpillar. It occurs to me that one reason for this may be that six weeks of intense frost seriously upset the balance of bird-life. In a winter when rabbits were forced to strip young ash-trees, roses, hollies, and fruit-trees as bare as bone, the death-rate among all birds must have been extremely high. Throughout the spring there seems to have been fewer nests than usual, and the dawn orchestra, leading off as early as three-thirty with the cuckoos, has seemed scattered and thin. In spite of pests, however, the promise of crops is excellent. Cherry-farmers, and in fact all fruit growers, have welcomed a dry, warm May, in which blossom has set to perfection. Hop-farmers were pleased by a steady, rather backward spring. Cereal crops have shown no sign of the sickliness that follows a wet May. And to me it was a rare pleasure to meet in one day three farmers, one fruit, one hops, one mixed, who were for once serenely satisfied with the state of their world.

7 June 1940

WASTAGE OF WOMEN

Nesca Robb

In the urgency and peril of the day all but our vast immediate problems are apt to be forgotten. Yet the need for planning our future efforts with the utmost vigour is not less but greater than in the past. Now is the time to look ahead, and to organise, with much else, the mobilisation of that second line of defence – the woman-power of this country. The whole question of women's part in the war effort has been shamefully neglected. It is nation-wide in its full implications; but at this moment those most painfully affected are the professional women, whose position is full of anomalies.

The war has in many cases swept away their peace-time employment. It has not, as yet, produced alternative work. Day after day Press and radio assure them that there is a burning need for their services; but when the individual comes forward all the facts appear flatly to contradict such assurances. For the young, able-bodied woman there are certainly openings in the land army, nursing, munition-work and the three women's services. The large temporary clerical and secretarial staffs in Government offices are also mainly recruited from the lower age-groups, a point which may be touched upon further on. But for the woman who is over age for the services, or unfit for heavy physical work, and for professional women of all ages whose qualifications are of a highly specialised kind, the situation remains infinitely depressing. The central register of the Ministry of Labour contains the names of some 96,000 specialists. Since the outbreak of war it has placed between 200 and 300 women. The others who lie buried in this august mausoleum of all the talents see little hope of a resurrection. There may be many reasons for this, but one undoubtedly is that our civil service system of entry at the bottom and promotion within the service – so admirable in peace time – is too inelastic in such an emergency. Intelligence and special knowledge which should be at the country's disposal have been allowed to lie idle.

The Ministry's supplementary register of less specialised workers also holds out few prospects, though some executive posts are filled from it, and its machinery functions adequately within limits. Neither this, nor the central register, makes any provision for giving help or advice to applicants. This is not the fault of the officials, who perform their often ungrateful tasks considerately; but it leaves the candidate with a growing sense of helplessness.

The Women's Employment Federation at Bedford College, and to a lesser degree the registers of professional bodies, are able to some extent to supply this deficiency; but they cannot supply work in anything like sufficient quantity. Many concerns, both public and private, are inclined to turn down highly qualified women who have earned good salaries on the plea that they would not accept the lower rates now prevalent. This is by no means true. Most of our professional women are willing to make great sacrifices so long as they can be of use. At the same time, in any large-scale mobilisation of women's services the problem of dependants will have to be faced. It is time to banish the comfortable belief that only men have such responsibilities.

To return to the search for employment, the professional woman who, ready to adapt herself to any form of service, presents herself at the labour exchange is likely to be told – sometimes with scant courtesy – that there is nothing for her. When she inquires about training for new types of work she finds too often that facilities are non-existent, or that such courses as there are are crowded out for weeks ahead. Her quest seems as bewildering and as maddeningly inconclusive as Humpty Dumpty's embassy to the fish. It would be ludicrous if it were not tragic. Tragic it is, because it reveals in yet one more sphere the sloth, the unimaginativeness, the waste, that have come near to be our undoing.

This article naturally emphasises the national rather than the personal side of the problem, but the writer is in almost daily contact with cases of individual hardship caused by the present deadlock. For the most part these are met with admirable courage; it is only when a sense of frustration and uselessness is added to the burden that hearts fail and defeatism begins to grow in those who should be a bulwark of sanity to the nation. There is real danger in such a state of things. It would have an excellent psychological effect if the Government, through responsible speakers, were to take the women of the country, as far as may be, into its confidence; show them that energetic measures are being taken for mobilising their services, and give some help and guidance to those who may still have to wait before their contribution can become effective. As yet we have had only the paralysis of peace-time activities, not the full diversion of power into new channels. The dilution of labour by women workers and the development that this may involve have hardly been even visualised. Let us approach these problems *now*, with daring, with imagination, and above all with speed.

Among practical steps that might be taken would be the provision of centres throughout the country where women could be trained for the existing services, for all forms of war production and for all essential civil work in which they will have to replace men. Instructors could easily be found among the hundreds of unemployed experts, thus helping incidentally to solve in part the problem of the professional woman in war time. Then, as the men are called up, there need be no slowing down of the national effort by the influx of wholly untrained workers. If equipment is not always available let us improvise what we can and go forward. The new recruits may have to drill with broomsticks till their rifles are ready. Very well; we will train with broomsticks too till better tools can be provided. Next, efforts should be made to use our reserves of woman power as effectively and as economically as possible. For instance, many young women who are at present employed as clerks and typists in Government and other offices could well be drafted into other more active work, and their places filled by some of the large number of older clerical workers, who cannot undertake heavy physical effort, and who are now unemployed and often a burden on the rates.

Finally, let us look ahead and plan, as far as is humanly possible, for

likely developments. As more and more women are absorbed into industry new problems are created. There may be, for example, increased need
for crèches and nursery schools, for canteens and communal kitchens,
for social services of every description. Hundreds of trained women are
ready and willing to undertake whatever work may be required of them; a
little intelligent forethought now may save costly inefficiency later on.
Today, of grim necessity and in a sense unknown to Aristophanes, 'War
is the care and the business of women.' Is it too much to ask that the experience, the knowledge, and the administrative powers of qualified
women in all departments of life should be used to the full in planning
and directing, as well as in carrying out this mobilisation? If time-honoured procedure stands in the way let time-honoured procedure be jettisoned. New means must be devised, and quickly, to meet an unexampled
situation.

21 June 1940

THESE 'LOST LEADERS'

E.M. Forster

SIR: W.R.M.'s epigram in your issue of June 21st impels me to ask
whether there could not now be a close time for snarling at absent intellectuals. About half a dozen of them – not more – are away in America,
and week after week their fellow-authors go for them in the newspapers.
The attacks are highly moral and patriotic in tone, but their continuance
raises the uneasy feeling that there must be something else behind them,
namely, unconscious envy; they are like the snarl of an unfortunate
schoolboy who has been 'kept in' and is aggrieved because the whole of
his class has not been kept in too, and therefore complains and complains
about those stinkers out in the playground instead of concentrating on
his own inescapable task.

And there is a further objection to this undignified nagging: it diverts
public attention from certain Englishmen who really are a danger to the
country. They, too, are few in number – perhaps again not more than half
a dozen – but they have influence, wealth and position, which intellectuals have not, and they shelter not in the United States, but in the City and

the aristocracy. Our literary lampoonists can here find a foe worthier of their powers. Let them leave their absent colleagues alone for the next fortnight, and denounce our resident Quislings instead. The consequences may be unpleasant to them, for Quislings sometimes hit back. But they will have had the satisfaction of exposing a genuine menace instead of a faked one, and this should be sufficient reward. – Yours faithfully, E.M. FORSTER

Reform Club, S.W.   *5 July 1940*

COUNTRY LIFE

H.E. Bates

Women's Land Army

Farmers have shown a reluctance to state their requirements for extra labour that has, apparently, confused both the Ministry of Agriculture and the Women's Land Army. An official appeal for another 5,000 women land recruits has resulted in 4,000 enrolments, and a further rate of enrolment of 500 a week. This is good, and means that there is now a surplus of volunteers. 'Many of them,' the WLA states, 'are from luxury trades. The fact that there are now more than 8,000 land girls on farms shows that they are making good.' As any farmer will tell you, it shows nothing of the kind. The organisation behind the WLA takes no account of the fact, apparently, that the English farmer is a conservative and prejudiced animal. He has a very deep suspicion of imported female labour; he assumes, and probably quite rightly, that a girl trained for a luxury trade will be out of place on a muck cart. He prefers one man to half a dozen women. Here and there one hears reports of city office girls who, as land workers, adapted themselves magnificently to the bitterest weather for half a century. Reports of others only confirm the farmer's attitude.

12 July 1940

'ENGLISH QUISLINGS'

F. Yeats-Brown

SIR: Mr E.M. Forster's letter asking for 'a close time for snarling at absent intellectuals' demands an answer from someone better acquainted than I am with these gentlemen, but when he continues that such 'undignified nagging' may divert public attention from certain rich and highly-placed English Quislings, I cannot restrain my curiosity, and must entreat him to name them. He says that these wealthy villains are a danger to the country. Who are they, and how would he deal with them? Does he approve of what is being done at present by Sir John Anderson?

May I give Mr Forster (and you, Sir) a specific instance? A friend of mine was recently hauled from his home under Section 18 B and thrown into prison. For the first ten days he was treated as a person awaiting trial on a serious criminal charge (except that he did not know what the charge was), and was allowed no razor, no tooth-powder except what could be taken in a paper bag (for no metal is allowed in the possession of dangerous characters), and he was confined in a solitary cell for 22 hours a day. Now his treatment is slightly better, in that he is (I think) allowed his razor; also two letters a week, and two visitors (who can speak to him only in the presence of a warder), and that he spends only 20 instead of 22 hours in a cell. He has been in prison a month. No charge has been made against him, and he has had no trial.

I wrote about this case to the Home Secretary, and received a polite answer that the matter was receiving attention. That was on June 14th. So far there has been no result. My friend must be wondering, as I am, who accused him, and of what? As far as I know his only crime is that in 1934 he was a member of the British Union of Fascists for one month. He is not a rich man like those Mr Forster has in mind, but a retired officer who fought by my side in the mud of Festubert in 1915. He volunteered again for service this war. If he is a traitor surely some proof could have been produced by this time. But if, on the other hand, he is only suspected of Fascist leanings, why are not pacifist and Communist sympathisers also arrested? – Yours faithfully, F. YEATS-BROWN

Bath Club   *12 July 1940*

'ENGLISH QUISLINGS'

E.M. Forster

Sir: There is a law of libel. It is unfortunately a bad law, a notoriously bad one, and I am not sufficiently wealthy to risk publishing the names of eminent English Quislings. I would like to think, with Major Yeats-Brown, that there are none, but I must point out to him that my suspicions appear to be shared by the Prime Minister: 'any traitors that may be found in our midst' was the phrase employed by him in his recent broadcast.

The rest of Major Yeats-Brown's letter develops another point: that of the treatment of persons during detention. Here I am glad to think that there need be no difference of opinion between us. His friend has, according to his account, been treated abominably. It is to be hoped that his representations will put an end to this, just as it is to be hoped that the protests of your other correspondents may ameliorate the unhappy lot of hundreds of interned refugees. – Yours faithfully, E.M. Forster

Reform Club, S.W.   *19 July 1940*

VOX POPULI

Dorothy L. Sayers

One of the strangest campaigns of the war has been fought and won. In its active phase it was a Blitzkrieg, and the victory was with the defence.

The preliminary movement of troops took place on the wireless, accompanied by a few skirmishing reconnaissances in print. Traitors and fools who talked too much were to be ruthlessly exterminated; and it was somehow implied that a number of us were possibly traitors and that most of us were fools. A kind of Gestapo of Silent Columnists were to be recruited for the purpose of browbeating their neighbours and reporting them to the police. Abusive epithets were employed and horrible threats brandished. The launching of the attack was announced for the third week in July; it would employ every known weapon of modern publicity.

I was out of town when the thing started. As it happened, I did have the opportunity of expressing my opinion, and took it; but it was only a personal opinion – I had no means then of testing the reactions of the people. On the Monday I was in London and made enquiries of a friend, who said that 'a lot of people were very angry about it'. The first advertisements had then appeared; another friend, whom I met on the Tuesday, had little to say about the Silence Campaign, though we agreed that the vagueness of the instructions about behaviour in case of air-raid or invasion was only thrown into relief by the intolerable archness of the phrasing employed. We refused to say to ourselves: 'This is where I keep perfectly calm and cool' – language like that, we said, made us blush to the toes of our boots. Apart from these encounters, I discussed the matter with nobody.

On the Thursday, my literary agent sounded me on the subject. I replied cautiously that, if this campaign had been a new theatrical show, I could only have said, in the professional jargon, that I 'did not like the feel of the house'. It might have been difficult to give my reasons. The newspapers were lying low and saying nothing; they could not very well say much, since they carried the advertising, and one does not openly quarrel with one's advertising appropriation. Besides, they were preoccupied with defending the freedom of the Press, which, as one organ rather naïvely admitted, meant in practice freedom of control by anybody *except* the advertisers. The British public paid singularly little heed to the complaints of the newspapers; it had other fish to fry.

In the meantime, a number of drunks and persons of feeble intellect had been clapped into gaol and given savage sentences for incautious exclamations, and a patriotic person had been arrested for saying 'to hell with Hitler' – the explanation being that another patriotic ass had mistaken 'hell' for 'heil'; thus, once again, as at Nicaca, the harmony of Christendom was split for an iota.

On Sunday there was a dramatic collapse: Mr Harold Nicolson apologised at a public meeting, and explained that nobody had ever meant to prevent the British people from talking as much as they chose. They had only been asked to be careful what they said. It was not explained why they could not have been asked with more politeness.

On Monday I rang up my agent and said: 'This thing is dead.' On the same day an evening newspaper, realising that the battle was over (perhaps the advertising contract had been cancelled?), came down heavily on the winning side.

On Tuesday, in reply to a question, the Prime Minister buried the corpse of the vanquished beneath the floor of the House.

Mr Churchill, who is nothing if not generous, appeared to accept some measure of responsibility for the campaign. It did not, he said, look so attractive on paper as it had seemed in prospect. The House laughed, as well it might. Nobody said that if Mr Churchill had put it on paper himself it would have looked very different. Mr Churchill knows how to be more insolently offensive, if he chooses, than any man living, but he exercises his unique abilities in this direction against the enemy, not against his own people. He never suggests to us that we are a bunch of fools and cowards who need to be incessantly scolded into resolution. On the contrary, he blandly assumes that we are a wise and heroic nation, and, since men become what they believe themselves to be, we are happy to take his word for it, and are encouraged to pull our socks up and behave ourselves. But the campaign was not put on paper by Mr Churchill, and, as he rightly says, it was not attractive. We did not like it at all.

What is more, we apparently said so. How? I do not know. Did we make a public uproar? If so, its echoes did not reach me. I do not think we wrote many letters to the papers, or, if we did, they were not printed. Perhaps we did, and they were privately conveyed to the spot where they could do most good. Did we hold meetings of protest? I was not invited to one, and I get invitations to quite a number of things. But there was little time to hold meetings; the campaign was over almost before it began. Did the judicature speak its mind? It is not unlikely. Did we badger our MPs? Possibly. Did they themselves, unprompted, divine our unspoken wrath? If so, they were fulfilling their functions as MPs should. Or was it the Prime Minister himself who, not finding the thing attractive on paper, informed his colleagues that he, too, 'did not like the feel of the house'? I do not know. The impressive thing is, precisely, that I, the common citizen, do not know how the battle was won. I only know that here was a thing which the people did not like, and that, mysteriously, with surprisingly little noise, the great, cumbersome machine of Government that conveys our wills and liberties went into action with the speed and force of an eighty-ton tank. The people were angry and the voice of their anger was heard in Parliament, breaking the cedar-trees of Malet Street and bringing the prisoners out of captivity.

We ought to be very much encouraged. Not encouraged to spread rumour in defiance of authority, for now that authority has eaten humble pie there is no temptation to such a superfluity of naughtiness. But we should be encouraged by this proof that the will of people and Parliament is still a living and a potent thing.

And we have gained much. We have been shown a very faint glimpse of the thing that we are fighting against, and now that we have seen it, we know for certain that we hate it beyond all imagination. To distrust our fellows, to become spies upon them, to betray them to the law, to go in a continual dumb terror for fear they should spy upon us – that is the thing that Nazi government means, and it is a thing that we will not endure. We would rather, indeed, 'see London laid in ruin and ashes'. We will endure restrictions upon our movements and upon our pleasures, we will tighten our belts, we will hand over our goods, and give our bodies to be burned, but this inner corruption of our liberties we will not tolerate, either from Germany or from anybody else.

2 August 1940

PRINCIPLES OF PEACE

C.E.M. Joad

I cannot believe that what I am going to say will not already be familiar to readers of *The Spectator*; that it is not, indeed, the last word in commonplace. Nevertheless, I propose to say it, if only for the good and sufficient reason that, commonplace or not, nobody else does say it.

I suggest that we make a public statement of the principles for which we are fighting this war. I say advisedly 'principles', not 'aims'. The word 'aims' suggests territorial and economic considerations; it involves a statement about Poland, Czecho-Slovakia, Norway, and, possibly, Colonies. As to whether it is expedient to make such a statement, I have neither the authority nor the knowledge to venture an opinion. But the word 'principles' indicates considerations of a more general order.

There are certain principles which form the heritage of our Western civilisation, principles which are derived partly from ancient Greece, partly from Christianity; so deeply are they woven into the texture of our civilisation that most of us have grown up as unconscious of their existence as we are unconscious of the air we breathe; yet just as air is an essential condition of physical existence, so the acceptance of these principles seems to me to be an essential condition of any tolerable political existence. Now these principles, taken so long for granted by ourselves that they have passed into political unconsciousness, are both denied and condemned by the philosophy of Nazi Germany, and if the Nazis were to win this war they would disappear from Europe as completely as the principles that inspired Roman law disappeared during the ages that succeeded the break-up of the Roman Empire.

What are these principles? They can be variously stated, but for reasons to be given in a moment, it is, I think, convenient to arrange them under four heads.

First, that the individual is entitled to respect as an end in himself, with a right to happiness in this life and a chance of salvation in the next. No claim of the State is entitled to override this right.

For, secondly, the State is made for man and not man for the State. Its function is to establish those conditions of order, law, security, justice and economic opportunity in which alone the individual can live the good life as he sees it, develop his personality and realise all that he has it in him to be.

Thirdly, that the individual should have a voice in determining the nature of the society in which he lives; that through his elected representatives he should make the laws under which he is governed, and that, if he disapproves of them and can persuade a sufficient number of his fellow-citizens to his view, he should be able to change them.

Fourthly, that he should not be arrested save for offences prescribed by the law of the land; that, if arrested, he should not be held in prison without trial, and that his trial should be by an independent judiciary.

What, it may be asked, is to be gained by publishing to the world a series of commonplaces? There are, I suggest, at least four gains. First, the principles are derived in equal measure from Magna Carta and Habeas Corpus, on the one hand, and from the French Revolutionary Declaration of the Rights of Man on the other. They are common, then, to England and to France which have jointly given them to the world. Hence, to publish them now establishes our claim to be fighting (at present alone) on behalf of the real France against a foreign Power which oppresses and a puppet government which betrays her.

Secondly, all the principles are embodied in the American Constitution. Hence, to publish them now establishes our claim to be fighting (at present alone) for the principles from which America derives her political being. Properly stressed, these considerations should enormously strengthen the force of our appeal both to Frenchmen and to Americans, indicating, as they do, that we are at the moment the sole defenders of a heritage which is common to all of us. Of the other potential defenders, one has been temporarily disabled; the other still stands aside.

Thirdly, all the principles are such as are consonant with Christian teaching, and the first we owe directly to Christ. Indeed, respect for the individual person as an end in himself constitutes the distinctive contribution of Christianity to political philosophy. Hence to publish these principles is to establish our claim to be fighting for Christian civilisation against a paganism which denies its postulates and denounces its values.

Fourthly, there is the question of the European countries now under the Nazi yoke. It is, I imagine, common ground among us today that the best way of winning this war is to provoke revolts against the Nazis in the countries now under their domination. In other words, if we are to win, we must turn this war into a war of European revolution. Now, while ideas are among the weapons of every war, in a revolutionary war the potency of the idea-arm is enormously increased. Indeed, revolutionary wars are fought and won by ideas. What, then, should be the ideas of the anti-Nazi revolution? They are to be found in the principles I have summarised, which embody the essential ideals of democracy, representative government and political freedom. It is difficult to suppose that these ideals are wholly dead upon the Continent, that in social-democratic Czecho-Slovakia, that in liberal Holland and bourgeois Belgium, that in republican France, that in a Germany which, less than eight years ago, was casting a majority of votes for social democracy and against Hitler, there nowhere survives a man who desires and demands the right to govern himself and to order his private life as he thinks fit.

It is obvious that there must be millions of such men. Our purpose should be to turn them into Fifth Columnists working against Hitler in all the countries which the Nazis dominate. These potential Fifth Columnists must be given a focus and rallying-point which can be found only in this country. It is from this point of view that one realises the importance of exhibiting England to the world as the manifest defender of the ideals which democrats and free men all over the world have in common. In other words, Czecho-Slovakians and Norwegians and Frenchmen and Belgians and Dutch, whom an appeal to fight for the British Empire, for British privileges, or for British tribute, would leave indifferent or hostile, would respond to an appeal to fight for freedom against oppression, for the right of the free individual against the all-embracing claims of the State, and for representative government against police law.

I add one final consideration. The principles that I have mentioned are, I should say, the indispensable requisites of civilised life in a civilised society. What is more, they are principles which are widely accepted among us. But though their acceptance is a necessary condition, both of European revolution and of the establishment of a civilised order after this war, it is by no means clear that it is sufficient. It seems to me inconceivable that after this war, we should ever again allow a single nation to threaten the world's peace; inconceivable that we should permit so destructive a weapon as the aeroplane to be let loose upon civilisation by the fiat of one irresponsible, sovereign State. I deduce that if civilisation is to avoid destruction, it must set up a Federal Government to control armaments and foreign policies. This means adding to my four principles, which are accepted, the principle of federalism, which is not. In effect, I should offer union on the lines of Mr Churchill's offer to France to whatever States in Europe are successful in throwing off the Nazi yoke, thus providing as a substitute for the artificial unity imposed upon Europe by German domination a spontaneous unity of free nations in which each unit retains its national functions and national characteristics, while surrendering to a common government the right which it at present possesses to plunge the world into war. This principle stands on a different footing from the other four, in that, while they are accepted, it is controversial; while they have been in operation for hundreds of years, this, in its application to Europe, is as yet untried. Yet it seems to me difficult to envisage a durable peace in the world unless this principle is coupled with the other four.

16 August 1940

THE WAR SURVEYED:
A YEAR'S FIGHTING

Strategicus (H.C. O'Neill)

Although it is the unexpected that happens in war, who, a year ago, would have dared predict that this anniversary would find Germany with a new ally facing a Britain without France? Under the conditions in which battle was joined, Poland, Denmark, Norway, Holland and Belgium were doomed; but who would have dreamed that France would stand up to the German attack scarcely a month? So many developments belong to the incredible that it is not easy to recognise what was at least implicit in the position from the first. Once Britain was involved it was inevitable the war should be fought on the oceans of the world; and Germany, for her own purposes, attempted to spread its stresses over the five continents. In effect it was a reconstruction of an old problem: how to defeat sea-power by a mighty army. Germany recognised and took up the challenge. She thought to solve it by overawing or overrunning Europe and spreading, through Italy, her power to Asia and Africa.

If these last developments are still latent, it is not for want of planning and resolution. It is because Britain at bay is recognised as so redoubtable a foe (and for our part it is to be regretted that she only becomes redoubtable when she is at bay). But in Europe Germany has seen a year of triumphs. Each of her campaigns has been planned with notable skill and developed with the boldest opportunism and resolution. It is true that much of her success has been due to the deliberate use of treachery, the scientific use of terrorism and the complete ignoring of every law and convention which mankind has evolved in order to prevent and limit war. It is impossible to disentangle them from the development of her strategy; and in the campaign which opened the war and seemed most brilliant they conditioned events absolutely.

By attacking Poland without warning she secured the advantage of fighting fully mobilised against an opponent only half ready; and history is eloquent of the chances that expedient provides. In the event, however, the scope of the advantage was greater than anyone had imagined. The aeroplane had invaded war to revolutionise it. The Germans concentrated two great air forces in Königsberg and Vienna respectively, and at the arranged moment these were set working according to the plan outlined speculatively by General Douhet. Aerodromes, centres of communication, staff headquarters, were bombed to at least temporary uselessness. When the two army groups threatening the sides of the salient Poland made in German territory were set in motion, they accordingly faced an opponent very largely deprived of all the direction which makes a body of troops an army. They struck, moreover, as an entirely modern army, with armoured divisions directed by the experts who had trained them, against an army of another era. Germany advanced on wheels and wings, while Poland struggled afoot. When, despite their heroic resistance, the Poles were reeling, the Russian army marched against their rear; and all was over.

So the internal-combustion engine gained its first victory; but the Poles fought against so many other handicaps that the French Staff, minimising their stubborn heroism, completely underestimated the influence of the armoured divisions, with disastrous results. In the Finnish campaign, for which Germany held the ring, even this assistance could not prevent the struggle developing into a contest between mass and morale. The evident skill of the last attacks in the Karelian isthmus could not change the character of the campaign. The big battalions won; and, though everyone recognised the splendour of the Finnish resistance, the mechanical theory of war secured still further impetus. It was while this struggle was taking place, however, that an event occurred in the South Atlantic that wrote a caveat to the theory. The battle of the River Plate should have given victory to Germany; but skill, the calm refusal to admit the peril of the big gun, and resolution, turned the scale without, however, seriously disturbing the French Staff's faith in 'the impregnability of the defensive'.

It was a by-product of the River Plate battle that led to the most inglorious of our exploits during the war. The *Altmark*, which carried the crews of ships sunk by the *Graf Spee*, was at length traced to Norwegian territorial waters and there boarded. It was this incident that indirectly led to the Norwegian campaign, since the Germans anticipated any movement we might make to deprive them of the use of territorial waters by occupying Oslo and the ports of Bergen, Trondheim and Narvik. They seized Denmark in order to control the doors of the Baltic; and, making all allowance for treachery, the occupation of Norway was a skilful and daring operation. But, placing the Germans in a position to challenge our blockade on better terms, it could not be tolerated; and an attempt was made by us to seize Trondheim. It is still not clear whether the keystone of the plan was deliberately taken out while the operations were in progress, or whether the capture of the fjord was not recognised to be the keystone. But what happened was only too clear. The operations had to face tremendous handicaps in any case without permitting the enemy to move in the rear of the operative arm of the attack. When this occurred all was over. The rest was anticlimax – even the prolonged struggle for Narvik, which had to be abandoned when taken.

But the debate on the evacuation was only just concluded when Germany attacked in force on the Western Front. With great ingenuity a force was landed in the rear of the main defensive line in Holland; and to assist the Dutch command to draw the obvious conclusion, the Germans delivered a barbarous bombardment of Rotterdam. In five days the army surrendered. But by this time the bridges across the Albert Canal, left intact by some oversight, had been used to fling a force into Belgium behind the main defensive system, and the Allies were, therefore, unable to take up their positions before their help was gravely discounted. More serious still, the French, falling back through Sedan, allowed the Germans to follow them over the Meuse Bridge, and at once armoured divisions were thrown across the river. They advanced westward, compelling the retreat of the Allied armies in Belgium, and southward, creating the utmost confusion behind the lines. General Gamelin never recovered control of his armies. In a few days there was a complete division between the units on the left and right wings, and while the former was attacked in front armoured divisions advanced up the Channel coast in its rear. The Belgian Army was beaten into submission, and after the splendid incidents at Calais and Boulogne there occurred the epic of Dunkirk.

What had happened to France? Attacked immediately on the Somme she maintained her positions for only four days, and four days later it was realised that she could fight no more. The rest, once more, is anticlimax. Italy had entered the war when it was quite clear that France was down and out; but so far, in the larger sense, her intervention has been a matter of gesture, though her operations have shown a very workmanlike character. It is the development of the direct offensive against Britain that is the most interesting and important feature of the end of the year. It is over nine weeks since the French armistice began, and Germany has been free to devote all her energies to Britain. In four she had compelled Holland and Belgium to surrender, and convinced France that an armistice was the only hope. What has Germany achieved in these nine weeks against the British Empire alone? She has made no serious advance in her blockade of Britain. In the first phase of her air offensive she received an undisguised check, and the second is still developing.

Indeed, we might also be tempted to a rash optimism if we took these facts apart from the moral of the French collapse. The imposing successes of Germany are due to intense (and, of course, unscrupulous) preparation and intense preoccupation with war. France was not prepared either materially or mentally. It seems impossible to interpret the abortive operations which Gamelin made in September to support the Poles, by attacking between the Moselle and the Rhine, as other than defeatist in inspiration.

How do we stand on the threshold of the second year of the war? We must guard against the dangerous illusion that we are the stronger for the defection of France. But we have certainly jettisoned much of our baggage-train that would have ruined us as it did France; for of course we now realise that France was beaten before she engaged. Our main strategy is intact, though the pressure of the blockade is weakened in some directions; and we have discovered how to invade Germany while the Channel which holds her off holds us in. We have discovered that at long last man will always dominate the machine, that numbers can be a deadly obsession, that quality is of more importance than quantity. If these are truisms they nevertheless belong to the obvious that is the last to be realised. So, stripped of illusion, fully recognising that we have only ourselves to count upon, we enter the second year strategically so placed that we can see no possibility of Germany defeating us and with reasonable hope that if we use our powers wisely, that is offensively, to the full we can bring her to ruin.

30 August 1940

A DECISIVE HOUR

(A Leading Article)

This has been described as the most critical week in the history of our realm, and impossible though it is to pass completely dispassionate verdicts in the midst of crisis, that description clearly falls little short of truth. It is the day of decision in the sense that if Hitler can break the spirit of this people by the concentrated and cumulative fury of his nightly assaults the last enemy will have gone down before him, and the lordship first of Europe and then of most of more than one other continent will be his. At such a moment there is a place for the reminder, which Mr Priestley gave his hearers on Sunday, that what has hitherto been the rather rhetorical declaration that every civilian is a soldier now has become sternly and grimly real. The shattered homes of East and South London tell how death may come unheralded to every doorstep, and tell equally how when he comes he finds his victims heroes and the survivors of the ordeal unshaken and determined still. The *ils ne passeront pas* of Verdun – ironic memory of Pétain the defender of the gate – has become in language no less resolute, 'he shall not get us down'. The civilians of London today, according to Mr Priestley, are London's men of Dunkirk, and the simile is apt if it serves to remind the civilian as he hears the bombs falling round him that at least he has a shelter or a basement to protect him. Between the German bombers and those crowded beaches and close-packed piers there was nothing but empty air.

The full purpose of the *Blitzkrieg* may have been more fully revealed by the time these lines are read. Its immediate object no doubt is to break morale. In that it will fail as other endeavours have failed from which Hitler and Goering are seeking now to divert attention. The first attack was on our shipping. It was so utterly unsuccessful that our convoys today go their way almost unmolested. The second was on our aerodromes. That was the approved technique. It was applied with spectacular success in Poland – thanks to the expedient of striking without notice at a nation against whom no war had been declared – and with hardly less effect in Holland. Against British aerodromes success was negligible. Many aerodromes were hit; that was inevitable; but on the day when the new phase of the *Blitzkrieg* opened not a single one had been made unusable. The blows against our ports and dockyards have failed. The blows against our munition-works and industrial plants have, as assiduous investigations by American correspondents have revealed, reduced our output by a negligible percentage. Now new tactics are invoked. Stark frightfulness, the traditional German *Schrecklichkeit*, is to achieve what relatively legitimate air warfare could not. London is to be desolated, its civilian population slaughtered, ordered life made impossible, by a series of promiscuous attacks that no longer even claim to be directed at military objectives. What we expected twelve months ago is coming now, and London and other cities that suffer like it must bear it as they were prepared to bear it then.

But the attacks on London may mean something more than that. This is the week in which certain natural conditions – a moon approaching the full, a calm sea and high tides about dawn – favour an attempt at invasion. That project, as both the Prime Minister and the Secretary for War have lately warned us, is by no means abandoned. The odds against its success are as great as they ever were, but Hitler is known to have set his mind upon it, and no sacrifice of men and ships and aeroplanes would deter him if he thought the chances of success were as much as one in five. Normally the defeat of the Royal Air Force, and in particular a wholesale destruction of its fighters, would be an essential preliminary. But in the circumstances a fanatical leader, faced with the need for that decision which, as Mr Churchill pointed out, Hitler cannot afford to defer, might disregard the indispensable condition and resolve to batter his way through in defiance of all the canons. In such a scheme the intimidation of London would play a natural part, in the double hope that disorganisation might be created at the vital centre and forces be detached to defend the capital that should properly be employed to repel aggression. Invasion may or may not be attempted – a very few days will answer that question one way or another – but, if it is, the assault on London will not have diverted a gun or a man or a machine from the protection of our coasts. A connexion between the two may exist in the mind of the assailant. There is none in the strategy of the defence.

The attack on London none the less raises grave questions. The hard fact has to be faced that no effective protection against night bombing at present exists. The comparative immunity our night-raiders over Germany have enjoyed week after week is proof enough of that. Anti-aircraft fire counts for something. So unquestionably does the balloon-barrage, which, apart from compelling the raiders to fly too high to pick out definite objectives, practically precludes dive-bombing. But it is not at present possible – the temporal qualification is important – to bring down, except by something little better than a fortunate chance, a machine that is not seen. For that reason an enemy bent only on destruction will continue to achieve destruction. The German pretext that the raids on London are reprisals for British raids on non-military objectives in Berlin is completely groundless. Our attacks have in no case been indiscriminate, as the report of pilots bringing back their bombs because weather conditions prevented them from finding their targets sufficiently testifies. We shall refrain from anything in the nature of reprisals in kind for two good reasons; the first that a nation fighting to save civilisation from barbarism cannot resort to barbaric methods, and the second that the RAF, by relentlessly and methodically reducing Germany's military and air strength by its daily and nightly attacks on aerodromes and factories, is pursuing tactics which must in time weaken the enemy's striking force, and ultimately compass his defeat.

Meanwhile there must be what adaptation is possible in view of the attacks on London. Simply to face the ordeal as we must is not enough. That may be actually playing the German game. Men and women doing valuable work do not help the country by being killed in London if they can work reasonably well elsewhere. A year ago elaborate plans were prepared for the evacuation of Government Departments and other public and private organisations in case of need. The need has now obviously arisen, and decentralisation should certainly be carried out in all cases where it is reasonably practicable. Concentration suits Hitler's book too well. The tide of school-children should flow back to the country. London is no place for them today. And with communications disturbed, and likely to be more so, the Government should be liberal in the matter of supplementary petrol allowances for good cause shown. To put it at the lowest, as many people as possible must live where sleep is possible. One other demand must be made of the Government, and there are signs that they are meeting it in advance. It is imperative that the fullest possible information regarding casualties should be published at the earliest possible moment. The truth will not depress or alarm the nation; wild and exaggerated rumours might, and there have been some examples of that already. We are fighting a savage and relentless enemy, whose savagery will not be intensified by knowledge of the number of his victims, because he is giving it its utmost licence in any case. The savagery is matched, and defeated, by the heroism it evokes, the heroism of the common men and women who know from the first moment the sirens sound

at night that they are potential victims, and the active and amazing heroism of the public servants, paid and volunteers, who are coping night
after sleepless night with fire and demolition, injury and death, as fire-
fighters, wardens, shelter-wardens, St John and Red Cross staffs and
all the rest. They would desire no higher tribute than the unstinted
gratitude and admiration they have inspired in every one of their fellow-
citizens.

13 September 1940

A SPECTATOR'S NOTEBOOK

Janus (H. Wilson Harris)

The efficiency with which daily papers are facing the present abnormal
situation is remarkable. But the weeklies have their difficulties too, and
it would not be astonishing if some mark of them remained on the face of
the finished article. They mostly work with very small staffs, so that any
defection creates a problem. *The Spectator* is no doubt a normal example.
In the course of Monday night the editor, with no worse than shattered
windows, had to evacuate his flat owing to the presence of unexploded
bombs, the assistant-editor (fortunately unhurt) had his house half
wrecked, another member of the staff, with the whole neighbourhood
evacuated owing to time-bombs, could not arrive at all. And so on. Of
course the posts, which bring copy, are utterly unreliable. Life therefore
proceeds under some difficulty, but it proceeds, and will. And if, as I say,
my colleagues' preoccupations leave some trace on the printed page,
readers who have suffered something similar themselves or worse will no
doubt make allowances. Carrying on will not get easier, but it is not in
sight of getting impossible.

13 September 1940

'THE SPECTATOR' IN WARTIME

The Editor (H. Wilson Harris)

The production of a paper like *The Spectator* is in the main its own affair. The business of its staff is to give its readers a finished article, for them to approve or disapprove as it may deserve. They, on their part, are concerned only with the thing as they see it, not with how it comes to be what it is. That, at least, is a reasonable view for an editorial staff to take who are well content to do the work that comes to them and not intrude their own personalities more than need be. But there is, no doubt, another side to that, and attention is called to it by a reader who asks for an article describing how *The Spectator* is produced each week, with something about the principal writers, on the ground that 'we who read the paper regularly feel almost like partners and would like your confidence'. No more persuasive argument could be invoked than that, for the words quoted indicate precisely the relationship which the producers of any paper would most desire to see existing between them and their readers. Here, then, is some response.

The normal make-up of the paper is familiar to all regular readers. It consists of some ten to twelve editorial notes on events of the week, a column of Parliament, two leading articles, the column and a half called 'A Spectator's Notebook', seven or eight middles, 'Country Life', a couple of pages covering the theatre, cinema, music and art, three or four pages of letters to the editor, six or seven of reviews, and a page or two of investment and finance. And, of course, there are advertisements, without which no paper would be an economic proposition. Normally the size of the paper each week is determined by the amount of advertisement space booked, for the editorial matter is kept fairly constant in volume. The average number of pages in *The Spectator* in 1939 was 48, though particular issues might run as high as 72.

A word about certain of these features may be apposite. The subjects of editorial notes and leading articles are chosen from the principal events of the week, listed as the days go by, and the notes are intended to contain both record and comment. The activities of Parliament, when sitting, are dealt with by a Member holding much the same Left Centre position as *The Spectator* itself. Middle articles do not just happen. Some of them are submitted by what may be termed 'outside' writers, more are written by arrangement by authorities on a particular subject which calls for discussion and elucidation. The aim is always to treat the 'middles' section as a whole, giving it as much breadth of interest and variety of theme and style as limits of space permit; under war-time conditions a good deal has to be sacrificed here.

Letters are a feature to which special importance is attached. The value of an open forum in which readers, often writing with peculiar authority on the subject with which they deal, can express views either consonant with or completely contrary to those of the paper, is very great; some discretion must, no doubt, be observed, and protests against the insertion of a letter embodying unpopular views may occasionally be justified. But, broadly speaking, controversy is healthy, and truth is attained and wisdom engendered by the cut-and-thrust of argument. Usually, of course, many more letters come in than there is room for.

The request for some details about the staff and the principal contributors can only be given a modified response. Of the Editor there is little to say, and perhaps the less said the better. He does what he has to do according to his lights, immensely helped by the proprietors of the paper, his colleagues and readers, both appreciative and critical. Interest in the identity of such contributors as Strategicus, Janus and our Parliamentary Correspondent must remain unsatisfied. They have their different reasons for preferring anonymity, leaving themselves to be judged by their writings week by week, and their wishes must clearly be respected. But regarding one regular and highly valued contributor no such reticence is called for. Sir William Beach Thomas has been writing a 'Country Life' page, reduced unfortunately for the present to a column, for nearly 20 years, and the value attached to it by readers has been unmistakably demonstrated by the flow of letters it evokes. Regret that Sir William feels that the time has now come for him to rest from his labours will be mitigated by the knowledge that he is handing his responsibilities over to Mr H.E. Bates, whose qualifications have been evidenced on the many occasions when he has taken temporary charge of the 'Country Life' page in the past few years.

So much for *The Spectator* as it normally is. But it is probably more useful to say a word about the abnormal conditions which compel its producers to see through the Press week by week a paper that is far from satisfying them. When war broke out we, like all such journals, were faced with the prospect of loss of staff, loss of contributors, loss of advertisements, loss of revenue, loss of circulation, a severe rationing of paper. Some of these apprehensions have proved groundless. Circulation, so far from decreasing, stands at a substantially higher figure than a year ago, and though paper restrictions often compel the painful decision to refuse lucrative applications for advertisement space, the financial position of the paper is sound. But on the editorial side difficulties have been manifold. The assistant-editor, Mr Goronwy Rees, enlisted before war broke out, and the literary editor, Mr Derek Verschoyle, has since joined the Air-Force. Fortunately it has been possible to replace them very adequately, in the one case by Mr R. A. Scott-James, formerly Editor of the *London Mercury*, and in the other by Mr Graham Greene, already well known through his reviews and film criticisms, and still more widely, of course, through his successful novels. Of regular contributors – most notably Mr Harold Nicolson – and reviewers at least 50 per cent have become unavailable. Some have joined the Government, some the expanded Civil Service, many, of course, are in one of the fighting services; some have most deplorably gone Trappist with Chatham House at Oxford. The paper has to be produced today by a narrowed circle.

There are, moreover, other problems. The chief concerns paper supplies. All such journals as *The Spectator* are permitted to use only one-third of their average pre-war paper consumption, and are prohibited from drawing on whatever reserves they may have been prudent enough to lay by. Since the average pre-war size of *The Spectator* was 48 pages, that would mean a reduction to no more than 16 pages if paper of the same weight and quality were still used. By substituting a much lighter and thinner paper we are able to maintain a 24-page issue, and hope to continue to do so, unsatisfactory though the expedient plainly is. That, of course, has involved dropping some features altogether and reducing others. There can now be usually only one leading article instead of two, five middles instead of eight (one of the five reserved, with the obvious concurrence of readers, for Strategicus), a column instead of a page of 'Country Life', fewer letters and fewer reviews, which is particularly unfortunate at a time when publishers are continuing, with great enterprise and courage, to produce books of a quality as high as ever. The competition goes, but the crossword remains. Advertisements have had to be limited, even though this involves considerable loss of revenue.

Various other dislocations complicate matters further. Most individual members of the staff have their own bomb-created problems, driving them in some cases to new and less convenient quarters. Interruption of communications often makes it impossible to reach the office at the usual hour, and a week or two ago first arrivals doubted whether it was worth reaching in any case. However, nothing more was wrong than shattered windows, blown-in doors, and no gas, and there is nothing at all fatal about that. But with the letter post completely incalculable, the parcel post so hopeless that it has been idle to send books to any reviewers out of London, or by any other means than special messenger, and with telephone trunk-calls unobtainable, there have been a good many disabilities to live down. There may well be many more yet, particularly if it becomes the habit to stop work in the early afternoon. Provision has been made for alternative accommodation in London if the present offices become untenable, or, if it should seem desirable, out of London. Problems multiply, but there is a certain satisfaction in solving them. Altogether there is so far little to complain of. Readers who are not getting *The Spectator* of a year ago, or *The Spectator* we should wish them to have, are singularly generous in their appreciation of our difficulties. The single purpose of the staff will be to give them, so far as is possible under the limitations set by the present emergency, the kind of paper they have a right to look for. Any moment may bring a new crisis, but there will always be some way round it.

11 October 1940

A SPECTATOR'S NOTEBOOK

Janus (H. Wilson Harris)

Opinions regarding Princess Elizabeth's broadcast seem to be unanimous. One professional critic, I see, speaks of the Princess as 'the most outstanding child radio personality I've yet heard'. I should not have put it quite that high myself, but it was an excellent performance, a clear and natural delivery being achieved without any shade of the assurance which would be out of place in a child of fourteen. It can hardly be supposed that the speech itself was composed entirely without assistance, but no word of it was out of keeping, and the 'Come on, Margaret' to the speaker's sister at the end was a touch of nature that came near being a touch of genius. And when the Princess declared that the future of the world rested with the children of today it was worth remembering that it was the next sovereign of these realms who was speaking.

18 October 1940

SIR JOHN REITH'S CHANCE

Clough Williams-Ellis

It is not yet clear what powers are to be given to Sir John Reith as our National Master Builder, but they will need to be quite unprecedented if they are at all to match the work that awaits them. It is a job that has awaited *someone* these hundred years, growing ever more daunting with every unplanned addition to our sprawling web of building, with every chance missed of unsnarling even some corner of our increasing tangle. It has long been a commonplace that nothing short of dynamite would ever remove the worst reproaches of our English towns. Hitler has clumsily and painfully inured us to large-scale destruction; it is now for Sir John to show us what dynamite can do when selectively applied by his own strong hands in the service of town-planning, civic regeneration and human well-being generally.

The last great chance for exchanging the haphazard sprawl of London for something fine, gracious and efficient was, of course, given by the Great Fire, a chance notoriously and disastrously missed. If Sir John's immediate function is no more than to act as a sort of burly commissionaire, restraining the queue of property-owners from pushing past him to set about rebuilding incontinently on their shattered sites, that is a very necessary task that will need all his relentless strength of purpose. 'Stand back, gentlemen, please. No admittance until the master-plan is accepted.' But that disciplining of the individual in the public interest, that civilised subordination of the citizen to his city, will only be one part of an almost endlessly complicated office which will need to take as much cognisance of World Affairs and Foreign Policy as of National Economics and Modern Technics. What sort of future, for example, are we to plan and build for? If that future is to be overshadowed by the bomber, then, if it is indeed worth while to build at all (except provisionally), we can scarcely set about it with much of that spirit of delight or that scrupulous care that can alone elevate mere construction into architecture. Once England had the chance of voting the bombing aeroplane out of existence. It chose not to. We now realise, perhaps, that the choice lies between bombers and most of the things that civilised people deem necessary for the good life. Yet the whole world will need re-civilising before the obvious choice can be safely made, if, indeed, we are ever given another chance to make it.

Then there are those 'property owners' – each intent on his own little parcel of land (too often a mere penny packet) to the exclusion of any wider interest in the general pattern of his town. Is effective, positive, town-planning possible at all whilst such private freeholds of urban land persist? That is a question that the new Minister and his advisers must face and report on pretty early in their deliberations, as, indeed, upon the private ownership of land in general.

Whatever their findings it is clear that such private ownership as may be allowed to survive must be far less absolute and irresponsible than heretofore. Now Sir John has the reputation of being an autocrat, and God knows he now has need to be. But in all his many positions of power he has never failed to seek the best available advice, and at least to consider it. He may be trusted to do no less in this the most difficult and dazzling post of his career. He will assuredly read (if he has not already done so) Lewis Mumford's *Culture of Cities*, Elizabeth Denby's *Europe Rehoused*, and the writings of Abercrombie, Sharp, Geddes, Reilly, Simon and others on the philosophy and technics of planning and building. He will, too, we may presume, put through his sieve a sufficient and representative number of those others who have been earnestly and effectively concerned with these things for many years, and whose public-spirited zeal for a better England is expressed in such foundations as the Housing Centre, the Council for the Preservation of Rural England, and a score of other kindred and equally active associations.

His data and his personnel are all ready to his hand; they have indeed been prepared against his coming these many years, and must by no means be overlooked. Doubtless his council will be fully furnished with accredited representatives from all the relevant technical and professional bodies as the custom is, but I think we may look to Sir John to pick his own team of actual advisers and executives himself on individual merit and performance, and on nothing else. From the very beginning he must be prepared to be a trouble-maker, hitting hard, and to hurt on all sides without fear or favour, if he looks to establish the new deal of an orderly, beautiful and convenient England as against the hugger-mugger *status quo*. An easy-going indolence has landed us where we are, and only a bracing spell of discipline can redeem us.

> All along of laziness
> All along of mess
> All along of doing things
> Rather more or less.

Have we not yet learnt that to go as you please is no way to arrive at what is pleasant?

Obviously and urgently necessary as it was to have a Minister of Works and Buildings, his actual appointment now is a heroic gesture as well as a wise provision – 'Sir John defying the *Blitzkrieg*.' But as suggested above, he will need to defy more than that; vested interests, inertia, bureaucracy and the Treasury itself.

In the past, on paper at least, a plausible *economic* case has invariably been made out against all proposals for public works in relief of unemployment. I doubt whether after this war, and what preceded it, that cock will ever fight again. It has never been quite the bird it was since Mr Maynard Keynes laid hands on it:

> There commenced in the eighteenth century and reached a climax in the nineteenth a new view of the functions of the State and of society, which still governs us today. This view was the utilitarian and economic – one might almost say financial – ideal, as the sole, respectable purpose of the community as a whole; the most dreadful heresy, perhaps, which ever gained the ear of a civilised people. Bread and nothing but bread, and not even bread, but bread accumulating at compound interest until it has turned into a stone. Poets and artists have lifted occasional weak voices against the heresy. I fancy that the Prince Consort was the last protestor to be found in high places. But the Treasury view has prevailed. Not only in practice. The theory is equally powerful. We have persuaded ourselves that it is positively wicked for the State to spend a halfpenny on non-economic purposes. Even education and public health only creep in under an economic alias on the ground that they 'pay'. We still apply some frantic perversion of business arithmetic in order to settle the problem whether it pays better to pour milk down the drains or to feed it to school children. One form alone of uncalculated expenditure survives from the heroic age – war.

Of course, there are and will always be all sorts of objections to every bold proposal – to a Master Plan for London and each town and city, to reinstating the Thames as a permanent citizens' highway, to coherent regional and 'neighbourhood' development, to satellite towns, to emparking slum areas and so forth and so on. Every conceivable plan for anything bristles with difficulties and objections, and we have been so mesmerised by such in the past that we have been intimidated into not planning at all – or not sticking to our plan when we dared to make one. Small wonder that we are now in desperate plight.

One will be interested in due course to learn the new Minister's views on many things – for example, the effect of an at first static and then steeply declining population, and the appropriate reaction thereto in planning and building metropolitan rail and air termini, municipal control and restriction of private motor traffic, school holiday camps, cohesive street elevations as against the competitively individualistic, the location of industry and of hospitals, professional 'Town Managers' (on the American model), the adequacy of our present municipal administration and of our local government bodies generally, arcaded streets, le Corbusier's 'City of Tomorrow', trolley buses . . . and so on.

It will be observed that I credit the Minister with as wide a charter as his office undoubtedly demands, and with the thoroughness that I know him to possess. Far from having a clean slate to write on, he is confronted by one bearing the confused scribblings of generations, now largely making illegible nonsense. Our slum-clearance efforts have rubbed clean a few little patches here and there, and our enemies have done a trifle more, but we ourselves must rub and rub again until our shameful places are every one expunged for ever. The great Wen of London that appalled Cobbett had been apprehensively foreseen by Elizabeth, and we have endured the monstrosity magnified a hundredfold.

According to D.H. Lawrence, 'The English may have great spiritual qualities, but as builders of splendid cities they are more ignominious than rabbits.' That was not always so. It is so now, alas, as for a hundred years past, but let it be so no longer. We change or we perish – as the dinosaur discovered. If this war does not serve to change us in more than that respect, we shall have lost it, whatever the military result. Another Peacehaven would be a sure symptom of our defeat.

18 October 1940

FELLOW PASSENGERS

H.E. Bates

All summer, in the south, the trains were crowded. It was only in August that I began to travel on them every day.

Already, by that time, the battalions of business men, travelling with the same cronies in the same compartments, regimentally pin-striped, hiding behind the barrage of *The Times*, the roses of financial success in their buttonholes, had been much thinned out. In their place now were travelling the real battalions: tired soldiers going home on leave, tired soldiers coming back. The weather was very hot, and they carried loads of kit resembling those of porters on a tourist expedition, and I used to get into conversation by handing round the morning papers, which none of them ever seemed to buy. ('Nothing in 'em, anyway. All the same.') It was clear that most of them were in strange country. Far from home, they had no idea how long the journey would be, no idea of place names, completely fogged as to how to get from Cannon Street to Paddington. One boy from Newcastle grew very excited on nearing London. Looking out of the window, he asked at every passing church, 'Is that Big Ben?' and when I told him no, I could see that for him it was a question of realising a life's ambition. So, as we crossed the Thames, I pointed out St Paul's instead, very impressive in the hot sunlight beyond the water. But he only shook his head, and I could see that it wasn't the same.

Soon I made a daily habit of it – getting into compartments crowded with soldiers, handing round the papers, getting them to talk about themselves, Dunkirk, the winter in France, giving what advice I could about crossing London. We were always crowded, always sitting on top of each other, always lively. Passing along the corridors, I would see officers, both men and women, sitting all alone in first-class state, bored, silent, out of touch. Sometimes there was a coincidence. Once I talked to a tough, regular Army sergeant, who had served in India and China. I wanted very much to hear about that, but he talked as if it had been a trip to Brighton. Instead he talked about Bedford – there was a little village up there, Yelden, quite pretty, with a little thatch-roofed pub. He'd spent Sunday there. Very nice, but now he couldn't remember the name of the pub. Now what was it? Damn it, what was it now?

He couldn't remember, so I told him. 'The Chequers,' I said.

'Well, blimey,' he said, 'how'd you know?'

'My aunt kept it,' I said, 'for thirty years.'

The making of friends has never been so easy. In the whole history of British railways there has never been, I should think, so much conversation and friendliness per mile as now. The air of silent refrigeration, the arid cross-examination of stares, the snoozing behind the fat peace-time blankets of newspapers – all that has gone. It has never been so easy to get all kinds of people to talk of themselves. I shall remember a long time the little Folkestone fruiterer – business gone to pot, three sons serving, all his Army pension sunk, few prospects. His life should have been broken in half. Instead, never a word of complaint. And as if to show me what adversity really was he told me reticently how, thanks to the last war, he had had thirty major operations on his stomach, and lifted his trousers' leg to show me a calf carved like a fantastic chair-leg by bullet holes. In peace-time we should never have met. In an hour, now, he had opened his heart to me.

This sort of thing went on for a month. All the time the *Blitzkrieg* was closing in on us. And yet all the time another curious thing was happening: evacuees from the coast were, in spite of everything, going back home. Two young women, the mother of one of them, and a frowsy brood of tiny children herded into the compartment on a suffocating afternoon. Dead tired from heat and travelling, they vowed and hoped, as long as they lived, never to go to Wales again. The babies grizzled and snuffled miserably, puffy-eyed, wet, hanging on laps like lumps of leaden dough. There was much threatening of bottom-smacking, alternate coddling, bottle-filling and despair ('If you don't be quiet that man'll come and git you'). The prettiness of one girl was still just visible, very dim, behind the dirty lines of poverty, weariness and a slight viciousness imposed by something at which I could only guess. 'My God,' she kept saying, 'my God, my God,' and I would have given my heart to know what lay behind it all.

Then changing circumstances turned me from the south. I began to travel north instead. The north of England begins, for me, on the platform of St Pancras Station. A new life begins there: the Luton hat travellers with their samples, the downright level-headed boot-and-shoe men, the right-on-the-spot lads from Leicester eternally playing cards on outspread newspapers, the hurrying high-tea Yorkshiremen who demand 'something more soobstantial' for tea. After years in the south it is impossible to mistake them.

Yet the very first afternoon I was, as they say in the Midlands, sucked in. The man sitting opposite me looked like the pale, down-trodden city clerk who is a popular cliché in fiction. I had grown so used to interesting fellow passengers that I was disappointed and immediately read into the pallor, the neat dark suit and the air of weariness a life whose foundations were a desk, a semi-detached, a Morris-Ten and a garden bounded by trellis-work. I was much mistaken.

In two minutes I was talking, not to a city clerk, but to a mining engineer home from the Gold Coast. The pallor had nothing to do with a city desk, but was the fruit of a climate whose humidity is too great to be measured, where nobody ever runs upstairs, where people conserve their strength by talking in whispers, and where all water is boiled. As the train went on I pumped hard. The working conditions, the natives, the social life, the colonial administration – I pumped out something about each of them. And lastly the gold itself. How was it worked, was there much of it, was it in danger of petering out? In answer he told me of mines in Ashanti that were too rich to be worked. 'Daren't work 'em,' he said. 'We keep 'em under lock and key. Can't have too much gold in the world. Oh! no, that wouldn't do.'

Next day, in a world in which gold was kept under lock and key while homeless people starved, and a nation struggled to find six million pounds a day for war, the train was crowded by people who literally no longer had a home. The tired young women with children I had seen going home to Dover were now repeated a hundred times. And not only young women, but old women, old men ('look after him, porter, see that he gets out at Sheffield'), a boy with his rescued tabby cat, whole families struggling as if on a Bank Holiday to get a seat on the over-crowded train. All needed sleep. There were more strange coincidences. I travelled twice with a man, the brother of a famous singer, before discovering his name was the same as my own. There was the country parson who, only the day before, I had found absorbed in the active restoration of his church, passionately reconstructing it with excellent taste, while in London the churches of centuries were being blasted to pieces. There were more cases of deceptive appearances – the little blonde office girl who had neither home, office, nor clothes, and on whom I almost took pity as destitute. She casually remarked as I left her that her fiancé was, or had been, a Dutch Cabinet Minister.

And finally there was the waiter in the restaurant car. I think of him as fighting for, indeed, risking his job for democracy. The train, as always, was crowded; the tea, as always, bad, late and expensive. At one table a man was clearly not playing the game by trying to keep one seat for himself, one for his bag, and another for his overcoat. The waiter pointed out the injustice of this on a train where three hundred people were standing. The man made some objection in reply.

The waiter at once delivered a speech magnificent in its fire-eating anger. Didn't the gentleman know there was a war on? Didn't he know there were three hundred people standing on the train? Didn't he know how difficult travelling was? If he didn't it was high time he did. Nor, said the waiter, need he think he could come on the train and throw his weight about. Times were difficult. People not only had not got seats, but many had not got homes. 'And finally,' the waiter said, 'not so much of your sauce, and not so much of your old-school-tie tactics. They'll get you nowhere here!'

Such a speech from waiter to customer struck us all completely dumb. It was the equivalent of a revolution, and was rightly regarded by all in the restaurant car as hot stuff. It was certainly something else that could never have happened in peace-time. In its way, dictated though it may have been by the weariness of the moment, it was a piece of high courage. In it spoke the souls of all waiters – and, I may say, a lot more of us besides.

As the daily exodus from London went on I found myself becoming interested in, sympathetic towards, attached to a great number of people. Death is a leveller; but death by bombing is, in more senses than one, the greatest leveller of all. It has smashed the silence of the English railway carriage.

18 October 1940

THE STRAYS

Henry Trench

There was no warning whistle when the bombs exploded; they tore the air like calico in our direction. The noise in the small basement-shelter was not so loud as one had expected, but the fourth bomb wiped away the house next door. There wasn't time to be afraid; only the silence afterwards was a little shocking, and the smell of hot metal. Then the wardens came and drove us out to find refuge in a strange shelter. It was our turn to be strays.

Strays had always interested us – uneasily – as their feet clattered on the area stairs and the curtain billowed. Just so, I suppose, do rabbits look up from their lettuces at the sound of an intruder in the burrow. Will it be buck or doe? aggressive or apologetic? For in our small shelter – which was comfortable but not reassuring with a beaverboard wall – there was only room for the regular population which came there every night. After a month of aerial war we had coalesced like a platoon; that was why we seemed to present a rather surly front to newcomers until they had proved friendly. Far more, I think, than bunks and free earplugs does this solidarity help to make life underground bearable – almost pleasant. A routine grows naturally like a plant; in the first week tea was always made after a particularly close explosion; later the close explosions didn't matter so much, so we had tea and biscuits at 9 (everyone paid a penny and took it in turns to supply tea and sugar); lights were shaded at 10, and snorers ceased to rouse angry feelings – toleration developed. Most wonderful of all a Pole learnt to make strong English tea.

For ours was a cosmopolitan world. It was as if, burrowing below ground, one evaded national boundaries. Three Germans had ended a long pilgrimage there: a mother and two children. The father had been an officer in the German army; he resigned when Hitler came to power, and they fled to Austria, and then to Amsterdam; the father had ended *his* journey in Australia. Vienna, Prague or Warsaw, Amsterdam, our burrow; these were familiar stations to others too. There was an Austrian, three Czechs and a Pole; the English were only a bare majority. Mattresses and deckchairs left little room for chance comers, and they usually went on to a larger burrow ten yards up the street: a raffish place where – we heard it rumoured – the police were sometimes called in to deal with drunks and gamblers. We never expected to find ourselves there, in those bleak halls, smelling of old sandbags, strays ourselves.

That night the raid started punctually to time, and everybody was happy (perhaps it was the tranquillity Peter Rabbit felt when he knew exactly where his enemy Mr Macgregor lurked at the moment). A Czech lady carried round a bag of sweets, and self-revealing conversations started up all over the shelter. Thick with personal dramas and philosophies, the atmosphere was usually a cross between *Grand Hotel* and *The Cherry Orchard*, but more Baum perhaps than Chekhov, for the plot was a violent one. Between the thuds of the barrage a young man explained to a girl the secret of contentment (he made it sound very easy); the Pole tried to improve his English, two women discussed babies, and a Czech told fortunes roguishly in a teacup. 'A bomb will fall,' he said, and everyone laughed.

Among the strays, too, the Baum and Chekhov elements predominated; there was, for example, the night of burglaries in the street above – which was unmistakably Baum. Three men came briskly down the steps at two in the morning, separated, and made for unoccupied chairs, then pulled other people's blankets up to their chins. They had tight suits and ugly ears, and looked shaved for action: once a policeman gazed in, and the cautious eyes watched him from the half-dark. They came once more . . . and there was a burglary that night too. One had a racking cough; he looked accustomed to cement floors and the heavy breathing of neighbours. Sometimes soldiers sat shyly out on the area steps with girls, and once – that was a Chekhov touch – an old philosopher with a white beard spent the night. He was a birdlover, and he had a little birdlime on his hat. It was a noisy night; when he left he said it had been an interesting experience – 'really very interesting'. He thought he would go into the country all the same, and sleep on a barn floor (if one had to sleep on floors one might as well sleep in a barn); there, he said, one could have peaceful thoughts. He handed round before he left picture postcards of himself with sparrows nibbling the food from his lips, and repeated that it had all been very interesting.

I like to think it was a tribute to our shelter, and now that we are strays ourselves, among the vagrant population moving restlessly up and down, I am glad to remember we welcomed at least one stray. Conscience pricks one for all the unwelcomed who tried – some with feigned indignation or nervous fantasies – to make a contact: irritation was better than indifference. There was the large woman in dusty furs who woke us at two in the morning, in the heart of the heaviest raid, to seek protection from an imaginary mouse – 'there it is, there it is' – but it was only a piece of grey fluff shifting in the draught of explosions; and there was the old drunk man who was scandalised at the sight of husbands and wives sharing mattresses. 'I'm a ratepayer,' he kept repeating, propped against the wall. 'If I hadn't seen it with me own eyes,' he said, shutting them firmly, 'I wouldn't have believed. Disgusting, it's disgusting.' Screwing his eyes tighter, he toppled sidoways.

Well, one can understand loneliness now. Sometimes one salutes at a distance another member of the old platoon, but we are individuals; the oolidarity is gone, and for the first time we are all aware of insecurity.

25 October 1940

A SPECTATOR'S NOTEBOOK

Janus (H. Wilson Harris)

Parliament the other day agreed in about five minutes to a vote of a further £1,000,000,000, to carry on the war for another four months or so, at the present rate of £9,000,000 a day. A comparison with the cost of one of Britain's other great campaigns is not without a certain sobering interest. 'William III's war,' writes Professor Trevelyan, 'had lasted nine years and had cost England an average of £3,500,000 a year. The War of the Spanish Succession was destined to last a dozen years and cost her an average of £4,000,000 a year or more ... William's war had run up a National debt of £14,500,000.' To this was added another £21,500,000 for Anne's war. So for £4,000,000 a year we got Blenheim, Ramillies and Malplaquet, to say nothing of Gibraltar. It seems reasonably cheap – even if £4,000,000 in Anne's reign represents £10,000,000 or more in George VI's.

1 November 1940

AIR-RAIDS AND THE ZOO

Julian Huxley

I have done various odd things in my time, but few odder than what I was doing early one morning recently. At that hour, rather dimly-lit by the light of fires, and to the accompaniment of the AA barrage, the hornet-like drone of German planes overhead, and the occasional whine and wallop of dropping bombs, I was pursuing a Grevy zebra along the Outer Circle in Regent's Park.

The Zoo had had its share of bombs that night, both HE and incendiary. Three fire-engines were in the grounds, with their crews, together with the Zoo's night ARP squad and three Boy Scouts who had appeared out of the darkness and were rendering very useful help. About midnight one of our men reported a zebra just outside the Office. It disappeared into the darkness, and must have made its way through the Tunnel into the Main Gardens, whence it emerged through the stores-gate, which was open for use of the AFS. A zebra in Camden Town, though not a dangerous animal, might have created surprise and even alarm, though probably not despondency; it was also a valuable animal (Grevy Zebras are rare, and the London Zoo has one of the few good breeding-stocks in captivity); so half-a-dozen of us set off in pursuit, leaving another group to block the animal's retreat. With some driving and coaxing, and generalship in the disposition of the man-power available, the beast was got back into the stores-yard and the doors shut. But he did not like the shed invitingly opened for his reception, and his jibbing was accentuated every time the neighbouring AA guns went off – which was very frequently. At one moment I confess to having been scared, when he backed until his hindquarters came within a couple of yards of myself, securely wedged in a corner. Next day I confessed my apprehensions to his keeper. 'Oh, you were all right, Sir,' was his answer, 'he's a biter, not a kicker.' But I hadn't known this at the moment. However, tact eventually prevailed, and he was safely recaptured.

After this a party of us went to look at the Zebra House. It had suffered a direct hit, and it seemed certain that half a dozen beasts must have been killed. As a matter of fact, not one was even injured – apart from a few abrasions and scratches. Two other animals had been liberated from their stalls, one into the paddock, while the other had sought shelter in the basement under the Hippo House; a pair of zebras had miraculously escaped damage when their roof came down – and that was all.

The comparative absence of animal casualties is indeed remarkable. Monkey Hill suffered a direct hit: but the monkeys were in their shelters inside the Hill, and did not exhibit even a trace of shock next morning. Damage was done to the wire netting at the end of one of the cranes' enclosures, with the sole effect of allowing one crane to get out and enjoy the dubious privilege of liberty in London for a few days before being recaptured. A Bird of Paradise was liberated from its cage into the public space, where it was caught up next day. One explosion wrought great havoc on the Zoo's abundant glass roofs, and allowed three humming-birds to escape. They were last seen happily flying about the Gardens, but will inevitably succumb to the winter.

The ordinary small incendiary bombs have on the whole been remark-ably ineffective in the Zoo. When a whole shower of them fell in the grounds one of the keepers describing the scene next day (I had happened to be at Whipsnade that night) said, 'Beautiful it really was. Only needed a bit of music to make it seem like fairyland.' One of them started a small fire in the bakery; we got it out with extinguishers, but only after it had kept flaring up again, in an annoying way, when by rights it ought to have been out. We later discovered that the bomb had fallen among a pile of rolls, which has provided a joke against the bakery-staff that will last a long time. Two other fires were more serious – one kiosk was entirely consumed (it was by the light of its flames that the escaped zebra was first sighted); and the upper storey of another building was badly damaged.

There has been still another cause of trouble in the Zoo – the detona-tion of unexploded bombs. I have on my desk a handsome piece of shell-casing, with very sharp and jagged edges, which descended in a red-hot condition much too close to a couple of keepers, and also a lump of clay weighing about 5 pounds which made a hole clean through the roof of one of the houses. Casualties to the animals are not quite non-existent – for example, to one goose which was, poor thing, blown high into the air, to fall dead into the bomb crater. A young giraffe was scared by a bomb falling near, and nervously refused to enter the house all night. This caused her a nasty cold, but that is now a thing of the past.

The animals' reactions were interesting. Many of the ruminants seemed scared at the whistle of descending bombs, and start running about; and the explosions themselves startle some of the more nervous. Others react with defiance: one donkey, for instance, brayed violently.

Once the bombs have fallen, some animals show a mild interest. A congregation of quadrupeds sniffing at a newly made crater made a peculiar picture one morning.

Finally a word of reassurance. Some of my readers will be asking why, if a zebra could escape, might not lions and tigers be liberated to seek prey in Albert Road or lurk in the shrubberies of Regent's Park? The Zoo authorities have naturally given a great deal of thought to this problem, and feel, after consulting the most highly-placed ARP experts, that their precautions are water-tight. All the really dangerous animals, notably the large cats, the Polar bears, and the full-grown apes, are shut up every night in such a way that it would take not one but two bombs to let them out into the gardens – one on their sleeping den and one on the bars of an outer cage. And the experts assure us that the mathematical improbability of this is so astronomically high that it can be disregarded. Other Zoo animals, if they did get out, could most probably be coaxed back by experienced keepers; and if they could not, and showed any signs of being dangerous, they would be shot by the trained riflemen who form part of the Zoo's ARP personnel.

Poisonous snakes and spiders and scorpions might elude capture if they escaped. They were therefore all destroyed in accordance with a decision taken in the late spring of 1939, within a few hours of the declaration of war. When I was in the USA last winter I was often asked if this was really true, and was told that the news had brought the war home to Americans more than anything else. A visit to Regent's Park at the present moment would, I think, convince a neutral observer, as much as any other single aspect of life, that London is carrying on with very reasonable efficiency in spite of the aerial *Blitzkrieg* and all its fury.

1 November 1940

AIR-RAID WARDENS' CLAIMS

Lady Violet Bonham Carter

During the year of lull before the *Blitzkrieg* started Air-Raid Wardens were generally regarded as a quite unnecessary and rather expensive nuisance. It was difficult to see what they were there for. They appeared to spend their days in basements, listening to gas-lectures in the intervals of playing darts, and when they emerged at nightfall it was only to worry innocent people about their lights. They occasionally held up the traffic by performing strange charades, pretending (as best they could) to cope with imaginary situations of wild improbability. And for this life of idleness and antics the public heard with horror that some of them were actually being paid.

As an (unpaid) participator in that year of waiting broken by antics, I felt some sympathy with the public. Our training was tedious; it often seemed academic, sometimes even absurd. I could never manage to persuade myself that, confronted with a bombed and blazing house from which gas and water were escaping and in which 'persons' were 'trapped', I should meticulously fill in an elaborate printed form (with block letters) describing under the appropriate headings not only what had, but also what had not, happened. Like many others I often longed for a less hypothetical, more immediate task.

Today we have our reward. We are conscious, as never before in our lives, of fulfilling a definite, direct and essential function. We are a frontline service, in action every night in the defence of London. We know that our neighbours in every walk of life turn to us in their hour of need and look on us as their friends. We would not exchange our job for any other . . .

8 November 1940

PEACE BY ECONOMICS

Balbus (Julian Huxley)

Most people would agree that absolute national sovereignty has become an anachronism, at any rate in overcrowded Europe, and must in some way be restricted if we are to minimise the danger of war. But there is little agreement as to the methods by which this desirable end could be brought about. Most of those who have concerned themselves with the subject have concentrated on political machinery, in which the precise degree of sovereign restriction is formally laid down. But though this *de jure* restriction is necessary in certain spheres, like the purely political, it may be suggested that in economic affairs a *de facto* restriction is more desirable and more likely to give results.

Modern war has become so technological and so total that it cannot be waged with any chance of success unless backed by an extremely high industrial potential. War could thus be made much less likely if we could set up in Europe an industrial organisation which cut across national boundaries and operated in such a way as to prevent the industrial potential of any great nation from being mobilised as a whole for armaments production. If you look at an economic geography, you will see that Nature has obligingly laid the foundations for such an arrangement. The largest concentration of heavy industry in Europe is based on the coal and iron ore distributed round the intersections of Western Germany, Lorraine, North-Eastern France, Eastern Belgium and Luxembourg. Again, the Silesian industrial region is by nature a unit, though politically divided (hitherto) into German, Polish and Czech sections. And there are many other examples.

The next step is for man to build on these natural foundations. Already steps have been taken in this direction. In spite of every obstacle, much has been done towards the pooling of ownership, policy and markets in various big industries. Examples are the European cartels for iron and steel and for aluminium, and the great chemical industries. Unfortunately, these have not been brought under any control in the public interest, and so have on the whole been irresponsible, with restriction of output and maintenance of the price-level as their main objective. This tendency towards regional and functional integration is probably inevitable in modern conditions, and has been accentuated by the Germans' elaborate organisation of the industrial resources of the huge area now under their control.

What is needful for our present purpose is to see that each such grouping of industry is independently rationed as regards the key raw materials it needs. And this will only be possible if a world-scale system of raw material control is set up after the war. Such a system could be readily developed, granted American willingness to co-operate, out of the positive side of the British blockade machinery, which even now is engaged on the constructive task of rationing neutral countries in accordance with their needs. Control schemes would be needed for those ten or a dozen substances which are both key raw materials and suitable for control. Iron, tin and copper are obvious candidates among metals, and rubber, cotton and sugar among primary products, while wheat is an obvious case of unsuitability. The separate control schemes would be supervised by some international body – shall we call it the Raw Materials Union? – representing all the countries willing to join in the scheme and admitted to its privileges; and steps would doubtless be taken to ensure that consumer as well as producer interests were taken into account.

But what concerns us here is the relation of the scheme to a non-national organisation of European industry. This could be arranged for along some such lines as the following. In each major area, such as Europe, industry would have to be organised on two levels. In the first place, single industries or groups of industries would be required to form a series of Regional Associations, so distributed as to cut across national boundaries whenever possible (though different industries would of course differ in their geographical set-up). Each of these would have to operate as a unit. The separate associations would have to submit their programmes of marketing and production to the second type of body. Each of these latter would represent a major area as a whole, and would act as a producers' co-operative entrusted with the job of buying the necessary substances from the raw material controls and distributing them to the regional associations. Let us call them Area Distributives.

Under such a scheme it would be impossible for any powerful nation, least of all Germany, to embark on a policy of autarky, or to concentrate its heavy industry behind an armaments programme. If the German component, say, of the Belgian-French-Luxembourg-Ruhr heavy industry association tried to use the raw material allotted to it for such illegal purposes it would not receive its rations and would be unable to function. In other words, the machinery for normal production and marketing would also act as machinery for sanctions. Thus economic sanctions would be automatic, and would not have to be built up each time, as under the League, out of many wavering national wills. Checks and counterchecks would have been set up between the economic and the political activities of Europe, just as they were set up by the American Constitution between the executive and the legislature.

It may be objected that such an elaborate system would be difficult to organise in the difficult years after the war. The objection is very pertinent. But it can be largely met by taking the process in two stages, of which the first would be temporary and adapted to the immediate post-war phase of reconstruction. The needs of reconstruction will be so urgent, the necessity for drastic action so obvious, that any scheme which holds out a real promise of meeting those needs will be readily accepted. What we must do is to use the needs of reconstruction as opportunities for a stable peace, and think out our post-war reconstruction machinery so that it could develop into a permanent organisation such as we have sketched.

This can be done if the entire business is entrusted to a Reconstruction Commission; through which alone raw materials and credits, as well as

other help, would be allotted, whether for the relief of hunger and disease, the rebuilding of devastated areas, or the development of industry.
Industry alone concerns our present purpose. Here, the Reconstruction
Commission, entrusted with the distribution of credit, with the machinery of the British blockade in its aspect of raw material distribution, and
of the British shipping control to ensure priority of transport to the more
urgent materials, would automatically be in the position of Area Distrib-
utive for Europe. With these powers in its hands, it could insist on imposing any organisation it wished upon European industry. If it chose to
insist on European industry grouping itself into Regional Associations
cutting across national boundaries, there could be no gainsaying it, and
in so doing it would have laid the firm foundation for a permanent
scheme.

The essence of the matter, in the economic as in other spheres, is to
regard Europe (as much of Europe as possible!) as a whole. We must at all
costs avoid the mistake of being hypnotised by the existing framework of
things into imagining that this has any intrinsic quality of rightness or
permanence. Most people by sheer habit, or if you prefer a harsher term,
mental laziness, start from the premiss of Europe as consisting of a mass
of sovereign Nation States, and try to work upward from this, comprom-
ising here, whittling away there. We must make the mental effort of
imagining Europe functioning in some way as a single unit, and then
work down from that major premiss towards its regional affairs, whether
in industry, or in the regional political units we call nations. It is often
said quite sincerely that Germany must inevitably and always be the
industrial centre of Europe. This is totally untrue. Economically speaking, Germany is an unnatural unit, which has imposed a purely political
unity on parts of numerous natural industrial regions. By divorcing economic from political powers this fact will at once become apparent. And
the same applies, *mutatis mutandis*, to all the other industrial nations of
Europe. In this separation of powers lies one of the main hopes of preventing war from arising in Europe.

15 November 1940

ON SLEEPING IN BED

Rose Macaulay

SIR: Every day one hears of fresh amenities to brighten public shelters (tube and other) – canteens, hot drinks, buns, bunks, concerts, libraries, &c. Before long they will be equipped with all the pleasures of a fun-hall. No wonder that railway officials complain to protesting *bona-fide* travellers that the tubes grow fuller each night. No wonder that parents refuse to send their children out of London because they are 'too useful in booking shelter-places and helping to shift bedding'. There seems no doubt that we are settling down underground, to be a race of troglodytes. It is said that the first question asked by evacuees to country villages is 'Where are the shelters?' When told there are none, because there are no bombs, they reply that, bombs or not, shelters there must be; shelters have taken the place of the cinema as an essential part of the good life. So the evacuees fire the natives with their troglodyte enthusiasm, and together they go round collecting materials for the erection of these charming dwellings, which, since there are no bombs, need not be strong, so are easily put up. The fact is that we are natural troglodytes by inheritance; as children we all wanted to make houses in caves, and now we have our chance. It is an amiable propensity, but has its dangerous side. Doctors and nurses tell us that this winter promises to be a grim season of diseases caught by infection and from foul air in communal shelters, or from cold, discomfort, sleeplessness and damp in Andersons and other private ones. Especially the elderly, delicate, and children will suffer – those children who cannot be spared because they are so useful in keeping places and shifting bedding. Already the tide of illness runs high: what will it be in a month or two?

Is it too late to try to stem it? To start a propaganda campaign for sleeping in bed? One does not want to be a kill-joy, but are all these incitements to the shelter life an intelligent idea? Mr Morrison lately spared a kind word for 'those calm people who sleep in their beds'; more such words might be timely. It is not that we who sleep in our beds are braver, but we prefer to face a different danger. Personally, though I value my life and limbs quite a lot, I am naturally philoclinic, and I find that it takes far less nerve to sleep in my flat on the third floor of a small and old-fashioned block of flats in a frequently bombed district than to adventure nightly into the foetid atmosphere of a comfortless unhygienic shelter crammed with people of whom many may have infectious illnesses, and many may not be particularly clean. It is a choice of risks; but obviously the chance of one's house stopping a bomb and oneself being killed, badly damaged, or buried longer than is healthy (I always hope I shall have the luck to be dug out in time) is a slighter chance than that of discomfort and illness from a shelter. Can we not concentrate therefore on urging parents to send their children out of London (accompanying them if they prefer to and easily can) and persuading the adult population to stay commodiously in their beds and take a chance?

By all means make shelters as little unwholesome as possible; but even at the best such closely and miscellaneously crammed dormitories cannot be health resorts, and not all the bunks and buns in the world will make them so. To keep children in London in order to help their parents to sleep there seems criminal. – Yours, &c., ROSE MACAULAY

15 November 1940

Part Three
1941

THE WORLD AND DOCKLAND

Margery Perham

Christmas morning, 3 a.m. in the shelter under the Church. It's a shelter-de-luxe, this, compared with most, but even here, as night goes on, the air becomes thick with the sickly smell of unwashed bodies and bedding. Three hundred pairs of lungs use and use again their small ration of air. The lights are on, and fall upon the stacked humanity in the bunks and the garish decorations looped over them. Many sleepers snore with great power: sometimes there is a word or a groan. In the babies' corner little pink forms lie in the dainty cribs they owe to American kindness. Above them presides a lighted Christmas tree.

Christmas Day, and dinner-time. The shelterers have come up from their refuge into the hall above, and sit at the long decorated tables. Turkey, sausage and Christmas pudding are served to them, the solid realisation of an idea conceived in Hollywood. Undergraduates, male and female, pacifists, responsible matrons from among the shelterers, social workers, permanent and migratory, wait on them with the scrambling eagerness of beginners. The feasters do their part stolidly amidst the altruistic bustle; dockers, labourers, city office-boys and charwomen, factory-hands. They pull their crackers and wear their caps and accept their cigarettes. Of what are they thinking? Of the donors in Hollywood? Of their broken houses? Of their evacuated children? Difficult to say. They seem only half aware of what 'they' are trying to do for them. Most of them seem to accept 'their' services as fatalistically as the bombs.

Christmas evening. There is a pantomime in the shelter. *Cinderella*. It is a home product. One of the clergy has written it – perhaps not up to the highest Hollywood, but admirable for its purpose, none the less; another plays the buffoon most excellently. The pantomime is true to tradition with its topical jokes and its knock-about fun. The ugly sisters, with the properly improper display of underwear, monopolise the cellar in an air-raid, and Cinderella is sent to sit, not in the cinders, but on the roof as spotter. At the royal ball it is not her slipper but her gas-mask that she leaves behind. Hitler is requisitioned to take the part of the bad fairy and appears at intervals in a flash of green spot-light to the music of the sirens, only to be worsted by two clowns with more than professional vigour. Ministers and officials who make wonderful promises about shelter reform get their share of caricature. 'Where's Mrs Brown? I want to see her at once.' 'She's just gone off on the Government evacuation scheme.' 'Oh, that's all right. She'll be back tomorrow.' The audience, perched thickly on its bunks, screams with delight. It catches up other jests too personal and local for the stranger. It joins with strength in the chorus of the dominant song:

> There'll always be a Christmas
> Whate'er the year may be,
> So let old Nasty try his tricks,
> He won't stop you and me!

That is only one shelter. There are plenty of others in this dockside borough. And shelterers need food. So it's cheering to see a large and fully equipped canteen coming down on tow from the West End. 'From the People of Sierra Leone to the People of Britain'. Admiring groups read out the inscription and pool their resources in geography. The Freetown Creoles in their cabins and the tribes inland must have put together their coppers and small silver for this welcome gift. So hands from Hollywood and negro Africa reach across two oceans to meet in London's battered dockland.

A few days later the new mobile canteen takes the road. It gets its baptism of fire, for this is the night of the great raid on the City. The East End receives its share. Those invisible pulsating machines spray their incendiaries as they pass, and the temporary stars which the shells add to the heavenly pattern descend in spatters of shrapnel. It's not the best moment to break down on the road. The young Indian barrister – bringing help from yet another continent – and the medical student, who make up the canteen crew, do their best in a darkness lit up only by the neighbouring fires. Two calm and effective locals, leaders in the near-by church, spring out of the pavement and lie on the muddy cobbles to coax the organs of the towing car. Here as elsewhere in England, the little human creatures at work under that incalculable sky are bound together by an excitement, almost an exhilaration.

On again, to the great shelter under the arches beside the docks. The canteen is very late. There are about fifteen hundred shelterers here, and many have had no evening meal. They do not know why 'they' bring a canteen or who 'they' are or where 'they' come from. But 'they' are late and that is cause for annoyance. There is a rush, and the table, set up with difficulty in the shelter to take the tea-urns and food, rocks dangerously. Hands tug at the canteen party, reach and clutch and wave their mugs in the dim light. Cockney voices shrill their orders. Appeals for restraint and discipline are not understood. Even the grown men do not respond. Disraeli's Two Nations are still two, and how is this one to learn courtesy, to feel a sense of solidity with the other from which 'they' of the canteen have come?

The rush dies down. There is time to look round. The air reeks from the crowds and the unsavoury bundles of bedding, some of which – for there are not yet bunks to go round – still lie on the damp floor. Water drips from the arches and down the walls. The Lascars foregather in one bay. Bill from Jamaica lies in his usual place with a pipe that contributes richly to the atmosphere. His house has been bombed. His wife lies in hospital with both legs broken. His own ankle has been smashed. His blanket has just been stolen – yet he smiles upon the scene with the benign humanity of the African patriarch. His low musical voice and gentle manner strike a deep restful chord in the Cockney crescendo. ('Yes,' admits a talkative matron, 'I've got good friends among the blacks and we say they make better 'usbands than our men. But some'ow I'd jest abaht kill my girl if she walked with one. Each class should marry into its own class – that's wot I say.') The mother of eleven justifies the whirlpool of dirty and tired children – it is nearly ten o'clock – which surrounds her by a drama of evacuation and of ill-treatment in far-away Cornwall. A dozen boys led by a magnificent little blue-eyed brigand worry through the crowd like a pack of dogs among sheep – so much voltage of human energy and intelligence running to waste or to mischief. The fifteen-year-olds, boys and girls, from such factories as are not charred shells, prick the blackness of the corridor with their cigarettes and enliven it with sudden giggles. When one of 'them' drags the canteen equipment through the passage with 'Excuse me, please – would you mind making way there,' the words are not out before the 'toff's' voice is being lavishly caricatured by a dozen unseen humorists.

'How is morale down there? Are the people really taking it?' 'Yes.' 'How splendid they are!' To those who have had even a glimpse of the grey proletarian square miles of dockland, seen the children playing in streets made but little more dreary by the casual devastation of the bomber, this conversation seems insufficient. The 'Yes' is true, but it is too short an answer. The real answer is a long story of which the most important chapter should be written immediately this war ends. Indeed, is it too soon to start writing it now?

10 January 1941

COUNTRY LIFE: CACKLE PIE

H.E. Bates

The cut in the meat ration is a depressing though not desperate thing, and it is a sad day for all of us, and for bird-lovers especially, when writers begin to advocate the shooting of gulls and small singing-birds as articles of food. I have before me a periodical in which a writer is at much pains to discuss the gastronomic beauty not only of sparrow-pie, but of chaffinches, bullfinches, fieldfares, red-wings, lapwings, woodpeckers, moorhens and curlew. Of gulls – which have always been considered unlucky birds to shoot – the article declares 'they will help to make a decent hotpot with sage and onions, and sausages if they can be bought.' It recalls that 'a Queen of England was specially fond of bull-finch pie'; it describes starlings, which are highly obnoxious creatures, as 'quite palatable'; it refers to pickled puffins as having been once widely eaten in this country; and it finally excuses itself with the naïve remark that 'we should, however, beware of killing too many of our birds.' The many bird-lovers who read this page will, I think, have their own answer to that. To me it only occurs that though there never seem to be too many birds, there are times when there seem to be just a few too many writers.

17 January 1941

BOMBED CHURCHES

John Piper

Correspondence columns have been full of suggestions about how to deal with the ruined City churches. Dr Julian Huxley has proposed that they should be rebuilt where they are; Mr Clough Williams-Ellis thinks that they might go to the Provinces; Mr Raglan Squire sees an opportunity for the younger members of the architectural profession with their 'more sensitive outlook', and Sir Reginald Blomfield has used the word 'modernismus' again. Yet there is only one sensible thing that *can* be done: the thing that was done (more or less) in Wren's time, and at all other times when people have shown any sign of an architectural conscience – take the advice of a good architect. One or two people have made suggestions that would be only funny if there was not a danger in this age (which has no architectural conscience) that they might be adopted. The most insinuating of these suggestions is that the ruined City churches should be rebuilt, stone by stone, in open spaces with plenty of grass round them 'so that they can, for the first time, be seen'.

Before the war, England was becoming a museum dotted with council houses. What nobody realised was that the museum exhibits in the open spaces – abbeys, churches, tumuli and so on – were as menacing as the council houses. For they were dying and being embalmed. For years the Office of Works has been taking the ivy off the ruined walls of abbeys and castles, shoring up fragments of cloisters and keeps, levelling and mowing the grass round them and infecting the remains with litter-baskets and turnstiles – a labour of no love except archaeological love, carried out with the deadening hand of supposed good taste. 'Protection and repairs are necessary,' they said, 'in these tourist days. Otherwise people would remove the stonework.' Necessary or not, the result is that most of these ancient monuments have died: they have lost all their relevance and all their beauty. They are now monuments of nothing but arrested decay, symbols of nothing but arrested taste.

The City churches were designed to stand among city buildings. Wholesale warehouses, towering offices and skysigns may not be ideal neighbours for them, but they are a good deal nearer the mark than level sweeps of grass. The Wren churches were designed by a genius for particular sites, and like all good buildings they belong to those sites. They were beautiful and serviceable once; rebuilt, they might conceivably be both those things again in time; removed to open spaces they would at once be follies, their only virtue an appeal to the museum-minded.

Among several burnt-out churches in a much-bombed West Country town there are two whose ruins are very tragic. One stood on a hill-top among terraces of charming stucco houses. It was planned to agree with them in style, and was built about 150 years ago. Its architect showed an ardour and a conviction that we ought to envy. Another, at the other end of the town, was built less than fifty years ago, and was of a highly original design which included a fanciful spire, a wide apse and Byzantine details. Both these churches had large congregations, but 'good taste' had decided against them – 'good taste' that allows the building of sham-

Tudor houses in Cornwall and sham-Cotswold manors in Surrey. The ruins are tragic because they have missed their day by ten or fifteen years. Very likely by that time they would have been visited as masterpieces. Today they are mourned by very few people beyond their incumbents and their congregations. Taste in architecture is flimsier than the most temporary wooden shack. The man to ask about the rebuilding or replanning of bombed churches whether they were mediaeval, or by Wren, or by Sir Gilbert Scott, is not the man in the street nor the committee-man nor *The Times* correspondent, but a good ecclesiastical architect. He will very likely be broken (even if he has the genius of Wren and the tenacity of John Nash) in trying to get his own way, but he is bound to be chosen in the end – and, when he has been, it would be better to leave him alone.

17 January 1941

FIRST DROP

Major Martin Lindsay

For four days there had been a strong wind. For four days I had felt as if my skin had been cleaned every morning with ether, in preparation for the surgeon's knife. The fifth day was calm. No breeze stirred the maple leaves. We went into the store and reached up to the shelves for our parachutes. We might have been going in to sit for an examination. Everybody was so very witty.

'Don't do like the man who made a hole in the Brighton Road. He pulled his tie instead of the rip cord.'

'. . . it's guaranteed to open. If it doesn't, they give you a new one.'

The small, stuffy, overcrowded room and my nervousness as we waited reminded me of sitting in the dressing room before a steeplechase. At any moment I expected a little man in a bowler hat to come in and say, 'All jockeys riding in the 9.30 out into the hangar please.'

We climbed into the aeroplane and sat on the floor of the fuselage. The engines roared and we took off. I knelt forward and peered out through a little porthole at my side. Spread out below me was an ordinary English countryside: fields and lanes, the odd farmhouse, yard and stacks, a strag-gling line of cottages, a disused brick kiln, a copse or two, the silvery line of a canal with the sun on it – typical of the England for which we are fighting, and in whose need we were making this fantastic experiment that morning.

I noticed how moist the palms of my hands were. I wished I did not always feel slightly sick in an aeroplane. The last time I had flown had been to Norway, dodging the Heinkels *en route*. I remembered the little cockney air-gunner with cauliflower ears who chewed gum and grinned at me, his finger on the trigger. Where was he now? I remembered another face: that of a man I met years ago in some bar; he told me that he had once been paid a pound apiece by the Chilean Government for testing thirty parachutes. 'Not enough,' I thought to myself at that moment. 'Not nearly enough.'

It seemed an age, but it cannot have been more than ten minutes, when the instructor beckoned to me. The Germans have a chucker-out in their aircraft, for the encouragement of nervous recruits. Flight-Sergeant Brereton, 6 ft. 2 in., would have made a good *absetzer*. I began to make my way down the fuselage towards him, screwing myself up to do so. 'Reso-lution,' I said to myself, 'your *something and your resolution will bring us victory*', was on the hoardings. But I could only remember the one word 'resolution', and kept repeating it to myself. I crawled on hands and knees into the rear-gunner's turret, the back of which had been removed. I tried not to overbalance and fall out nor to look at the landscape speeding across below me, as I turned to face forward again. Hitherto it had been a mental struggle; now it was a physical struggle, to squeeze past the flight-sergeant's legs and turn in that narrow place, hampered by the parachute pack strapped to my back. Without the flight-sergeant to help me to my feet I could scarcely have managed it. I now found myself standing on a small platform about a foot square, at the very back of the plane, hanging on like grim death to the bar under which I had had such difficulty in crawling. The two rudders were a few feet away on either side of me; behind me was nothing whatever. As soon as I raised myself to full height I found that I was to all purposes outside the plane, the slipstream of air in my face almost blowing me off. I quickly huddled up, my head bent down and pressed into the capacious bosom of the flight-sergeant.

The flight-sergeant held up his hand for me to watch. I was about to make a 'pull-off', opening my parachute which would not pull me off until fully developed – a procedure which was calculated to fill me with such confidence that I should be only too ready to leap smartly out of the aircraft on all subsequent occasions.

The little light at the side changed from yellow to red.

'Not long now!' he shouted to me with a grin, looking over my shoulder at the country beneath.

'Oh, God!' I said to myself. 'Oh, God!'

I was undeniably frightened though at the same time filled with a fearful joy.

The light changed to green and down fell his hand.

I put my right hand across to the D-ring in front of my left side and pulled sharply. A pause of nearly a second, then a terrific jerk on each shoulder. I was whisked off backwards and then swung through nearly 180°, beneath the canopy and up the other side. But of this I was quite oblivious, having something akin to a black-out. At any rate the first thing I was conscious of after the jerk on my shoulders was to find myself, perhaps four seconds later, sitting up in my harness and floating down to earth. The only sensation I registered was one of utter astonishment at finding myself so suddenly in this remarkable and ridiculous position.

I looked up and saw the silken canopy billowing in the air-currents – a thing of beauty as the sun shone on and through it. I reached down and eased the harness straps from the more vulnerable portion of my anatomy. I looked down at the ground. Green tops of trees and sheep tracks across the green turf stretched below me. I saw the smoke flare that had assisted the pilot not to drop me in the lake. I saw the ambulance on the edge of the landing-ground. I saw some cows and just had time to decide that they were Jerseys. Little knots of people were running about beneath me. But mainly I watched the smoke flare. Suddenly I realised that the ground was coming up very rapidly towards me. The smoke had shown me that I should fall over on my right side. I made myself limp and prepared to fall in that direction. Before I knew what had happened I was sprawling on the ground, having taken a bump but no hurt.

As I got to my feet a feeling of exhilaration began to fill me. 'There's nothing in it,' I said to myself. This fearful bogey was dead now, another dragon slain. Then I realised I was wet. I ran my hand down my side: a thick and slimy substance met my fingers. The exhilaration swiftly melted away. People came running up and I found myself an object of ridicule. What an anti-climax!

'Your morning tea, Sir!' said Private Wells, who in private life is a Fellow of Balliol.

So it had all been just a dream, I said to myself. Of course it never could have been true.

'. . . a nice morning,' his voice droned on. 'And what will you be wearing today, Sir? Shall I put out your new tartan trews or your canvas overalls? If you are contemplating another descent today, Sir, I should recommend the overalls. I have cleaned off all the – ah – the – ah – *excretum vacci.*'

And overalls it has been ever since.

21 February 1941

ISLE OF FORGOTTEN MAN

René Elvin

All has been said about the injustice, the muddle and the damaging unfairness of the internment 'policy'. What is more, and better, it has been said by Englishmen, at a time when England was facing the worst dangers she has known for centuries. It would therefore be more than unbecoming for an alien who, though neither German, Austrian nor Italian, was interned for nearly six months in the Isle of Man, to add fuel to a discussion the rights and wrongs of which are by now, anyway, known to everyone. Yet, it may perhaps not be without interest to have a few first-hand impressions of a life which, to one internee at least, was one of the most instructive of experiences.

I shall never forget that beautiful July morning when two (very decent) CID men came to 'collect' me, and my wife hastily and tearfully packed into the one small suitcase I was allowed to take along a few clothes and some fruit as my only viaticum. Nor can I put out of my mind the look of utter dejection of the fifty-or-so fellow-prisoners I found already milling in the common-room of a police station, wretchedly waiting for the Black Maria to take them to their unknown destination. This proved to be the Kempton Park racecourse, under whose draughty grandstands and paddocks, surrounded by a luxuriant vegetation of barbed wire, we were to spend the next week. The less said about the squalor of these first few days, the miserable food, the filthy palliasses which were our only furniture, the undignified treatment, the better. Nor do I wish to expatiate on the nightmarish journey from there to the Isle of Man: 'things like that, you know, must be in every famous victory' – and the prisoners taken in the successful raids on the enemy positions in Hampstead and Golders Green were, after all, the biggest haul the British had made up till then, so that a condignly numerous military escort, with fixed bayonets and all the trappings, seemed indicated. It was none of the soldiers' business that many of their charges were old, sick, or infirm: they had to deliver a certain number of prisoners, and that was all that mattered.

After these tribulations, Mooragh Camp looked to us, if not like Paradise, at least like an acceptable Purgatory. It was almost empty on the day we arrived: the ship that brought us took away a thousand hapless young men, on their journey to deportation abroad. Our quarters were cheerless, dirty, and badly overcrowded, but they were as many challenges to our ingenuity and spirit of fellowship. How we slaved, displaying hitherto untapped resources of husbandry, and acquiring a knowledge of household management which would have surprised our wives. But alas, after three weeks' disappearance, they had no more news from us than we had from them, nor had we any information about events in the world outside. This, inevitably, gave rise to the most ghastly rumours and to gnawing anxiety over the unknown fate of our families, many of whom were entirely dependent on our earnings. All other hardships of internment would have been bearable but for this. The ensuing distress, heartbreaks, and personal or family catastrophes were certainly not intended, but, in effect, the incompetence of embattled officialdom proved in some cases almost as cruel as the deliberate and systematic brutality of the Gestapo.

And yet, curious to say, some of the internees, especially the unattached, enjoyed their internment, at least during the summer months. Bathing was allowed, sun-bathing could not be forbidden, and, beyond the barbed wire, the sea, in its evergreen newness – *la mer, la mer, toujours recommencée* – was the very symbol of our existence, monotonous certainly, but not devoid of a certain modicum of variety and even excitement. For our mutual entertainment and instruction we had only ourselves to look to, and right nobly did many of the internees rise to the occasion. For the most remarkable thing about the Camp was the incredible variety of talents collected there: it was almost as if a careful selector had presided over their gathering. Painters, writers and musicians of world-repute, first-class doctors and specialists, scientists and scholars in all possible branches of learning, were there galore, and so were craftsmen whose many-sided skills covered every necessity of life. Their learning, however, was not matched by an equal mastery of English, so that those of us who were slightly more proficient at it were much sought after, either to give lessons and lectures, to edit the Camp's newspaper (which, twice a day, brought the latest BBC bulletins), or to act as 'Foreign Secretary' in the relations with the authorities and with those influential people from whom every one of us expected his salvation, i.e., his release.

For myself, I found that being an internee was thus a full-time job and that I had very few moments either to get bored or even to read those books on the 'must' list I had always vaguely kept in reserve for just such an occasion. Nevertheless, things of the mind were far from being neglected: every evening lectures, concerts, recitals, theatrical or variety performances of a very high standard were given to almost pathetically appreciative audiences. The adult internees were so eager to improve their minds that they even crowded the Camp 'Extension University', which was actually meant for the Camp youth. The subjects covered there varied from English and French to Assyrian and Chinese, from history and geography to differential calculus and astronomy. Most lectures were followed by discussions which often proved even more fascinating than the lecturers' lessons, as the bearded 'pupils' were frequently only slightly less well-informed than the teachers. I never attended more illuminating introductions to music, nor any which were more thoroughly and brilliantly discussed, than those given by a young genius who was not only an excellent pianist but also a profound musicologist, and many other courses of our 'University' were of a similar quality.

With such a gathering of talents and skills, even if it *was* a *Zwangsgemeinschaft*, a community based on compulsion, some of us imagined that a valuable social experiment might have been attempted. Here we were, each of us with some sort of useful qualification, all comparatively free from worry about our daily bread and shelter, all equally rich in that priceless commodity – time: in fact, presented with all the material requirements to build up a latter-day 'Abbaye de Thélème', a lay monastery, a modern utopia. It was not to be. Too many of us were – shall we say – too irremediably individualistic for the necessary submission to the common weal. But I cannot help feeling that the spirit of high endeavour which animated the best of us was destroyed mainly by one factor, the same which gradually transformed our stay in not altogether unpleasant and certainly safe surroundings into an endless abyss of boring drudgery: it was simply the lack of that today almost obsolete notion: freedom. The barbed wire which, to many of us, became an obsession, an *idée fixe*, was the very symbol of all we are fighting against. We shall not win the brave new world after which we are striving until we do away with it and all it stands for.

28 March 1941

WAR PAINTINGS AT THE NATIONAL GALLERY

Osbert Lancaster

The English are a nation of illustrators, a fact to which the last three generations of art-critics never succeeded in reconciling themselves. For us 'art for art's sake', 'significant form', &c., are far less potent and productive slogans than 'every picture tells a story'; all our best artists, or nearly all (Rowlandson, Hogarth and frequently Sickert) are raconteurs. And as war, whatever its inconveniences, seldom fails to be a first-class story, we can always look forward with some degree of confidence to a recurrent Renaissance as soon as the guns go off.

However, one should not assume that the National Gallery has filled up with masterpieces overnight. All that has happened is that a number of painters who have hitherto been wandering aimlessly between Fitzroy Street and Provence, constantly haunted by the fear of being thought 'literary', have at last been freed from their inhibitions and enabled to settle down and become, if not great artists, at least competent illustrators. The modern painters' pathetic appeal, once so pithily expressed by Mr Piper as 'Wanted, an object', has at length been answered. Future generations may not find that the present war has produced many Goyas, but it seems at least quite probable that it may have revealed a considerable number of Callots.

Before discussing the Callots, it would be as well firmly to state that there are two exhibitors at the National Gallery who are potentially of the Goya calibre – John Piper and Paul Nash. The former's 'Coventry' in the big room is a staggering production, a crackling, molten *tour-de-force* which, I am convinced, could have been produced by no other living artist; while the latter's big oil painting of the crashed bomber has all the calm and certainty of really great art. The same artist's series of watercolours in the next room, despite the occasionally rather tiresome persistence of the buff ground, may be said to have done for aeronautics what Degas did for ballet-dancing.

Of the Callots, the one with the most immediate appeal is undoubtedly Mr Ardizzone. On second thoughts, it may occur to the unbiased observer that the robust old English tradition is here perhaps being carried on with rather too self-conscious a fruitiness, but in the little picture of the two girls in black called 'East End', and in 'Shelter Entrance', this artist does display a personal and true, if limited, vision. In the old-fashioned bird's-eye-view Van der Meulen tradition of battle-piece Mr Eurich scores another popular success with his 'Air Battle at Portland', and it is no disparagement to say, both of this picture and his earlier 'Dunkirk', now no longer here, that one would probably like them even more as steel engravings. Eric Ravilious has produced nothing new, but his faithful, controlled records of the various aspects of Naval warfare, personal and owing nothing to any past tradition of martial-art, are as refreshing and, what is more important, as informative as anything here. Frank Dobson is represented by a quite extraordinarily vivid water-colour of a fire at Bristol, which makes most of its neighbours appear very small beer; a not altogether welcome development as one of them is Vivian Pitchforth, who is rapidly becoming very good indeed. For the rest, the usual cohorts of over-life-sized chunky airmen by Mr Kennington still stare down at one, gaining by contrast with Mr Eves' muddy military notables, but not by contrast with anything else. Mr Freedman's pictures get larger and larger, and Mr Cundall gets more small figures into any given area of canvas than anyone else. Indeed, in his version of the French refugee-ships arriving at Falmouth, close inspection would probably reveal that he had managed to include every journalist who claimed to have come out on the last boat, Auntie Geneviève Tabouis and all – an achievement which makes Tintoretto's 'Last Judgment' look like a landscape with figures.

28 March 1941

FLYING FOR THE FLEET

A Pilot

'Aircraft of the Fleet Air Arm ... have made a torpedo-attack on units of the Italian fleet, have dive-bombed enemy shipping off the Norwegian coast, intercepted an air-attack on a convoy, sunk a submarine, located a German raider, bombed a port ...'

The official report is strictly accurate, but it leaves a good deal to be filled in.

The shriek of the wind and the incessant thunder of engines are unheard. Nor is there any reminder of the empty sea, seen through a slightly oily windscreen, and a pair of anxious eyes searching for the home carrier – the speck on the waste which means warmth, safety, the sparkle of light on a glass, food, and, above all, sleep. The activities of the Fleet Air Arm make a short story with a lot in it, and it has not yet had time to be written – nor for that matter has a pen been nimble enough to keep pace with it. But hearing of its exploits, people ashore are aware of a new force.

I can recount a minute part of the story, because every day I help to train the aircraft crews upon whose skill – particularly in navigation – the success of the air-branch depends. We are no more like the Royal Air Force than the Tank Corps. Our aircraft are different: our men are different: and nine times out of ten our problems are different. As men, we are Jacks of all trades. That two-stripe in the corner of the ward-room is probably as handy with a torpedo from 1,000 yards as he is with a bomb at 10,000 feet, or a machine-gun at 100 yards, a pair of binoculars at 10 miles, or with a pencil and a tricky navigation-problem in a failing light, when he knows he has to locate the carrier or 'ditch' himself and his crew.

The aircraft in our hangars are versatile, too. If you could squeeze into the cockpit beside me – which you couldn't, because it's a shoe-horn fit for one – you would observe the fire-button like that on a Spitfire, the bomb-selector switch like a Wellington, a fuel-tank capacity like an Anson; and a few additional extras such as a neat little handle for releasing a torpedo and another for an arrestor-hook. Then if you climbed out again and transferred yourself to the back premises, which are slightly more commodious, and are designed for a crew of two, you would find a lot more – for instance, a set of navigation-instruments whose mathematics would give a liner-captain food for thought, a machine-gun or two, a big wireless set, a bomb-sight, and near at hand a few trifles such as a rubber boat, flares, emergency rations, first-aid sets and fire extinguishers. Don't think that there is anything very startling or new in any of these things. Your surprise will be that they are all housed in one aeroplane and that the aeroplane has only one engine, and – just to make it homely – folding wings.

You ought now to be appreciating that Fleet Air Arm aircraft and their personnel are not like anything else in this war. They combine the qualities of the fighter, the bomber and the reconnaissance-machine, and visually they may suggest some such phrase as 'flying bricks'. I would not have quarrelled with this description a few months ago. But then I was only a civilian pilot, with a profound contempt for big biplanes which tried to look like flying fortresses. Since then I have flown them in all weathers, and I can assure you that they are the sort of aircraft suitable for teaching your maiden aunts to fly. I don't only mean that you can grip the stick between your knees and doze, with 'hands off', but that you can do such wicked things as climbing turns in a stalled position. I doubt, for instance, whether that maiden aunt could crash such an aircraft as a Fairey Swordfish if she tried.

The young men whom I have been flying around during these last few months are mostly youngsters from the universities who have particularly impressed My Lords with their intelligence. In one sense, the problems with which they are faced in the air are not very profound, but when they have to be worked out at a great height to the non-stop racket of an aero-engine they assume bigger proportions. No doubt many readers of this paper could successfully answer the following simple question:

'You leave a carrier at 10.00 at a speed of 100 kts. with orders to make good a track of 090 for 150 sea-miles. The carrier is steering 135° at 10 kts. and the wind is blowing at 20 kts. from 225°. What is the course the pilot must steer to intercept the carrier after he has completed his orders, and how long will it be before he is over it again?'

This is the sort of practical problem which arises every day, and which must be solved correctly unless the crew are prepared to swim for it. It can, of course, be complicated by the addition of further courses, but the principle remains the same.

The young men who to me are only voices down the speaking-tube become amazingly proficient after a few months. We meet each other in the morning, looking like mummies in our full flying-kit. We nod. We are levered upwards by a willing crew into our places, and after that they become voices who order me courses to fly. So we take off, and I sit watching my gyro-compass, and then long afterwards the voice will say, 'Our position in two minutes' time will be directly over the "carrier".' It rarely is, of course, but on the other hand, an error of more than a mile is not unusual.

When these young men finally leave me, the operational pilots whom they will join are safe in their hands. What is more, the Admiral knows that his fleet has a few more eyes which he can rely on as completely as the navigator on his own bridge.

9 May 1941

A NOTE ON HESS
Walter Tschuppik

The explanation of the Hess flight to Britain here offered gains in probability, if it is the fact that a communication – whether actually by or on behalf of Hess – was addressed to the Duke of Hamilton the moment when the defeat of Germany in the Battle of Britain had become obvious. – Ed.
THE SPECTATOR

In 1921 Rudolf Hess, today a prisoner of war in Britain, won a prize essay at the University of Munich on the theme, 'What must be the qualities of the man who will restore Germany's greatness?' Rudolf Hess, the student, a pupil of Major-General Karl Haushofer, who, after returning from the army, was appointed professor of political geography at Munich University, was even then a supporter of Adolf Hitler, at that time making his first demagogic speeches in Munich beer-halls. In answering the question set by the prize essay, young Hess drew a picture of Germany's future saviour which was in the exact image of Adolf Hitler. Much that Hess recommended and foretold has come to pass, and the textual reproduction of this remarkable thesis would contribute much to our understanding of the Hess case, and of the psychology of the Deputy-Führer. For present purposes, however, it will suffice to draw attention to certain passages which, read in conjunction with Rudolf Hess's subsequent career, tell us much of the man's real mentality, his deeply-rooted convictions and his hidden aims.

Here are a few quotations from his prize essay which deserve to be specially noted at the present time: 'The man who means to restore Germany to greatness must not hesitate, if necessary, to spill blood. To attain his end he will even walk over the bodies of his closest friends. He must also be prepared for the sake of his great cause to appear a traitor to the nation . . . A terrible justice will overtake those who have betrayed the nation both during and since the war . . . He is acquainted with nations and with influential individuals. As circumstances dictate, he will either stamp with the jack-boot or, with sensitive fingers, spin threads stretching out to the Pacific Ocean. By one means or the other the enslaving treaties will collapse. The day will dawn when the new Greater Germany will arise and embrace all that are of German blood.'

Exactly twenty years have passed since Rudolf Hess wrote these words, and in all that time he has never left Hitler's side. Throughout those twenty years he has not had to retract one word of what he wrote in 1921. All through these two decades he has approved of all that Hitler has done. He knew no hesitation, nor needed long reflection. Blindly he followed a programme constructed from Hitler's own ideas and under Hitler's influence.

There is no evidence of any difference of opinion between Hitler and Hess in all that long time. On the contrary, there is abundant proof of Hitler's complete trust in Hess, and, even more, that Hess put unbounded faith in Hitler, was his, indeed, body and soul. Hess's personality, his character, tendencies which he tried to repress in youth – and these explain certain traits such as a noticeable shyness, a leaning towards mysticism, &c. – marked him out as 'the prophet's first disciple'. For many years Hess went by the nickname of 'Fräulein Hess'; the name hit off not only his innate tendency, but still more his bigotry, which made something of a religion out of Hitler and Hitlerism. In those days of June, 1934, Hess played a leading role, and stood firmly by Hitler during the mass-executions. At no time did he ever protest against the brutalities of the *régime*, and he was always on good terms with Himmler. He avoided all partisan quarrels among the followers of Goering and Goebbels, but tried always to exercise a mediating influence.

It is not very difficult to imagine what was passing in Hess's mind when he decided on May 11th, 1941, to fly to Britain. He must have been revolving this hazardous plan for a long time, from the moment, indeed, when Hitler realised that Germany could not win the war, that is to say, since last autumn's Battle over Britain, that abortive prelude to the intended invasion of England. From that moment on Hitler had irrevocably lost all hope of ending the war by a lightning stroke. His armies might win victories on the continent, but this could not bring the war to a speedy close. The prolongation of the war, with all that it involved, soon led to discussions within leading political, military and economic circles in Germany. Hitler is today in exactly the same hopeless situation in which he found himself just before he decided to fire the Reichstag and pose as the 'saviour of civilisation from Bolshevism'. From the many critical situations in which he has been placed, Hitler has always had the same means of extricating himself – blackmail. The years between 1926 and 1933 were an unbroken series of acts of blackmail, intimidation and terrorisation. The Reichstag Fire was intended to present an intimidated German public and Europe with the choice between Bolshevism and Hitler. The massacres of June 30th, 1934, were similarly justified as offering the alternatives of anarchy or Hitler. And it is perfectly clear what Hitler now aims at in his policy towards Soviet Russia. Once again he hopes to blackmail and intimidate the world: 'International chaos or Hitler.' On the one hand, he threatens to join hands with Stalin (he once said that he would see the world in ruins before he surrendered power in Germany); on the other hand, he offers the world 'peace' as a prelude to marching against Russia.

There are many signs that opinion among leading Germans on this development of events is divided. It is well understood that the world puts no further faith in Hitler's promises. The arrest of a leading industrialist, Director-General Friedrich Minoux, formerly organiser of the Stinnes concern, and until today a prominent figure in the steel industry, belongs to this chapter. Responsible military and industrial circles in Germany are afraid that Hitler is contemplating an adventure the outcome of which is viewed more and more pessimistically. These circles also receive first-hand information from Hitler's business-agents in the United States to the effect that in the long run German economic strength cannot stand up to America's resources. They fear the destruction of German cities by the latest American bombers, the inevitable ruin of all Germany.

Although a great part of the German public is not, of course, informed of the true state of affairs, and is inclined to see in the victories of German arms a guarantee of a successful issue to the war, military and industrial quarters are alarmed at the prospects that loom ahead. This explains not only Hess's risky undertaking, but also the embarrassed and contradictory comments upon it by German propaganda. Rudolf Hess's whole record, his position and his psychological make-up, show that it is of no importance whether he made the journey with the tacit approval of others, or whether he acted on his own initiative. For in either case he is as much the representative of the *régime* as Hitler himself. The idea of visiting Britain, a scheme surpassing the maddest escapades of history, is proof of the helpless bewilderment which prevails in high quarters in Germany. Rudolf Hess could not calculate the effect of his flight. It has proved to be a triumphant exposure of the whole appalling German adventure summed up in the word 'Hitler'. By flying to Britain, Rudolf Hess has, in a sense, sought international police-protection against Hitler himself.

The British Government has received Hess as a prisoner of war as though the deserter were not the Führer's deputy, but an unknown German soldier. This says much. It is symbolic, for Hitler himself and Hitlerism are history's prisoners of war. According to the Berlin correspondent of a Swedish newspaper, Franz Leidgen, Rudolf Hess's chief aide-de-camp, is supposed to have said, on being arrested, 'Why arrest me? Arrest rather the course of events.'

6 June 1941

BRITAIN ALONE

Strategicus (H.C. O'Neill)

In a few days' time it will be a year since the British Empire found herself alone in the struggle against the might of Germany and Italy. The position at that moment was almost desperate. The British Army had been evacuated from France, but had been compelled to leave behind practically all its heavy equipment. The greatly superior German Air Force lay across the Channel ready to deliver the attack preparatory to invasion. From Narvik to the north coast of Spain the ports and seaways of Europe were in the hands of the enemy. The numerous bases within easy reach of England in effect represented an immediate and heavy reinforcement of his submarine attack upon the sea communications which support the life of the country, supply its overseas military effort and afford the means by which the main part of its war potential can be mobilised and concentrated in the theatres of war. The Italian Fleet threatened the great seaway through which passes one of the most important lines of Imperial communications and two large armies were ready to deliver converging attacks upon the chief nodal point in it.

How does the position look after a year of war? Mr Lees-Smith said the other day that since the fall of France we have been engaged in 'a great delaying action'; and that is an accurate summing-up of the operations. But, first, we had to keep our main base inviolate, and this was achieved in the splendid victories of the Royal Air Force last autumn. The struggle to keep our main communications open is logically an extension of the same battle, since otherwise Britain would be a beleaguered garrison which must be reduced in time. This struggle, the 'Battle of the Atlantic', as it has been called, has been more successful than perhaps we could have expected. We have lost shipping and valuable cargoes very heavily, but not so vitally that they have reduced the standard of living dangerously, or gravely affected our war effort. It cannot be questioned that they have influenced the latter since, operating upon external lines, the reinforcement of the Near Eastern and Far Eastern theatres bears very heavily upon shipping; but so far their effect has not been vital anywhere.

The shipping losses have also had their influence upon the main strategy. The Royal Air Force offensive against the German industries, bases and communications, which is the chief expression of British offensive action, has had much success, and its power is increasing; but it might have been developed much farther if our sea communications had been completely free. The enemy's night-bombing attacks have not gravely affected the production of bombing aeroplanes; and, in fact, it is the lag in deliveries from abroad that is more responsible than either. The other means of offensive action against the enemy is the blockade. This is now almost as effective as could be expected. Between the air offensive and the British blockade there is a shortage of several essential commodities in the enemy countries. Wheat, fats and oils and several minerals must be replenished if Germany is to fight out victoriously the long war which Hitler now evidently foresees. The lack of these necessities tends increasingly to colour his strategy. Whatever be the meaning of the present concentration on the Russian front, it must reflect Hitler's need of commodities which Russia possesses and he lacks.

The enemy's attempt to break and ours to maintain the blockade have led to several naval actions, and in these Britain has been almost completely successful. The *Bismarck* is at the bottom of the sea. A second pocket-battleship is out of action. The *Scharnhorst* and *Gneisenau* are immobilised in harbour, where the *Prinz Eugen* keeps them company. In the victories of Taranto and Cape Matapan the Navy dealt even more drastically with the Italian Fleet. Smaller craft have suffered more than the capital ships. The British Navy has paid little for these successes. Apart from the loss of *Hood* it suffered little outside the narrow waters about Greece and Crete. It is once again operating steadily in the Near East and there seems little reason to doubt that it will be able to continue that close co-operation with the Army that has led to such clear-cut victories as those of the Libyan campaign.

If Italy's reputation as a military power is now in the dust it is mainly owing to the series of defeats inflicted upon her armies in Africa. These campaigns have never yet received the appreciation they deserve. The tendency is to depreciate them because of the supposed ease with which they were carried out. The same criterion is not applied to Germany. She is seen to be in possession of almost the whole of Europe and that is taken to endorse her claim to invincibility. But in Africa General Wavell had to

face problems which were in many respects graver than any that confronted Germany. When France went out of the war she left Britain alone
to hold the Near East. Mussolini had placed two picked armies in Africa
to deliver a converging attack upon the Suez Canal. Each of them was
equipped in the most modern way, each commanded by a soldier of
repute. Each of them was so placed that it could operate from a strong
base at no great distance from places whose capture would have
resounded throughout the East.

General Wavell found himself at a disadvantage, numerically and
materially, so profound that it still seems inexplicable that he was able to
hold off Marshal Graziani and the Duke of Aosta. At the beginning he
had not a tenth of the force arrayed against him and not a twentieth the
number of guns. The two Italian armies numbered in all about half a million men. Today both armies have been destroyed. With very small loss to
himself he has inflicted about 400,000 casualties upon them. If the ter-
rain in which these campaigns were fought is considered they seem the
more remarkable. The frontiers of Abyssinia measure about 4,500 miles.
One of the British columns had to cover 1,200 miles to reach the capital;
and during the campaign, apart from a number of stiff engagements, six
major battles were fought. Everywhere in that colony were almost insuperable obstacles. Liaison between the separate columns had to be
effected by aeroplane. The bush could only be penetrated by means of
tanks. Water had to be carried immense distances. Rarely have such
problems of administration confronted any staff. Those who are 'sick of
defeat after defeat' would be well advised to study these campaigns,
which were almost invariably fought against odds.

There have, of course, been defeats. The withdrawals from Greece and
Crete cannot fail to rankle. But Mr Lees-Smith said no more than the
truth when he spoke of 'delaying actions'. It is natural but unreasonable
that they should rankle so much. If Germany after six years of preparation cannot for some time dispose of overwhelming force, upon what
foundation is our hope of victory based? The actions in Greece and Crete
established one important point: they convinced everyone, even the Germans, that man for man the Imperial troops are at least their match. And
were these actions complete defeats? There is now evidence that it was
due to them that the Germans could not assist Rashid Ali in his attempt
to hold Iraq for the enemy. The importance of this failure is that the
entry into Syria could be effected with a column or columns co-operating
from Iraq. Without the reduction of Iraq the Syrian operations could not
have been safely undertaken at all; and, unpalatable as they are, Syria had
to be occupied.

The one retreat which yielded no advantage was that from Benghazi;

but the risk of a surprise stroke was the condition of our intervention in Greece. We lost, however, the possession of aerodromes and bases which materially affect the defence of Egypt and it may be that General Wavell is attempting to redress the situation at this moment. The exact scope of these operations is difficult to estimate; but it is clear that the first effect of the local advance about Sollum was to carry the imperial detachments to Cappuzzo and cause the enemy to bring up reinforcements from Tobruk. In Syria the attempt of General Wavell to avoid inflicting the casualties entailed by a ruthless attack is meeting with little assistance from the Vichy forces. Sidon has been occupied, and the imperial forces are pushing on towards Damascus; but there have been sharp counter-attacks in the centre, and, unless the advance from Iraq can be reinforced, the operations seem likely to be long drawn out.

Of that prospect it is impossible to foresee the development. But who that knew the exact circumstances of the situation in the Mediterranean and the Near East a year ago would have cared to predict that General Wavell's negligible force could have effected such a revolutionary change? If we are strongly placed in Egypt, and have been able to reinforce the Far East, that is the reassurance of the future that we most need. If there is a great distance still to go, a year's fighting alone against two great Powers has reinforced the prospect of victory. We have preserved all the main essentials of our position against the heaviest odds, and we have defeated and destroyed great armies and the striking power of two great navies. If there is shade as well as light over this year, the light predominates and grows brighter.

20 June 1941

THE TWO FRATERNITIES

Mervyn Peake

In death's unfelt fraternity the cold
And horizontal dead bestrew the world.
And you and I must add our little quota
To the globe's veneer.

What is more ghastly than death's brotherhood?
This doomed, this fragile life, this pounding blood,
This hectic moment of fraternity,
This *you* . . . this *me*.

8 August 1941

MARGINAL COMMENT

Harold Nicolson

The harvest is now upon us, one of the finest harvests which England has ever seen. Further volunteers have been called for from the industrial North and Midlands, and north-country voices are heard among our Kentish lanes. Under the Kent threshing-scheme some 400 girls have come down to the soft South. I met two of them yesterday in the wet fields. They were sisters from Mansfield, and they were striding along in their dungarees with sickles in their hands. All day they work, hardening new muscles and waiting for the moment when the great red threshing-machines will start to shake and hum. This is their first knowledge of the land, since hitherto they have worked only in a cotton-cleaning factory, running cotton off from one bobbin on to another, from left to right. Now, when they return aching to their beds, two new movements will weave patterns in their half-sleeping minds – the motion of cutting bonds, the motion of hoisting sheaves.

Mr Hudson is now calling for two thousand more land-girls to cope with the increased acreage now coming under plough. Will the time come when the hop-gardens, our hanging vineyards, are swept from Kent, leaving the oast-houses to swing their cowls unused? Even for such sentimental losses there will be compensations. Or will there? A year ago fifty London children came to settle with us like a flight of sparrows. The rooms were cleared for them, the glass and ornaments stored away, the lighter furniture removed, until only the books and the oak-tables looked down upon the rows of little heads which lined the walls. They were pale and heavy-lidded in those days, with scrannel wrists and violet circles round their eyes. Today they yell and shout and have bramble-scratches on their large red knees. Will they remember the smell of sweetbriar and the bark of foxes in the wood? Or will the unconquerable gregariousness of the Londoner wipe out these memories and benefits, and will they return with unashamed delight to the paving-stones and the loud voices of the street?

15 August 1941

THE CIVILIAN'S NERVES

A Medical Correspondent

Psychoneurosis has been far less prevalent in this war than in the last. This is a much more remarkable fact than may at first appear to the layman. In one sense it is decidedly the most remarkable fact of any that has emerged from the struggle to date. It establishes the existence of a national morale which is a surer pointer to ultimate victory even than the steady increase in the numerical strength of the RAF. Its true significance may be better understood if I speak in terms of shell-shock and bomb-shock. The latter is really the modern description of the condition diagnosed when, in the last war, a soldier suffering from psychoneurosis was said to be a shell-shock case. That is to say the mind had been disordered without there being organic disease in the brain. It was caused by exposure to danger or subjection to terrifying experiences, such as narrow escape from death following a violent explosion.

That risk was confined almost exclusively to the fighting forces overseas. But this time the entire population of these islands, men, women and children, are subjected to the risk. It was thought that civilians, not disciplined to war, untrained in defence, helpless targets of enemy bombers, must crack up on a wholesale scale. Even mass-hysteria was feared. But nothing of the sort has happened – anywhere. Despite the vastly greater numbers subjected to war-risks, psychoneurosis, or bomb-shock, is less prevalent than in the last war.

That is something to be proud of. A fact on which we may well congratulate ourselves is the advance in psychotherapy (the treatment of bomb-shock) since the close of the last war. That has been due in a large measure, so far as London is concerned, to the establishment of the Tavistock Clinic in 1920. It quickly developed into a flourishing centre of research and training for doctors specialising in psychological medicine. Psychological treatment is now accepted as a medical science, and is provided in both civilian and military hospitals. Many remarkable cures have been effected, and many facts important to future research have been established as a result of recent experience thrust upon us by the Luftwaffe.

One is that women are less prone to bomb-shock than men. The ratio is 18 women to 30 men. It may be true that women are more emotional than men in romance, but they are less so in air-raids. Their protective instinct for those they love is actually a shield against the nerve-shattering effects of warfare noises. They perform the job in hand with calmer deliberation than men. Men get through the job all right, but they work in a state of mental excitement – often consciously suppressed – which, in time, takes its toll. Women also recover under psychological treatment more quickly than men. Part of the treatment is the re-telling of their experiences, and it has been found that women can recall details with greater ease than men and are more willing to talk about them. Repetition in this way invariably tends to rob the experience of its initial horror, which is an important aid to complete recovery of normal self-control. One woman was actually cured of fits by the shock of bombs which fell near her home in the East End. She felt so much better after the raid that she insisted upon remaining in that vulnerable area. Her doctor verified her statements and she has the special permission of the local authorities to stay put.

It has been found, too, that air-raids rarely induce bomb-shock in men and women who have not previously shown psychoneurotic traits. But some such men have been turned into heroes by service under conditions which might be expected to produce the reverse results. In fact, there is a mass of evidence supporting the view that activity in civil defence services is the most effective antidote to the fear capable of producing hysteria and bomb-shock in an air-raid. A remarkable example is provided by the case of the young London dental mechanic who was rejected by the Army on the ground that he would break down under any strain. Justification for the rejection seemed to be proved by the neurotic symptoms he revealed in the next twelve months. During that time he was a member of a rescue-squad belonging to a first-aid post. Then the raids began, and almost automatically, it seemed, the neurotic symptoms disappeared. As soon as it became his nightly job to rush to bombed buildings and help in rescuing the trapped, he was able to do so again and again with complete disregard for his own personal safety. He became a real war-hero.

Men, as I have already mentioned, will not talk so readily as women of their terrible experiences. Sometimes it is due to forgetfulness induced by shock. But all the time the subconscious mind is activated by the memory, and this is liable to produce varying forms of hysterical paralysis. I remember the case of an insurance-clerk who was admitted to hospital for a suspected fracture of a collar-bone after being buried with his wife when their shelter was bombed. It turned out that he had no physical injury, but was suffering from an hysterical paralysis of the left arm. 'Everything happened in such a mist of pain and blackness I don't remember it properly,' was all he could say. Simple persuasion to talk, such as is possible in some cases, was not enough to rid him of the paralysis. Hypnotism might have been tried, but an anaesthetic was chosen. On coming round he spoke quite readily and with an emotion entirely lacking before. While he was still under the influence of the drug he was vigorously assured that he would be all right; that there was nothing to stop him using his left arm if he wanted to. When he awoke he was persuaded without difficulty to try to use the arm, and he was delighted to find it absolutely normal. After that he made a rapid recovery and was soon back at work. If he had not been enabled to tell his story he would not have recovered.

Even the BBC has been brought into the psychological experimental field. Working to medical specifications, technicians have made records of sirens, the firing of AA and machine-guns, the sound of planes, dive-bombing and explosions. These were used in experiments in what is described as 'de-conditioning'. The idea is to reproduce warlike sounds and disturbing noises until the patients regain their normal reactions. Records have also been made which combine 'reassurance' talks with actual bombing-noises. One patient in a military hospital who complained of trembling, palpitation and loss of control during air-raids since the Dunkirk evacuation was conditioned to warfare-noises in a week, and during subsequent air-raid alerts was no longer disturbed. Another soldier at first reacted so strongly to the sounds that he rushed screaming from the room. But at the end of six days' treatment he was perfectly calm and showed no reaction whatever.

Equally successful has been the psychological treatment described as occupational therapy. This is a process of re-education by giving the patient something to do – regulated work specially chosen to meet individual needs. Where colours are likely to occur, as in the case of rug-making, it has been found that wools in startling and decided colours, reds, blues and vivid greens, are vigorously rejected. Softer shades and pastels are nearly always acceptable. Psychological research of the past twenty years has undoubtedly proved a blessing in this ordeal of modern aerial warfare, but the end of the road in this department of medical science is still a long way off.

5 September 1941

FEWER 'SPECTATORS'

'Northerner'

SIR: It is with a deep sense of regret I read the notice, under this heading, as to the effect of the latest paper-rationing scheme in further restricting the sale of *The Spectator*. As a regular subscriber for just over 50 years I feel that it is a catastrophe that such a fine medium of public opinion and comment – in my view the best conducted in this country – should be so drastically dealt with by the Paper Control. A newspaper-proprietor myself, fully conversant with the necessity of conserving paper-stocks, I am confident that the supplies of many publications, using huge quantities in comparison with yours, might well be further curtailed with more justification, and no real loss to the community.

I may add that after reading my *Spectator* it is posted to a member of the Air Force, and then by him to a friend in the Forces overseas. – Yours faithfully, 'NORTHERNER'.

10 October 1941

COUNTRY LIFE: WINTER LAND-GIRL

H.E. Bates

As October comes, many of the newer land-girls look forward to winter with misgiving. Many of them came into the country in summer, to find the days of hay-time and harvest long but pleasant. The isolation of winter is their great dread. In many villages they see no evidence of communal life except the public-house. They want friends, and friends in the country are hard to make. To be isolated, friendless and cut off from sympathetic activities, in the heart of winter, can be a painful thing. Yet in many villages there are not enough land-girls to form their own clubs, and one wonders if there is any solution to their problems except the simple solution of neighbourliness. In addition to these problems of environment and isolation, it seems to me that the land-girl has genuine grievances. Arriving late at night at a railway-station, for example, tired out and hungry, she finds that the ordinary Services' buffet cannot serve her. Hers is not recognised, apparently, as an auxiliary service, and so she is denied these simple Service privileges. If this is true, and I am assured by a very intelligent land-girl that it is, then it is a wrong that very quickly needs righting.

10 October 1941

MARGINAL COMMENT

Harold Nicolson

I met the other day a citizen of a neutral country who had for two months been travelling through Europe. He had been in Germany and Italy and had spent much of his time visiting the occupied territories from Oslo to Bucharest. I did not wish to question him too closely, since his mission had been one of mercy. He appeared saddened by his experience and in his eyes there was a haunted look, as in the eyes of those who have seen dreadful things. 'When you get back,' I said to him, 'when the sounds and voices which now echo in your ears die down to a half-forgotten murmur, what will be the final impression that remains?' He thought for a moment and the expression of distant pain faded from his eyes. He leant towards me. 'I did not know before,' he said intently, 'that hatred could take so many different forms.' I understood what he meant. There was the bewildered helpless hatred felt in Italy, there was the fanatical hatred felt by the Poles, there was the watchful hatred with which the Czechs must now be seething under the blond beast Heydrich, there was the Austrian resentment at betrayal, the panic-hatred of the Rumanians, the sullen hatred of the Bulgars, the heroic hatred of the Greeks, the dumb loathing of the Danes and Norwegians, the experienced hatred of the Belgians, the sturdy detestation of the Dutch, the combative hatred of the Jugoslavs, the outraged indignation of the neutrals. 'Had you been a German,' I asked him, 'which of all the different hatreds would you have found it hardest to understand?' 'French hatred,' he answered at once. 'It is the most disconcerting of all the hatreds, since it is unexpressed. The French look straight through the Germans and treat them as if they did not exist.' 'There is little hatred here,' I added. 'No,' he answered, quietly, 'not yet.'

Some months ago a diary was found upon the body of a young German officer. He had been in Poland and in Norway. He had visited Oslo. 'I have to thank my Führer,' he recorded, 'that I can now walk the streets of foreign capitals with the firm step of a conqueror: There will be no need hereafter for any German to feel embarrassed.' Those words were written in the first flush of early victory, when the wine of triumph had for the moment stilled the whisperings of self-distrust. One of the most attractive qualities of the Germans has always been their pathetic longing to be liked. One of their most unattractive defects is the readiness with which they can change that longing into a harsh determination to be feared. They find many excuses for such relapses into barbarism. 'The moment in which we are living,' writes Friedrich Sieburg, 'compels us to be brutal to ourselves and even to have recourse to spiritual self-mutilation, although our cruelty is mitigated by our mourning.' 'Our sense of what is harmful,' he writes again, 'has been impaired . . . We have acquired a sense of impregnability and live in a state alternating between extreme objectivity and suicide.' There are moments when the Germans take such mumbo-jumbo seriously, and like to feel upon their cheeks the wind of the wings of madness. But there are other and more frequent moments when the exercise of force leaves even them with a feeling of exhaustion and when they become terrified by the hatred which they have aroused. It is this terror which in the last few months we have been able so successfully to exploit.

17 October 1941

LOSING ONE'S BOOKS

Rose Macaulay

It happened to me last May to lose my home with all contents in a night of that phenomenon that we oddly called *Blitz*, though why we should use the German for lightning for attack by bombs I do not know, unless to appease by euphemism, like calling the Furies Eumenides. Anyhow, whatever the thing was called, it destroyed my flat, leaving not a wrack behind, or, rather, nothing but wracks. Of furniture, books and pictures nothing stayed but a drift of loose, scorched pages fallen through three floors to street-level, and there lying sodden in a mass of wreckage smelling of mortality, to trouble me with hints of what had been. Here was a charred, curled page from one of the twelve volumes of the Oxford Dictionary, telling of hot-beds, hotch-pots, hot cockles, hotes and hotels; there, among a pile of damp ashes and smashed boards, were a few pages from Pepys, perhaps relating of another London fire, a few from Horace Walpole, urbane among earthquakes, revolutions and wars, knowing that all things pass. But no book remains; my library, with so many other libraries, is gone.

When the first stunned sickness begins to lift a little, one perceives that something must be done about lost books. One makes lists; a prey to frenetic bibliomania, I made lists for weeks; when out, I climbed my ruins, seeking in vain; when in, I made lists. A list of the books I had had; that is the saddest list; perhaps one should not make it. A list of those one cannot hope (for one reason or another) to have again. A list of those that one hopes to replace one day, but not yet. Another of those to replace at once, directly one has shelves again – the indispensables. Another of the good riddances. One has, by inadvertence, all kinds of books; some are better gone; I had some like that, and they went.

I had not a grand library, full of costly firsts. Plenty of firsts, but usually poor firsts, like my *Athenae Oxoniensis*, of which the later editions were much better, or Fuller's *History of Cambridge*, or Thomas Heyrick's *Miscellany Poems*, which no one had bothered to reprint often (I seldom found anyone to like this Heyrick much except myself and his patrons, who prefaced his book with their flattering views in verse), or torn copies, such as Hooker's *Ecclesiastical Polity* and Raleigh's *History of the World*, or books so popular that the first edition was enormous, like Fuller's *Holy and Profane State*, or books that no one would dream of ever reprinting at all, like the essays of my great-great-great-grandfather on *Revealed Religion* or my great-grandfather's notes on the antiquities of his parish (as I have said, I had a lot like that, and they went). And, naturally, plenty of the first editions of my contemporaries, but they scarcely count as firsts. I had a few real firsts; I had *Tom Jones* and Bentley on *Phalaris*, which was terribly dull, and Baker's *Chronicle*, and Holland's Pliny's *Natural History*, and Purchas his *Pilgrimage* (1613), and Johnson's Dictionary, apparently stolen by my great-uncle from the library of St John's College, Cambridge, and a few obsolete poets and essayists of small merit, and *Leaves of Grass*; but no collector would have thought anything of my library. I have never had any particular feeling about firsts, and would as soon have read a book in any vaguely contemporary edition published, say, in the first fifty years. When they lack title-page and date, I rather like the disputes by experts often pencilled on the inside of the boards, as in my *Arcadia*, to which Professor Dowden had ascribed one date, my father another, and some earlier and more innocent owner the date of the first edition.

To return to my lists. First I thought I had better do the ones I saw little prospect of getting again, then I could forget them. Some I knew to be out of print and unprocurable even by their authors; of these were Dr Gosse's *Gathered Together*, Logan Pearsall Smith's *Cornishiana* and *How Little Logan Came to Jesus*; these three little books seem irrecoverably gone, with a lovely edition of Gerard Hopkins's *Mermaids*. So do the *Purefoy Letters*, whose publishers exasperatingly remaindered it to some wholesaler who got his stock burnt. And a quantity of old numbers of the *Modern Language Review*. And Purchas his *Pilgrimage*. Not his *Pilgrimes*, of which I then had the Maclehose edition in 20 volumes, and which could be got again when I could afford them. They went on the next list, of books now barred from me by price, but which might be replaced if ever they should turn up cheap somewhere, or if ever some money should turn up. This list was long; it was headed by the Oxford Dictionary. I grew up with this dictionary, I grew with its growth, for my parents had subscribed to it from the first; my copy was full of my father's annotations and additions and my own later ones. I had not yet led a life without

it, but such lives can be led and are; in any case it was not a book to be
bought by the totally bombed and totally uncompensated. (But, through
the munificent generosity of a friend, I now have it.) Also on the list of
farewells-thou-art-too-dear-for-my-possessing were the Paget Toynbee
Horace Walpole, Wheatley's Pepys, Birkbeck Hill's Johnson (Boswell,
Piozzi, Letters and Miscellanies), Dr Keynes' Sir Thomas Browne,
Topsell's *Four-Footed Beasts and Serpents*, Holland's Pliny, the Encyclo-
paedia Britannica, Jowett's Plato, the Blackwell *Poly-Olbion*, several
Nonesuch Press books, and plenty more.

Then there were the books to look out for in the second-hand
bookshops, in case they turned up cheap enough. (For the encouragement of others in like case, I should add that many of them have.) Among
these were the Cambridge *English Literature* (in 15 volumes, not in one),
Sylvester's *Du Bartas*, Burnet's *Theory of the Earth*, Bishop Wilkins's
Mathematical Magick, John Swan's *Speculum Mundi*, Professor Living-
stone Lowe's *Road to Xanadu*, Tyndale's and Coverdale's Bible transla-
tions, a lot of diaries (Evelyn, Anthony Wood, Hearne, Fanny Burney,
&c.), a lot of letters (Verney, Conway, Pope, Gibbon, Mme de Sévigny,
Byron, Jane Carlyle), Gunning's *Cambridge Memories*, Aubrey's
Miscellanies and *Antiquities*, *Elegant Extracts*, Hone's *Every Day Books*,
Ovid's *Metamorphosis* translated by several gentlemen c. 1700, the *Phoe-
nix Nest*, Camden's *Reviews*, and so on. (I have not listed books by friends,
as it did not prove necessary; tell your friends you have been bombed and
you tap in them a most admirable generosity, both about books they have
written and books they possess, or even buy: this is the brighter side of
getting bombed.)

Then there was the list of indispensables, to be replaced at once, either
new or second-hand – Shakespeare, about twenty other poets, Herodotus,
Jane Austen, Aubrey's *Brief Lives*, some edition or other of Browne, Pepys,
Horace Walpole, Boswell, *The Spectator* and *Guardian*, Isaac D'Israeli's
Curiosities of Literature and *Calamities and Quarrels of Authors* (out of
print and proved hard to find), the Authorised Version of the Bible, the
Book of Common Prayer, Arber's *English Garner*, de Fontanelle's *Plurality
of Worlds* (preferably John Glanvill's translation), Burton's *Anatomy*,
Hakluyt's Voyages, Gibbon's *Decline and Fall*, Johnson's *Lives of the Poets*
(all these five last are in Everyman; why is not Walton's *Lives*?), Norman
Ault's *17th Century Lyrics* and *Unfamiliar Lyrics*, a Shakespeare concord-
ance, Smith's *Greek and Roman Antiquities*, the Greek Anthology, some
foreign dictionaries, *South Wind*. Then, to look out for at leisure, a great
number of travel and exploration books of all periods, a number of modern French books (not just now replaceable), some contemporary books
by writers I know too slightly to raise the subject with, or don't know at

all, or else they are poor, or dead, or their publishers are bombed. And Quarles's *Emblems*, Clarendon's *Life*, most of the Restoration plays, Sheridan, Goldsmith, Defoe, all kinds of Coleridgeiana, Milton's prose (or about half of it), *Piers Plowman* (but not the Everyman edition, which is a very strange one), and a number of history-books, and biographies of all dates. And a lot of island literature – Beebe, and *Robinson Crusoe, Coral Island, Swiss Family Robinson, Masterman Ready, Suzanne et la Pacifique*, and so on.

Among the irrecoverables were my own MS notes on places, books, and the character and behaviour of animals in literature. This last was a large file, the result of about ten years of spasmodic research, that would in about another ten years have become a book. The sources of my own notes and extracts are now largely inaccessible, and even if they are ever again within reach, I shall not have the heart to begin all that again; it was the book I really wanted to write, but it is gone, with all the other notes and MSS I had. And with all my maps and guide-books. I had a good collection of these – all the Michelin sections of France, much of Italy, Spain, and the Americas and West Indies, and many large-scale maps of foreign towns, and 6-in. ordnance maps of a lot of England, but you can't get these now, it would help the Germans for you to have them. And Baedekers one can't get much, or only antiques, and anyhow travel is over, like one's books and the rest of civilisation.

One keeps on remembering some odd little book that one had; one can't list them all, and it is best to forget them now that they are ashes.

7 November 1941

MARGINAL COMMENT

Harold Nicolson

I am not, I trust, unduly sentimental on the subject of internment. The denial of liberty is one of the greatest ills which man can inflict on man, and so many of these unhappy men and women have been imprisoned for no sin. It is no sin to be patriotic, and it is a fierce calamity, at a time when one's country is in peril, to be prevented from sharing danger and suffering with one's kin. Yet I know that in all wars internment is necessary, and I recognise that in this war the net of internment must be wide and meshes narrow and strong. In former wars only those were interned who, if left at liberty, might escape to serve in the armed forces of the enemy. Hitler's employment of the Fifth Column has taught us that the enemy may be within our gates. We cannot afford to risk the stratagems which he employed at Oslo, at Rotterdam, or in France. I can understand also, although I cannot approve, the panic measures which we took in the summer of 1940, with the example of France still seething in our minds. The danger was immediate, the enemy had pierced our outer defences, we had retired to the keep; we could not risk the presence of enemy agents within the inner fortress; confusion and injustice were inevitable. To a large extent that wrong has now been righted. But now that the moment of ghastly peril is over, it is healthy to examine our actions and to realise that in our necessity we were forced to behave unlike ourselves. Such episodes as the brutalities inflicted on the internees in the *Dunera* should not be suppressed as too shameful to mention, but remembered always as a warning that even among our own people cruelty can exist. I still feel that the public should be told the full story of the *Dunera*, and informed of the punishment inflicted upon those responsible for that disgrace. Public opinion – the final guarantor of our reputation in history – should be vigilant in such matters. Let all who are regarded as of possible danger be confined in such a manner as to prevent them escaping or communicating with the enemy. But, subject to these precautions, let them be treated in such a manner as will enable them hereafter to respect their gaolers and not to hate them.

5 December 1941

A SPECTATOR'S NOTEBOOK

Rose Macaulay

There seems a rather unnecessary fuss going on about getting women for national service. An adequate men's army cannot be raised without conscription, as was proved in the last war, so why expect that a women's can? A certain amount of nonsense has been talked about women not

wanting adventure; as a matter of fact, most young women in the economically higher classes (there does seem to be an economic distinction
here, due, I think, to the over-domestic bringing up of girls who have to
help in the house from a young age) do like adventure; they travel,
explore, ski, fly, drive ambulances abroad, as well as their brothers; but
are they offered much adventure in the women's services? I know of
women who walked out on the Auxiliary Fire Service when they learned
that they would not be allowed to drive the engines, man the pumps, or
climb the ladders, but would have to drive staff about or type or sit at telephones. Necessary work, but dull; people should be ordered to do it, not
cajoled, for it obviously lacks glitter and appeal.

12 December 1941

LONDON 1941

Mervyn Peake

Half masonry, half pain; her head
From which the plaster breaks away
Like flesh from the rough bone, is turned
Upon a neck of stones; her eyes
Are lidless windows of smashed glass,
Each star-shaped pupil
Giving upon a vault so vast
How can the head contain it?

The raw smoke
Is inter-wreathing through the jaggedness
Of her sky-broken panes, and mirror'd
Fires dance like madmen on the splinters.

All else is stillness save the dancing splinters
And the slow inter-wreathing of the smoke.

Her breasts are crumbling brick where the black ivy
Had clung like a fantastic child for succour
And now hangs draggled with long peels of paper,

Fire-crisp, fire-faded awnings of limp paper
Repeating still their ghosted leaf and lily.

Grass for her cold skins' hair, the grass of cities
Wilted and swaying on her plaster brow
From winds that sweep along the streets of cities:

Across a world of sudden fear and firelight
She looms erect, the great stones at her throat,
Her rusted ribs like railings round her heart;
A figure of dry wounds – of winter wounds –
O mother of wounds; half masonry, half pain.

12 December 1941

MARGINAL COMMENT

Harold Nicolson

My memory of the last war tells me that these moods of nervous depression come in waves. For no very particular reason one passes through dark zones into lighter zones, and it may well be that when the snowdrops come I shall be snapping all my shoe-laces with delight. It is a constant solace also to consider how infinitely preferable is the lot of any Englishman to the lot of any German. I often reflect in solemn sympathy upon the spiritual torments through which any German of my own age, temperament and experience, must now be passing. For us, as for the Americans, this war was wholly inevitable; for the Germans it was not inevitable. What should I have done between 1933 and 1939 had I been a German politician of liberal sentiments and humane understanding? I should have shared with my fellow-countrymen a sense of humiliation over the defeat of 1918, and a belief that the great practical virtues of the German people entitled them to the position and authority of a Great Power. I should have been distressed by the failure of the Weimar Republic, and I might even have felt that the Parliamentary system was not that most suited to the German genius. I should have doubted the efficacy or even the fairness of the League of Nations, and I should have felt that

Germany would always be slighted so long as she remained in a position
of physical inferiority. I should have feared also that the evident weakness of the central government, and the increasing audacity of the dis-
ruptive elements, might well lead to chaos and even anarchy. I should
have regarded Hitler as a ridiculous demagogue, but at the same time I
might have recognised that Germany was ripe for revivalism, and that
any revivalist was better than none. Consciously or unconsciously, I
should have been terrified of a second inflation, and should have put up
with many limitations of my liberal doctrine if only so great a disaster
could be evaded. I should probably have been a supporter of Hitler in
1933. But when from 1933 onwards, disillusion turned into distaste and
distaste into acute alarm, what attitude should I have adopted? I might
have resisted and faced the rubber truncheon; I might have escaped and
faced the bitterness of exile. Yet I should probably have remained silent,
hoping vainly that things would improve, passing almost insensibly
from self-deception to self-deception. Only today I should see quite
clearly the approaching ruin of my country; and I should know that this
ruin had come about because people such as myself had not been honest
enough and brave enough in time. To the bitterness of disaster would be
added the bitterness of self-reproach. What, in comparison to so terrible
an indictment, is the blame which we can lay upon ourselves?

How strange it was to be in London last week and to realise that the public (stunned as they were by our naval losses) seemed unaware that two
decisive events had occurred. The fact that the United States have
entered the war against all our enemies means in all certainty that Germany cannot win. The fact that Congress has almost in the first hour
voted for the creation of an American expeditionary force means that
Germany is certain to be beaten. It may be that for the next eight months
we shall suffer bitterly; but when that grim period is past the road to victory stretches clear ahead. The British public did not realise the import of
these great events. There was no jubilation, nor did the Stars and Stripes
float from our public buildings. Twelve months from now, when we look
back upon that amazing week, we shall say that Sunday, December 7th,
of this year marked the end of all the Axis hopes. I trust that our American associates have not been offended by our temporary absence of mind.
The BBC were the first to recover their sense of proportion and their
'salute to America' on Saturday night was a reminder of what our cause
has gained these days in spirit and in power. They quoted the 'American
Letter' of Archibald MacLeish which I have already sought to bring to the
notice of readers of The Spectator. 'America,' writes MacLeish, 'is a great

word . . . a shining thing in the mind.' It is a word which will strike fear in Germany, a deep, corroding fear.

19 December 1941

Part Four
1942

**Expressions
of
Satisfaction**

"It's a piece of Cake"

It's "a piece of cake" to the R.A.F. boys when it's a job they can finish with satisfaction—a job they can get their teeth into.

A piece of cake was always something good. Today when so many good things have vanished it is doubly appreciated.

Cake is a splendid food, containing nourishing ingredients that the body needs.

A piece of Cake
is satisfying

CVS—116

SHOVING THE LITTLE MEN OFF

Murray Sayle

Tokyo

This weekend we might easily have had enthusiastic crowds feeding the pigeons in Tokyo's historic Singapore Square, with incense rising, Nikons snapping and Emperor Hirohito waving benignly from his balcony. In the end, things went the other way, and only a handful of greying Japanese privately recall the 40th anniversary of the most dazzling of Japan's victories. On the other side, fewer survive to mourn the greatest disaster ever to befall British arms. The fall of Singapore on 15 February 1942 certainly ranks as a date to remember, like the loss of Constantinople to the Turks in 1453. The cosmopolitan hub of a rich and powerful empire overrun by barbarians, as both seemed at the time; a long decline suddenly made manifest, an old order swept away for ever, as we can see now. Either way, another great turning point to torment schoolboys yet unborn.

Britain and Japan, once the best of allies, fell out in the Thirties over trade, the stickiest issue being the best way to pick the bones of China. Britain favoured the 'open door' policy, meaning a fair ring of the cash register for everybody, which unfortunately included the Japanese. Japan, having the military means to do it, inclined more towards the 'closed door' policy, with themselves inside the door and all non-Asiatics outside. In July 1937 Japan went to undeclared war with China, and the following month a Japanese fighter (a forerunner of the promising new Zero) shot up the car of the British ambassador, Sir Hugh Knatchbull-Hugessen, outside Shanghai, using the large Union Jack painted on his roof as a convenient aiming point.

With Hitler's star rising in the West, Britain was in no position to make war either in or over China. A deal seemed indicated, raising the age-old, ever-new problem of who is in charge in Tokyo. 'I only wonder whether it would be possible to get in touch with the forces that in fact direct Japanese policy,' the Foreign Secretary, Anthony Eden, wrote to his ambassador in Tokyo in September 1937. 'It is conceivable that statesmen in Tokyo may have moderate and long-sighted views, but have they any influence on events, and with the passage of time are they more likely to regain ascendancy?'

When the search for moderate Japanese statesmen failed, Britain's fall-back position in the Far East was the great naval base at Singapore. Begun in earnest in 1933, the base was intended to support a fleet of battleships, the ultimate weapon of the trading and seafaring nation which had carried through the first industrial revolution. But the Japanese are ambitious islanders, too. At first they bought British, then started building their own warships. By the early Forties the Japanese fleet included super-battleships of the Yamato class, 64,170 tons, nine 18-inch guns, nearly twice the size of any comparable British ship, bigger than anything the Americans could bring through the Panama Canal. With this ultimate weapon the Japanese navy planned a super-Trafalgar, to be followed by their turn at a world empire.

Singapore was bluff, even from the beginning. The dry docks, the oil storage tanks, the workshops and the shore batteries of 15-inch guns cost £60 million but they protected nothing, not even themselves, without a fleet of capital ships. The fleet was to be sent from Malta, from Alexandria and from Britain to deal with 'an emergency in the Far East', meaning war with Japan. But sanctions against Italy over Abyssinia, followed by the outbreak of Hitler's war in Europe and the fall of France, meant that no big ships could be spared. Then in the summer of 1941 the American government applied long-threatened sanctions against Japan, cutting off oil supplies until the Japanese gave up their war in China – a move described as putting the Japanese in 'quarantine'.

With great misgivings Britain was persuaded to join in. 'What does he mean by "putting them in quarantine"?' Neville Chamberlain wrote cautiously to his sister Hilda, when President Roosevelt first proposed the scheme. 'Seeing that patients suffering from epidemic diseases do not usually go about fully armed, is there not a difference here, and something lacking in his analogy?'

At the Foreign Office, Charles Orde, himself no great admirer of the Chinese ('such inveterate wrigglers and self-deceivers'), nevertheless advised a strong line with the fractious Japanese: 'When they have a case and have learned to state it properly and reasonably, we will, I do not doubt, be prepared to listen to them with respect and magnanimity. But meanwhile we shall have to let them see we are not to be intimidated. Of course,' Orde added, presciently, 'there is a point at which they may go off their heads, and sanctions may be that point.'

They were. The carrier force which was to attack Pearl Harbor sailed secretly from Japan on 25 November 1941. The Japanese 5th and 18th

Divisions and the Imperial Guards Division, fresh from the war in China, were already assembled in Saigon and ports in southern Indochina, practising with landing-barges. Some 700 front-line aircraft had arrived from Japan. Opposing them in Malaya was a scratch collection of British, Australian and Indian troops, plus the Malayan volunteers, two and a half divisions in all, and 336 aircraft – Buffaloes, Sharks, Swordfish, Wildebeeste, an aeronautical *salon des refusés* of obsolete types and designers' mistakes – all that could be spared from the war in Europe.

On 2 December the long-prepared-for British ships arrived in Singapore. The new battleship *Prince of Wales* and the battle-cruiser *Repulse*, a veteran of the First World War, were intended to 'overawe' a Japanese battle fleet eight times their size. 'Thus,' said Winston Churchill, 'we stretch out the long arm of brotherhood and motherhood to the Australian and New Zealand peoples' – who were, indeed, getting distinctly uneasy about Japanese intentions. The aircraft carrier *Indomitable*, also intended for Singapore, had run aground off Jamaica and was being repaired.

At 1.15 on the morning of 8 December a telephone call from General Arthur Percival, GOC Malaya, woke Sir Shenton Thomas, Governor of the Straits Settlements, in his bedroom at Government House in Singapore. The Japanese, the general reported, were coming ashore at Kota Bahru, the northernmost port on the east coast of Malaya. 'Well,' said Sir Shenton, 'I suppose you'll shove the little men off!' (Governor and general were both tall, thin men.) Two hours later the first Japanese air raid hit Singapore, killing 61 people and wrecking Robinson's new air-conditioned restaurant in Raffles Place. At dawn GHQ in Singapore issued its first communiqué, reporting that the Japanese had met stern resistance. 'The few troops left on the beach are being heavily machine-gunned . . . and all surface craft are retiring at high speed,' said the communique – as indeed they were, to fetch more Japanese from the transports lying offshore.

The same afternoon Rear-Admiral Sir Tom Phillips set out from Singapore with *Prince of Wales, Repulse*, four destroyers and no air cover, in the hope of getting among the transports. He missed them, and early on 10 December a Japanese aircraft spotted the British ships. Three hours later both had been sunk by Japanese army bombers from Saigon. Phillips went down with his command, although most of the ships' companies were picked up by the destroyers, the Japanese not interfering.

At this point Singapore lost whatever influence it may have had on the outcome of the war. Nevertheless reinforcements – British, Indian and Australian – continued to pour in, jostling with rubber planters and their families going the other way. The Japanese High Command allowed 100 days for the capture of Singapore. In fact it took them 70 – a melancholy story of strong points by-passed, lines of resistance pierced and isolated units outflanked and enveloped by roads not blocked and bridges never blown.

Against any determined opponent who controls both sea and air the loss of a long, thin peninsula, especially one leading from nowhere to nowhere, can only be a matter of time. The Japanese arrived with bicycles, split-toed rubber shoes and nippy, Honda-sized tanks, weighing only ten tons and narrow enough to slip between rows of rubber trees. The Japanese troops were well practised from their days in China where, fighting stubborn guerrillas, they became thoroughly brutalised as well. Numerous well-attested massacres of wounded and prisoners took place, mostly the work of the highly politicised guards division whose junior officers were among the keenest exponents of the Japanese variety of fascism.

On 20 January Churchill sent a stern message from London: 'I want to make it absolutely clear that I expect every inch of ground to be defended, every scrap of material or defences to be blown to pieces to prevent capture by the enemy, and no question of surrender to be entertained until after protracted fighting among the ruins of Singapore city.'

On 30 January the last troops in Peninsular Malaya withdrew into Singapore and the causeway spanning the half-mile between the island and the mainland was blown, leaving a gap barely four feet deep at low tide. There were nearly a million civilians inside the city, whose Chinese shopkeepers, not liking the look of things, had suspended the age-old chit system and were now demanding cash for every purchase. Singapore did not have its own water supply, and for that matter, still does not – which is why the present republic of Singapore to this day maintains an Israeli-trained armoured force with the mission of nipping up the main road and seizing the reservoirs on the mainland in the event of another 'emergency in the Far East'. In February 1942 the available water would last the besieged city, bloated with refugees and under constant air and artillery bombardment, no more than two weeks.

The first Japanese came ashore in rubber boats on the night of 8 February. On 14 February the Municipal Engineer reported that only 24 hours' water remained. Next morning General Percival asked the Japanese for terms. The parley, held in the boardroom of the Ford car factory, was brief, an exception to the normal Japanese fondness for interminable conferences. 'Do you accept our terms of immediate unconditional surrender, yes or no?' barked the bullet-headed, bemedalled General Tokoyuki Yamashita. Percival, thin and drawn, had little option. Wearily

he signed, surrendering the city and garrison of 85,000 men to an attacking force of 30,000. The Japanese lost less than 10,000 killed and
wounded in the campaign. After the war the reason for Yamashita's
brusque manner emerged: he was almost out of ammunition, and a sortie
from Singapore might have delayed the end a week or two. The Japanese
general was later hanged by the Americans in the Philippines for his
activities there, when the Japanese in their turn were fighting a hopeless
defence.

The survivors of Singapore had scarcely been marched off to a brutal captivity before the search for guilty men began. Recriminations have, in
general, come under three broad headings:

(1) Whisky-soaked planters. It is true that this class of Malayan resident drank heavily, as civilians behind the lines in wartime generally do
if the stuff is available, on the gather-ye-rosebuds principle. Singapore
under siege was a kind of giant Harrods with the Goths at the front
entrance, and drinking was one way of denying it to the enemy. As it was,
one and a half million bottles of spirits and 60,000 gallons of home-made
Chinese gin were destroyed to dissuade the Japanese from staging
another drunken rape of Nanking. The planters' boozing could, however,
hardly have decided the outcome.

(2) The guns pointed the wrong way. This, the best-known of all Singapore theories, appears to have originated with Winston Churchill himself. One of the more opulent passages of *The Second World War*
expresses the Prime Minister's shock/horror on hearing that the guns of
the naval base pointed out to sea and asks, 'What is the use of having an
island for a fortress if it is not to be made into a citadel?' What, indeed. But
this simply continues the myth of the Thirties, that Singapore city and
Singapore island were the fortresses, not just the overpopulated neighbours of the empty naval base. Even the most amateur strategist would
reject a teeming tropical town as a suitable site for a 'citadel'.

What, then, was the Former Naval Person on about? He was, of course,
also a practising politician, indeed an arch-imperialist, unable to the end
of his days to accept what Singapore demonstrated so clearly – namely
that Britain no longer had the resources to protect her Empire against all
comers. On this harsh truth his entire world view foundered; hence the
need to blame the unknown idiot who sited the guns, especially as he had
done so under a previous government.

(3) Hopeless generalship. General Percival and his Australian second-
in-command, Major-General H. Gordon Bennett, were certainly not
Napoleon and Ney, or even Haig and Robertson. Indeed, the losers at Singapore get a section to themselves in Norman Dixon's penetrating work,

On the Psychology of Military Incompetence. A former Royal Engineer turned scientist, Dixon advances the view that the military profession positively attracts persons who, probably because of unloved childhoods and overstrict toilet training, are psychologically unfitted for high command.

These people are not, however, the heads of oak of popular view, specially selected for dimness by military promotion boards. On the contrary, although suspiciously fond of 'bull', spit and polish, they are usually highly intelligent and eager to please, and hence rise rapidly in the service. They lack, however, any penetration into their own self-deceptions, and are unable to modify their plans with the changing circumstances inescapable in war.

So, Dixon argues, when Percival forbade his engineers to build fixed defences with civilian labour the length of the Malayan Peninsula on the ground that this would be bad for civilian morale, it was actually concern for his own morale that he was rationalising. 'In the case of Percival and Gordon Bennett, to erect defences would have been to admit to themselves the danger in which they stood,' writes Dixon, describing this reaction as 'helpless resignation in the face of same-species aggression. Whereas the brown rat, that most ferocious of fighters, will turn and attack any large predator, it makes no such attempt to defend itself against a concerted attack by fellow rats. At a human level such behaviour could well be part and parcel of appeasement tendencies.'

We may well have here at least a partial explanation of why generals of great intellectual distinction sometimes fail, and boneheads often win. Certainly General Percival impressed everyone he met with his intelligence, and in 1937 he even wrote a brilliant staff paper predicting with considerable accuracy the direction from which the Japanese would come, and the unorthodox methods they would use. As to the controversial General Bennett, who wore a neat moustache, he certainly seems to have had a well-developed sense of self-preservation, not necessarily a bad thing in a soldier. After ordering his command, the Australian Eighth Division, to hold fast Bennett and his staff escaped by boat to Australia, where the chief of staff of the Australian forces was frostily unimpressed by the argument that his experiences at the hands of the Japanese were of unique value. Bennett never got another active command.

Another view expands from the love of ritual and disinclination to face the facts to the entire direction of the empire. No serious preparations, it is argued, were made to defend Malaya in case the preparations themselves might attract attack. Without the callous warrior spirit, on this view, empires cannot be long maintained. Percival would therefore emerge both as a faithful reflection of his times and a decent man of considerable moral courage, at least, in surrendering his command to avoid useless loss of life, despite the voices from afar urging him to hold on.

Suppose, in the end, things had gone the other way? Both Germany and Japan were developing nuclear weapons, both were convinced that they were the master race, and neither was averse to intra-species conflict. Their joint victory would, no doubt, have been followed by a cold war, and with Germany ruling Russia and Japan India they would be colliding about now in the vicinity of Afghanistan. Both Singapore Square and Stalingradplatz would have giant fallout shelters. In Japan's case, at least, there have been considerable practical advantages to being on the losing end.

13 February 1982

MARGINAL COMMENT

Harold Nicolson

I propose this week to write about books, and to discuss some of the difficulties to which literature in general, and publishers in particular, are today exposed owing to the shortage of paper, and the dearth of labour in the binding trade. Of the many legends which bemuse the public mind, one of the most unfair is that which represents publishers as sharks. There are few publishers in business today who have ever behaved really badly to any author; there are few authors in business today who have not, at some time in their lives, treated some publisher with ingratitude, duplicity and greed. How many of our writers could boast that they have remained faithful to the publisher who first greeted their dawning talent, and who risked his capital upon the uncertain venture of their earliest books? The publishers themselves treat these acts of treachery in sorrow rather than in anger, ascribing them to the impulsiveness of the *genus irritabile vatum*; and those who write the lives of our literary heroes slur over such material matters as being irrelevant to the noble character which they are seeking to portray. Thus when George Eliot, after the success of *Adam Bede*, abandoned Blackwood, who had fought and paid so nobly for her during the difficult days, we are left to assume that she had a mind above pecuniary details, and that it was

George Lewes who engineered this act of treachery; yet in this case the
'pecuniary detail' was a firm offer by Smith Elder of the sum of £10,000.
The publishers remain silent; the authors and their biographers are very
vocal. And thus the public are unaware of the principles which inspire
British publishers as of the great contribution which the bulk of them
have made, and are still striving to make, to the cause of English letters. I
have always been on the side of oppressed minorities, and I regard British
publishers as a minority which for generations has been unfairly
exploited, vilified and oppressed.

Nobody who has examined the question of book production in wartime
could contend that there has been any real absence of good intention,
either on the part of the publishers, or on the part of the authorities concerned. From the first days of the war the publishers offered to cut down
their production to 60 per cent, and to reduce the paper consumed both
in size and weight. The authorities for their part have not been unaware
of the importance of books to national morale at home and national
prestige abroad. The Chancellor of the Exchequer readily gave way to
Parliamentary pressure and exempted books from the incidence of the
purchase tax. The Paper Controller has never been unenlightened or subjected book-production to a purely quantitative test. The Ministry of
Information and the British Council have done all they can to support
the interests of the book-trade, and to confirm the principle that books of
high quality are one of the most valuable forms of British export. The fact
remains, however, that, in spite of goodwill in every quarter, the book-
trade will, unless further steps are taken, suffer grievously in the present
year. The paper ration allowed to publishers has been reduced progressively from 60 per cent to 50 per cent, to 42 per cent, and now to 37½ per
cent. Most publishers have by now run out of such stocks of paper as they
happened to possess, and can no longer find chance reams of paper in odd
corners. Enemy action has added to the shortage. More recently an agreement has been reached under which publishers are given some extra allo-
cations of paper to replace such losses. But this allocation is only 7½ per
cent of the amount destroyed. The effect of this shortage of stock is
already apparent in the present famine in text-books or in those cheap
editions of the classics for which there is a constant demand. Take, for
instance, a great national institution such as the Everyman Edition; of
the 970 books published in Everyman, something like 500 are today
unobtainable at most booksellers. The demand also for popular text-
books today far exceeds the supply, and the complaint goes up from every
quarter that our young people simply cannot obtain the text-books
which they need.

I am aware that the shortage of paper is not the only, not even perhaps the most serious, disability with which publishers have to contend. Even if they obtained double their present ration of paper they would still be faced by the acute congestion in the binding trade. Before the war there were some seventy firms which specialised in binding books for the market, and of these some twenty have been put out of action, whereas the remaining fifty have lost half their labour. The suggestion is often made that the shortage of strawboards for binding might be met were all our books to be published in paper covers, as is the practice in France. This suggestion does not really solve the difficulty since different types of machinery would be needed for binding in paper covers, and this machinery cannot now be obtained. Many publishers have sought to mitigate this difficulty by reducing the weight of the strawboards used for binding; yet such *ersatz* bindings are apt to curve and cockle if exposed to the comparative warmth of a February sun. And thus it comes that even the most lavish bookseller will inform us with a wan smile – that the book we ask for is 'being bound'; one knows what that means; it means that the book has been caught in the great bottleneck which it will take many a weary month to disencumber.

This shortage of supply has coincided with an enormous increase in demand. It is not merely that elderly people find in reading some occupation for the long dark evenings of wartime and some distraction from the painful preoccupations of our present discontents. It is also that young men and women have developed a thirst for information, and that this thirst cannot be assuaged from the summer-dried fountains of the book-trade. As a symptom of this admirable craving it may be mentioned that the numbers of those joining the London Library (which provides lavish reading on generous terms) has risen during the last nine months to an almost unprecedented degree. This is a symptom of an increased need for information, and an increased taste for reading at which we should all rejoice. But the fact remains that of the current books available in 1939, as many as 37,000 are already out of print. It is to the credit of our publishers that in spite of this urgent demand for reprints they persist in assigning a high proportion of their ration to the publication of new books. Most publishers could keep the machine turning over by merely reprinting former books for which they know there is a stable demand. The fact that they all of them seek to expend a large portion of their ration upon new and uncertain ventures shows that they are no mere book-merchants, but people anxious to risk something for the benefit of English letters as a whole.

20 February 1942

SINGAPORE HAS FALLEN

Kate O'Brien

The clock chimed four, and an elderly gentleman entered the lounge. He moved an armchair close to the fire, and also a small table with a copper top. The fire was bright and hot. The elderly gentleman sat down and folded his hands. He was very handsome, and his knickerbocker suit became him well. He looked about him slowly, and at the clock. He did not seem pleased.

Some ladies came in, bright and sociable. One of them came and sat beside the elderly gentleman.

'Tea is late,' he said to her.

She laughed merrily.

'My poor darling, of course it's late.' She threw a gay glance over the lounge to her lady friends. Her large torso was shaped like a Christmas pudding; she wore a salmon-coloured jersey. 'My poor husband, with his touching hope of getting tea *on time!*' she said.

'Dear Sir James,' said a lady in a pixie hood. 'Still dreaming of perfection, after eighteen months of this hotel!'

A waiter and waitress were hurriedly putting buns and bread-and-butter on the copper-topped tables. The waiter had a limp, and wore very thick glasses. The waitress was a neat, nimble child of fifteen.

'It's seven minutes past four,' Sir James said, clearly, to each of them in turn.

Salmon-coloured Jersey pulled a toasting fork out of a large embroidered bag, and set to work to toast a bun.

'Two years, Mrs Hollingsby,' she corrected her friend in the pixie hood. 'Sir James and I are the oldest inhabitants now, I think. We were among the very first to realise that Surrey was going to be *quite impossible!* Besides, with that great house, we were simply terrified of evacuees, my dear!'

'And how right you were!' said a lady with *pince-nez* and a double chin. 'And yet, when one thinks of all one's beautiful things in store.'

'Oh, let's keep it cheerful!' said the pixie hood.

Salmon Jersey took a little tin out of her bag, and buttered the bun.

'Begin on that, you poor darling,' she said to Sir James.

'And here *is* tea, actually arriving! Miraculous!' said Pixie.

The teapots went round. Everyone began to eat and drink.

'I stored everything,' said the double-chinned lady. 'Absolutely every-thing. My lawyer advised me to. "Store everything, Mrs Buckshott," he said. And so I did. Even my dressing-table things, if you'll believe me. Beautiful enamel, of course.'

'Oh, one can't be *too* careful, I always say,' said Salmon. 'Here is your second bun, my pet.'

Sir James took the second bun, which was spread with jam.

'Have you heard of the management's new ramp with our soap cou-pons, Lady Drimble?' asked Pixie.

'Have I not, my dear! Really, don't you think we should *all* protest, *en masse*? The jam scandal was bad enough, and I still don't see why we stand for it—'

'Nor do I,' said Double Chin. 'Considering what we pay here. The profi-teering must be criminal, and I know for a fact they have *enormous* hoards of jam.'

'If the place was clean, one mightn't grudge them one's household cou-pons!' said Pixie, with a tolerant laugh.

'Yes – but how *is* one to manage on three ounces of toilet soap?' asked Salmon.

'Have you brought the new cake downstairs?' Sir James asked her.

'Yes, darling. I must say,' said Salmon, as she plunged into the bag again, 'I must say it's a comfort that I am still able to get these home-made cakes sent on from Surrey.'

'Time they were sending another chicken,' said Sir James.

'The menu does pall in this place,' said Double Chin. 'Even in wartime you'd think that with just a *little* imagination—'

'Oh, my dear,' said Pixie, 'don't you know that these West Country people are bone from the ears up? Take the Clubhouse, for instance. Pamela and I went up this morning, and there wasn't a caddie in sight. Not one. It was a bit cold to play, anyhow, so we just thought we'd stay and knit. But do you know that those radiators were *stone*-cold? With today's temperature!' Everyone shivered sympathetically. 'And that wretched stove thing was smoking. Actually smoking.'

'Disgraceful,' said Double Chin. 'I really can't imagine why we are all spending so much money in this hole of a place.'

'Oh, let's keep it cheerful,' said bright Pixie. 'Pamela had the blues this morning. Her brother was at Singapore, you know.'

'Yes, indeed, poor girl. But really, to listen to poor old Pamela, you'd imagine that her brother was the *only* person serving in this war!' said Salmon.

'No self-control,' said Double Chin.

'I want more cake,' said Sir James.

'What I'm very hot on in this hotel,' said Pixie, 'is the wine racket.'

'How right you are,' said Salmon.

'Of course Dudley buys a good deal of stuff, and we have plenty in our room, so it doesn't matter to us really, but just on principle.'

'Well, when it comes to 11s. a bottle for Hungarian hock that was 4s. 6d. a year ago,' said Salmon.

'Exactly. Dudley ticked the waiter off good and hard last weekend over the price of brandy here. There's a ramp, if you like!'

'I'm very partial to a good Nuits-Saint-Georges,' said Double Chin, 'and I happen to know, through my lawyer, that there is plenty of it about still.'

'Dudley says he's given up drink for Lent,' said Pixie.

'Well, that's very good of him, really,' said Salmon.

'Oh, he'll have forgotten about it by this weekend,' said Pixie, merrily. 'If ever there was a time when a few drinks were absolutely essential—'

'Exactly, my dear,' said Salmon. 'Heavens, no more milk? What a war!'

'What a war, indeed!' said Double Chin. 'It gets worse every minute. Why, only last Easter – I was at Torquay then – we were still having "bubbly" parties. Several people gave them.'

'How lovely! You *were* gay at Torquay! Have you had enough cake, darling? Shall I put it away?'

'Well – be sure you shut the tin *properly*,' said Sir James. Then he settled himself in his chair and fell asleep.

The waiter and waitress began to remove the tea-things from the copper-topped tables. The lounge was quiet and hot. The clock chimed the half-hour.

'What about a spot of bridge?' said Pixie.

                                                                    27 February 1942

'SHIBBOLETH'

Eric Baume

The Australian sergeant leaned against the bar at the Al Manir, near the Cecil, and looked out through fly-spotted glass at Alexandria's outer harbour. He squinted at a signal coming up on the halyards of a Vichy battle-cruiser, yawned in the middle of the operation and leaned more heavily. A fat Greek woman walking with a tall naval petty officer intrigued him for a moment. Three little boys came up with begging whines, and he shifted them with his foot without hurting them as he would have done to a dog at Marree. He yawned again. The afternoon sun was hot. The air was sticky, grease-filled, seemingly after its rush across the Iraqi desert from Habbaniyeh having lost the dry keenness of its warmth once it zephyred down from Haifa. Outside someone began a noisy argument about the Koran. Was it possible, asked an old coffee-drinker, for a non-orthodox Moslem to say the blessing 'Bismillah' when drinking forbidden alcohol with a non-believer? The resultant argument would have done credit to a musical broadcast in Arabic. The sergeant grinned again. Then he turned to Vassilios, the Athenian bar-keeper.

'Another beer,' he said. 'Cripes, it's been hot ever since Tuesday's air-raid.' Vassilios, who liked the sergeant, was concerned. 'Too hot,' he answered; 'but those air-raids are too hot. My cousin Lepidos was telling me about those nights at Crete. You got it worse in 1941, eh?'

The Australian sergeant leaned more comfortably, crossing his legs, letting the bar support his lanky body at the diaphragm, pivoting his body on his right elbow, holding his beaker with his left.

'Yairs,' he said, 'Crete was a hot place when they dropped the 500-pounders, but your blokes were okay-doke; that's why we give 'em a hand here whenever they give us a "hoy".'

Vassilios smiled. Even Prince Philip of Greece, himself a serving officer in the Royal Navy, had watched Australian soldiers in Egypt, running to aid Greeks caught in some Quarter fight. There was a friendship which would not blow cold, and many a big steak would be eaten at Greek restaurants in Australia at some reunion of far-off days to come.

He waved away two piastres for the beer. 'After all, sergeant,' he said, 'you are my cobber.' The sergeant nodded smilelessly. There was a warmth of gratitude in his swallow.

Outside a naval patrol passed, clumpily. One of the Koran polemists lost his temper, threw down his coffee-cup, left. A beggar with a stinking leg was urged on with curses by Kobu, the black doorman from Djibai on the Persian Gulf. In slow eddies the smell of the Alexandria waterfront assailed the sergeant's nose. It drifted out when he had lit a cigarette. Cripes, he thought, how much bloody longer before Libya or home or both or bloody none? He ordered another beer and paid for it, as well as for one which Vassilios drank. Three sirens from a destroyer broke his boredom for a second. Five Sunderlands roared down to anchorage. Up towards Rosetta ack-ack guns coughed for a few minutes. But there was no alert.

'Quiet, sergeant, isn't it?' The sergeant pivoted on his elbow. A captain of the Royal Engineers had come in quietly enough. 'Yairs,' said the sergeant. If the poms wanted to talk, o.k.

'Been here long?' asked the captain, ordering two beers.

'Couple 'er days,' said the sergeant. 'Long enough.'

'Waiting to go up, eh?' the captain smiled, and raised his beer. 'All the best.'

They drank. 'I heard you chaps were coming down from Syria. Good show. Your infantry's some of the best we've got. I thought I recognised your battalion.'

The sergeant studied his beer. 'Those are divisional patches. Yairs, I reckon we had enough rest up in Palestine.' He leaned further against the bar. The captain was most friendly. 'I wonder whether my friend, Lt-Col. Jenkyns, is with you? He had the 35th battalion when last I heard of him. Fine chap. Weren't they Eighth Brigade?'

'Yairs,' said the sergeant.

The captain thought for a moment. 'By jove,' he said. 'I've read a lot about your country – especially the chaps from out-back. Or was Jenkyns with you up in Palestine? Or was he 45th battalion? Hard to remember, isn't it?'

'Yairs,' said the sergeant.

The captain snapped his fingers. 'I know, 45th battalion had those new anti-tank rifles from Sydney. Now I remember. Are they with your brigade now? They'll give Jerry a bit of hurry-up.'

'Yairs,' said the sergeant, leaning further across the bar.

The captain bought another beer. 'I've read plenty about your out-back,' he said. 'I've seen pictures of it so often. Herrgott Springs, for example, in northern South Australia, and that song of Pat Dunlop about Yarravonga.'

'Yairs,' said the sergeant. Then, winking at Vassilios, he smacked the captain on the chin, dropped him and held him while Vassilios ran for rope and tied the captain's hands and feet.

'What beats me, sergeant,' said Major Hendren, Chief of Security Police, 'is how you suspected him. Instinct, eh, you old bushman?'

The sergeant grinned. 'Yairs,' he said, 'you see, I come from Marree. Before the last war it was called Herrgott Springs. That bloke wasn't old enough for the last war, so he must of read about it all in Germany, and, cripes, when a bloke calls Yarrawonga, "Yarravonga" . . . there's something crook about him.'

The major poured the beer, now.

'Another won't hurt, sergeant? In fact, it might do good with that mention you're going to get in despatches.'

'Yairs,' said the sergeant, 'yairs.'

2 October 1942

THE GUNNER-GIRLS

Major D. Rees Williams

One by one the strongholds of male isolation have been sapped. We rather thought in the Gunners that our bastions would be the last to fall, but we were mistaken, and when it was announced that girls were to be trained in the technical work of anti-aircraft batteries we were at first incredulous and then inclined to scoff. By chance I saw the first team of women to control the fire at a target at practice-camp. They were carefully selected and had had considerable experience of practice-camp conditions. A gunnery instructor had trained them on the instruments in his and their own time and the results were good but not, we felt, conclusive. This was a year ago.

It was with considerable interest that I learnt a few weeks ago of my posting to a training regiment where girls are instructed in their duties as members of a mixed battery. In such a unit the girls form the instrument detachments and the men the gun teams. I found that almost all my forebodings were without foundation and that the girls were most promising. The instructors seem generally to be of opinion that the girls pick up the work quicker than men do but in a different way. The men learn their duties by the discipline of an exact drill. The girls learn it in a way of their own. They are apt to get depressed when they find technical matters facing them such as they have never previously experienced. Any impatience or brusqueness with them at this stage would result in tears and despondency. The instructors therefore take care to assure the girls that with patience and without worrying the subject can be mastered. In a week or so the girls find that their tasks become clear to them and they are then, to use their own expression, 'On top of the job'. On the parade-ground their drill is exceptionally good. They hold themselves well and march with a short, precise step. Their well-fitting battle-dress gives them a soldierly appearance. Their bearing and turn-out is all that could be desired.

It is strange, indeed, how soon one becomes accustomed to look upon them as soldiers; soldiers of rather a special kind, of course, but soldiers fitting themselves to take a vital part in the defence of this country. The bad weather we experienced a few weeks ago does not seem to have affected the women to the extent that might have been expected. The sickness percentage is low and the Medical Officer informs me that most of her sick parades are chiefly concerned with foot trouble. A good deal of this is probably due to the shoes worn in civil life, but it is brought to a head by marching drill. Their feet soon harden up and the girls love drill. It is a sight as refreshing as it is novel to watch the evident enjoyment of a squad of girls on marching drill, and the zest with which they move as one across the parade-ground. I do not remember noticing this same delight on the faces of men soldiers throughout my years of service but possibly they were more adept at concealing their feelings. The wearing of battle-dress for work has been an excellent idea. It has made the girls feel, I am sure, that on the gun-park there is no differentiation made between themselves and their male comrades.

The reports from the gun sites of their work have been satisfactory. Since the mixed batteries were first formed there has been little enemy activity over this country, and consequently they have had little opportunity of proving themselves in action. No one doubts that when the time comes they will do so abundantly. The work of women as ambulance drivers, nurses, ARP personnel and so on is beyond praise, and what they have done, so will the gunner-girls do. In a mixed battery the women officers, though primarily concerned with the administration of the women and their well-being, are being trained in an operational role, so that they can release their male colleagues for other work. The responsibility for directing operations is, however, in the hands of the military officers.

These women officers are a good lot. With the thoroughness, attention to detail and loyalty of women they look after their troops in every way. The jibes one has heard about the behaviour of the ATS are so false as to be ludicrous. No mother need be afraid of entrusting her daughter to a gunner unit; she will be very well provided for. Most of the officers, and all the junior ones, have been through the ranks and know well the special needs and problems.

24 April 1942

LIFE AND DEATH

Freya Stark

As to triumphant arms
Life leaps to death,
And ends her daily harms
With quiet breath,

She brings earth-gifts as dower.
Where strong death waits
Life, fragile as a flower,
Unlocks the gates.

The heavy gates scarce swing
So slim she goes,
Lightfoot as wind of spring,
Transient as rose.

The dull gates open free,
To zodiac height;
Like a wave to its waves of sea,
Like a star to its night,

Like a maid, but enriched with desire,
Like a summer's breath,
Life flees to her funeral pyre,
The bride of death.

5 June 1942

UNDERSTANDING RUSSIA

Sir Bernard Pares
(Lecturer on Russian history)

The publication of the Anglo-Soviet Treaty was sure to be greeted with intense satisfaction. This is what has been eagerly asked for at innumerable public meetings which I have attended in every part of the kingdom, by platforms representative of every shade of political opinion, from Conservative to Communist, and often enough the most eloquent expression of our tribute to Russia's contribution in the war has come from the Conservative. This has nothing to do with any political theory. It is the grateful recognition of the immense burden shouldered by a great and gallant people in our common struggle against the forces of evil, together with the earnest wish that after the war there should be a continuation of this close friendship, without which no lasting peace in Europe is possible.

This war is a war of peoples, and they sweep aside all that interferes with their security. In 1935 Mr Eden said in Moscow that he could not see any conflict of interests which need divide us. Once in the past we fought Russia – in the Crimean War. It was a war fought with great chivalry, but it was from start to finish a war of muddles, and it did no good to either side, except that by implication it led straight to the emancipation of the serfs in Russia. On the other hand, this is the fifth time that the two countries have found themselves side by side in a struggle against a world aggression.

It is well also to emphasise the importance of the accompanying engagements of common effort and of support in supply. Twice, with a capricious or emotional Tsar, we lost the alliance because our help came too late; and even in the last war the munitions that flowed from the chivalrous crusade of Mr Lloyd George reached Russia, as I know too well at first hand, only when the Russian regular army had been pounded to pieces, and was no longer there to use them.

So obvious is the strong identity of interests between the two countries that ever since the unification of Germany in 1871 it has been the settled policy, not only of her government, but of her Press, and even of her scholars, to keep Britain and Russia in perpetual misunderstanding with each other. Throughout my forty-odd years of study of Anglo-Russian relations, without any animosity against the German people, I have always had to recognise that we had this set purpose against us, which is the reason why I have always tried to direct our attention to the cardinal importance of the study of Russia: we must see Russia for ourselves, without the intervention of this most untrustworthy tutor. Anglo-Russian misunderstanding was the object of Bismarck, of the Emperor Wilhelm II, and, more emphatically than with either, of Adolf Hitler. He deluded simple souls here by always holding in front of us the picture of a Russia unchanged since that poignant moment when, in the passions and sufferings of the last world war, a dead government was removed from the body of a live people. Those who listened to him could not see that, nationally, they were simply playing into his hands.

Those who would see the true picture should read with care that quite admirable book (reviewed in last week's *Spectator*), the record of Mr Joseph E. Davies, American Ambassador in Moscow from 1936 to 1938. It is a picture of neither the heaven nor the hell which Russia has been represented to us to be, but of fallible human beings, ready to learn from their mistakes, amidst enormous difficulties, and without any former precedents or experience, trying to build up in one of the most backward countries in Europe a new human society in which the chief consideration of the State goes to those who had so far received so little of it in the past, but were at the same time the great mass of the population.

It is most essential of all that for the first time we should understand what followed immediately in Moscow on the peaceful end of our own General Strike of 1926, which entirely failed to disrupt our unity here. This was an outcome which Radek, as a world revolutionary, compared at the time in *Pravda* to the effects of a bomb for the internationalist leaders of Russia in that period. There followed at once a bitterly fierce duel between two men who were political opposites, Trotsky and Stalin. The first had lived most of his life outside Russia, engaged in building a school of world conspiracy. The other had stayed at home and fought the Tsar on his own ground, and was out to replace the old broken-down system with a new construction in Russia itself. Stalin was and is a home statesman, who will go down to history as the transformer of Russia. It is he who has armed his country against foreign aggression – a task in which Trotsky did everything to obstruct him. He sought peace because his tender young plant was bound to suffer in any new convulsion, and he offered his co-operation to those who were as much interested in peace as himself. Now he has had a terrible setback, and the work of regaining the ground lost is enough to take up the rest of his life. It is, undoubtedly, to this task that he desires to return.

The blankness of our misunderstanding of all this is one of our troubles even at the present time. Trotskyites, conscious or unconscious, are ready enough to cash in on the credit of Stalin, as brought home to us by the magnificent resistance of his people on the battlefield. They would like to assure us, just as Hitler has done, that friendship with Russia means world-revolution here on the model of 1917–21. We have to remind them of their heavy defeat and their exclusion from Russia – that it was precisely they who were the victims of those drastic purges which we now find it more easy to understand.

The engagement into which Britain and Russia have now entered should be the answer to the doubts of some of us as to Russia's attitude to the rights of smaller nationalities after the war. The question is more complex than some realise, and claims understanding. Very much as in the British Empire, there are 180-odd lesser nationalities in Russia. Stalin belongs to one of these, the Georgian, and his first official post was as Commissary for the rights of all of them. He himself was the drafter of the new federal constitution of the Union of Soviet Socialist Republics which guarantees those rights. He has discriminated carefully between the federal functions and those of the constituent units, leaving to these last a greater measure of responsibility than that of an individual State in America.

On the other hand, some of these units passed out of Russia in the complete social breakdown which followed the abdication of the Tsar, when she lost nearly everything that she had conquered since Peter the Great; and these particular units – the only ones that have engaged our close attention – are precisely those which lie between Russia and Germany, and could not be expected to defend themselves against either. In time of war they were bound to be a *glacis*, falling inevitably to the one or to the other. Some of them, Estonia and Latvia, had never been on the map of Europe as national States, until the breakdown of Russia and her absence from the Peace Settlement made their independence possible in 1918. Poland, on the other hand, had already been lost to Russia in the war, and no sensible Russian would wish to revive the old position in which a partitioned Poland was a running sore on the frontier of each of the three great pre-war empires of Eastern Europe and a constant encouragement to future wars.

I think we must bring ourselves to recognise as soon as possible that the situation of 1919 could only be temporary, that both the German and Russian peoples were bound to revive, and to renew their old rivalry, that the authority of Britain and France, which for the time seemed to extend to the frontiers of Russia, was no lasting safeguard to these smaller units, and that to attempt to link them together by paper agreements under our leadership could not alone provide a solid barrier to future German aggression. The result of some twenty years of diplomacy on these lines ended by our having to defend our own shores in 1940 with hardly a single ally in the field. If all this is realised, I see no insuperable obstacle to a lasting peace in the future. A subject Poland – or, still more unthinkably, a subject Czechoslovakia under Russian rule – could offer no possible security to Russia, and could only be an encouragement to a new German aggression. Even the neighbourhood of an independent Finland can be tolerable enough to Russia if she is so well grounded in the friendship of Britain and America as to be able to feel sure that Finland will not again become a springboard for German aggression on Leningrad. On the other hand, the smaller peoples, more than any others, can only find a lasting security in that joint guarantee which is the object of the present Anglo-Soviet agreement.

19 June 1942

THE DYNASTS IN WARTIME

Siegfried Sassoon

I may as well say at once that in my opinion those of my readers who have not read or re-read *The Dynasts* since September 1939 would be wise to do so. To the uninitiated this may appear a somewhat laborious undertaking, since its five hundred pages contain a certain amount of pedestrian writing, especially where political speeches had to be paraphrased into blank verse. On the whole, however, *The Dynasts* is by no means difficult reading. In fact, it carries one along so potently that one is liable to move too rapidly past its many beauties and profundities. I have been making the experiment myself, and the effect has been invigorating and illuminative.

Among other things, it is just as well to be reminded that what we non-combatants have endured in the last two years was unprecedented only in its mechanical concomitants. (By non-combatants I mean those of us who are obliged to sit still and think about the war instead of taking an active part in attack and defence.)

It is somehow comforting to say to oneself that Wordsworth and Jane Austen were kept awake at night by comparable anxieties in 1805 –

anxieties which impelled Wordsworth to exclaim:

'These times strike moneyed worldlings with dismay',

and resulted in the works of unwittingly immortal Miss Austen preserving a ladylike and consistent silence on the subject of Bonaparte's rampagings around Europe.

I have been wondering, by the way, how some of Hardy's poetical contemporaries would have reacted to the total international tragedy of today. Browning, Meredith and Swinburne, for instance, all of whom he deeply admired. We can be certain that Swinburne would have exerted his astonishing virtuosity in a torrent of invective against the Teutons and their leader, which wouldn't have helped us any more than his diatribes against Louis Napoleon, whom he designated 'The one most poisonous worm that soiled the world'. Browning, who was mainly a retrospective writer, would probably have stood aside and continued to do what his genius naturally dictated to him. Meredith, with his passion for freedom and his faith in the upward trend of civilised humanity, might well have been vocal, though it is difficult to imagine how his optimism could have been sustained. In a sonnet 'On the Danger of War' he described it as 'the down-slope of the lunatic'. But necessity has made lunatics of us all.

> The hunger for embranglement
> That gnaws this man has left us optionless,
> And haled us recklessly to horrid war.

I am inclined to think that Meredith's philosophic and verbal elaborations would have gone over the top of our agonised realities.

Hardy, on the other hand, would have got close to the circumstances and showings of the cataclysm, just as he did with the loss of the *Titanic* and the signing of the Armistice. His imaginative observation would have made the summer night-skies of 1940 his own in a few museful stanzas. Searchlights and the sound of aeroplanes would have been described with exactitude and sublimated by that tragic intimacy of thought and expression of which he held the secret.

Meanwhile, *The Dynasts* can help us towards a sense of proportion and perspective when we try to acclimatise and adapt our minds to the biological struggle for survival in which we are involved, seeing – as we now begin to – some sort of surmisable outline in the violent sequence of events. I am not competent to offer even a tentative opinion on the analogies between 'the First and Second German Wars' – or whatever we choose to call them – and those of the Napoleonic Period. Hardy himself, when completing his Epic-Drama in 1908, can have had no expectation that history would repeat itself in the twentieth century, or that 'The

Little Corporal' would have a claimant-successor. In presenting what he called 'The Great Historical Calamity or Clash of Peoples, artificially brought about some hundred years ago', his implied – though never stated – purpose must have been to warn us against the futility of war. Always compassionate, he clung to his hope that 'earth was bettering slowly'.

I once heard him remark – in his wistfully modest way – that had he foreknown 'The Great War' he would not have thought it worth while to write *The Dynasts*. This need not be taken as having signified anything more than a passing mood of discouragement. Anyhow, it can reasonably be asserted that there is in *The Dynasts* a timeless and unsupersedable quality which makes it illuminate the dense and elemental darkness of today. Reading it as an indirect commentary on the present world conflict, one feels more at home in the melting-pot of the Nineteen Forties and gets a glimpse of the way out of it. Certain passages can, of course, be applied appositely to our wartime conceptions of what we are fighting for and against. It is superficially consoling when we fit to our arch-enemy the words:

> Such men as thou, who wade across the world
> To make an epoch, blast, confuse, appal,
> Are in the elemental ages chart
> Like meanest insects on obscurest leaves . . .

But *The Dynasts* brings us much more than that. It is a panoramic masterpiece which shows us all in relation to our tormented chapter of history. And it encourages one to take a meteorological view of the matter. World weather is unreliable, and we happen to have struck a bad patch in the cosmic calendar.

During the summer of 1940 I several times overheard myself thinking 'How that reminds me of something in *The Dynasts*!' That something was usually an essentially countrified episode or state of affairs – something simple and permanent in the English rural scene. Not always, though. Motor buses were passing my front gate one perfect June evening. There was a noise of singing, uproarious and apparently exultant. It was the soldiers returning from Dunkirk. Hardy, I thought, would have listened attentively and made something memorable of it afterwards.

The Home Guard were immediately recognisable as prototypes of their predecessors when 'Boney' was waiting across the water. Betaking themselves at dusk to the shepherd's hut on the down for their night watch, they were – with a few exceptions – a modernised version of 'The Bang-up Locals'. I don't suggest that their conversations up on the hill were in the vernacular of Hardy's simple-minded wiseacres. The BBC had put them a long way ahead of that. But I found it plausible to infer that the sentiments they expressed could have been translated into something ancestrally related to the talk of the malt-house villagers in *Far From the Madding Crowd*. Which affords me an excuse for reporting what might have been uttered in the malt-house. 'This Hitler, I figure it,' remarked Joseph Poorgrass, 'have a brain-pan chockfull of most disrespeckful ambitions, and would dang-well destroy us and all we ever knowed, could he but find a footing on our shores.' 'Ay,' answered Smallbury, 'there be little comfort for us plain folk in such gallivanterings and goosetings about the globe. And all to no more purpose than a mampus of crazy dumbledores in an unmown meadow!'

There is an hour-glass on my table – one of those large ones which used to stand on pulpits during eighteenth-century sermons. It belonged to Thomas Hardy, and I have seen him turn it over to watch its pale-fulvous sands heap themselves to a subsiding pyramid. Englassed between slender columns of worm-holed wood, they are doing the same now. They measured the hours while Napoleon came and went. They will make their casual contribution to Chronometry when aggression has once again received its proper repayment. With which self-evident observation I will conclude . . . There is, however, something quietly Hardyish about that hour-glass.

6 February 1942

MARGINAL COMMENT

Harold Nicolson

In Odette Keun's recent book, *And Hell Followed*, there is a passage which is strange and welcome to me as coming from one who in the past has been so angry, and even rude, about the imprecisions of the English character. 'I do not,' she writes, 'envy Britain – or any other country – anything; no race in the world seems to me worthy of provoking pride; no people lives up to my notion of civilised man. But I wish – yes, I wish – that I could call the RAF mine.' She is writing, of course, about the Battle of Britain, about those anxious days when our fighters traced gigantic question-marks against the sky, and when we watching below them became day by day more fired with the wild surmise that victory had been won. Since then the RAF have gained other laurels and struck mightier blows. Yet none of their many episodes and adventures has filled me with such elation as Flight-Lieutenant Gatward's recent visit to Paris. The account which he himself gave of this expedition was a masterpiece of modest glee. I listened entranced. And next day I read the whole story again in the newspaper *France*, which printed every word he said. I found that to read his talk in French gave it an added significance, partly because one was conscious how deeply it would move the homesick exiles and partly because the French words brought out the extreme 'Englishness' of Lieutenant Gatward's story. He told us how he and Sergeant Ferns had hedge-hopped across France, flying so low that their photographs showed the surprised eyes of horses grazing in the fields below. '*Nous n'avons pas,*' continues the French text, '*trop dérangé ces chevaux, ni le bétail.*' This phrase had not struck me particularly when I heard it on the wireless; but when repeated in the mirror of the French language, how English it seems, how gentle!

For what more delicate gesture could an airman conceive than to risk his life in dropping the flag of France upon the Arc de Triomphe? I like to feel that this story has been read by every French exile, and that the whisper of it has spread mirth and wonder throughout occupied France. Assuredly this dramatic act will not be wasted; there was something more significant and important in the flight than anything that the RAF themselves might call 'shooting a line'; to us it seems a gay piece of daring; to the French it will mean more than this, for they understand to the full the meaning of the word *panache*. This, so he informed us, was Flight-Lieutenant Gatward's first visit to Paris; it lasted only six minutes. I share his hope that at some future date he will be able to revisit the scenes of his exploit with 'his two feet upon the ground'. The windows of the Ministry of Marine which he shattered will by then have been repaired, and the lovely house which Gabriel built will have returned to its lawful owners. He will be able to see from the ground the Orangery in the Tuileries Gardens, the sole remnant of the former palace, which in those fantastic minutes he photographed excitedly before wheeling to swoop upon the Place de la Concorde. And the streets, which seemed to him so tragically denuded, will once again echo to the traffic of the finest city in the world.

26 June 1942

OUR FUTURE HOMES

Jacquetta Hawkes

The Land and Planning. By F.J. Osborn. (Faber. 1s.)
Planning and the Countryside. Edited by F.J. Osborn. (Faber. 1s.)
New Towns after the War. By F.J. Osborn. (Dent. 4s. 6d.)
Living in Cities. By Ralph Tubbs. (Penguin. 1s.)

These four booklets, so modest and slender in appearance, expose with
shocking clarity the obstructions and conflicts which still make the field
of physical reconstruction look more like a battleground than a building
site. The first pamphlet lays bare the particularly baffling obstacles
represented by the words 'compensation and betterment'. Proper control
of the land is, of course, a first essential, without which all extensive
planning schemes are likely to be wrecked. Unfortunately, the host of
private individuals who in one way or another control a large proportion
of our acres are not all so thoroughly deserving of retribution as in our
most black-and-white moods we like to picture them, nor can their
claims to compensation when their possession is threatened be wholly
ignored without ill-effects on the community at large. The hope that
individuals whose holdings were bettered by public development could
be made to help compensate those who suffered from it has proved
largely illusory. It is so easy for one man to show that he has been
unjustly robbed of his fair profits, so difficult to convince another that he
has got more than he deserves. It seems, in fact, that the collection of
'betterment' dues will never meet more than a small fraction of the
claims for compensation. Yet the ill-used private owner must have some
recompense, even though it might well be rather less generous than Mr
Osborn suggests, and the best ways and means must be decided in
advance.

It is perhaps still more disquieting to recognise that even were these
technical obstructions removed tomorrow and the land made free for
national planning, it would be found that there is no agreed master-
scheme to inspire it. What kind of mould do we wish to construct for the
reception of the molten mass of a demobilising population? The
remaining three books well represent two great factions opposed on this

all-important issue. Mr Osborn is well known as a seasoned leader of the Garden City movement, while for Mr Tubbs such places are only 'little patches of suburbia'. The conflict between them is whether the main effort of national reconstruction is to be directed towards a revolutionary reconstitution of existing great cities or towards a large-scale dispersal of the population from these old centres into new small towns, and, granted that at least a few new towns are desirable, whether they should be sister Welwyns or small cities truly urban in design.

There is no question that Mr Osborn burkes the problem of what to do with the existing wens, those obtrusive memorials of an age of *laissez faire*. If, as he suggests, five million people are decanted into new centres there will hardly be resources left for essential renovations to the towns that have already spread concrete over so many square miles of our country. There is a strong case for concentrating effort on these areas: on reclaiming wasted spaces within the cities, on raising lofty commercial premises, rationalising the siting of factories and laying out residential areas in a true urban pattern. Terraces, squares and crescents for those who want houses, imaginatively planned blocks for those whose needs are better served by flats.

During the eighteenth and early nineteenth centuries we had a distinguished tradition of urban architecture, aesthetically delightful, admirably suited to the national needs and temperament. What Nash and his predecessors could do in their manner and with their materials we can translate into modern terms. Many believe that this conception is as sound for the planning of small towns as for great cities. If it is harsh to refer to Garden Cities as 'patches of suburbia' when they are in fact decently laid out and provided with amenities, it is equally wrong to try to damn flats by referring to them as tenements, to encourage in-dividualistic houses at the expense of street design and to think always of the number of heads per acre rather than of the open spaces which modern planning can provide even where population is dense. If we are to be obsessed with the 'everyman his house and potting-shed' view of life, it is likely that we shall waste more of our limited countryside, neglect existing cities, and fail to provide the proper mould to give form and dignity to urban living.

26 June 1942

POLITICS AND THE PUBLIC

Jennie Lee

I wish something could be done to narrow the gap between what politicians say and what they do. I don't make that remark querulously. It is a very serious matter. There are millions of people in present-day Britain who, for the first time in their lives, are taking an interest in public affairs. They are trying to understand what the various political parties and their spokesmen stand for.

But this is not easy. For almost everyone in public life talks the same generalised blah-blah. All tell us we are fighting a People's war for a People's peace. All talk of post-war planning and reconstruction. All promise a new world order in which the economic inequalities of the past, if not entirely eliminated, will certainly be vastly reduced.

What are we to make of all this talk? If we could accept it at its surface value we could go about our wartime tasks in a state of subdued excitement and contentment. But it would be nonsense to say that that was the present mood. We are dubious, sceptical, unconvinced. Most political pronouncements, especially vaguely idealistic ones about after the war, leave us with a feeling that we are walking on mush.

I have a great respect for men and women in public life who use language that is concrete and particular. They are the true democrats. Whether Tory, Liberal or Socialist, by saying clearly and unequivocally what is in their minds, they behave towards their fellows seriously and honourably. They create the kind of atmosphere in which democratic government can flourish.

It is the furtive, evasive type of politician who does the mischief. By perpetually trying to appear to agree with everyone he serves no one. He makes democratic institutions farcical. And he is impertinent. He assumes that we, the electorate, are children, imbeciles, irresponsibles who have to be humoured, cajoled, even downright lied to in order to keep us placid and compliant.

The duty of a public representative, as I understand it, is something quite different. It is to give us his point of view and his reasons for holding it. Other representatives with conflicting viewpoints then have their say. The clash of opinions and the arguments advanced in support of each is the means by which the public is put in possession of the facts.

There you have the groundwork of a vigorous, effective democracy. But it is happening less and less that way. It becomes progressively more difficult to know what is really going on. The party machines are co-operating to create a political paradise for the storm-trooper type of representative who fears responsibility and is happy only when shelter-ing behind the coat-tails of his party führers. Decisions are being made not in open debate on the floor of the House of Commons, but behind closed committee-room doors in a hush-hush unwholesome atmosphere.

I instance the recent coal debate. There could be no plainer example of this disquieting trend towards government by caucus and conspiracy. By the time the issue reached the floor of the House some hundreds of Members of Parliament were forced to vote contrary to their private con-victions. They were forced to perjure themselves. Men who believed that the coal-pits ought to be nationalised and nationalised now, not after the war, failed to state their real point of view and failed to vote in accordance with their convictions.

Why did they behave in this way? I am not arguing for the moment the case for or against the immediate nationalisation of the coal mines. All I am saying is that a considerable number of MPs who believed that imme-diate nationalisation was the wisest policy both for meeting wartime pro-duction problems and for making a beginning to solving the post-war problems the mining industry will have to face, gave no indication in the debates nor in the division lobbies that such was their point of view.

Their party chiefs forbade them. National unity, it was alleged, could not stand the strain. National unity apparently can stand the strain of legislation that does not necessarily meet the views of a majority of the community, but it cannot stand the strain of offending the coalowners of Britain.

The reflection on the coalowners is a serious one, and I, who have attacked them all my life, in this instance come to their defence. I refuse to believe that if the Parliament of Britain after a free discussion and a free vote had decided to nationalise the mines, British coalowners would then have become Quislings. No doubt they would have heartily disliked the decision just as many others of us heartily dislike the present controls and management of the industry. But we don't stop fighting Hit-ler because we don't get all our own way in domestic legislation. Nor would the coalowners have behaved less well. They would have had to acquiesce.

I am not, of course, assuming that in a free discussion and vote nationalisation would necessarily or even probably have been carried. But MPs would have had to stand on their own feet, make their own decisions, vote as their mind and conscience dictated. The eager, forward-driving, experimental mood that you find in the rest of the country would have had its legitimate reflection in the Houses of Parliament.

No country in the world has a steadier, more responsible population than Great Britain. It is sheer fiction to suggest that it is necessary for the party chiefs to conspire to prevent free discussion and voting on issues of this kind that would in no sense weaken the resolve that you and I and all the rest of us have taken, unitedly, to maintain the military front.

In May 1940, when the National Government was formed, the leaders of the Tory, Liberal and Labour Parties reached a standstill agreement. But if there is one thing that public opinion has NOT done between then and now it is to stand still. There has been a marked leftward swing. The *blitz* months began it. They taught us to value property less and people more. They taught us that if we were left alive after a night of terror, with those dearest to us still around us, we were millionaires. They taught us that all the material possessions in the world counted for nothing against loss of family, of friends, of neighbours. We wanted to do something to enshrine that new attitude. In those days we set high standards for ourselves. Two years later we know we have not yet fulfilled those standards. That is the dichotomy that goes right to the heart of the present mood. Nor does talk of all the fine things we may or may not do at some unspecified time in the future assuage present discontents. Rather such talk is an added source of irritation. It is a breeding ground for cynicism. Ours is not a nation of morons. We know quite well that we are capable of greater competence, generosity, fair dealing between man and man, than wartime legislation has as yet caught up with. We know equally well the difference between social and economic changes that can come only when the shooting war is over and those that would be doubly effective if put into operation here and now.

The people I meet may be unrepresentative. I don't think they are. At any rate, they come from all parts of the country, every kind of occupation and income level. If I am to risk generalising about their attitude to public affairs, I would say that most of them don't want to be Conservatives, but they have no faith in the Labour Party and don't know where to look for leadership. The Liberal Party they regard as an historical hangover, the Communist Party as solely the instrument of Soviet foreign policy, the Independent Labour Party as cancelled out of reality by its anti-war stand.

Where is this restive, unanchored, leftward tending public opinion to come to rest? It is too numerous to be ignored. And it is in no mood to be trifled with. It is deeply serious and less and less disposed to be tolerant of mere party hacks among public representatives. There are great possibilities in the present situation, but also great dangers. Disastrous military news sharpens the public demand to be told the truth about what is happening, why it has happened, and what can and is being done to improve matters. Meeting this mood involves certain risks. But to thwart it, political leaders taking refuge behind the need to prevent the enemy benefiting by some of the information disclosed, is to court disaster. Rumour, scandal, disgruntlement then have the field to themselves. Nothing could be worse than that.

This country has been nurtured in a tradition of free discussion and independent thought. We are by no means a perfect democracy, but the passion to be treated as responsible citizens whose point of view must be consulted and considered has taken too deep a hold on too many of us for it to be safe for any national leader or combination of leaders to try to belittle it. It is no use trying to lead us into battle with blinkers on. They worry us and anger us. They most certainly don't steady us.

In a time of mortal crisis a people must try to be its own best self, not a crude ineffective imitation of the thing it is fighting against.

10 July 1942

THE FORGOTTEN PARENT

Roger Clarke

At last the educational reformers have got the ball at their feet. Everyone seems agreed that the school-leaving age must be raised after the war; everyone seems agreed that there must be more physical training and more instruction in leadership; everyone seems agreed that there must be an extension of the provision of school meals, school medical services and the rest of it. Doubt exists about the scale and pace of these reforms, but about their desirability no body from the House of Lords to the Labour Party, nobody from the President of the Board of Education to the lowliest class-teacher seems to have any doubt at all. Nobody except the average parent. The ordinary working-class mother and father of children in elementary schools have not been consulted about all this. Probably they would be inarticulate if they were to be consulted, yet it is fairly certain that their attitude would not be favourable to the reforms.

We have all forgotten – we the intellectuals, the reformers, the com-
mittee-members, the administrators, the teachers – that compulsory
education involves compulsion. Parents are compelled to send their children to school, all their children from the age of five to fourteen – a longer
period of compulsion than that enforced in any other European country.
In the vast majority of cases they are compelled to sent them to the
'Council' school and to one particular Council school, the nearest. It may
be a school in which the teacher is untrained or even incompetent, the
conditions insanitary or even vicious, the equipment inadequate or even
dangerous, the discipline repressive or even cruel. No matter; the parent
must send her child on pain of the penalties of the law (her child, because
in working-class families it is the mother rather than the father who is
concerned with the children's education). For middle- and upper-class
parents, of course, the wind of compulsion is tempered. They have choice
of school, and if they decide not to send their child to school at all their
competence to educate him at home is usually recognised. But the working-class parent has no such privileges. If she thinks the influence of the
nearest Council school to be bad, her only alternatives are to move house
to the vicinity of a better school or to send her children a long journey
every day. The working-class parents are compelled. They must send
their children to a school over which they have no direct and no effective
indirect control, to be educated on lines with which they disagree and for
ends of which they have no comprehension.

This does not mean that the average parent is in revolt against the school
system. She is glad to have the child out of the house and off her hands.
But she resents both the compulsion and the system, and her resentment
shows itself in the attitude of parents as a whole towards teachers as a
whole. Everyone who is in contact with the working class notices the
jealousy of teachers' long holidays, of their high pay and of their airs of
superiority. Working-class parents are glad for their children to become
teachers – it is the quickest way out of the working class – but they resent
and to some extent despise teachers all the same. The root of resentment
lies in the fact of compulsion and in the complete divorce between the
ideals of the parents and those of the teaching profession.

Parents' resentment of teachers is exactly balanced by teachers'
resentment of parents. To the average elementary-school teacher the
parents of their pupils are a nuisance and a disgrace: ignorant, selfish,
benighted beings with no sense of social values, no ideals, no dis-
interestedness, anxious only to get their children a training which will
enable them to earn more money. In any gathering of teachers you will
hear complaints of parents – their fecklessness, their unreasonableness,

their failure to keep their children clean and punctual. The teachers would like to control the feeding, dressing, hygiene, health and sometimes the religion of the children, as well as their class-teaching. For all the extra work it lays on them, they welcome the provision of school milk, of school uniforms, of school dentistry and of Youth Clubs. The parents would prefer to have the milk delivered to their homes, the clothing-provision made in the form of money to be spent on boots and coats of their own choice, the dentistry put on a panel system which would give them choice of practitioner. Most of them accept what benefits are offered, but they resent them; and being working-class parents their resentment is inarticulate.

How is the barrier between parents and teachers to be broken down? The first move should surely come from the teachers. Their superior education and their professional position alike demand that they should make the overtures. They must go out of their way to recognise that it is the parents, not the teachers, who are primarily responsible for the children. They must consult them, collectively as well as individually. In every elementary school there should be a Parents' Conference, meeting, say, one evening a month to discuss the affairs of the school, and holding regular consultations with the authorities, school-managers and teachers. The profession might look on this as a way of educating the parents; the parents would certainly look on it as a way of educating the profession. Once the barriers were down, the way would be open to educational progress along the lines of true democratic community.

Do I exaggerate the barriers? The class distinction between parents and elementary-school teachers is as sharp as any in our class-ridden society. Though they come from the same homes, the teachers regard themselves as members of a higher class than the parents. In a way they have been taught to regard themselves so. They have been segregated from the mass of the working class ever since they went to a secondary school, probably at the age of eleven. When they left the secondary school they went to 'college', usually to a training college, where everyone was preparing to be a teacher. The training college is the opposite of a university; universality is absent; the future teachers meet no students in other faculties, no research-students, no foreigners, often no member of the opposite sex. When they take up their first appointments they are already accustomed to wearing blinkers which many of them retain for the rest of their lives. If the first move must be towards parents' conferences and parents' councils, the second must be towards the liberalising of teachers' training, perhaps through the transformation of training colleges into departments of universities and technical institutes.

*

But there is a third step to be taken, a step which involves not so much organisational change as sheer straight thinking on first principles. The present trend in education is all towards totalitarianism. Reformers want the leaving-age to be raised; they want compulsory powers first, after which they will begin to think how to use them and towards what end. They would no doubt like compulsory school feeding, compulsory school dressing, compulsory school dentistry and diphtheria-immunisation. Already there is talk of compulsory religious instruction (quite undenominational, quite undogmatic, of course) and of compulsory inculcation of a 'sense of social purpose'. The totalitarian trend is most obvious in the new Youth Movement which is growing at such a pace, especially in certain rural and semi-rural districts. The idea is to enrol adolescents in clubs. Hundreds of Youth Organisers (ominous title!) have been appointed already. Some authorities look forward frankly to the day when every adolescent will be enrolled in a Youth Club. But nobody has decided in what direction the movement is to move.

The definition of purpose with which most reformers and authorities would agree is, perhaps, the following: 'We shall first care for the physical side. Our second task is the forming of character and the implanting of a feeling of responsibility and duty. Through the youth we will shape a new generation ready, if necessary, to defend the country in arms. The third task will be to instil knowledge.' (The definition is that given by Stang, a Nazi Youth Minister.) Education may be moving towards equality, but liberty is being lost in the process and the totalitarian trend is obvious.

Working-class parents know all this, and the knowledge lies behind their resistance to so many contemporary reforms. Give us milk in our homes, they say; we know how to use it to the best advantage of our children. Give us money to feed the children properly, then you won't need to pull out so many teeth. Give us decent houses and gardens and a bit more leisure, then you won't need a Youth Movement to get the adolescents off the street-corners. Give our men the prospect of good jobs, then we won't want to take our children away from school early so as to get some of their earnings for housekeeping money. All you are doing with your educational reforms, with your compulsory this and semi-compulsory that, is to patch up the holes in your rotten social system. You treat the symptoms and neglect the disease.

The forgotten parent must be remembered if we are to get any straight thinking on the aims apart from the methods of education. Granted the parent is selfish, granted she is ignorant, granted her vision is as unsocial as that of the lioness-with-cubs; the fact still remains that there must be a balance between the claim of the parent who thinks of the child as a member of the family and of the educationist who thinks of him as a member of the State. At present the scales are weighted on the side of the State. In this third year of war against Fascism we are laying up for ourselves a totalitarian future in education.

17 July 1942

PRISONERS AND CAPTIVES

Eiluned Lewis

One of the petitions of the Litany gathers together a small company of oddly assorted people, bound to each other by their common peril. *All that travel by land or by water, all women labouring of child, all sick persons and young children.* And then, a little apart from this group, asking not for safety but only for pity, the company of *all prisoners and captives.*

There they stand, the Elizabethan travellers in doublet and hose, looking to their weapons before mounting their horses, or stepping aboard their galleons with every prospect of scurvy, shipwrecks, pirates and maroonings; sick people awaiting the ministrations of the barber-surgeon; little children in stiff ruffs and farthingales, and women facing the fierce pains of childbirth without anaesthetics. But it is when we turn to the prisoners and captives that the scene darkens. Damp, ague-ridden straw, and in the half-darkness the shape of the rack; the fear of being forgotten in the lair of an Algerine pirate; the livelier fear of being remembered by the Inquisition of Spain.

Time was, when we were young, that the grim prisons of the past seemed quaint anachronisms. We were taken to see them on fine Saturday afternoons (children half-price), and no doubt our elders, as they jerked their way back through the turnstiles into the pleasant light of day, were soberly thankful that such things had ceased to be. Now night has fallen again on lost mankind, and thinking of the vast, unreckoned number of captives the world over, we ask if they are all the more in need of God's pity and such help as sinful man can devise. Families and friends of prisoners of war can take comfort in knowing that conditions in the camps are still ordered by military convention and observe the decencies of agreed international treatment. The enemy, one suspects, is more within than without; the sense of futility, the nightmare Life-in-Death, is the fear that looks over each prisoner's shoulder.

That the spirit can triumph over captivity we know. The most poignant of St Paul's epistles were written from his Roman prison; the visions of a tinsmith in Bedford Gaol have been translated into more than a hundred languages, and the gayest book in the world came into the head of a man chained to a bench in a stinking pirate ship. Was there something common to the condition of all three that fostered their genius? It is possible, even probable, that in these tragic years some saint, poet or wit, concealed as Prisoner of War, No. 4321, is sharpening the sword of his spirit.

One of the manifold duties of the Red Cross is to see that the minds of our prisoners are kept from rotting, and that whether a man be tinsmith, poet, or both at once, the right books reach him in his camp. Quite a number of them are the tinsmith's lineal descendants, the engineers and metallurgists of today. But the list of subjects studied comprises the whole scale of human activity: physics and diamond-boring, jute manufactures and Old Provençal, campanology and orchestration, shipping and paper-making – it covers sheets of foolscap, this catalogue of things that a man would like to be doing.

From small beginnings and by way of countless obstacles, the scheme has grown and developed, and now the blue official forms and the parcels of books have become a bridge joining the prisoners to the world they have left behind. For the time being they seem dwellers on another planet, and we are surprised to find them studying hotel-keeping and advertising, just as we should be if we discovered these occupations among the Martians. There is a Stalag in Germany which boasts an English school with a syllabus of sixty-three subjects, ranging from Diesel engineering to music and first-aid. Are patience and fortitude in the list, one wonders, or are these compulsory subjects which each man must learn for himself? One of the Oflags has a university divided into six faculties, and holds classes in twenty-two languages, including Albanian and Tamil. By grace of various educational authorities on our side of the bridge, examinations can now be held in the camps, with properly appointed invigilators. Special papers in Malay and Chinese have recently been set up by the School of Oriental Languages.

Most men are eager to pursue the callings they followed in civil life. An Australian captured in Crete wants to study the design of clothes, and another man asks for a handbook on boxing. On the other hand, who among us would dare label as escapist the ship's-stoker who wishes to take up pig-farming, the infantryman with a taste for hieroglyphics, and the man, requesting books on gardening and general knowledge, who adds, 'Don't send me a book on humour. I get plenty here'?

Almost one thinks of them sometimes with envy as the only people in the world today with leisure to study. Perhaps it is true to say that their lives are simplified, but there ends their advantage. Even leisure, it seems, is scarcely in the day's routine, and there are difficulties, such as delay in the arrival of books, shortage of paper and overcrowding. It is not easy to concentrate in a room containing forty men. Then with the shortening days come lengthening cares, for light is precious, and when daylight fades on the glimmering page the differential equation, the orchestral score, and the intricacies of pig-farming look very much the same. This is a blackout which we in this country have not yet contemplated, when five o'clock may ring down the curtain on knowledge, and only thought be left. What do they think about then?

> If I have freedom in my love
> And in my soul am free,
> Angels alone, that soar above
> Enjoy such liberty

sang the Cavalier poet behind the bars of his gaol. Perhaps in the end it is the prisoners and captives who will be best equipped to carve out the new world, but we must see to it now that they are furnished with the right tools.

31 July 1942

MARGINAL COMMENT

Harold Nicolson

It is time that those of us who have hitherto regarded General de Gaulle with admiration but perplexity should clear our minds. Our admiration for his military qualities has always been unstinted. The young lieutenant who was three times wounded in the last war, who fought so valiantly at Douaumont, became during the interlude between the two German wars the prophet of mechanised strategy, a prophet who was without due honour in his own country. His books, and especially his prophetic vol-

ume *Vers l'Armée de Métier*, were carefully studied in Germany, but pronounced 'dangerous' by the French General Staff. As commander of the
fourth armoured division he won a dashing victory over the Germans on
June 2nd, 1940, when he penetrated their columns to a distance of fourteen miles. Appointed Under Secretary for War at the very moment of
disaster, he refused to share either the panic of Tours or the capitulation
of Bordeaux. At the time when the people of France were stunned by
defeat a resolute voice spoke to them upon the ether. On June 18th, 1940,
late at night, those who in shame and in despair turned to the British
wireless for hope heard the resonant words: 'It is I, General de Gaulle,
who am speaking to you from London.' 'Today,' he said, 'we are overwhelmed by mechanical force: tomorrow we can conquer by superior
mechanical force; therein lies the destiny of the world.' We realise today
that these words were no rhetorical gestures flung upon the air to comfort a defeated people; they were words of prophecy. We realise today
that it was no idle boast on the part of General de Gaulle that he and
those who joined him were the saviours of France's honour and the van-
guard of France's resurrection. We realise that in the twenty-six months
which have passed since he issued his call to arms he has become not
merely the symbol of hope but the organiser of power. Many people
know today that General de Gaulle commands an army of trained fighting men; that there are many hundred French airmen under the direction
of General Valin; that the Fighting French Navy contains many valuable
vessels of war; and that the Free French Merchant Marine helps the common cause with more than one hundred ships. But how many people are
aware that today territories of the French Colonial Empire representing
an area fifteen times the size of Great Britain have hoisted the cross of
Lorraine? General de Gaulle's attitude in June 1940 was one of supreme
moral courage; he has shown since then that he also possesses great
organising capacity.

Yet we were perplexed at first and hesitant; it has taken us two years to
understand General de Gaulle. Our democratic prejudice against all
soldier-politicians led us to wish that General de Gaulle would confine
himself to purely military matters and would not aspire to the role of a
political leader. We see today that this leadership was thrust upon him,
and that had he remained no more than the officer commanding the
French volunteers his representative function would have been diminished. We regretted that he should be so difficult, so unaccommodating,
so authoritative; we see today that unless he had asserted himself in season and out of season he would have become no more than a foreign officer in the pay of the British Treasury. We distrusted those by whom he

was at first surrounded, and disliked the methods which on occasions they pursued. We realise now that he was bound to improvise his National Committee, and that today it is composed of men whom all can respect. We were hurt by the emphasis which he placed upon his own independence, attributing his criticism of our methods to some dislike of English ways; we see now that his determination to remain essentially and combatively French was a wise determination, and that when he returns he will not return in the baggage of the Allies. Had de Gaulle sought always to be convenient he would have ended by being ignored; the force of his personality, highly inconvenient though it has proved at moments, renders it impossible that either he or France can ever be disregarded. The fears that we once entertained lest he might on his return establish some military dictatorship have been dissipated by his own utterances and by the wider composition which he is now seeking to give to his National Committee. We see today that the apparent arrogance of his person embodies and defends the wounded pride of France; and in his faithful ruminative eyes is reflected the eternal patience of her wisdom.

14 August 1942

A SPECTATOR'S NOTEBOOK

Clusius (Rose Macaulay)

It would be interesting to know the real motives of those diehards who object to compulsory fire-fighting for women. A variety of odd reasons are trotted out, none of which seems valid. It is dangerous, say the aldermen and others. But why not? Is there any reason why women should not be exposed to as much danger as men? To think this is, surely, 'thinking with the blood', i.e. with feeling divorced from reason. Women are not soldiers because, generally speaking, they would not make nearly such good soldiers as men, being less physically and nervously tough. For the same reasons, they are not miners, navvies, firemen, hard labourers, or anything else that requires tremendous physical strength and stamina. Most of them would probably crock up and go sick after a few weeks' hard campaigning. This does not apply to fire-fighting, which, in fact, very many women are already doing, with no ill results. There is absolutely no reason, as Miss Ellen Wilkinson points out, why women should not face the same dangers from bombs and fire as men. Then, say the aldermen, there are moral dangers. These are unspecified; but, whatever they may be, should not women face them with the same intrepidity as men? And are they, as a sex, more likely to be overthrown by them? History and experience do not so indicate. It is a pity that people will not cease from talking nonsense on important subjects.

2 October 1942

ALL YE THAT PASS BY

Mrs Edgar Dugdale

In March 1942, Himmler visited Poland, and decreed that by the end of this year 50 per cent of the Jewish population should be 'exterminated' – in plain English, put to death – and the pace seems to have been hastened since. Now the German programme demands the disappearance of all Jews, men, women and children, natives of occupied Poland or deportees from Western or Central Europe. Mass-murders on a scale unheard-of since the dawn of civilisation began immediately after the order was issued. At first the details of these were hardly believed, even in quarters capable of judging the reliability of the news that percolated from behind the dreadul barriers of the 'sealed ghettos' all over the country. But the accounts were confirmed again and again, and it became evident to those who received them that the German genius for organisation was being applied methodically to the slaughter of Jews. Nevertheless, it was not until the Gestapo Chief reviewed the results in person this summer that Nazi efficiency reached its peak. The exact date of highest achievement, in the Warsaw ghetto, the biggest of all, was July 24th, 1942, when ten thousand Jews were assembled for so-called deportation. The curve then declined for some time to seven thousand a day. By September 1st some 250,000 people had disappeared. For that month 120,000 Jewish ration-cards were distributed in the Warsaw ghetto (entitling the possessor to a pound of bread per week and very little else). For October only 40,000 such cards were deemed necessary. Now the Warsaw 'deportations' sink as low as three thousand persons in a day. Before I go on to give an idea of what happens to them, the origins of these appalling reports must be named. There is a spontaneous reaction against 'atrocity-stories' and a desire to believe them exaggerated, which is rooted as much in the healthier forms of incredulity as in the instinct to spare oneself pain. But my facts and figures are quoted primarily from documents issued by the Polish Ministry of Information in London dated December 1st.

If support were needed it could be found in a speech delivered recently in New York by Dr Stephen Wise, the well-known Jewish leader, based on information given him by the State Department in Washington. No room seems to be left for doubting the reports, tallying as they do with things known to responsible Jewish bodies in the Allied countries. The facts do indeed surpass imagination. Here is one sample from the Polish Government Report. It describes what happens after the daily quota of victims has been assembled at the clearing-stations. They are carried off to death with the 'maximum of suffering'. A hundred people of both sexes and all ages are packed into trucks that would hold forty and the floors covered with unslaked lime. To enhance the effect of this, the deportees may be ordered to take off their boots. The trucks are sealed before they are started on their journey to the camps of execution at Belzec, Sobibor and Treblinka, places east of Warsaw. There the Polish peasantry can hardly endure the continual stench of putrefying flesh, for when the trucks are opened they reveal a mass of the dead and dying, standing upright for lack of room to fall down. Those who still breathe are shot, electrocuted or gassed. The Germans do their butchery assisted by Ukrainian, Lithuanian and Latvian Fascists, but they do not attempt to use the Polish police even for rounding-up the victims.

These things have been happening all through this November of cheerful memory. They are happening now. Scepticism cannot much longer serve as excuse for inaction, as the burden of providing proof shifts from those who believe that such crimes are being committed to those who refuse credence. So the question arises of what to do, or rather of whether there is anything that can be done while the war lasts. Certain it seems that Polish Jewry will be beyond help if the murder-campaign cannot be stopped before the war ends. But the spectre of defeat may already be lying in wait for the German people. Now is the time to enlist its help, for the argument of fear is one which Germans understand more than most.

The United Nations have sworn to exact full retribution for war crimes. Let them now repeat the pledge with specific reference to the Jews in occupied countries, and so remove any possible idea that atrocities against Jews will be punished less severely than those against peoples who are not in a minority everywhere. The Polish Government have given a lead in their efforts to secure publicity for facts, and this honour is rightly theirs, for the Jews in German-occupied Poland are their citizens or deportees within their borders. But it would be a shameful thing if the British Government, Parliament and nation were to remain supine or mere critics of what others try to do on behalf of tortured people. The German system is not in full operation in every country under German influence. The jaws of the trap are not closed everywhere – at any rate not yet. We know now what will happen if, or when, they shut, and that knowledge lays a heavy responsibility on the Governments and nations who have it in their power to provide refuge. The Jewish communities in the free countries are willing and able to carry the financial burden of the old, the sick and the children. Palestine has an acute labour-shortage due to its contribution to the war-effort. But Palestine is not the only place within the British Empire where safety awaits those who succeed in escaping. Men who do not open doors to those who are hunted by murderers participate in the crime.

11 December 1942

BEVERIDGE AFTERTHOUGHTS

(A Leading Article)

It is rather more than a fortnight since the Beveridge Report was published. In that interval the report has almost eclipsed the war itself as a subject of discussion in the country; it has been keenly debated by British troops overseas, and in the Dominions and the United States it has markedly increased the prestige of Britain as indicating an imaginative and courageous attempt to grapple, even in the midst of such a conflict as this, with those problems of social security which, so formidable before the war, may be even more formidable after it. Meanwhile the Government has the scheme under consideration, and it will be debated in the House of Commons after Christmas. That is, of course, most necessary and desirable. But it is no less necessary and no less desirable that everywhere where concern for the betterment of social conditions in Great Britain prevails discussion among the ordinary citizens whom it affects should be initiated. A letter printed in another column purports to give news of the first local group formed to study the Beveridge Report systematically. That is an example that should be widely followed. The report costs no more than two shillings, and there could be no better school of citizenship than its three hundred pages provide. Time devoted to study and discussion of the problems it raises would not be wasted even if no single one of the solutions Sir William Beveridge proposes ever materialised. For, if these solutions are not adopted, some others must be. Criticism of the scheme should be welcomed undisguisedly, provided always that it is constructive, and directed towards demonstrating not only where the Beveridge proposals are wrong, but how they can be improved on.

The discussions so far engaged in have brought various misapprehensions to light. One Labour MP has complained with some bitterness that this is not the pure gospel of Socialism. It is not. It would commend itself much less to many people if it were. But it resembles so closely what the Labour Party has constantly demanded in the past that expressions of dissatisfaction with the scheme come a little oddly from that quarter. Elsewhere Sir William is criticised for basing his proposals on the assumption that unemployment will somehow be kept in hand (not abolished) and making no attempt to show how that can be done. On that it may be observed that if any man in the country is capable of indicating methods of coping with the unemployment problem it is the author of what is still the standard work on the subject. But to complain that Sir William Beveridge, given a specific, searching and comprehensive task by the Government, did not on his own account shoulder another not less comprehensive that lay completely outside his terms of reference is less than reasonable. There is nothing in those terms about schemes to avert unemployment, and the comment that the Beveridge scheme will only work if unemployment is abolished, and in that case will not be needed, is simply a facile and completely unsubstantial attempt at epigram. The degree of unemployment will, of course, affect the finance of the scheme, as it has always affected the finance of the existing Assistance Board. The actual figures suggested by Sir William are based on the assumption of an average total of 1,500,000 unemployed. That may argue optimism or pessimism. It certainly does not argue blindness to the problem.

All the Beveridge figures, of course, are tentative, and it is nowhere suggested that the scheme must be either taken as it stands or sidetracked altogether. What Sir William has done is to produce a plan for putting the population out of the reach of want. If there is no sufficient desire to achieve that elementary reform or if it is found that to achieve it would involve expenditure which, by reacting on our internal and external trade, would actually create more evils than it cured, then we shall have to be content with a more modest advance than Sir William has inspired us to attempt. Parts of his scheme could be postponed for the present, or indefinitely – such, for example, as the proposals for a comprehensive national health service. Here, as elsewhere, strange misunderstandings seem to exist. Sir William Beveridge, someone has written, has promised free and equal treatment for all without consulting the doctors. On that it may be observed first, that the doctors through the Planning Committee of the British Medical Association, have proposed something very like this themselves, and secondly that Sir William, of course, has in fact promised nothing to anybody. It was no part of his business to promise anything. All he was asked to do was to consider how certain schemes of social insurance are at present working, and suggest any possible improvements. That he has done, in a document that can already be termed historic. With regard to the details of any plan for a national health service, he specifically expresses the view that they should be worked out by the Department, presumably the Ministry of Health, concerned with the health of the people. The importance of such a scheme, if only on hard financial grounds, is sufficiently demonstrated by the statement made by Sir Farquhar Buzzard in last week's *Spectator* that sickness and disability is at present costing the country some £3,000,000 a year.

But to recognise that everything in the Beveridge plan is open to discussion and revision does not mean that the plan can be simply shelved. Certain features of it could, no doubt, be dropped but certain others must by general consent be adopted. Families are going hungry today because there are more children than the wage-earner can support adequately. No part of the new plan has been hailed with more enthusiasm than the proposed provision of family allowances. That part of the Beveridge scheme will inevitably materialise, though not necessarily in the precise form, or on the basis of the precise figures, recommended there. Old age pensions, again, will unquestionably have to be increased. There is no more pathetic figure in the community today than the man or woman of over 70 struggling to maintain life somehow on a maximum figure of 19s. 6d. a week, subject to a means test, against the 24s. to 25s. which the most experienced authorities regard as the minimum necessary for subsistence. Our responsibilities to that section of the community are not to be ignored. As regards medical treatment, again, steps will indisputably have to be taken in the direction of the goal which the Beveridge plan contemplates. In the article already quoted Sir Farquhar Buzzard recalled the promises made by the Minister of Health regarding co-ordination of the hospital system of the country, and added that under the Regional

Hospital Scheme which the Nuffield Trust has been working out it was found essential to include private practitioners. It is only necessary to add that an immense load would be lifted not only from workers' but from middle-class families if the immensely expensive surgical or institutional treatment to which they may have to have recourse at any moment were made available under such a comprehensive insurance scheme as the Beveridge Report has proposed.

It may well be that here, as so often in life, what we want we cannot have. It would be absurd to disregard the financial aspect of the question or treat it as subordinate. But to assume forthwith that the financial obstacles are insuperable is as gratuitous as to assume them non-existent. It is impossible to foresee what economic conditions after the war will be, and impossible in particular to know how far standards of life everywhere can be raised by international action – a most material consideration when there is danger that an increase in labour costs here, as the result of expensive social reform schemes, may put us at a disadvantage in competitive export-markets. All that may be conceded. In resolving to go to the utmost limits of the possible, we must recognise that beyond them an impossible may lie. But at least we can determine not to stop short of that limit, wherever it may be. Even if we would we dare not, for demands will be made when this war is over that cannot be ignored. Men and women in the Services and munition-factories today will not tolerate the social conditions that prevailed before the war, with the hazards of old age and ill-health and unemployment overhanging them still; a question of social security in two senses will arise. For better or worse the Beveridge scheme has already aroused great expectations. The only practical, as well as the only humane, policy is to go to the utmost length to satisfy them, and, so far as that is not possible, to be able to show convincing reason why. The first step is to create a Ministry of Social Security to concentrate on the whole problem.

18 December 1942

MARGINAL COMMENT

Harold Nicolson

It is generally assumed that in wartime there must exist a certain tension between the soldier and the civilian, between the combatant and the non-combatant. It would seem natural to suppose that those who after long encounters with death and suffering are accorded a few days at home should look upon our comforts, or our small discomforts, with enmity or contempt. It would seem inevitable that the boy who returns from some trans-Alpine flight, or from the cold darkness of a Murmansk convoy, should view with displeasure his soft-skinned uncle mumbling about the blackout from a warmed armchair. Certain it is that we, the elderly, are acutely sensitive to this difference, and feel embarrassment and shame when we catch in young, once restless, eyes the taut look of experience. Yet in fact, the warrior on leave is so anxious to remember peace that he is almost grateful to those who ignore war. The crusader must have been pleased rather than irritated on his return from those years of salt-marshes and scurvy to find his women folk still weaving the tapestry which they had begun the day he sailed. It was not with resentment or envy that on the eve of Agincourt King Henry referred to the civilians; it was in terms of regretful sympathy. Nor can I recall that in the last war any displeasure was expressed by those who returned from Flanders to the music-hall gaiety with which the lights of London were then lit. The civilian should remember that the young warrior who has fought in Crete or at Alamein is not in the very least impressed by the tiny inconveniences which his parents may endure; the wise parent should avoid all semblance of a common sacrifice, knowing it to be grotesquely disproportionate, and should seek only to create for those few days the sweet illusion that home at least is much the same.

18 December 1942

DECEMBER. (To F.H.)

J.R. Ackerley

We never knew what became of him, that was so curious;
He embarked, it was in December, and never returned;
No chance to say Good-bye, and Christmas confronting us;
A few letters arrived, long after, and came to an end.

The weeks dragged into months, and then it was December.
We troubled the officials, of course, and they cabled about;
They were patient but busy, importunities without number;
Some told us one thing, some another; they never found out.

There's a lot go like that, I suppose, without explanation;
And death is death, after all; small comfort to know how and when;
But I keep thinking, now that we've dropped the investigation:
It was more like the death of an insect than of a man.

This beetle, for instance; I lower my foot now and crush it,
And who's to connect me, correct me? Who is to know?
I do not ask whether the other beetles will miss it,
Or God will say 'Where is my beetle, Where did it go?'

The life and the tiny delight, the sublime fabrication
Of colour, mechanics and form, I care nothing for that;
I am man, with his mind, the master, the lord of creation;
This beetle obstructs me, offends me; I lower my foot.

And that was the way he went. Yes, I see the rejoinder:
He was bound with us, armed with us – man in his violence and pride.
What use now to speak of his kindness, the gentle remainder?
But he was my friend, and that was the way that he died.

25 December 1942

Part Five
1943

In the BLACK-OUT

The Railways are giving as much light as they are permitted. You can make the black-out "lighter" if you —

- Keep the blinds down.
- Tell your fellow passengers the names of the stations.
- Be sure your train is at the platform before alighting.
- Close the carriage door after you.
- Have your ticket ready at the barrier.

RAILWAY EXECUTIVE COMMITTEE

A SPECTATOR'S NOTEBOOK

Janus (H. Wilson Harris)

The death of Richard Hillary has sent me back to his book *The Last Enemy* – the only one he lived to write. Whether he would have reached the same high standard in another who can say? As it is, he will live in memory as the author of one of the outstanding books on the war. Passage after passage, as one re-reads it, is charged with a bitter poignancy, and the description of what Hillary suffered after his accident, when in operation after operation his burned face was being built into something new, makes it unspeakably tragic that after all that had been achieved by the surgeon with such skill, and borne by the airman with such courage, death should so swiftly and finally obliterate it. Hillary ended his book with the reflection that if he could not fly again he could do one thing – write. 'If I could do this thing, could tell a little of the lives of these men, I would have justified, at least in some measure, my right to fellowship with my dead, and to the friendship of those with courage and steadfastness who were still living, and who would go on fighting until the ideals for which their comrades had died were stamped for ever on the future of civilisation.' He did write. He wrote the book of which these sentences are the concluding words. And he did fly again after all for a few months. Last October I heard him speak at a luncheon in London (I understand that what he said appears on a later page of this issue), when he talked little about flying, but suggestively, gropingly, about the heart of men, and about men in society. Such deaths drive deep into the consciousness realisation of what a price is being paid for victory.

15 January 1943

THE ARTIST AND FASCISM

Richard Hillary[1]

It has been said that the artist, the scientist and the truly religious are the three greatest bulwarks any country can have against Fascism and Hitler. Of the scientist and, even more, the truly religious, that is certainly true. I cannot presume to any knowledge of artists, but it is not of artists in the strict sense of the word that I wish to speak, so much as of those of us who would truly love to be creative artists but who are not, those of us who are authors, art critics, columnists, not because we have something in us which must come out, but because it is the thing we do best, because we have the facility and it gives us a certain position and a certain power. I mean all of us with a taste for music, painting and writing, who can see a table and realise that it is not really a plank on four legs, and that there are semitones in life and that everything is not really black or white, as opposed to the factual. It is we, I suggest, at this moment who are primarily in the position of being a bulwark against Fascism and Hitler. A true artist, a creative artist, is always an individualist, and although I realise it is dangerous to generalise, I think it is true to say that if he has any political leanings at all they are really always towards anarchy. Surely nothing could be further from Fascism.

I myself – if I may take myself – as an artist or pseudo-artist, have always believed that man's salvation lies in his own hands and I have always avoided any form of control from above. I have always been, and still am, a passionate believer in free trade, private enterprise and *laissez faire*, and I should like to see the day when a government realised that its only proper function was to vote itself out of existence. But I know that day, or anything approaching that, is very far off – so far off, in fact, that it can never be until man is willing to satisfy his material needs by economic rather than by political means: in other words until he realises that it is to his advantage to produce and exchange, rather than to wait for somebody else to produce something and then to take it away from him. In view of the present state of the world today it does not seem likely that

[1]This article is the substance of an address given by the late Flight-Lieut. Hillary, author of *The Last Enemy*, at Foyle's Literary Luncheon on October 22nd, 1942.

he will come to that realisation in our lifetime. Therefore, as I see it, after this war some form of planned and organised society is absolutely inevitable, and however much one may cry individual liberty in a planned society, it is a contradiction in terms.

Facing up to realities, then, what of the state of mind of the individualist when he realises that he can no longer go his own sweet way, but must conform to some pattern of an organised society? Those of us of a certain education, who before the war prided ourselves on our responsibility, thought personal relationships the most important thing in life, second only to the state of one's own mind and the realisation of oneself. And we did not lack encouragement in that belief either. Remarque, who wrote *All Quiet on the Western Front*, was asked if he liked Germans, and he replied, 'No.' Then he was asked if he liked Frenchmen and he said, 'No.' Then he was asked if he liked Englishmen and he said, 'No.' He was then asked, 'Whom do you like?' 'I like my friends,' he replied. That was a suitable and human answer before the war. Now, I suggest, it is not enough.

Let us now assume, then, that belief in self-realisation and personal relationships. We are asked if we believe in humanity. 'Yes,' we say, paying lip service but continuing to live entirely for our own small circle of friends. We are then told that we must accept the fact that man is basically good, that there is, or some day will be, such a thing as *homo sapiens*, that we must accept mankind as a whole or else call ourselves Fascists. We feel we are being critical and we agree to that, too. Do we then accept the Australian aborigine? Have we no responsibility towards him? No, certainly we have not; why, one was brought over here at the age of three months and educated up to the age of eleven, and at the age of eleven his mind slipped and everything stopped; he is a beast. Yet I suggest it is not such a very big step from him to the sweating crowd at Marble Arch tube station, that crowd that gets into the tube and clogs all the restaurants when we come home on leave. In peace-time we could have avoided it, but now we cannot. The world is closing in and will continue to do so. And this is the point: these people we would like to remove, and every thinking man, have something of the Fascist in them. What are we left with? Our own small circle of friends again; and that is where, in every country now in Europe, we have to take a big step to this – that it is no longer a question of whether so and so is a friend, speaks the same language, has the same tastes, and went to the same school: it is a question of what, in the last analysis, do I fight for? Do I shoot you or do you shoot me? Which side of the fence are you on? In applying that form of reasoning to ourselves and in reducing this argument to its logical absurdity, what we are prepared to fight for with our backs to the wall is our own small circle of friends – and that, we must realise, is putting ourselves straight into the Fascist camp, because that is exactly what they say. 'Think as we do; act as we do; believe as we do, and you are all right. Otherwise—!' That is an appalling and terrible fact to face up to.

Now assume for one moment that we lost this war and had a collaborationist government in this country, as in France, or even that we have not lost the war but have a Fascist government here under another name. What, then, will our position be? At this moment there are many artists, musicians and journalists, together with those of us who profess and call ourselves intellectuals, who are in the Services, men who before the war had a position in a certain sphere. Let us take from among them a completely imaginary example. Let us imagine someone who before the war was an art critic, with a column admired in some newspaper. Now, let us say, he is in the Air Force. Nobody reads his column, nobody knows his name, he is a cog in the machine, and he does not like it, and despises his dull companions with their lack of awareness, perception and sensibility. Let us suppose he is sitting in the mess, feeling awfully bored by a garrulous and rather drunken species of station medical officer, who before the war had a large and very brilliant practice, a man who, according to our friend, has no subtleties whatsoever, but who, in his own way, is completely orientated towards medicine. He also is bored by the dull pilot on his right with a pint of beer in one hand and the *Daily Mirror* in the other, that pilot whose emotional reaction to the most cultivated woman or the local barmaid is identical – to him they are simply women – but that boy's life lies up in the sky. Our friend would say that he had no sensibility, but how wrong he would be.

What we usually think of when we speak of a man's sensibility is somebody with a keener awareness of life than the average, of the spiritual rather than the factual, the unseen rather than the seen – and that pilot has that awareness, acquires that sensibility through the combination of great mobility and great power, alone with wind and stars. He may be boring on the ground, but neither he nor that garrulous and slightly drunken medical officer will go Fascist. Each is far too well orientated in his own sphere.

But what of our friend? It seems to me that in his intellectual frustration he approaches very closely to a character of Miss Dorothy Thompson in an admirable article in *Harper's Magazine*, a character who, given a chance, would make the most perfect Goebbels of a budding Fascist movement. If his life cannot be apart from those he despises he cannot ignore them and will seek to dominate them, for the man who despises those around him who have power but not his intellectual attainments, those who attained that power by birth or marriage, feels it is his right to wrest that power from them.

I suggest that that man is perhaps representative of all of us, of the subconscious of all of us anyway, of all of us whose art is not a thing big enough of itself but simply a means to power. Let us remember two things: one, that Fascism is not a national creed but a state of mind; two, that all those who love power more than people will go Fascist if and when Fascism is a majority movement. Finally, let us not go around and look at our friends and say, 'Oh, he will be a Nazi.' Let us rather ask ourselves – what is *my* position? And if we can answer that question fairly, then I think that that itself is a not inconsiderable war aim, and if, after having looked into our hearts and seen the danger, we can honestly say it is all right when the day comes, I shall feel then we shall have a spiritual armour which, come what may, will see us through to the end.

15 January 1943

THE CRY OF THE JEWS

The statement made by Mr Attlee in the House of Commons on Tuesday regarding the action of the British and Allied Governments in face of Hitler's threats to exterminate the Jews carried matters no further than previous statements have done, saying merely that 'the Government was now engaged on consultations with the other Governments most immediately concerned to see what further measures it was possible to take to assist those refugees who made their way to countries beyond German control'. One obvious measure is to let such refugees into this country, and help them to get here. As to what more might be done, that whole question is discussed in detail and in a strikingly temperate tone, having regard to the fact that the writer is himself a Jew, by Mr Victor Gollancz in his recent threepenny pamphlet, *Let My People Go*. Whether it is of the smallest use to approach Germany through neutral countries or the International Red Cross may well be doubted, for it seems probable that Hitler in his sadism is determined to destroy Jews, not merely to get rid of them, but the attempt at worst could do no harm. One practical suggestion is that shipping should be provided at Lisbon, so far as any can be

spared, to transport from there any who can escape from hell to that free
and neutral country. Poignant though it be, the pamphlet is a document
which concentrates in some thirty impressive pages all that needs saying
about one of the most terrible happenings of the war. To read and consider it is a painful duty, but a duty.

22 January 1943

STALINGRAD: 1942

Norman Nicholson

The broken sandstone slabs litter the shore
Like gingerbread; the shingle, pink and grey,
Slants to the runnels of the rocky floor
Where seaweed greens the red edge of the sea.

The tide rides up from Ireland, and a peel
Of sun curls round the axles of the waves;
The rough tongue of the water like the steel
Tongue of a limpet strops the kerb of caves.

Stalingrad now has stood the flood of fire,
Three moons of tide, for more than eighty days;
And this for more than eighty hundred year
Has borne the barrage of the western seas.

Whatever names wash over Stalingrad,
Or salt corrodes its stone, or torrents shock
Its cliffs, the city will not change, though blood
Settle like ore in the red veins of rock.

5 February 1943

MARGINAL COMMENT
Harold Nicolson

It is said that the modern generation has no sense of wonder. In 1843, for instance, the Vicar's little boy at Market Harborough would have thought of the ocean as some silver cloth patterned with golden crowns, and of the Lord Mayor of London as something super-human; as a large turtle, in fact, dressed entirely in fur. The same little boy in 1943 would be subject to no such visions; at the local Odeon or Regal he would have seen the north seas curling in dark rage, or the south seas shimmering with flying fish and dolphins; and on Sunday evenings, sitting by the vicarage fire, he would have heard the Lord Mayor proclaiming the Week's Good Cause. It is inevitable, I suppose, that the imagination of the young must today be much diluted; they have seen the fingers of Papuan fishermen drying their nets under the palm-trees; they have watched the sappers in the Libyan desert auscultating for land-mines with the gestures of a housemaid working the electrolux; for them nothing is so remote as to be unfamiliar, nothing so unusual as to be unexpected, nothing so impossible as to be improbable; there exists for them no lovely barrier between the known and the unknown. The war itself invades their privacy; what did the Vicar's little boy know of Liao-Yang, or Magersfontein or even of Gheluvelt? Today his bed will make a little leap on the linoleum, and next morning he will find the cucumber-frame a shatter of broken glass. We have become accustomed during this war to the intrusion of the extraordinary upon the ordinary, and we read without surprise of the destruction of rooms or buildings of which from childhood we have known the very feel and smell. It was not always like that. Even in the last war we were startled when the flame of battle came to scorch areas within our own orbit of familiarity. It was so different from the Modder River; so different from Omdurman.

19 February 1943

RETURN TO LONDON

E.H.M. Relton

One expected, on returning to England after eighteen months spent in Canada and the United States, to find things altered. We had kept, of course, in vicarious touch. But correspondents were scared, a little, of the censor; experience of newspapers had taught us to read between the lines; and if, perhaps, our most reliable informants were those who followed us out, even *they* contradicted each other. Some facts we knew. Soap had been rationed since we left; fuel-targets had appeared; the basic petrol allowance had been stopped. Clothes-rationing, which we saw introduced, had had time to take effect. The bread had turned an off-white, if not definitely brown. Food, on the whole, we gathered, was in some respects scarcer; but in others, we believed that an ingenious trick, known as dehydration, had caused an improvement. Our absence had seen the dwindling of air-raids and rubber, the conscription of women, and the invasion of our island by the American army. With such older institutions, such as the blackout and the earlier food-rationing, we had lost touch. What were our impressions on returning?

My own, at least, were unexpected. I had imagined, I think, a distinctly shabby lot of people (men in patched suits, women in bare legs or cotton stockings) with the backs of their hands perhaps a little grained, people whom a shortage of soap and hot water might, for all I knew, have compelled to offend in a way which even their best friends would shrink from openly criticising (if, indeed, being in a similar state, they were able so to do). I was looking for the usual stoic gloom, for cynicism, for apathetic, for fatalistic, resignation. I was even prepared to see my countrymen *enjoying* themselves in a queer, perverse way – a sort of mass-masochism, like the Germans.

I saw none of these things. Londoners, far from being shabby, had a clean, prosperous air. (Whence came, I wondered, all the beautiful clothes?) The streets and houses were neat. Nearly two years' immunity from air-raids had wrought a form of super-organisation of which the incredible punctuality of trains was but one example. Food was sparse but, to ensure health, adequate; in the case of those who, like myself, abhor carrots and potatoes, it appealed less to the palate than to the appetite. Everybody seemed very brisk and purposeful and tough.

This toughness, indeed, was extremely remarkable. It compared with the flabbiness that I remembered in pre-war London, with the decadent and pallid faces that have slowly vanished with sports cars and roadhouses and char-a-banc outings and women of leisure. It was different, too, from the intermediate stage, from the demeanour of the blitz or period of training. Then, apprentice war-mongers, mere fledgling savages, we were bruised and bewildered, resentful but resolute. Then, in the fields of our agony, was sown the seed of hate which now is ripening for the harvest.

London has an air of tenseness. Something is about to happen. Something big, but you don't know what. Men and women are grim, seriously determined, steeling themselves for action and sacrifice. Restrictions, discomforts, official supervision that smacks in some degree of Fascism — these we suffer but do not enjoy. Nor do we discuss them. But they are felt; they are very definite; they form the powder-charge to the shell of personal fury against the German people which is shortly going to explode with devastating effect, somewhere. There is no sign, I thought, of apathy or resignation. Instead, there is a healthy impatience, a straining at the leash. This is a nation in its fourth year of total war. It has done with play-acting, and it will brook no shirkers. It is still kind, but now also it is stern. Its democracy is being stretched to its limits, but it is still democracy.

If London has not, in these days, the same infectious air of gaiety, of fast and furious well-being, as New York, it is very crowded, and there is still, I found, plenty to do, if you can afford it. Money buys the privilege more of privacy than of luxury. You can take your lady friend out to dinner and a dance, and pay five pounds or one, but the food and wines you have are the same either way. Many attempts of rich people to spend money are both futile and wasteful. Members of dance-bands are old, slack and appallingly inefficient. Waiters are decrepit. Women military police look funny. It was odd, I thought, to see the grimy, drily humorous cockney bus-conductor replaced by a conductress from Roedean.

Britain, once more, has acquired character. Into the soul of a people which, for well over a year, alone defied the fury of the Axis world there has entered again the iron of pride, the cold steel of arrogance. Self-assured, self-controlled, we have put on our old armour of reticence. The people walk with dignity; the humblest private, the poorest waitress or shop-girl, is a Churchill in miniature. Is all this, I wondered, to impress the Americans?

Above all, I detected a new spirit, a fresh and rather complex awareness of Britain's destiny, which was totally absent when I left. It is a strange, struggling, contradictory, inarticulate spirit; half-formed; a revolution, a first groping towards the new era. It is the spirit which can acclaim the Prime Minister's (and therefore its own) declared resolve, in face of a good deal of criticism from America, to hang on to the Empire. It can, while still being able to stomach the neutrality of Eire, be stern enough to allow the leader of the Indian Congress Party to starve himself, if necessary to death. In the middle of this grimmest of all wars, a war of survival, of total victory or total defeat, it can take time off and, over a beer, as it were, in a pub, praise and rationally discuss such a kindly revolution in social economy as the Beveridge Report. These contradictions lead nowhere; the paradox cannot be explained. The only clear issue is that our attitude is changing. A democratic New Order is emerging; a wider and better emancipation, it seems, might be won, in combination with an enlarged sense of national and international duty, a sterner personal discipline. Britain is aware of her responsibility. It may be that at present she is unsure of her rightful place in the world after this war; but on the issue of deciding what sort of a world it will be she will yield, unless I am mistaken, to nobody.

2 April 1943

'GO, WORDS, ON WINDS OF WAR'

Siegfried Sassoon

Go, words, on winds of war. Let invocating breath
Adjure what ruthful influences on earth remain
Wherefore our common kindness should be done to death.
  No answer comes. The Germans drub their desolate drums.

Ask of recording angels what can glory gain
When the bombed city burns, the sinking ship explodes:
Compute the mutilations; number off the slain.
  Comes no reply. The Germans mutter, marching by.

Ask of the armoured columns whither bend their roads,
And what the factory's output fruitfully achieves:

Question the Stuka squadron wherefore it unloads.
  No choice, the Reich responds with guttural radio voice.

The souls of men are lost upon the storm like leaves,
Or crucified on faiths which once undid despair.
Only of retaliation the mass-mind conceives.
  One fact we understand. This feud was German-planned.

Return, words voiced in vain, on war's unanswering air . . .
Pride, that denied compassion, will find full payment there.

                                                    2 April 1943

MARGINAL COMMENT

Harold Nicolson

The most prominent accusation made against the evacuees by their hosts in the reception areas was that of personal uncleanliness. This accusation, to a really horrible extent, was justified. No less than 65,292 of the children evacuated from London were found to be in verminous condition. A similar discovery was made in regard to 20.8 per cent of those evacuated from Liverpool, 19.8 per cent of those evacuated from Middlesbrough and 17.3 per cent of those evacuated from Manchester. Certain other discoveries were made. It was found that even when evacuees had been deloused in the country they again became infested after a visit from their parents. It was found that the highest degree of infestation was found among children of pre-school age. It was found that although 40 per cent of boys under three years of age were verminous, very few of the older boys or young adult males were infested. Conversely, in girls there was practically no decrease before the age of 13, and many girls over that age were found to be verminous. The suggestion is made that the older girls refrain from combing their hair for fear of disturbing the permanent wave. Dr Kenneth Mellanby, for instance, in his study of *The Incidence of Head Lice in England*, reports that even little girls under ten years of age are given permanent waves and dissuaded by their parents thereafter from combing their hair. The incidence of skin disease such as scabies, impetigo and ringworm is also analysed. In

Sheffield, for instance, there were 14,500 cases of skin diseases in a school population of 55,000, and in Birmingham nearly 11,000 in a school population of 118,000. Nor were these the only complaints. The hosts in the reception areas were astounded by the insanitary habits of their guests. Bed-wetting may well be excused as due to psychological causes, such as home-sickness and loss of confidence, but there are other habits recorded in this analysis which throw a harsh light upon the home life of our urban population.

Apart from this major accusation of uncleanliness, there are other facts disclosed in this book which indicate that parents in the poorer classes are ignorant of the simplest principles of child welfare. It was found, for instance, that many people were totally indifferent to the importance of sleep. No habits of regular bed-time had been inculcated into the urban children, who were allowed to go to bed whenever they chose. Many parents appeared totally unaware of the basic principles of nutrition, and would spend money on sweets or comics which would have been far better devoted to the provision of food. It was found that many of the evacuated children had never sat down to a meal and did not know the use of forks or spoons. Their diet seems to have consisted almost exclusively of fish and chips, pickles, ice-cream and sweets; many of the children had never seen their mothers cook and had never had a hot meal at home. Vegetables to them were unknown and therefore distasteful. They regarded the country diet with suspicion and alarm. The remedies for these defects are obvious. They include housing, sanitation, water-supply, more day-nurseries, more British Restaurants, more hot meals in schools, better school premises in urban areas and, above all, education for parents in the elements of child welfare. The task is immense, but the disgrace is great. Bad conditions will not be remedied if we pretend that they are incidental, inevitable, or non-existent.

The evacuation of September 1939 was not only a terrible disclosure, it was also a great opportunity. Many evils have been disclosed, but much permanent good has been done. I know of one house in Kent which since the war has been turned over to the Save the Children Fund, and in which some fifty little children from London have been cared for and trained. In September 1939 they were indeed a squalid little bundle of human miseries; it is a delight to see them today, clean and rubicund, banging their spoons on their porridge bowls, tumbling like puppies on the grass. Nor has every host in the reception areas found his guests intractable or uncivilised. Even the parents, sometimes, have shown understanding and something approaching appreciation. And, above all, this great disclosure has profoundly affected the public conscience. It has taught local authorities that conditions in the areas under their control are not always as admirable as they seem in the reports, and it has taught the citizens of this country that we cannot claim to be a civilised community so long as such conditions are allowed to persist.

16 April 1943

PEACE PLAN

W.J. Turner

'Television at £15 is Peace Plan.' DAILY EXPRESS, *March 23rd, 1943.*
>After the war a new world,
>A new world and a new man.
>Yes, but tell me if you can
>What is new in your world plan,
>Have you murderers, police and jails?
>Yes, and we have bargain sales.
>Do the mediocre thrive
>While the best can scarcely live?
>Yes. Do power and honour go
>To those who how to seize them know?
>Yes. And are men poorly schooled
>And everywhere by humbugs fooled?
>Yes. And is the public taste
>In cities, homes and arts disgraced?
>Yes. What's new then to be found?
>Television at £15.

16 April 1943

THE MATCHLESS EIGHTH

Quintin Hogg, MP

At the point where the Desert Road between Cairo and Alexandria meets that between Cairo and Mersa Matruh the Western Desert may be said to begin. From there the road stretches past Alamein, Mersa Matruh and Sidi Barrani to Sollum, thence north and west past Bardia to Tobruk, from Tobruk west and south to Benghazi past the fertile Green Mountain and the pretty Roman coastal towns. South of the coast there is no metalled road, but there has been much travelling, and the desert is scored with thousands of tracks.

And when you have got to Benghazi you are only half-way to Tripoli – so long the seemingly impossible goal of our ambitions – and the worst half of that road, they say, is still in front of you. From Alexandria to the escarpment above Sollum is as far as from Scotland to the south; to Benghazi is as far again. And from Tripoli you have to traverse a whole country before you get to Tunis. Alexandria is almost due south of Moscow, Sfax of Cologne. And the way between is not by any means straight. The greater part of the journey lies through waterless desert. The railway which traverses part of the route is itself largely the creature of the British Army. But neither the road nor the railway marks the way they went, over the bumpy desert, rock and sand and scrub. There are few ports, and those there are are battered and poor. The desert has been called the tactician's paradise and the quartermaster's hell.

General Montgomery has expressed a doubt whether we have ever possessed an instrument of war equal to the Eighth Army, which has fought its way over this vast battleground. In the last war we had armies on a grander scale, but less fully equipped, and with adequate rail communications; and the rate of casualties deprived the young men of experience, the nature of tactics of mobility and campaigning knowledge. South Africa and the Crimea were small matters compared to this. Wellington's Peninsular veterans provoke a closer comparison, but men and transport lived on the country. Marlborough's Army was British only as to the equivalent of less than a modern division. Cromwell's Ironsides were perhaps as efficient but not so glorious, and before that we must go back to Crécy and Agincourt.

It is no slight to General Montgomery to say that the Eighth Army is not the product of one leader or of one campaign. Our desert force was born in 1940 in the desert between Sidi Barrani and the frontier wire. It began with a few picked units stationed in the Middle East before the war. From the first they knew each other well, and thus from the first the battle formations avoided all trace of rivalry between units or different branches of the Service. Such as there were were soon smoothed out in the intimate life of the mobile column.

The men who formed the core of the Eighth Army form, in the main, part of it still. As new units and new personnel came to be drafted out or joined the desert army from East Africa, Greece or elsewhere, they found it already a well-tried fighting force. The new formations were welded by battle experience and judicious posting into a complete unity. Many of the original units had found their way into the Seventh Armoured Division, of all formations perhaps the highest in *esprit de corps* – delighting in their characteristic totem, the red jerboa on a white background. This gave them their honoured name of 'Desert Rats', and they resented the use of the name of the same humble creature by the Australians of Tobruk – who, however, had earned a just title to it by reason of the terms of a derisory German broadcast.

The Western Desert Force bequeathed to the Eighth Army much battle experience and invaluable administrative technique. They taught the newcomers desert navigation by day and night, how to build a desert latrine, how to wash, cook, shave, drink, launder and fill your radiator on anything down to half a gallon of water a day, how to form leaguer at night after dusk and break it before dawn the next morning, that it is useless to try to brew tea on a twenty-minute halt, that there is no place too desolate for flies, how to murder gazelles with a truck and a tommy-gun.

They bequeathed also the priceless results of their early trials in interservice co-operation. At first the RAF had played a gallant but small part. There was a time when a small number of dilapidated Gladiators gave the only air-cover, and a later moment when anxious but hopeful messages were sent for the intervention of the Hurricane. When more aircraft arrived the technique of co-operation had to be learned for the first time on the field of battle, and the overwhelming superiority and flawless co-ordination of which they are now proud are the fruit of much bitter experience.

They had their legendary leaders, some of whom have died, but will not be forgotten. Jock Campbell, a huge Rupertlike figure, dashing about the desert upright in a pickup – fighting his own guns, with an infantry company officer on a neighbouring armoured car acting as his FOO – or pouring out over the wireless an almost incoherent jumble of orders to a subordinate column-commander whom he called by his Christian name. Strafer Gott, calm, cultivated and bespectacled, Aristotle's μεγαλόψυχος personified, with a touch of Christian humility, refusing orders to go on leave until the last rifleman in his division had had his five days in Cairo. Others, already legendary with the Italians by 1941, though less well known here: Goschen (now a PW), who used his twenty-five-pounders like brigantines on incredible predatory expeditions behind the enemy lines, and more still of whom personal friendship makes it impossible to write.

It is important to say that this army, always outnumbered in the beginning, out-tanked and out-gunned, never regarded itself as a beaten force. There were bitter reverses, less well understood here than in the Middle East, and disappointments as at Sidi Rezegh, long and heart-breaking withdrawals as that from Knightsbridge. But there never was a time when the Desert Army did not know by experience that, man for man, it was better than its opponents; and it never failed to keep its individual identity with the small force which had withstood the first Italian advance, held it at Sidi Barrani and driven it back in hopeless rout to Agheila in 1940. The secret of its success lies in battle experience, in the quality of its junior leaders, in highly developed desert discipline and administration, and finally in the inspiration of its army commander himself. But it is true to say that at most times the Desert Army had leaders it loved. In the early days General Wilson, the Army Commander, and Wavell the C-in-C; thereafter General Auchinleck and now General Montgomery.

Its final triumph came when at last to individual superiority was added superiority in quality and quantity of equipment, and finally of numbers, together with an adequacy of supplies and air support. But these by themselves could not have availed. The use of tanks, guns and aircraft in desert warfare is not an art which can be learned at once, and it is no criticism of the Army Commander's achievement to say that the weapon he has used so well was not forged in a night.

The morale of the Eighth Army is, perhaps, not its least wonderful characteristic. These men have many of them slept in the open for many months, fought in the desert for, literally, years. Their mail from home has often been infrequent and the news not always good. They have gone without sleep for nights on end and short of it for many months. They have been short of water and, occasionally, of food. But they remain the same, good companions and loyal friends. Here is a young officer's letter written within a few days of Alamein: 'You are quite right. *Den bösen alten Rommel haben wir mit brennenden Zungen am Arsch geleckt.* I have just been back to the Alamein battlefield to count the pick-up and write a historical record. Remaining on the ground were twenty-seven burnt-out tanks of various types and six other vehicles. But a certain number of burnt-out hulks have been removed and we are officially credited with thirty-seven tanks burnt out with other vehicles in addition. Actually we brassed up a round fifty tanks. It was an amazing day. For the first time we really saw the German tanks really foxed. They didn't begin to know what was happening – came lolloping up to within 200 yards of our six-pounders and then getting blown to smithereens before they'd even seen us. Highly satisfactory, but rather breathtaking, and rather tragic casualties. We are delighted with the Colonel's award (a VC). He is the nicest, simplest, most loyal and conscientious regimental officer, extremely kind and modest to a degree. Puts the professional cynics like myself unutterably to shame. There'll be a number of other awards (not quite such glorious ones) later.' This was the reward of nearly three years' campaigning. They are now nearing Tunis. Soon perhaps they will be elsewhere.

No account of the Eighth Army will be complete without a note of what we owe to them – to bring them home when the situation permits. Here are two quotations. They need no comment. 'Mind you ask *stinking* questions in the House if the "rats" aren't given home leave.' 'For your information, the principal after-the-war grouse you hear here is a fear that Eighth Army and ancillaries will be sent East and the Army in the UK disbanded; while that is patently absurd, I do think that a word or two by someone who has the ear of the newspapers, if not the PM himself, to allay that fear would do a lot of good, especially in base areas.' *Verbum sapienti.*

                                                                    23 April 1943

MARGINAL COMMENT
Harold Nicolson

When the stern strokes of Big Ben hush their vibrations on the still air, we listen in anxious excitement to the calm voice of the announcer as he tells us of the battle of our two great armies and of their French and American allies. Tunisian names float across the ether – names which have only become known to us during the last six months or names which evoke faint tourist memories of the hotels which were illustrated on the posters and in the folders of the Compagnie Générale Trans-atlantique. Yet we are aware also that this gigantic battle is now reaching historic ground, that our tanks already churn meadows once stamped upon by the elephants of Juba or Hasdrubal, and that the sappers auscultate for mines along roads once traversed by the legions of Belisarius and Caesar. Already perhaps some corporal in a county regiment has seen the distant stain in the hot air, a stain of green and white, which marks the gardens and palaces of what to the ancients was known as 'shining Tunis'; and already from the hill of Keftouro the French have seen the sun glint on the wide lagoon which marks the site of Hippo Zarytus, or Bizerta. Already our men have passed the battlefield of Thapsus, where Caesar dealt his final blow to the Republicans between the marshes and the sea. As I write these words the Eighth Army may already be in Hamamet, or Neapolis. Already the two great promontories of Hermes and Apollo have shimmered through the haze; already our Spitfires have swooped round the cliff where Dido bewailed Aeneas and where the great citadel of Carthage rose above the gulf. Three times in history have those few square miles witnessed the destruction of great armies; and on this fourth occasion it may be given to us, between the mountains and the sea, to win one of the world's resounding victories.

7 May 1943

SONG

Alun Lewis

I lay in sheets of softest linen
Sleepless and my lover spoke
The word of Death within her sleep
And snuggled closer and awoke
And wrapped me in her snowwhite cloak,

And clasped me in exhausted arms
And swore I should not go again.

Her lips were writhing like a moth
Burnt in the steady lamp of pain.
But I was young and fain.

I heard the daylight wind its horn,
I saw the cloudy horsemen ride.
Alas! my lover lacked the strength
To keep me by her side
And I went forth in pride.

I clasped the burning sun all day,
The cold moon bled me white;
Then all things ended suddenly.
I saw the world take flight
And glitter in the starry night.

28 May 1943

THE WAR DISEASE

Col. L.W. Harrison
(Adviser on Venereal Diseases at the Ministry of Health)

What various chances in Life, what seeds conveyed this strange disease, unknown of any through long centuries, which, in our own day, has raged throughout Europe, through portions of Asia, and through the cities of Africa; but which broke into Italy through the grievous wars of the French, and took its name from that race.

Thus runs the translation, by Wynne-French, of the opening lines of *Syphilis, sive Morbus Gallicus,* the poem in which Girolamo Fracastoro, in the year 1530, gave syphilis its name and at the outset associated its spread with war. The pandemic to which Fracastoro referred began in 1495, with the occupation of Naples by Charles VIII of France and the subsequent return of his mercenaries to their own countries; it is perhaps the outstanding example of the fact that war always promotes the spread of venereal disease.

Such an increase during the war of 1914–18 hastened the birth of the Public Health (Venereal Diseases) Regulations, 1916, which mainly govern the anti-venereal measures in this country today; they apply to syphilis, gonorrhoea, and soft chancre. Good general descriptions of these diseases are available in booklets published by the Central Council for Health Education, and here it must suffice to say that, amongst a multitude of evils for which they are responsible, syphilis and gonorrhoea do an incredible amount of harm in the production of domestic misery, individual inefficiency, ruin of families by death of their bread-winners in the prime of life, sterility, mortality of infants, and grave physical disability of children, adolescents and young adults at the outset of their careers.

During the last war the number of British and Dominion soldiers treated for venereal disease was 416,498, of whom about 102,000 had syphilis and 271,000 gonorrhoea. The increase of these diseases in the civilian population at that time is unknown, but some idea of it may be gathered from the number of service men who were infected and from the facts that in 1917 the mortality of infants certified as due to syphilis was nearly twice that in 1913 (ten times that in 1939), and that in 1938 the crude mortality of women from aneurysm of large blood-vessels, a disease most commonly due to syphilis contracted many years previously, was two and a half times the mortality from the same cause in 1921. The contrast between this large increase in women and the relatively small increase in men is attributable to the fact that during the last war, whereas a high proportion of the men who contracted syphilis were treated for it in service hospitals, only a very small proportion of the women infected then can have received this protection. Syphilis kills by many other means than aneurysm; but, for a number of reasons which cannot be given here, aneurysm is the only one which reflects at all clearly (albeit on a very reduced scale) changes in the incidence of the syphilis which remained untreated in its early stages several years previously.

Under the 1916 Regulations already mentioned (similar measures apply in Scotland and Northern Ireland) the County Councils and County Borough Councils had by 1939 set up in England and Wales 187 free-treatment centres (118 in voluntary hospitals), and there were 13 hostels for the care and rehabilitation of girls rendered homeless through their infection becoming known to their parents or their employers; there was also provision, in 99 approved laboratories, for the free examination of specimens from persons suspected of suffering from these diseases. These measures had achieved a notable degree of success. Thus there was good evidence that in 1939 the incidence of early syphilis in

England and Wales was less than one-third of that in 1920, the number of early cases dealt with in the centres (which treated the very great majority of the infected) being 4,986; the rates in the fighting services stationed at home supported the civilian figures. Less was known about the incidence of gonorrhoea because a much greater proportion of those infected with this disease were being treated privately, but, as in other countries, the success was probably not substantial. The discovery of new remedies within recent years had, however, raised a reasonable hope that gonorrhoea had become as controllable as syphilis, and it can fairly be stated that under modern methods of treatment, the three official venereal diseases (soft chancre is unimportant in this country, besides being easily curable) were rapidly becoming only a minor public health problem.

War conditions have caused a sharp reversal of the downward trend of incidence, as was not unexpected. In the first half of 1939, in conferences with medical officers of health and venereal disease medical officers which I arranged in different parts of England to discuss measures for coping with the inevitable accentuation of the venereal problem in the event of war, it was emphasised that, through the shift of large sections of the population into areas hitherto unprovided with treatment-centres because of the absence there of any venereal disease, through disruption of families, and through the usual lowering of moral sexual standards which affects a country at war, social conditions would favour the spread of these diseases. Plans for the creation of more centres as required were discussed at each of these conferences, but the prospects of preventing a large increase in venereal diseases did not seem bright, having regard to the slowness of the statutory machinery for creation of treatment-centres and to the fact that the number of specialists in this branch of medicine was not much greater than was required to staff the existing centres, without allowing for reduction by the demands of the services. The prospect would have been more depressing if it had been known that social conditions here would become more favourable to the spread of venereal diseases than probably in any war that has ever afflicted any country.

Venereal diseases are, of course, spread by promiscuity, and this is promoted principally by absence from home with only remote prospects of returning there; reaction from mental strain; boredom; the possession of money to burn; 'gold-digging'; indulgence in alcohol in dosage a little higher than is customary for the individual; and, in some societies, custom and example. We have here multitudes of temporary exiles from their own homes, many of them receiving very high wages, and amongst them, as also amongst our own nationals, are very large numbers who periodically undergo intense mental strain and excitement. We have also multitudes of reckless, unstable girls who drink far too much and are determined to have a good time come what may. When to these factors, and to others which will doubtless occur to many readers, is added the fact that the density of population (always favourable to the spread of venereal disease) is greater here than in most countries, it is not surprising that in 1940 early syphilis cases (including infections of British service men in this country) were 31 per cent, in 1941 70 per cent, and in 1942 120 per cent more than in 1939. The figures for gonorrhoea are not known so accurately, but there is no reason to suppose that they were significantly more favourable.

The measures adopted to cope with the situation include: expansion of treatment facilities; revision of hours of sessions to ensure – as far as is practicable in difficult circumstances – that they are sufficiently convenient for the patients; Regulation 33B, about which so much has recently been published; and intensification of efforts to enlighten the public on the nature of the venereal diseases and the importance of infected persons seeking treatment. In the expansion of treatment facilities, to the cost of which the Ministry of Health contributes 75 per cent, the general aim is to have these within ten miles of any infected person, and the number of centres has been increased to 209; also, under a new arrangement, 110 practitioners with certain qualifications have been enrolled in 79 areas in 13 counties to treat venereal cases in their own surgeries, the fees being paid by the local authorities. A useful gauge of the needs of any area in respect of treatment facilities is provided by the numbers of service infections stated to have occurred there and by the number of contacts reported under Regulation 33B. One great defect in the existing arrangements is that the proportion of infected women brought under treatment is too low. This is due partly to their carelessness, partly to ignorance of their condition (the symptoms of gonorrhoea and of syphilis in women are often so mild as almost to pass unnoticed by the affected person), and partly to inconvenience of treatment arrangements. Serious handicaps to the working of the scheme are the difficulty of obtaining premises for treatment-centres and the relative scarcity of medical practitioners for the staffing of new centres, or qualified and willing to undertake treatment in their own surgeries.

On the other hand we must be thankful that we are aided by powerful remedies in making the infected non-infectious quickly; but for these, the position would indeed be serious. But more than remedies for the disease are needed. Behind the disease lie the conditions that promote it. The essential is to find remedies for the conditions that favour sexual promiscuity. That is a problem for the ordinary citizen to reflect on.

11 June 1943

MARGINAL COMMENT

Harold Nicolson

The majority of young men and women in the Forces today surrender themselves without conflict, and sometimes even with relief, to the loss of individuality which war discipline implies; there are some even who welcome a system which relieves them of all personal responsibility. But if these be the majority, they are not a very interesting majority: the interesting problem exists for those educated or intelligent young men and women who constitute a very important minority in our citizen Forces. Why should these sensitive and valuable people regard themselves as 'forsaken'? This submerged generation hovers, as we know, between two worlds – 'one dead, the other powerless to be born'. It is a truism to say that they 'lack faith', which can mean little more than that they have as yet been unable to find or to define their absolute values. They have been brought up in an age of denial rather than in an age of affirmation, and they are not exposed, as my generation were exposed, to the pressure of conventional habit. It is not only that they lack leaders; they have no heroes; although they behave heroically, they scarcely believe in heroism. They have an instinctive suspicion of all the older patterns of achievement, and the men whom they most admire are those, such as T.E. Lawrence, who deliberately abandoned their own success. It is customary and right that the younger generation should repudiate the standards and conventions of their predecessors; but the tragedy of our submerged generation is that, as yet, they have evolved no standards of their own. They possess qualities of energy and intelligence greater than any we possessed, yet they float sullen and dispersed upon an ocean of disillusion.

The major element in this disillusion is distrust. There is distrust, in the first place, of the older generation and all the several systems, theories, aphorisms, fictions and dogmas which the last century evolved. But the distrust between 'we' and 'they' (the age gulf, the class gulf, or the even more significant gap which widens between the products of the primary and secondary schools) is not the most important form of modern distrust: far more operative in the disquiet of the young is their distrust of themselves. It is natural, I suppose, that young people should suffer from some lack of self-confidence; but the diffidence of the submerged generation, and the irritated helplessness which it produces, are beyond the normal. In my day we were able to conceal and assuage our diffidence by impudently attacking the conventions of our elders; yet heresy becomes a vapid thing if unaccompanied by faith; nor is much fun to be derived from attacking systems which one believes to be already dead. In my day we felt that we were being comfortably carried down the river of existence, and it was most amusing to fling insults at the people on the banks; today the river is reaching the open sea, the banks have receded, and ocean fogs come up to obscure the buoys and beacons. The young today find themselves carried out in little boats towards an uncharted sea. It is not surprising that they should feel forsaken and alarmed. It is not surprising that the more sensitive and intelligent, such as Richard Hillary, should come to feel that in all this uncertainty the only positive certainty is death.

16 July 1943

A HOPE TO DIE FOR

E.L. Woodward
G.V.M.

SIR: A short time ago there appeared in the Press extracts from a letter written, before leaving England, to his parents by a young Englishman who was killed in his first battle in the North African campaign. As I think that many people may like to read this letter in full, I have asked permission to send you a copy of it. The writer of the letter was an undergraduate at New College, Oxford, in the years immediately before the present war. During those years I saw much of him, and thought him unusually fortunate in his home, his friends and his happy disposition of mind. He was physically strong and of good ability. In ordinary times I should have forecast for him a long and successful life.

His letter sums up very simply the positive ideals for which he and so many others of his generation have fought, and are fighting, in this war. I need add no comment, unless it be to repeat the words attributed to Pericles about the young Athenians killed in war: 'They are gone from our city as though the spring was taken out of the year.' – Yours truly, E.L. WOODWARD

All Souls College, Oxford.

'... I should like you to know what it is I died for, and for that reason I am going to try to express my feelings and hopes. There is, I feel, both in England and America a tremendous surge of feeling, a feeling which, for want of a better word, I shall call "goodness". It is not expressed by the politicians or the newspapers, for it is far too deep for them. It is the heartfelt longing of all the "middling folk" for something better – a world more worthy of their children, a world more simple in its beliefs, nearer to earth and to God. I have heard it so often among soldiers in England and America, in trains, in factories in Chicago and in clubs in London, sometimes so poorly expressed that one can hardly recognise it, but underlying it all there is that craving for a new life. This feeling is no less powerful or significant than the Renaissance was, and will, I hope and pray, surge over the whole world in a tidal wave – that is the ideal for which we are fighting. Now let me try to express it in practical terms.

'First, there must be friendship between nations, for on the maintenance of peace all other things depend. This, I believe, with fanatical zeal, depends entirely on the co-operation between the British Empire and the USA. This, indeed, is my personal inspiration, something worth living for, something worth dying for. From it may arise untold happiness, without it I regard the war as lost, regardless of the fate of Germany and Japan. I love the American people, for I truly know and understand them, and it is my lifelong ambition to spread that understanding.

'Secondly, we must try to improve the lot of the poor. No sacrifice is too great for the rich to make to ensure that the poor of England have decent houses, good education, social security and a chance to live a happy life. If we in England could set out to conquer not poverty, but its attendant and unnecessary miseries, as we set out to beat Hitler in 1940, the dream world would soon come to our hands. Lastly, and perhaps most important of all, let us return to God. These last forty years we have drifted away too far; led astray by "realism" and "practical living". Let us return to the fold and guide our lives by His principles and no others.

'To accomplish this task we have one great weapon – the inherent goodness of man. I love people. I am sure that the good far, far outweighs the bad. Simplicity is stronger than cynicism and kindness than cruelty. Let the power of the world be in the hands not of the rich or of the poor, the old or the young, but the simple, the honest and the good. They are to be found in all classes, all creeds and all ages; but, and so often, their very goodness holds them back. That is what I am fighting for . . .' G.V.M.
Home Forces.

16 July 1943

COASTAL JOURNEY

Norman Nicholson

A wet wind blows the waves across the sunset;
There is no more sea nor sky.
And the train halts where the railway line
Twists among the misty shifting sand,
Neither land nor estuary,
Neither wet nor dry.

In the blue dusk of the empty carriage
There is no more here nor there,
No more you nor me.
Green like a burning apple
The signal hangs in the pines beside the shore
And shines All Clear.

There is no more night nor evening;
No more now nor then.
There is only us and everywhere and always.
The train moves off again,
And the sandy pinetrees bend
Under the dark green berries of the rain.

23 July 1943

MARGINAL COMMENT

Harold Nicolson

The enemy wireless, until Monday morning, throbbed with indignation at the bombing of Rome. The invective with which we ourselves (in an admirable feature entitled '*Ritratto d'un assassino*') assailed that evil person, Carlo Scorza, was almost complimentary when compared to the insults which were hurled at the leaders of the United Nations. The shrieks of rage which spread from the Italian transmitters across Europe and the world were echoed by Dr Goebbels in a comparative undertone of sighs. The Italians drew a telling contrast between the inordinate brutality of President Roosevelt or Mr Churchill and the awed delicacy shown by Alaric in 410 and Attila in 451. Dr Goebbels spoke in sorrow rather than in anger. The dark ages, he explained, were now in danger of returning: if any proof were needed, here for all to see was a patent demonstration that the treasures of European culture were at the mercy of the barbarians of the West; a people who could wantonly destroy Goethe's Gartenhaus at Weimar were capable of abolishing one by one the monuments of European history and culture; all good Europeans therefore must rally round the German standard and defend their common heritage: for years he (Dr Goebbels) had been trying to reveal to the world the true nature of the Plutodemocracies: Europe was now aware that his had been no empty imprecations; the tiger had at last disclosed its frightful fangs. This propaganda was reinforced by long lists of those objects in 'Europe's heritage' which Anglo-Saxon bombers had destroyed. In Germany the list included not merely the Cathedral at Cologne, but such valuable buildings as the State Opera in Berlin, the Martin Cathedral at Cassel, the Margrave's Palace at Karlsruhe, the Cathedral at Lübeck, the Elector's Palace at Mainz, the old Pinakothek at Munich, the Pilatus Haus at Nürnberg and the Nikolai and Petri Churches at Rostock. In Italy the list contained nine palaces at Genoa, the Cathedral and Church of St Zita at Palermo and the Cathedral at Syracuse.

These catalogues of disaster have without doubt been exaggerated. We know, for instance, that Cologne Cathedral has not been destroyed, although some damage has been done to the north transept. Nor can I

believe that any Allied aviator, except by some almost inconceivable mis-
chance, damaged the little summer-house which Goethe built for himself in the pleasant valley of the Ilm. The fact remains, however, that in
many of the more ancient towns of Germany and Italy there exist buildings of immense historical and artistic interest; and that even if the
greatest care is exercised some of these buildings are liable to be damaged
by incendiaries, explosives or blast. It is irrelevant to contend that many
of our own finest buildings have been similarly destroyed. When I walk
daily through the fragments of the Temple, observing how reminiscent
of Pompeii or Palmyra are the bases of the shattered columns, it is no solace to me to reflect that one day a similar fate may reduce to rubble the
tracery of the Zwinger at Dresden: nor if Oxford were reduced to ashes
should I wish such a tragedy to overwhelm Siena. One cannot acquire
any mental comfort by drawing up a balance-sheet of right and wrong;
the tit-for-tat frame of mind is a rotten frame of mind. Neither do I derive
comfort from the thought that some at least of the buildings destroyed,
such as the Hedwig Kirche at Berlin or even Cologne Cathedral, possess a
local or sentimental value greater than their intrinsic importance. This is
mere casuistry. It is a bad thing to destroy even a fifth-rate work of art.

There are, I know, many arguments which run counter to such an assertion. There is the argument (which I accept) that our enemies cannot be
allowed to conduct military operations under the shelter of works of
artistic or historical importance. There is the argument that were we to
give immunity to the capital or main cities of Italy and Germany we
should be depriving ourselves of an effective means of shortening this
war. I admit this argument also; and, indeed, I have no doubt that the
retirement of Mussolini was due in no small measure to the knowledge
that the cities of Italy could not expect to remain immune. There is the
contention that our pilots and navigators are carefully briefed and
instructed to avoid all non-military targets; this also, with certain obvious reservations, is undoubtedly correct. There is the argument that it is
unfair for civilians to cast doubts upon the value of the tense and difficult operations which our bomber crews have to execute. I am impressed
by this argument. It is, I know, no fun at all to fly through the night from
England to Turin. It is no fun at all to wait hour after hour for the summons; to huddle into the dark tumbrils which take one to the plane; to
see the faint fields of England slide below one as the searchlights spring
to anger along the Dutch and Flemish coasts; to throb through the dark
over shrouded cities and mountains glistening in the moon; to search for
one's target through cones of searchlights and avenues of flak; to feel
danger clustering around one and safety far away; and to realise that

within a day or two the whole horrible adventure will begin again. I do not suppose that our pilots and navigators are agreeably impressed by the criticisms of those who have never shared the perils of the night.

Yet if we must remain unable to solve the problem completely to our own satisfaction, we can at least seek to avoid all unnecessary confusion of thought. The attack upon Rome, for instance, has given to vague perplexity a most unreasonable slant. I have been distressed during the last few months by the number and nature of the questions which have been put to me at public meetings on the subject of the bombing of Rome. It was not sufficient to explain that circumstances had not yet arisen in which the military advantage of an attack on Rome would justify the political and other disadvantages which such an attack would inevitably entail. Some of my questioners believed that I was one of those archaisms who prefer the mouldering past to the resplendent future. Others suspected that I was in some way subjected to the nefarious influence of the Catholic hierarchy. I was of the opinion and I remain of the opinion that such centres of civilisation as Rome, Florence and Venice should not be bombed unless such action can be proved to furnish an overwhelming military advantage. I am convinced that our Government were well advised to delay such attacks until the moment when the advantage became obvious and immediate; nor could any reasonable man deny that the attack when it came was well-timed, well-directed or that it contributed to important results. It was most unfortunate that the raid upon the railway system in the south-west corner of Rome should have occasioned damage to the Church of San Lorenzo fuori le Mura. It may be true that the damage affected only that part of the basilica which had been largely reconstructed in 1864; but it is also true that San Lorenzo was founded by Constantine, that it contains the tombs not only of Honorius III, but also of Pio Nono, and that it is one of the seven pilgrimage churches of the Eternal City. Damage to such a basilica is much to be regretted.

It is foolish none the less to allow sectarian prejudices to distort the incident. It is unreasonable for any Catholic to suggest that the damage to San Lorenzo represents an affront to the Holy See: their indignation should be turned against the Fascist Government who refused to declare Rome an open city. It is equally unreasonable for Protestants to suggest that the Pope's letter on the subject was an unneutral act. It is customary for bishops to sympathise with their diocesan officials when a religious building is destroyed; nor was there a word in the Pope's letter which was more embittered or more partisan than the protest which he raised against the destruction of Malta's sacred edifices. Let us hope that it will now be possible for Italy to retire from the conflict with only a small fraction of her buildings destroyed; but if that retirement be postponed unduly, we can rely on Bomber Command to give to the phrase 'discriminate bombing' a specially accurate interpretation.

30 July 1943

JARGON

Vansittart

My husband 'fell' in forty-two:
   The Jerries bombed him out.
I did what most brave women do:
   Yes, Sir, I did without.

Next year I 'gave' my only son;
   He was shot down in flames.
How could I get another one
   Except by 'failing' James?

I've been to church, I've been through hell.
   God holds his comforts high,
High as my head, and none can tell
   How long I took to die.

I starved the flesh till it grew faint.
   Too withered to transgress.
Yes, Sir, I am the village saint.
   And am I bitter? Yes.

6 August 1943

MARGINAL COMMENT

Harold Nicolson

The other day, in a garden near my home, we held the village fête. Notices in red and blue chalk were hung along the drive indicating with crude arrows where one should go in. The iron-wrought gate in the yew hedge stood open, flanked by two Boy Scouts who gripped their staves in firm lictorial fashion. Beside the gate was a kitchen table and a chair on which was seated a pillar of the Women's Institute, who received the sixpences of the villagers as they poured in. The great trees beyond threw their vast shadows, not only upon the hayfield which had once been lawn, but upon rows of little tea-tables and a vast tin urn. Upon their solemn trunks were tacked further notices: 'Tea 4d.' And around that large and varied garden, in among the flower-beds and the limes, were arranged all manner of side-shows. There was Aunt Sally with her pipe already broken, with her scant skirt already disarranged, facing with black and dog-faced fury the missiles which we hurled. There was the skittle-run, and over there the treasure-corner, and in the shade of the beech tree a fish pond where with trembling wands we guided the hooks into the eyes. The statue of Minerva, backed by her neat semi-circle of yew, gazed upon this scene with dignity and distaste. Tucked roughly into the clematis of a high garden-pier an amplifier relayed to the assembled crowd the music of a hidden gramophone. The village maidens, in an ecstasy of poise, danced upon the sward. The children paraded in their fancy clothes. And as I strolled from booth to booth, I came upon three targets, bearing in black charcoal the semblances of Hitler, Mussolini and Tojo sketched upon large sheets of paper pinned to boards. For the sum of 2d. one could hire six darts wherewith to assail the enemies of mankind. Hitler and Tojo, when I got there, were already riddled by the pin-holes of expended darts. The Duce was practically immune. 'You have not,' I remarked to the man who ran the show, 'done well with Mussolini.' 'No,' he answered, 'they prefer Hitler and the Jap. Now that Musso's down and out they say, "It seems hardly fair somehow."' Once again I stood amazed by the unerring instinct of the British people.

13 August 1943

A SPECTATOR'S NOTEBOOK

Janus (H. Wilson Harris)

The five days between September 3rd, when Italy definitely surrendered, and September 8th, when the news was made known to the world, were an anxious period for the relatively few Allied soldiers and statesmen who had the momentous secret in their keeping. It was imperative, if possible, to keep the news from the Germans while the Allies made their new dispositions with, if not Italian connivance, at least the certainty that there would be no Italian opposition. It was necessary to invade Italy, for Badoglio could hardly surrender his country before an Allied soldier had set foot on its mainland. Actually the surrender and the invasion took place on the same day. Then fighting had to go on with sufficient vigour to avoid arousing German suspicions; but I fancy the main concern of the Allied Air Forces in Calabria (Naples is another story, for other reasons) in these last days has been to harm as few Italians as possible. It seems hardly credible that the Germans should not have realised what was happening; but it looks as though that really was the case, largely no doubt because so many rumours were rife that there was no more reason for believing the only true one than the many false. The actual announcement on Wednesday only came after various alarms and excursions. Mr Eden imparted the news that afternoon to M. Maisky and Dr Wellington Koo, as representing the major Allied Powers, and then to the representatives of the other Allied nations, among whom it is a peculiar satisfaction to mention specially the Ethiopian Minister Belata Ayela Gabri. The release to the Press, fixed for 5.30, was jumped by the New York Radio, which had sent out the news before five. Anxiety about a last-moment hitch prevailed up to the zero hour, and it was not till the BBC monitoring service reported that they were listening to General Eisenhower giving the news himself from Algiers that it was certain that everything had gone well.

10 September 1943

MARGINAL COMMENT

Harold Nicolson

In the excitement of the last few days, when triumph or disappointment have succeeded each other almost hourly, Adolf Hitler's speech of a week ago has received but scant attention. Yet how significant, in fact, was the change both of tone and substance. Gone are the days when, at Nüremberg or at the Sportspalast, his every phrase was followed by the rhythmic panting of 'Sieg Heil!', that dreadful chorus which was as incisive as a steam-saw screaming in the wood-shed, as sad and sinister as a vast sea tearing at the shingle of some northern beach. Gone are the days when, to the accompaniment of bands and banners, his high scream of hatred and vituperation would echo through the amplifiers, driving, as he himself confessed, 'the broad masses into an ever more precipitous hysteria'. Gone are the days when the whole world listened with bated breath to the pronouncements of a creator of destiny. In place of this we had the monotone of a disillusioned man, gabbling with incomprehensible speed through the manuscript before him. The miracle of the wireless never ceases to confound me. There was the Führer sitting before the microphone in some distant Pomeranian or Bavarian castle spouting his piece so breathlessly that one could hear, across those miles of ether, the very inhalations of his lungs. And there was I, crouched above the receiving-set in an English cottage, while outside the sullen September day waned across the Weald of Kent. From the latticed window at my side I could see down across the fields towards the hop-garden, already half-stripped so that on the eastern half the poles stood naked, while on the western half the hops still clustered. A little owl settled clumsily upon a branch of an oak, and as I listened to the Führer rattling along in his Bohemian accent I could see its round head and twin ears sharp against the sunset. Only once did Hitler raise his voice above a tired monotone. He spoke of the ring of steel forged round the German homeland. 'Niemals,' he shouted, 'werden sie es zerbrechen.' At that moment only did the old Hitler return. And as the light waned over the Weald of Kent the proceedings were concluded by the singing by some Berlin choir of that horrible Horst Wessel Lied.

•

As I listened to Hitler speaking on Friday I forced myself to imagine that I was a German hearing, in this hour of calamity, my leader's words. I should have known that, whatever happened in central Italy, the British had secured command of the Mediterranean; that their airfields were creeping ever closer and closer; that the U-boats had for the moment been defeated; that vast new armies and unlimited equipment were being amassed for invasion; that the Russians, in their summer campaign, had inflicted grave losses on the German forces and occupied vital areas of land. I should have detected no note in the tired voice of my leader of any certitude of victory; I should have heard only an appeal to stand or die. And I should have known that nothing which could happen could improve the situation, and that everything which would happen was sure to make it worse. And if an owl, as I listened, had perched upon the oak, I should not have recognised the bird of Pallas Athene; I should have seen the harbinger of doom.

17 September 1943

FROM ONE GENERATION . . .

Kate O'Brien

The church in our village is a beauty – mainly Gothic, but with a Norman doorway and a lovely little Renaissance chapel; its inner walls are crusted with memorials to local grandees who died in their beds, and also to young men who died in the Peninsular War, or in the Crimea, or in South Africa. Shreds of silk flags from old campaigns hang in dust above family tombs; and outside, on the dark grey wall, facing the eastern sky and the huddled tombstones of departed worthies, we have our memorial tablet of 1914–18 – still seeming white and new amid so much ancientry.

'In Grateful Memory of 42 Men of this Parish who died for us . . .'

The names listed below – Thomas Wicks, George Latter, Albert Crabbe, Frederick Woodman, Samuel Dawe, and so on – are the same which are borne now by our milkman, our postman, our blacksmith, our hedger and ditcher, and our landlord at the 'Dog and Partridge', over the road.

Twenty-four years ago the fathers, uncles and brothers of our present village got their names inscribed on the east wall of the church, and now those who came back are in a fair way to get their sons', and their daughters', names – if not their own – immortalised in the same way, having 'died for us'. For Sammy and Will Dawe from the inn are in the Navy; and George Latter, who two years ago was the loudest-whistling milkman for miles around, is a Sergeant Pilot; Gladys Woodman is on an AA gun somewhere on the coast; and the postman, who went through the other war, is on Civil Defence in our nearest town, and his rheumatic old-maid sister brings us our letters now – in her own good time. So there we are. Anyone knowing the village could go right down the list of 42 names and find this repetition of design.

There's a handy short-cut from my cottage, through the churchyard and Sid Wicks' orchard, to the bus-stop. On days when the news is bad, if I look up at the War Memorial as I pass it, I tend to lose heart. For these forty-two names stand for an enormous sacrifice from a little place, an immeasurable grief – and now, the same names are asked so soon again for the same surrender, for greater sacrifices . . . even closer, more constant and more terrible griefs.

One very bright morning, not long after the loss of Tobruk, when the eight o'clock news had told of a terrible count of bombers not returned from Germany, Sid Wicks overtook me as I passed under the 1914–18 stone. His brother Tom is listed there – and got a posthumous MM. Sid himself was in the Yeomanry, and by some trick got out to France in 1914, before he was seventeen. He went all through the four years on the Western Front. He is a farmer in a small way, kind and easy. His daughter is in the WAAF, his son Tom is an Air Cadet, and he has two kids still going to the village school. He is in the Home Guard.

I saw his eyes flick sideways to the Memorial as we passed it.

'I always try to give a thought to old Tom when I pass it,' he said simply. 'It's the least I might do.'

The view from the churchyard and the top of Sid's orchard is wonderful – a long, wide valley of a thousand sleepy colours, ending in a far-away blue smudge of hill and sky. I looked at it sadly.

'The news is bad,' I said.

'Bound to be. No use getting rattled. They'll take a hell of a lot of beating, same as they did last time. But we'll get 'em taped all right, like we did before.'

'Think they'll invade, Sid?'

He looked down the valley; a smile spread over his gentle face, and I knew that he was thinking of the scene before him with a devotion he would never dream of putting into words.

'They might and all. It'd be one quick way of showing 'em, too – and it might save our chaps a lot of time and trouble.'

'It'd be pretty bad, though. They have so many terrible new dodges.'

'Aye – bad enough. But they don't change all that much. I knew that when I heard Freddy Woodman talking after Dunkirk. They're the same old Jerries. They don't change – no more than we do. We can handle 'em all right. Nice and steady.'

He smiled very gently, and went his way.

It was Saturday morning, and there were a good many people at the bus-stop. Mrs Dawe, of the 'Dog and Partridge', made us laugh about her mother – a wonderful old lady of ninety-three, but with all her faculties, only a bit wandering-like in the mind, as you might expect. She often mixes up her grandsons, Sammy and Will, with their Uncle Joe that was killed at Zeebrugge, and makes jokes to them about Kaiser Bill; and some-times she thinks they're fighting the Zulus, like her own brothers did; but last night she capped all by confusing them with her old Uncle Bob, that died at Balaclava! A wonderful old lady, to be sure!

The bus was late. A fighter plane – a yellow-painted trainer – came hedge-hopping along, and roared down alarmingly low above the Post Office. Miss Spandril, the schoolmistress, shook her umbrella at it.

'It'll be that show-off, Bertie Crabbe, again!' she cried. 'From his con-duct, I declare you'd *never* think I laid a birch to his back!'

'He's a good lad all the same,' said Mrs Dawe. 'And the very spit of his Uncle Bert that he never knew, that was killed at Wipers. Did you ever see such a likeness, Mrs Woodman?'

'That I never did. It's sad someway,' said Mrs Woodman.

The bus came in sight round the bend of the lane and in an orderly queue we got on to it. I looked at the women about me. All of them had suffered one way or another from the waste and griefs of the first Great War, and now, through the errors and follies of the interim in which they had grown up and raised another generation, they were being asked to risk and suffer more than ever. But they would meet tonight, as eager as children, to learn about field kitchens, or any other thing that, in their little place, might make them useful to their fellows in emergency or danger. And before they began their lesson they would sing – very badly – their Women's Institute song, 'Jerusalem'. Miss Spandril would give them the note – optimistically – with a tuning-fork. And they would sing, with heart and will: 'I will not cease from mental fight, Nor shall my sword sleep in my hand . . .'

We have a long way to go, all of us – and even if we were all in deadliest earnest, maybe we shall not see a New Jerusalem. But the heart is there for the journey, and the innocent hope. The people in the villages are not visionaries or geniuses, but they have courage and good sense. They will see their bit of history through, 'nice and steady'; they will give what they have to give, to finish a job begun when they were young, by 'forty-two men of this parish, who died for us'. Sid Wicks is right; people don't change – and that can be good news as well as bad.

'I always think the village looks its best from here,' said Mrs Dawe to Mrs Woodman.

It looks lovely from here – old and calm, with the old grey church at its heart, and the white memorial shining on the east wall in the sunlight.

8 October 1943

MARGINAL COMMENT

Harold Nicolson

It is sad and strange that Oxford, whose very motto is one of illumination, should be the darkest city in all the land today. In other towns some glow-worm lamp does at least reflect a pin-point on the pavement, indicating where the way to Grimsby cuts the Great North Road. But, when sunset passes, the blackout gathers Oxford firmly in its arms, muffling every eye and orifice, shrouding the spires in impenetrable dark. The visitor on arriving at the station finds the platform a medley of struggling forms composed almost entirely of bicycles and the Army. A distant light, with brown paper tied around it, indicates the wicket at which the collector receives the little squares of cardboard which we thrust into her hand. And beyond that dim portal is darkness impenetrable pierced by the shouts of forlorn men calling cabs. Grasping my suitcase I tottered out into the night. I suppose that in the world there are other towns as dark and damp as Oxford in wartime. Zhitomir, for instance, can scarcely be garish at this time of year; and I assume that even the oil lamp outside its bath-house has for security purposes been dimmed. It may be also that the Pripet marshes, on a November evening in the rain, can emulate and perhaps even surpass the damp of Oxford. Yet as I walked along the road which leads from the station – bumping into Americans, bumping into Canadians, bumping into other human beings of whose nationality I was unaware – I reflected that in no other area of the earth's surface could it

rain in just the same way as it rains at Oxford. For when the waters of the
upper air mingle with the waters of the Isis and the Cherwell a general
liquification results; the rain ceases to fall downwards but creeps
sideways and upwards from the streets. And all this wetting process happens silently, without a single sound. Not a splash is heard in the surrounding darkness; one is aware only that one's very thigh-bones are
being slowly soaked.

I have sought in all sympathy to understand the sorrow of the young
intellectual who has been caught, and displaced, by the war. It is no doubt
a tragic and bewildering experience to discover that the *élite* into which
one was born, and to which one was educated in boyhood, would seem,
during one's own absence upon a most unprofitable adventure, to be losing its authority. Scholarship, intelligence, even experience, appear to
have become less important; and the old tests and standards of eminence
seem to be threatened by the rise of an internal and external proletariat. I
fully recognise that the men and women who in 1939 reached the age of
twenty are in an indefinite position. The men of my father's generation
believed quite simply that creation was moving towards an event which
was not only Divine, but also far-off; their actions and ambitions were
guided and controlled by the belief that Providence had decreed that a
certain class of Englishman should rule a quarter of the globe and furnish
an excellent example to all other men. In my own generation we were
content to expose the moral fallacies of our elders and to put in their
place a belief in intellectual integrity. After the last war the young men
who returned to the Universities sought to recompense themselves by all
forms of self-indulgence for the hardships and dangers to which they had
been exposed. They were followed by a generation of austere men and
women who believed quite sincerely in the existence of the economic
man and who derived much spiritual and intellectual solace from the
perfected logic of the Marxist theory. But the young people of today
neither believe nor disbelieve in any theory; they have come to learn that
the world is a highly intricate organism, and that most of what has been
said about it is either partially or totally untrue. And since they dismiss
the wisdom of the ancients as being fallacious and the advice of their
immediate elders as savouring of 'propaganda', they are left naked with
their own horrible but slight experience and a deep consciousness of the
enormous intricacies of life.

With the tiny torches of their own knowledge they grope amid the majestic ruins of the past. I am not surprised that they should feel 'forsaken'.
Yet if they can believe in no absolute theories, they can at least know that

courage, truthfulness, energy, scholarship and kindness are virtues and that their opposites are vices. With their little torches they can see and illumine these great absolutes. Guided by such stable landmarks, they can find their way through the dark, wet fog which surrounds them. And in the end, I suppose, they will find warmth again, and laughter and light.

3 December 1943

ON A DUTCH FLOWER-PICTURE

V. Sackville-West

Darkest December, when the flowers fail
And empty tables lack their lucent lading,
And far beyond the window's rainy veil
The landscape stretches, into twilight fading,
And all seems misted, moribund, and pale,
The past too far away for recollection,
The present vacuous, forlorn, and stale,
The future far for hope of resurrection,
– Look, then, upon this feast, your eyes regale
On this impossible tumble tossed together,
This freak of Flora's fancy, this all-hail
Regardless of the calendar or weather.
Here is the daffodil, the iris frail,
The paeony as blowsy as a strumpet,
The fringéd pink, a summer's draggle-tail,
The gentian funnelled as a tiny trumpet.
Here is the hundred-petalled rose, the hale
Straight streakéd tulip curving like a chalice,
The lily gallant as a ship in sail,
The sinister fritillary of malice,
All towzled in a crazy fairy-tale
That never blew together in one season
Save where romances over sense prevail,
– Yet even here behold the hint of treason:
The small, the exquisite, the brindled snail

Creeping with horny threat towards the foison,
Leaving a glistening, an opal trail,
A smear of evil, signature of poison . . .

31 December 1943

MARGINAL COMMENT

Harold Nicolson

In the gap between Christmas and the New Year, the gap between the Dionysia and the Lenaea, six days seem to be but discards from the pack of the year, mere idle playing-cards, at which one scarcely glances and then pushes aside. It is a period when wise people rearrange the books upon their shelves, and put in correct order the loose leaves of their diary, pausing from time to time to read again the hopes and fears, the expectations and the disappointments, of the twelve tremendous months that have passed. Few years indeed can furnish such a succession of excitements. The Russians took Kharkov in February, lost it again in March, and recaptured it in August. Stalingrad, in circumstances of the most intense drama, was relieved. At the same moment the First Army was in danger at Tebessa and Sbiba and many anxious days passed before the Germans retreated from the Kasserine. Then came Montgomery's attack upon the Mareth line, the first disquieting check, and the swing round by El Hamma and the final breakthrough. At the end of April the First Army again took the offensive and captured Longstop Hill, and thereafter, day after day of victory followed, and upon our maps we traced with rising excitement the seizure of Mateur and the entry into Tunis and Bizerta. It was at midnight on May 12th that the great news came. 'The long African campaign is over. Von Arnim has been captured.' In July we invaded Sicily and on July 25th came the astounding news that Mussolini had resigned. The Italian landings followed and on September 7th came the news of Italy's surrender. Cold autumn winds came to nip the excitement of these adventures. Mussolini was rescued from the Gran' Sasso and the battle of Salerno went ill indeed. Kesselring laid his iron hand on Rome; our Dodecanese landings were a failure; and the soft under-belly of the Axis proved, as Mr Aneurin Bevan so unkindly remarked, about as sticky a backbone as one could find. And then came the Cairo and Teheran Conferences, the intensive destruction of Hamburg, Frankfurt and Berlin, and the certainty of enormous things to come.

It is not easy, even when we look back upon this wonderful year, to assess which of these victories was the most decisive. The battle of Hammam-Lif was undoubtedly one of the most brilliant of all British feats of arms, and will live for long in our military annals. But it did no more than complete, with extreme neatness, a story already written by the First Army in the Mejerda Valley or by the Eighth in its amazing march from Alamein. The Russian offensive was undoubtedly a decisive offensive, from the effect of which the German armies cannot hope to recover. Our bombing attacks will have done much to diminish both the capacity and the will of Germany to wage a protracted war. Yet all these dramatic acts and energies would have proved uncreative had it not been for the immense labours of the British and American peoples in the factories and in the fields, and had it not, above all, been possible for our naval forces to keep open the high seas. It will be said, presumably, by those who in after years study this great year of 1943 that the most decisive of all our many campaigns has been the campaign against the U-boats. And it is a fitting conclusion to the year that the Royal Navy, whose skill has been so great, whose endurance so superhuman, whose resource so inexhaustible, should at last have received a dramatic triumph of its own, and added the sinking of the *Scharnhorst* to labours which, through night and day, have been unseen and ceaseless, constant but unnamed. It is this aggregate of unrecorded effort which has given us our victory in the end.

It is encouraging at such a moment of retrospect to consider what must be the apprehensions of the average German when he considers the circumstances, the changed proportions of power, which exist as 1943 glides off into 1944. When I was in Sweden recently I met a Swedish politician who had spent much time in Germany during the present war and who had observed with care their reactions of this year between the month of January and the month of September. He said that the year 1943 would be known in Germany as the year in which the legends were destroyed. The first legend was the legend of Hitler's invincibility; the belief that this daemonic corporal possessed some genius for strategy which enabled him to defy the laws of warfare and to disregard the advice of senior and more experienced strategists. That legend had been destroyed at Stalingrad. There was not a German who did not know that Hitler had insisted on the retention of Stalingrad, long after his military advisers had told him that a withdrawal was inevitable. This error did not mean that Hitler had lost his hold upon the German imagination; it meant only that their former confidence in his judgement had been replaced by a deliberate form of belief in his destiny; a far less durable form of faith. The second legend had been destroyed at Alamein. It was not that this great battle had convinced the Germans that the British soldier, if properly equipped, could defeat German armies in the field: whatever their propagandists might say, the Germans had never had any doubts about the fighting qualities of the British armies. The lesson that Alamein had taught them was, my informant assured me, quite a different lesson. It had destroyed a second of their comforting legends: the legend of the U-boats. Until then they had been assured that, however enormous might be the productive capacity of their Western enemies, only a mere trickle of guns and ammunition would be able to reach the fighting front. The great barrage of Alamein blew that legend into fragments. They learnt at Alamein that the unconquerable resources of the Western factories could be transported across half the world. That was a most alarming lesson.

'And what,' I asked my Swedish friend, 'was their third legend?' 'Their third legend,' he replied, 'was the legend of Germany's own invulnerability. You people seem to underestimate the significance of this particular legend. But at the back of every German's mind is the belief that war for Germany is a profitable thing, since while, owing to their efficiency, they are able to invade and despoil the territories of their neighbours, their own home country, their fields and factories, remain untouched. The American and British bombers have destroyed that legend most completely.' 'And are there any more legends?' I asked him. 'Yes,' he said, 'there are two more legends, and if you manage to destroy them also, you will have destroyed the will of Germany. You will be left only with Germany's despair – which will offer another, and perhaps scarcely less potent, difficulty.' The fourth German legend, according to my friend, was that in modern warfare the command of the seas is of little value except in the widest oceans. The invasion of Sicily, the bombardment at Salerno, had done much to shake that legend; but it had not as yet been destroyed. And the final legend was of a political nature. It was the conviction that, if the worst came to the worst, Germany could always make a separate peace, with Russia against the West, or with the West against Russia. 'That sounds,' I said to him, 'rather a Ribbentrop sort of legend.' 'Not in the least,' he answered, 'it is a legend which many serious Germans will cherish to the very last.' And this may well explain the almost panic fury with which Dr Goebbels treated the Teheran Conference.

*

These short grey days at the fag end of the year hang sadly round us. We are conscious of the weariness of the past and the anxieties and efforts of the future. But we know that our legends – and we were glad enough of our legends in 1940 – have miraculously come true. The Germans know that their own legends are fantastic and that they have built upon them an edifice of fear and hatred which will be terrible in its collapse. The months in front of us will be months of sober anxiety. But they will not be months either of hopelessness or remorse. Our pride has been justified and our faith fulfilled. I am glad that I am not a German when 1943, and all its legends, fades wanly into 1944.

31 December 1943

Part Six
1944

THE EVACUEES

Norman Nicholson

Four years ago
They came to this little town
Carrying their bundles – women who did not know
Where the sky would lie when their babies were born, mothers
With children, children with sisters and brothers,
Children with schoolmates, and frightened children alone.
They saw the strangers at the station, the sea-mist on the hill,
In the windless waiting days when the walls of Poland fell.

Winter came
And the wind did not rise; the sky
Withheld its threat of thunderbolt or bomb.
The women were lonely. Thoughts began to bend
To Northumbrian voices high as a seagull's cry,
To the smell of the North Sea in the streets, the foggy air,
The fish-shops and the neighbours. The tide of fear
Flowed back, leaving weary empty sand.

The women returned
To the Tyneside husbands and the Tyneside coal,
And most of the children followed. Others stayed and learned
The Cumberland vowels, took strangers for their friends,
Went home for holidays at first, then not at all,
Accepted in the aisle the bishop's hands,
Won scholarships and badges, and were known
One with the indigenous children of the town.

Four years ago
They came, and in four childhood years
The memory shrivels and the muscles grow.
The little girl who wept on the platform then
Now feels her body blossom like the trees,
Discovers tennis, poetry and flowers,

And under the dripping larches in the rain
Knows the first experiment of a kiss.

Will they rest,
Will they be contented, these
Fledglings of a cuckoo's egg reared in a stranger's nest?
Born of one people, with another bred,
Will they return to their parents again, or choose
The foster-home, or seek the unrented road?
Grant that in the future they may find
A rock on which to build a house for heart and mind.

21 January 1944

MARGINAL COMMENT

Harold Nicolson

When I ask my constituents what they really mind most about the war it is always the blackout which comes first in their list of evils. The second tribulation, especially for women, is shopping. For me this ordeal is intermittent rather than constant. It is inconvenient, of course, to run out of soap, carbon paper, razor blades, and clothes. It is sad that my washing should be collected and delivered so irregularly, and that my underclothes, when they eventually return, have ceased to be my underclothes, but have shrunk to the shape of Little Black Sambo's pants. I quite see that were I a housekeeper (which I thank Heaven that I am not) these difficulties would assume enormous proportions, and that I should almost envy in my black despair the irresponsibility of those who labour at Anzio or in the Garigliano river-bed. But for those who have constantly to move from one place to another, and according to a rigid time-table, the second of war ills is certainly transport. It is all very well for those who can appear early at a station, and who on arrival can, in the eighteenth century manner, go to bed; but for those who have to dash for a train, make a speech on arrival, and then return in the evening, the conditions of modern transport are an ordeal which frays the nerves and debilitates the frame. St Pancras station on a wet midnight, and after three hours in a packed corridor, makes one realise that this is, in fact, a total war.

In this great darkness there is a shining light, namely, the amazing good-temper of the British people. After a night journey recently the dawn broke cold and grim upon a packed corridor. People had taken it in turns to sit upon their luggage, but when morning broke other people emerged from the compartments and picked their difficult way towards the end of the car. Those who had to rise at their passing did so with a wan smile of forgivingness upon their sleepless, haggard faces. 'You observe,' I remarked to a Polish officer who was standing next to me, 'how good-tempered are the citizens of this country?' He had stood the strain of the journey less well than my compatriots. He ground his teeth with rage. 'They are like sheeps,' he said furiously. 'Oh, no,' I said, 'it isn't that at all.' He grunted, unconvinced. My admiration for these patient, patriotic, courteous people knows no bounds. I pray with all my soul that they are right in thinking that we are now passing out of the last winter of the German War.

4 February 1944

MARGINAL COMMENT
Harold Nicolson

During the past few weeks there has been much discussion, in the Press and elsewhere, of the problem whether military necessity can justify the destruction of buildings of religious, historical or artistic importance. Those who regard the mortal as more important than the immortal fail to separate eternal values from momentary hopes and affections: whereas those who consider art to be more important than individual lives are unable to distinguish between what is desirable and what is practicable. I am not among those who feel that religious sites are, as such, of more importance than human lives, since religion is not concerned with material or temporal things; nor should I hesitate, were I a military commander, to reduce some purely historical building to rubble if I felt that by so doing I could gain a tactical advantage or diminish the danger to which my men were exposed. Works of major artistic value fall, however, into a different category. It is to my mind desirable that such works should be preserved from destruction, even if their preservation entails the sacrifice of human lives. I should assuredly be prepared to be shot against a wall if I were certain that by such a sacrifice I could preserve the Giotto frescoes; nor should I hesitate for an instant (were such a decision ever open to me) to save St Mark's even if I were aware that by so doing I should bring death to my sons. I should know that in a hundred years from now it would matter not at all if I or my children had survived; whereas it would matter seriously and permanently if the Piazza at Venice had been reduced to dust and ashes either by the Americans or ourselves. My attitude would be governed by a principle which is surely incontrovertible. The irreplaceable is more important than the replaceable, and the loss of even the most valued human life is ultimately less disastrous than the loss of something which in no circumstances can ever be created again.

It is indeed a catastrophe that the most destructive war that Europe has ever witnessed should have descended upon the loveliest things that Europe ever made. It is a reproach to democratic education that the peoples of Britain and America should be either indifferent or actually hostile to these supreme expressions of human intelligence. It is a reflection upon our leaders that they have shown but a perfunctory awareness of their responsibilities. And it will be a source of distress to our grandchildren that we, who might have stood firm as the trustees of Europe's heritage, should have turned our faces aside. To hope for a change of heart among the people or their rulers is, however, to hope for something which is quite impracticable: all we can do is to induce in them a slight, uneasy and recurrent sense of shame.

25 February 1944

NOT A CRIME BUT A BLUNDER

Nigel Nicolson

Twenty-five years ago the huge monastery of Monte Cassino was destroyed by Allied bombers. My brigade was then in the hills about eight miles away. We had not been warned of the attack, and were not directly involved in the battle that followed. But we could see the monastery clearly. It dominated the whole valley and the whole battle. Two American divisions had already smashed themselves against its defences. We were glad to see it go, and imagined that the way to Rome would now be open. It was thrilling to witness from a safe distance so dramatic a display of power; to see so massive a target hit fair and square. But was it fair, and was it square?

The demand that the monastery be destroyed originated with the soldiers of the 4th Indian Division who were about to attack it. The divisional commander, General Francis Tuker, claimed that 'Monte Cassino is a modern fortress and must be dealt with by modern means.' Whether the Germans were actually in occupation of it or not, in the last resort they would be bound to take refuge within its walls, and use it as a rallying-point for sorties and wounded. It was impossible to make a tactical distinction between a strongly fortified mountain and the buildings which crowned its summit. The monastery was an integral part of the German defence system. Tuker's argument was endorsed by Freyberg, passed on a little hesitantly by Mark Clark (the army commander) to Alexander, and there the buck stopped. Alexander took the final responsibility.

'When soldiers are fighting for a just cause,' he wrote in his memoirs, 'and are prepared to suffer death and mutilation in the process, bricks and mortar, no matter how venerable, cannot be allowed to weigh against human lives. In the context of the Cassino battle, how could a structure which dominated the fighting field be allowed to stand? The monastery had to be destroyed.' I remember him saying much the same thing when he visited our brigade a few weeks after Cassino fell. 'A commander, if faced by a choice between risking a single soldier's life and destroying a work of art, even a religious symbol like Monte Cassino, can make only

one decision. Otherwise the moral problem would become insupport-
able.' He said this with a sincerity that was impressive.

We now know that the Germans were not occupying the monastery.
Their fortifications were on the hill around it, but no closer than 200
metres from its walls, and they posted sentries outside the main gate to
prevent any troops entering the monastery itself. The German corps
commander, General von Senger, told me in London after the war that
Kesselring's policy, like Alexander's, was to spare religious monuments
whenever possible, and he had informed the Vatican that Monte Cassino
would not be occupied by his troops. Unfortunately, the version of this
declaration which reached the Allies was that 'no considerable body of
troops' was in the 'immediate vicinity' of the building, which left the
matter in doubt.

The Allies could scarcely believe that any commander would resist
making use of so formidable a fortress in the very centre of his line. Von
Senger, however, saw it differently. Apart from his strong personal feelings about the sanctity of the place (he was a Catholic from Bavaria), he
was unwilling to bottle up his troops in so obvious a target when they
could occupy the shellproof emplacements which had been prepared on
the surrounding hillside during the previous three months. To the Allies
looking up from the valley it seemed that a German observer must be stationed behind each of the monastery's thousand windows. But to the
Germans the upper part of the hill below the walls afforded even better
observation, because it was unrestricted and concealed. To add fifty feet
to a hill already 1,700 feet high gave them no extra advantage. 'Even
under normal conditions,' von Senger wrote in his autobiography,
'Monte Cassino would never have been occupied by artillery spotters. So
conspicuous a landmark would be quite unsuitable.'

Fred Majdalany, in his book on the Cassino battles, argues that it was
irrelevant whether the Germans were in the monastery or not. He calls
the question 'the great red herring'. The troops who were to attack it
thought that it was occupied, and that was all that mattered. They could
not be asked to undertake so dangerous an assault while this menace
hung over their heads. But was the question so irrelevant? If the monastery were destroyed, and the Germans could prove afterwards (as they
did, by the widely publicised statement of the Abbot) that they had
respected its neutrality, there would be four results. The bombing would
be wasted, since no enemy soldiers would be killed by it nor military
installations destroyed. The ruins would make an even more formidable
strongpoint than the intact building. The Germans would then have the
pretext to occupy it immediately. And world Catholic opinion would be
deeply shocked.

This is just what happened. The occupation of the ruins ('a far finer defence position than it would have been before its destruction', wrote von Senger) made the Allies' task more difficult. The bombing bolstered German more than Allied morale, after the first impact had passed. There had been insufficient coordination between the air attack and the ground attack, for the assault troops had been warned to expect the bombing a day later, and were not ready. Three months were to pass before the monastery was captured by the Poles, and then they bypassed it to the north. So, in the end, the bombing helped nobody, except the Germans. To them it seemed nothing more than a petulant gesture by the Allies in compensation for their previous failures to capture the position. The tough parachutists in Cassino town were cock-a-hoop.

The bombing of Monte Cassino, like the bombing of Dresden, worried the Allied conscience at the time, and still worries it. Mark Clark, who had said neither yes nor no to the Tuker/Freyberg request but left it to Alexander, wrote after the war that the bombing was not only an unnecessary psychological error but 'a tactical military mistake of the first magnitude'. All other Allied commanders, supported by Churchill, have defended the decision in retrospect, and so have the majority of historians. My own view is that it was a blunder, but not a crime. The question of German occupation was highly relevant to the decision, but it was treated as secondary, and the evidence for it was based upon chance observations from ground and air, not on repeated and specific inquiries through the Vatican, which in such a matter could have afforded an exceptional channel of communication between enemies. Nor was it fair to leave the decision to Alexander. It should have been taken at the highest political level.

If the troops could have been assured by their commanders that not a single German soldier was in the monastery, they would have been as relieved as by the information that a major blockhouse on the Normandy beaches was unoccupied. If they had known that only the Abbot, five monks and some hundreds of peasants had taken refuge there, the monastery would have been neutralised in their minds as well as on the ground. It was possible to fight the battle round the hill, as indeed it was fought, without damaging the monastery by more than a stray shell.

I say that the bombing was not a crime because these facts were not known, and because Alexander was certainly right in his definition of a commander's responsibility for his men's lives. The Pope told him, after the capture of Rome, that he fully understood the necessity for it.

My father wrote in The Spectator a week after the bombing, 'I should not hesitate for an instant to save St Mark's from destruction even if I were aware that by so doing I should bring death to my sons.' I read that

ırticle in Italy with mixed feelings, and heard to my delight that it
ıroused strong protests in England. 'The loss of even the most valued
human life,' he went on, 'is ultimately less disastrous than the loss of
something which in no circumstances can ever be created again.' Well,
the monastery has been rebuilt around the cell and tomb of St Benedict
which miraculously survived untouched. Religious sites are in a sense
always more replaceable than works of art, since religion is not concerned with material or temporal things. Still, the monastery at Monte
Cassino was both, and it could have been spared. How easy to say this
now! I think back to that February morning in 1944 when I watched the
bombs explode, and I remember my elation. I know, too, that had I been
Alexander, I would have acted as he acted.

21 March 1969

MARGINAL COMMENT

Harold Nicolson

It is sometimes said that this war, unlike the last, has produced no outstanding poet. I doubt whether this is a correct assertion. The poetry of
Sidney Keyes, for instance, is certainly valuable poetry; once we have had
time to assimilate it, we may pronounce its value to be great. There is little of it to judge by, and yet that little is complete in itself. We have the
volume called *The Iron Laurel* which Routledge published in 1942. We
have the collection of poems which the same publisher issued recently
under the title *The Cruel Solstice*. There must exist in some form the
morality play which Keyes wrote and produced at Oxford in 1941. There
are memories and letters. It is possible, even from this scant material, to
form some impression of the quality of his genius and to trace the development of his mind and taste. The first point about Sidney Keyes is his
astounding precocity; he acquired the mastery of his inspiration and
technique when scarcely more than a child. His poem, for instance, on
The Buzzard, with its very intricate geometrical scheme, is handled with
complete and muscular assurance. I have been told that he composed
that poem, and very rapidly, when he was no more than a schoolboy of
seventeen. It was written to fill a blank space in the school magazine; his

tutor, to whom he showed it, saw at once that it was worthy of a more discriminating audience and advised him to send it to some London periodical. In his innocence and modesty Keyes sent the poem by the same post to three different editors; to his astonishment it was simultaneously accepted by all three; difficult explanations followed. The story is illustrative of boyish diffidence and underlying certitude of mind. For in truth his poetic gift was born fully armed: while still a stripling he strode in iron intellectual armour across the stones.

It is not his amazing poetic skill only which differentiates Sidney Keyes from so many of his contemporaries, but above all his grave acceptance of the tragedy to which his youth was destined. It is not war only which appalls him:

> The captive brain, the feet that walk to war
> The ironbound brain, the hand unskilled in war
> The shrinking brain, sick of an inner war.

He has a firm sense of courage:

> The fifes cry death and the sharp winds call.
> Set your face to the rock; go on, go out
> Into the bad lands of battle, into the cloud-wall
> Of the future, my friends, and leave your fear.

But he is obsessed by the dread of pain, the certainty of death:

> See
> How I believed in pain, how near I got
> To living pain, regarding my lost image
> Of hard perfection, sexless and immortal.

And a tragic import is given to his poetry by his deep premonition that he also must die in Africa: 'and the tall miraculous city that I walked in will never house me':

> The bright waves scour the wound of Carthage.
> The shadows of gulls run spiderlike through Carthage.
> The cohorts of the sand are wearing Carthage
> Hollow and desolate as a turning wave;
> But the bronze eagle has flown east from Rome.
> Rome remember, remember the seafowls' sermon
> That followed the beaked ships westward to their triumph,
> O Rome, you city of soldiers, remember the singers
> That cry with dead voices along the African shore.

A man of his intellect, a man of his poetic certainty, might have pierced the cloud of uselessness which keeps the sunshine from our younger men. Sidney Keyes was killed before he reached manhood; but he has left behind him something that is most powerful and lovely:

> A boy's voice flowering out of silence
> Rising through choirs to the ear's whorled shrine
> And living there, a light.

24 March 1944

NEWS OF THE WEEK

Forty-eight hours after the launching of the first attacks on the beaches of Normandy the British official report was that operations were running to time and going as well as could be expected. The German report was that the battle was going as well as could be expected from the defenders' point of view. The two verdicts are not necessarily in conflict, for they are passed on operations which at this stage must be indeterminate and indecisive. Certainly the attack could not have had a much better beginning. Misgivings about General Eisenhower's decision to launch the assault in weather which would be bound to subject a large proportion of the troops to that most disabling of temporary ailments, sea-sickness, were largely dispelled when it became clear that the Germans' scepticism about an assault in such conditions provided a considerable element of tactical surprise. The improvement in the weather since Wednesday is perhaps the best news the Allied forces could hope for. As for the actual operations, the capture of Bayeux is welcome. The capture of Caen, where fighting has been in progress since early on Tuesday, would be more welcome; news of that may arrive at any moment. From the very guarded British statements and the much more expansive German *communiqués* it is clear that the Allies are concentrating their attention on the Cherbourg peninsula. It is the obvious strategy, and appears to be meeting with considerable initial success. Full success would give the invasion an invaluable start. For that reason Rundstedt will exert every conceivable effort to rush up sufficient troops to hold the great naval port. The Allies can bring in reinforcements by air faster than the enemy can by land, but not with the same heavy equipment. Here, possibly, as in a later stage almost certainly, the air-arm may be the deciding factor. Whatever the strength of the Luftwaffe may be, the German air-force must inevitably be destroyed whenever it goes fully into action. Rundstedt's supreme problem must be to choose the moment and conditions when that sacrifice will bring the greatest return.

Organising an Invasion

In these days when everyone knows something of the meaning of 'total war' it hardly needs demonstrating that masses of trained men cannot be thrown on to a hostile shore without elaborate organisation on a colossal scale. In an operation of the size of the western invasion hundreds of thousands of men, performing specialised activities of hundreds of different kinds, have to be trained for exactly this task. Ships have to be provided, timed, and depart in orderly synchronisation from many harbours for specified objectives. The Royal Navy has its escorting duties and its attack functions, while the Air Force provides cover, attacks targets near and far, and keeps reserves available for any emergency. But all of this indicates no more than the last stage before the invasion itself, the stage for which preparations have been going on in planning units, in factories, in depots, and in the transport services for years before the whole thing takes its final shape. From the moment when the authorities began to reorganise the troops rescued from Dunkirk this country, as Mr Churchill has never ceased to make us aware, has been directing its war-policy with the ultimate intention of reconquering Europe; and from the moment when it began to plan the divisions into which a striking force would be divided, and the various units with specialised functions which would form part of the divisions or be ancillary to them, the vista of military organisation on a literally unprecedented scale was opened up. At different stages of the war planning passed more and more from the general to the particular, and finally took shape under the conception that United States forces and other Allied fighting units would be operating side by side with our own. An invasion requires trained men, ships, aeroplanes, tanks and guns – and how much else? – assembled from thousands of places to marshalling yards and embarkation points, each unit having just its right proportion of essential equipment, ammunition and food, with reserves behind coming in from day to day as required. The operation, as a military authority has said, is like transporting the population of two of our greatest cities overseas and keeping their personal and military needs fully supplied day by day. The miracle is being punctually performed.

9 June 1944

WALLOWING TO UTAH

Julian Spiro

This piece, written a few days after the event, describes the little-known role played on D-Day by Thames lighters, engineless flat-bottomed barges operated on tidal rivers by lightermen using wooden sweeps, or bargepoles. From 1942 onwards hundreds of the barges were given engines and loading ramps so that they could be used in the invasion. The conversion did not, however, produce a very seaworthy vessel. Julian Spiro's flotilla of 18 barges was seconded to the US assault forces landing on Utah beach. The US Navy Captain instructed his officers: 'Give these barges a wide berth, they are a menace to shipping.'

Towards the end of May our flotilla sailed from our base to Poole. Landing barge crews normally sleep ashore but from then on officers and men lived aboard. Everyone was sure that things were about to get moving, but no one knew when or where. Guns were tested, stores checked, emergency rations loaded, engines carefully tuned – but all this with a sense of urgency and the feeling that this time we were not preparing for just another large-scale decoy exercise in the English Channel.

Without being told to, each man took extra care. They had seen the hundreds of craft massing in the ports. Confidential charts were delivered by hand of officer, sealed TOP SECRET and with instructions to be opened only on receipt of a certain signal.

The other landing barge flotillas in X Squadron were still being loaded by the army, but we had a special cargo and pumping equipment, to refuel the assault craft after their first run-in. From D-Day until D plus 4, our flotilla was to keep the entire naval assault force off our beach-head supplied with petrol and diesel – everything from LCAs up to destroyers. We expected to be busy.

As the barges in the other flotillas finished loading they came and moored to the trots of buoys allocated to our squadron. We had always regarded the barges as silly trundling old things, undoubtedly the lowest form of marine life. They had never been designed to go to sea. But now, looking down the trots of buoys at the hundreds of barges stretching away up the estuary, we felt quite pleased with them. Singly they were rather stupid, but collectively they acquired a sort of clumsy strength.

Then one morning the officers were summoned ashore – we were going to be briefed. It was a stifling hot day, yet the briefing-room windows were tightly shut, the doors were locked, and armed sentries were on guard outside. The senior officer began: 'We are going to land on the east side of the Cherbourg peninsula. D-Day is next Monday, the 5th. H-Hour is 0600.' We received our copies of the operations orders, and examined the chart overlays showing the course we were going to take. We would set sail on D minus 1 at 1600 hours.

Back on board, we were immediately 'sealed up', and all shore leave was stopped. When a party of men had to go ashore for stores they were accompanied by an armed officer. The town was strictly out of bounds, and conversation with civilians was a criminal offence.

On Sunday 4 June we received a signal that D-Day was postponed 24 hours owing to bad weather. On Monday the sea was still rough and I was terrified that it might mean a further postponement, for the crews had now been briefed and after all the waiting everyone wanted to get on with it.

But there was no postponement and at three o'clock on the Monday afternoon on 5 June the signal went up, 'Prepare to weigh.' Hundreds of barge engines immediately sprang into life and the mighty roar they made seemed to express our relief at getting going at last. As barge after barge switched on engines all down that long line the roar increased to a fury of sound that must have been heard for miles inland.

At exactly 1600 hours our flotilla received the signal, 'Take up formation single line ahead.' We slipped from the buoy and started down the estuary with the other barges peeling off from their moorings and taking up station astern of us in prearranged order. The line of barges, an ensign fluttering from each one, stretched away as far as the eye could see. And still they kept coming – taking a full hour to get clear of the estuary.

As we approached the rendezvous point off the Needles a couple of hours later we fairly gaped, for ahead of us lay what was surely the greatest mass of shipping ever assembled. And this was only one of scores of assembly points all round the coast of Britain. Great carriers, troop transports, ships and craft of every size and description were converging from all directions. Four Hunt-class destroyers came belting out of the Solent, picking their way through the hundreds of craft scattered about before turning in succession to port, keeping station magnificently at high speed. A light cruiser shot past us at full speed, on her way to meet a convoy that was still only a forest of funnels and masts on the horizon.

Indeed, so great was the general sense of excitement that I only now fully realised one fact – that the sea was rough. This meant little to a real ship with a keel to cleave the water but it meant a whole lot to flat-bottomed barges that would roll on wet grass. And it was blowing up, too. We, who had never been allowed to exercise in more than a force four wind, were now rolling around in at least force five or six.

Now one of our escorting MLs rolled up and signalled 'Follow me'. Well, this was it! All that great mass of shipping was still at anchor, but we had to start out many hours beforehand because of our slow speed. Rather like the kids being packed off to bed while the grown-ups still sit around talking, we threaded our way through the maze of shipping keeping close on the heels of our nanny the ML.

Our station-keeping was lousy. It was impossible for barges to keep station in that sea. Those long months we had spent in practising cruising dispositions at sea went for a Burton. The barges just lurched and rolled drunkenly in the waves, following the leaders as best they could. And remembering those Hunt-class destroyers I reflected that this was an awfully undignified way to go to the second front.

Leading our flotilla was an armed trawler whose duty it was to take in tow any barge that might break down. It is recorded that the trawler's skipper, who had never seen one of our barges before that afternoon, kept looking back at them from his bridge with a mixture of incredulity and pity, murmuring repeatedly: 'The poor cunts . . .'

It was twilight now, and as the Channel coast receded into the distance I realised that the next time I stepped ashore it would be onto a French beach. We were taking a sweeping zigzag course so as not to disclose our eventual destination to the enemy reconnaissance craft. As darkness came down, the ML circled round exhorting us through her loudhailer to keep closed up.

Very soon after dark came what we had been expecting. On our starboard beam a cluster of star-shells went up. E-boats! Almost at once there followed streams of red tracer bullets describing their graceful leisurely arcs.

It's amazing how a flare at sea on a dark night makes you feel naked and exposed. We had our orders: only to open fire if directly attacked, so as not to give away our position. The escort was to deal primarily with attackers. Our gun crews were closed up and all lifebelts inflated. I thought of our cargo tanks each carrying 12,000 gallons of 100-octane. It would only require one armour-piercing bullet.

The battle lasted half an hour. The trawler's bridge got hit, and so did a few barges – but not, thank the Lord, in the fuel tanks. The casualties weren't heavy. Then the E-boats cleared off – no doubt they had spotted better game. The barges must have been a very difficult target in that sea as they sat very low in the water and were hidden by waves half the time. In the darkness they were still lurching and wallowing in the heavy sea. A few were straggling, but somehow that amazing convoy kept on its course. (I made a mental note to travel first-class on the boat when visiting France after the war.)

The sea grew rougher. Two hours later the trawlers had their hands full, towing at least three barges apiece. Other barges were straggling badly and the ML kept ploughing on through it, gunwales awash, indeed submerged most of the time. Now two barges reported they were shipping water faster than they could pump it out and were sinking. The Squadron Commander's yacht came alongside them and picked the crews off. It was a magnificent piece of seamanship in that heavy sea. The yacht was as light and frail as a cockle-shell compared with the heavy plunging barges, and a knock from them would have holed and sunk her instantly.

The dawn light revealed some mines floating around. It revealed too that three of the stragglers were missing. Whether they filled up and sank, or got picked off by E-boats, or struck mines, we don't know. Those three barges were never seen or heard of again. The heavy weather had reduced our already slow speed, our snail-like progress in striking contrast to the invasion fleet now whipping past us and the air fleets passing overhead.

We travelled along the coast to our beach-head amid an inferno of noise. Battleships of the Home Fleet were pounding hell out of the coast batteries, mines were going up all around us, enemy shells rained down. But the sea calmed down, the sun came out, and we thanked the Lord for being delivered from that nightmare voyage amidst the perils of the sea into the peace and security of the battle area.

9 June 1984

NEWS OF THE WEEK

On the ninth day of the invasion the length of the Allied line is something over eighty miles and the depth of its greatest penetration some twenty miles. The advance, moreover, in spite of the growing intensity of the fighting, still continues. An enemy counter-offensive might have been expected before this, but so far Rundstedt has been capable of mounting only local counter-attacks. Montgomery's tactics of ceaseless attack appear to have compelled the German command to throw in its armour prematurely, and the tanks cannot now disengage to re-group for a concerted offensive. It is too soon to decide that no such offensive can now materialise, but the general situation is not only as good as could have been hoped but rather better. There are large Allied forces in the beach areas still to be thrown in, to say nothing of the reinforcements being ceaselessly ferried across an English Channel which to all appearance is as safe as if U-boats had never been invented. It is true that the naval guns have been of immense value to the invading forces, which will soon be moving beyond their range, but the air arm is always there, and its destruction of communications may prove the major ingredient of victory. The achievement of landing some hundreds of thousands of troops, with heavy as well as light equipment, on open beaches in heavy weather against fortifications elaborated not through months but through years is something unparalleled in military history, and it would hardly have been believed possible if it had not been proved so. Marshal Stalin's generous tribute is as merited as it is welcome; there is characteristically sardonic humour in the reference to Napoleon's fruitless and futile procrastination in the invasion of Britain, and 'Hitler the Hysteric's' failure even to attempt to carry out his loudly-trumpeted threat of invasion, as contrasted with the Allies' triumphant achievement in Normandy. There has hardly been sufficient recognition here – though the omission is obviously only inadvertent – of what is owed to the British Minister of Defence in that capacity.

16 June 1944

ONE MAN'S D-DAY

Iain Macleod

I had graduated from the Staff College early in February 1944, and had had exactly one day out of my leave when the telegram arrived. I was to report with the rank of Major to an address in Ashley Gardens, near Victoria Station. There were no other details. When I arrived, I found myself an extra DAQMG (Deputy Assistant Quarter Master General) on the planning staff of the famous 50th (Northumbrian) Division. 50 Div., as everyone knew them, had been brought back from the Sicilian campaign to take part in the assault on France. The attack was now planned on a five-division front with 50 Div. in the centre. On our right two American Divisions of the American 1st Army; on our left the 3rd British and 3rd Canadian Divisions. 50 Div. was almost the size of a small Corps when it landed. A fourth infantry Brigade and an Armoured Brigade came under command. So did a crowd of artillery units, and a proportion of the 'comics' – special units often with Heath Robinson-type equipment designed for a special task. In all, there were about 40,000 men.

I did not in this planning stage expect to land with the Division. Probably when the planning was over I would either be given another appointment or, more likely, be held temporarily in Montgomery's pool of staff officers to wait for the inevitable vacancies that the assault would bring. But under the strain of the planning the AA and QMG fell ill. Tom Black, the divisional DAQMG, was promoted in his place and I took over Tom's job. I studied the landing sheets again. H plus forty, I saw, was 'my' time. In other words, I was due to land forty minutes after the first wave of assault troops went in. I did not know when D-Day was, but by an odd chance I learned where the invasion was to take place. Thumbing through a file in the Headquarters of 2nd Army I saw a receipt for a map marked 'TOP SECRET OVERLORD' (the invasion code name). To most people the receipt would have meant nothing, but I had just come from the Staff College at Camberley and recognised the map sheet number as the one, based on St Lô, which we had used in a staff exercise. I took the receipt away and burned it. So we were not to land in the Pas de Calais, but in Normandy.

Slowly order began to emerge from chaos. We met our Naval Force G at Weymouth, and the staffs wove the plans together. We rehearsed endlessly at Studland Bay in Dorset. And in due course in the last two days of May a tide of men and machines began to roll towards Southampton. By June 1 we were afloat. No more telephones, and very little to do. If we hadn't thought of everything already, it was too late. We knew now when D-Day was to be – June 5. We knew exactly where we were to land, exactly where the different headquarters were to be established and, above all, what the objectives were for the Division on D-Day. I spent most of the time (and nearly all D-Day itself) with Lieut.-Colonel 'Bertie' Gibb, then ADOS in charge of Ordnance Supplies, and of many other things. Even by 50 Div. standards, Bertie was an exceptional staff officer. He is my only check on the accuracy of my memory, for I kept no written record of the landing. I have also confirmed the outline of the attack from Major Ewart Clay's book.[1] But my account does not pretend to historical accuracy. It is, as I remember it, one man's D-Day. The day of course belonged, above all, to the fighting infantry. No praise can be too high for them. I was only a staff officer. But I was there.

D-Day itself was postponed for twenty-four hours until June 6. Even so, the weather was cold and the sea was rough. General Eisenhower took the greatest gamble in all military history when he launched his armada on such uncertain seas. He was proved right.

The Divisional HQ was split between two ships, and I found myself with men of the 1st Hampshires of 231 Brigade. For the Division this was the second seaborne assault. For 231 Brigade, the third. Moreover, the 50th Division, which had been the last Division to leave the beaches of Dunkirk, was now one of those chosen to be the first to land in Normandy. I had not been with them in 1940, but I had, in fact, been away from France for a few days less. It was about June 10, long after Dunkirk, that I had left St Nazaire in a hospital ship. Four years later, and in the company of the finest fighting Division of the Army, I was going back.

Perhaps I was helped by my early voyages on the Minch, but I slept soundly enough through the rough night, and came on deck somewhere around first light. The waves were still choppy and the landing was going to be a hazardous and in part a haphazard affair. But the day was becoming warm. The coast of Normandy began to take shape through the haze. And then as full light began to come one saw the ships and the planes. It was a sight so paralysing that tears came to my eyes. It was as if every ship that had ever been launched was there, and even as if the sea had yielded up her wrecks. It was as if every plane that had ever been built was there, and, so it seemed in fantasy, as if the dead crews were there too. There had never been since time began such a rendezvous for fighting men: there never will be again. And I remember reciting, not in scorn, but out of sheer delight at being part of that great company in such a place, 'And gentlemen in England now abed . . .'

As the fire from the naval guns began to blot out the shore defences, and the endless drone of the planes and the whine of their bombs rose to a crescendo, so came H-hour. 50 Div. were to assault on a front of two brigades, the 69th on the left and the 231st on the right. The Hampshires were to land just east of Le Hamel and to take the village and then the other coastal villages, especially Arromanches which was earmarked as the site of the artificial port called Mulberry. It meant for them a day of heavy fighting and severe casualties. The commanding officer was

[1] *The Path of the 50th.* By E.W. Clay. (Gale and Polden, 1950.)

wounded, and the second-in-command killed. But it was also a day of glory for the regiment that must rank high, perhaps first, among all the Hampshires' battle honours. Watching the LCAs (Landing Craft Assault) carrying the Hampshires pull away and switchback to the shore, and while waiting for our own sea taxi, I thought that as a martial gesture I would load my revolver. When I unbuttoned my ammunition pouch, I found that my batman, who knew more about war than I did, had filled it not with bullets but with boiled sweets. He was quite right. They proved much more useful.

Few things went exactly as planned, and the biggest disappointment was the failure of the secret waterproofed tanks to negotiate the heavy seas. They were supposed to paddle through the last few miles to the beach and provide covering fire for the assaulting companies. In view of the weather, it was then decided to take the craft to the beach, and disembark the tanks. The same dilemma came to the Americans assaulting the strongly-held Omaha beach to our right, but here a different and a tragic decision was taken. In spite of the seas, sixty-four tanks were launched and all were swamped. Nearly all the crews were drowned and, of course, the cover fire was lost.

Presently Bertie and I climbed with elderly dignity down the scrambling nets that were slung over the ship's sides and dropped down into our LCA. We began to cruise in to the beach. Something now went wrong. Perhaps the naval officer in charge decided that too many craft were trying to get ashore at once, perhaps the underwater mines obstructed us. In any event, we began to circle a few hundred yards away from the beach. Quite a long time passed. The sun grew hotter, and I began to doze. Suddenly and equally for no reason that I could see, we stopped turning and ran straight for the beach. The landing ramp smacked down and one stepped or jumped according to taste into the thigh-deep water. Bertie and I stepped, and waded carefully ashore.

The beach was alive with the shambles and the order of war. There were dead men and wounded men and men brewing tea. There were men reorganising for a battle advance, and men doing absolutely nothing. There were even some German prisoners waiting patiently for heaven knows what. There was a whole graveyard of wrecked ships and craft and tanks of every size. It was like an absurdly magnificent film by Cecil B. de Mille. It was like war.

We wandered over the beaches and climbed the dunes behind them. Everything seemed oddly quiet. The minefields were most carefully marked ('Achtung Minen') and wired. The villages to left and right of us were still German-held, although we did not realise it at the time. We must have taken a sand track between them.

We met very few people on the way to the orchard at Meuvaines which was to be our D-Day headquarters. Only a motley collection of vehicles had arrived, but one of them was the intelligence truck and in it a staff officer was busy marking up the reports of the progress of the leading battalions. We were about a mile and a half inland.

The rest of the day is a patchwork of memories. There was a flurry of shots into the orchard from a small nest of Germans we had overlooked. There was a journey back to the beaches to see the build-up. There was a journey on the back of a policeman's motor-cycle to find the forward brigades, and establish contact with their staff captains. I can't remember when I ate, but I remember what I ate. We had been issued with twenty-four-hour packs of concentrated dried food. I expect they had a taste as evil as their appearance. But I don't think many people in 50 Div. tasted them. 50 Div. were used to looking after themselves. From somewhere my batman produced both the great delicacies of 1944 – tinned steak pudding and tinned Christmas pudding. These and whisky were my food.

Night began to fall. Nearly all our objectives had been taken. Patrols were moving into Bayeux, which was to fall next morning. The St Leger feature was in our grasp. The 47th Royal Marine Commando (under our command for the landings) had started its successful battle for Port-en-Bessin. Hideous close fighting in the Bocage lay ahead, but at least on the 50 Div. front the day had gone well.

My batman had secured a corner of the farmer's barn for me, and I was thinking of snatching some sleep when the door opened and Tom Black looked in:

'Is Iain here?' I followed him outside.

'What's up?'

'Nothing. I thought we'd have a drink.'

We stood under the trees, drinking from his flask and looking back towards the sea. A few fast German fighter planes were making a tip-and-run raid on the beach, and the red tracer bullets climbed lazily into the sky after them. I looked at my watch. It was exactly midnight. I had lived through D-Day. We had expected anything up to 40 per cent casualties in the landing, and somehow I had been convinced that I would be killed. Now, equally unreasonably, I became convinced that I would live through the war. I would see our second child, who was to be born in October. There would be a life after the war. D-Day was over.

5 June 1964

ON THE OTHER SIDE OF THE HILL

General Leo Freiherr Geyr von Schweppenburg
(Commander-in-Chief, Panzergroup West, in 1944)

In a peaceful room in St Germain in the early summer of 1944 I was sitting with the Chief of Staff of von Rundstedt's Western Army Group. Once again our conversation turned to the question of the invasion.

'Our intelligence service has just received a warning from one of the London embassies that the invasion is now imminent,' he remarked. 'But I am not at all sure that this whole business of invasion is not an enormous bluff.'

Indeed, knowing the British intelligence methods, one could seldom tell what was the truth and what was a hoax; but this time I was sure. 'No,' I replied, 'the British, from the Prime Minister down, are prepared to use anything as a hoax, with one exception. That exception is the Crown. The King has seen the troops off. Believe me, the invasion is coming.'

The danger of opinions such as that expressed by the Chief of Staff seemed to me so great that I asked if I might put my views personally to von Rundstedt. The Field-Marshal listened in silence. Such was the lethargy in the Army Group Headquarters that I also warned the staff as energetically as I could of the dangers of air attack, and in particular of airborne landings. I knew General Browning from my time in London. I knew his job at that time was training the airborne troops. Slessor I had not then known personally, but I was well aware of his important and dangerous military teaching.

By 1944, the Hitler regime had seriously undermined both the spirit and the principles of the German command system. In the old army, teaching on the subject of command depended upon a cold and sober assessment of every situation, and relied upon the competence of every subordinate to carry out his task in whatever manner seemed best to him. This was replaced by 'intuition' from Berchtesgaden, and by a strict control of every smallest detail from the top. Contrary opinions were not entertained.

Hitler hated the General Staff. He succeeded in splitting it, and reducing it to a monstrous Saints and Sinners Club. Such few Saints as remained by 1944 he hanged after July 20.

No Allied soldier can understand what the atmosphere of Hitler's madhouse was like. His influence affected everyone – the leading military men as well as those of weaker character. To understand it one must have experienced it oneself. People who have had no experience of the destruction of complete families and the concentration camp cannot fully understand.

The German soldiers who fought and died bravely behind the fictitious Atlantic Wall made a sad picture. The infantry divisions could scarcely be called even third-rate. It was not their loyalty or their courage that was in question, but their physical condition and their equipment. Again and again these formations had been combed out to provide replacements for casualties on the Eastern Front. Almost one-third of the strength of the infantry divisions of the Seventh Army in Normandy was made up of Russians; they lacked all mobility, and their equipment simply did not compare with that of their enemy. At no time could the so-called Atlantic Wall ever seriously have impeded an Allied landing on the Continent.

The panzer divisions, on the other hand, were well trained. The commanders had for the most part had a longer command training than even those of the Waffen SS. It was reckoned later on, by a number of experienced officers, that at this time the panzer divisions were still at least one-third as powerful as they had been in September 1939.

The whole basis of their training lay in recognising the enemy air superiority over the battlefield. They depended upon fast movement by night and in the twilight, on really accurate shooting, and on the quick and reliable passing of orders. Enemy airborne or parachute landings had to be dealt with immediately, even if they turned out to be dummy landings. Where infantry tactics were concerned, I had ordered a demonstration battalion to be formed in 21st Panzer Division, to show British infantry tactics. These were watched by all the panzer troops.

These fine troops were overwhelmed by weight of numbers. The words of Marshal Timoshenko – 'The steel of the German Army must be melted in the holocaust of the Russian onslaught' – applied once more.

Old Field-Marshal von Rundstedt in St Germain, though highly respected, was ailing. He had become lethargic. He had no command over either the Luftwaffe or the German Navy, and armoured tactics were not his strong point. Difficult decisions were avoided. His Chief of Staff tried to iron out differences of opinion by negotiation, even when no compromise was possible and only a tough decision would do.

Before the arrival of Rommel, Field-Marshal von Rundstedt had laid down clearly the role of the panzer forces in defence of the Western Front. They were his only really battleworthy formations. Rundstedt had followed the recommendation of his responsible adviser on the subject – in this case myself. The main force of the panzer divisions was to remain well back from the coast, but north of the River Loire. South of the river were three panzer divisions which I had newly formed into the 58th Panzer Corps. It was impossible to tell at this stage whether the invasion would come first from the Mediterranean or from the Channel, but with this deployment, with the SS Panzergrenadier Division Götz von Berlichingen on the Loire, an immediate reaction either northwards or southwards could be achieved.

Rommel, however, brought a new idea. He required the invaders to be pushed back on to the coast. His experience of the very powerful British Air Force in Africa had convinced him (wrongly) that the movement of large mechanised formations was no longer a practical proposition. For months there had been a protracted controversy between him and myself as the adviser on this subject to the Commander-in-Chief. General Guderian, Hitler's highly experienced but often unheeded armoured adviser, supported my opinion without question.

Rommel's ideas, being clearly defensive in concept, were undoubtedly out of keeping with proper armoured tactics. He did not see the difference between the open expanses of the desert and the thickly covered countryside of Normandy. On the other hand, by adopting a more mobile concept of operations, a concentrated counter-attack could at the very least have achieved a temporary victory against the Allies. The insistence on the defence of the coastline threw away from the start the mobility of the panzer formations; worse, they were committed in the impossible hedgerow country, hemmed in by minefields and marshes.

The endeavours of the leading armoured experts to hold a proper force in reserve had two main purposes. The first was to retain some possibility of manoeuvre, and the second was to avoid, in the event of an airborne landing, the breakdown of our whole supply system by cutting us off from our petrol. Due to constant casualties to our supply columns caused by air attacks, our supply system never worked well from the start of the campaign.

Perhaps the last word in the story of this great argument about the employment of the armour comes from one of Rommel's personal orderly officers whom I met briefly (much later) on Stuttgart railway station. He told me that shortly before Rommel's injury on July 17, 1944, the Field-Marshal had remarked to him: 'It would perhaps have been better after all to have held the panzer divisions back.'

At the time, the ultimate solution to this lengthy argument came in the form of a directive from Berchtesgaden. This solution was the worst possible: it was neither one thing nor the other. Half the force was to be moved at Rommel's disposal, to the coast; the remainder would stay inland 'for the time being'.

Remember the wise Moltke's maxim: 'Mistakes in preliminary deployment are difficult to correct.'

As to where the Allied landings would take place, Rommel, Jodl and von Salmuth were all in agreement; the main landing would be in the Pas de Calais. Rommel clung firmly to this belief, even after the battle on the Cotentin peninsula had been fought for some weeks.

Early on June 6 I heard from my Chief of Staff that the invasion had begun. The army group had ordered the panzer divisions which had been held back north of the Loire to move to the coast. I had not even been asked.

I requested immediately that the Panzer Lehr Division should not move before nightfall. My request was refused; or rather, I did not even receive an answer. The armoured grenadier battalion of this division, which was the only one that was properly equipped, was heavily attacked from the air during this daylight move.

On the morning of the invasion a young German pilot had succeeded in carrying out a particularly courageous operation and had flown over the Allied invasion fleet without being detected or engaged. Unfortunately, *his report never reached the High Command*. Had it done so, it would have removed any doubt that this landing in Normandy was in fact the real thing. On June 7 I was ordered from the Headquarters in St Germain to take command of the Caen sector under the direct command of the Seventh Army and indirectly under Rommel's command. (Whatever one may say of Rommel's tactical ability, he was a brave and tough soldier, and his constant appearance at the front line demanded respect. This made it possible for the more senior officers to accept his orders.)

The area around Caen and the neighbouring coastline were well known to me. I had had the job of planning the operations of 24th Infantry Army Corps as the follow-up formation in Operation Sealion (which was the intended invasion of England in 1940).

The boldness of the enemy airborne operations achieved full success – as boldness always does. The landing of the 6th British Airborne Division near Caen was most successful.

A request was sent at once to Rommel's headquarters to allow the 21st Panzer Division to operate against this landing. Unfortunately Rommel was away in Germany at the time, and he had given strict orders that the

21st Panzer Division should not be moved without his own specific order. He had estimated that there was no danger of invasion at this time because of the state of the tides. It was not until eight o'clock on the following morning that his Chief of Staff gave permission for the division to move. By this time it was too late.

When I visited the courageous infantry divisions on the coast north of Caen I found that they had been practically wiped out by the Allied bombardment. On June 8 and 9 I visited the three panzer divisions which had by then been committed. They were fighting a very hard battle. I had received clear orders from the Seventh Army on June 8 in the best traditions of the old German Army; however, shortly afterwards I received conflicting orders from Rommel, from the Army Group Headquarters in St Germain, and from Berchtesgaden. What a state our army had reached!

On the morning of June 10 I visited a regimental headquarters near an abbey on the top of the hill just north of Caen. From there I saw a panzer regiment in action against the Canadians. It was hellish, but in this case the hell came from the sky. The British and Canadian troops were magnificent. This was not surprising when one knew the type of man, and when one knew that a large part of them had been trained by that outstanding soldier (and old friend of mine) General Sir Bernard Paget.

However, after a while I began to think, rightly or wrongly, that the command of these superb troops was not making the best use of them. The command seemed slow and rather pedestrian. It seemed that the Allied intention was to wear down their enemy with their enormous material superiority. It will never be known whether Montgomery had received a private instruction from his Government to avoid for the British troops another bloodbath such as they had suffered in the First World War on the Somme and at Passchendaele. However, it seemed to me that the command of the British and Canadians failed to make the best use of these magnificent troops.

One serious problem which faced us was the dropping of agents by parachute. As soon as they landed they were swallowed up by the local population. Many years later Chester Wilmot told me that from the moment that my headquarters had left Paris it had been continually shadowed; I could well believe him. The subsequent destruction of my whole headquarters in the late afternoon of June 10 was no doubt the result of the highly organised intelligence service run by the British. Only a few moments before an air attack wiped out my operational headquarters, Rommel and I had left the very command vehicle which was destroyed. I was lucky in that, being 'off-side', I was only slightly wounded.

The command of the Caen sector was then taken over by 1st SS Panzer

Corps under General Sepp Dietrich on the orders of Seventh Army. Dietrich had been a Bavarian cavalry sergeant. He was brave and friendly and to me he was always most loyal. However, in a fast-moving and attacking battle he was not up to his job.

The counter-attack which I had planned to take place on June 10 had to be cancelled. Then the British 7th Armoured Division made its appearance. The Desert Rats first started to make life unpleasant for us in the area of Bayeux.

In accordance with my orders I went off to Paris to reorganise my new staff. By about June 23 I had taken over my new command which consisted of three panzer corps and one infantry corps. I was under the direct command of Rommel. As soon as I took over command I called together the four chiefs of staff of these formations. They were all well-trained and experienced soldiers and I had no reason to think that any of them were suicidal maniacs. I then put to them a question to which I required the answer Yes or No. The question was: 'Do you think it possible to push the Allied invasion back into the sea?' Nobody would answer for fear of the results. For this, although it was Hitler's dream, was in fact nothing short of cloud-cuckoo-land.

I felt it my duty to send an honest report about the situation. Fortunately I took the precaution of keeping a photostat copy of this report. Both Rommel and Rundstedt agreed with my opinions. My neighbour, General Hausser, the Commander-in-Chief of the Seventh Army, also supported me.

Rundstedt and I were as a result relieved of our commands, and Rommel, who was good enough to try to support me, told me that he expected to be the next to go.

The most clear-thinking soldier on the Western Front, General Dollmann, latterly the Commander-in-Chief of Seventh Army, soon disappeared from the picture. Luckily for him his sudden death saved him from a subsequent court-martial. In any case he, as a practising Catholic, had always been suspect, as was I. By seniority I should have been his successor, but I was superseded. In a sworn statement made subsequently, Rommel's Chief of Staff said that Hitler had always mistrusted me. He was right.

In ending these notes on the invasion, I must stress that what I have said is far from the whole story. No landing or lodgement attempted by the Allies could ever have been defeated by us without an air force, and this we utterly lacked. The command organisation set up by Rommel and von Rundstedt in the West was not unlike the Roman system of changing command daily between the two consuls. The result, of course, was Cannae.

The differences of opinion throughout the German High Command at the time of the invasion put one in mind of a story told by Field-Marshal Lord Ironside in his memoirs; these had been written, it must be remembered, four years before by a member of the other side! He tells how General Gamelin had warned the French politicians in the hour of emergency that endlessly sitting round a table, thousands of miles from the scene of the battle, would never produce any better answer than the strategists of the Café de Commerce. The German café strategists were at this time sitting in Berchtesgaden.

The effect of Hitler's and Rommel's coastal defence policy on the German troops echoes the bitter remark made to Lord Ironside by the French Commander-in-Chief on the Western Front in 1940, General Billotte: 'Nous crevons derrière des obstacles.' ('We are rotting behind our defences.')

To think that these were the tactics chosen by the successors of von Schlieffen! They do not deserve the title of 'strategy', for true strategy is always bold. But one thing is certain, no matter how bold our strategy had been, the final result in the West would never have been changed. The war had already been lost at Stalingrad, in Africa, with the destruction of the production lines for the air force, and, indeed, with the destruction of the Luftwaffe itself. The invasion was the final act in the tragedy of the Third Reich. The remainder of the war after the success in Normandy was only a prolonged epilogue, in which the events of July 20 were no more than the final spasm before the old Germany breathed her last.

5 June 1964

NORMANDY'S HORROR

Colin Welch

In vain 25 years later I searched with my son for the brickworks and the nearby wood in which, in June 1944, I was introduced to my new platoon. 'It must have been here . . . No, it doesn't quite fit. Perhaps there . . .'

Restored, smiling once again, Normandy has effaced nearly all traces of her agony. Memory has to work almost unaided. It brings back to me now the soldiers' faces looking up at me from their slit trenches, apprehensively wondering what fate had allotted to them for an officer in place of the one (or two?) they'd already lost, wondering perhaps what the cat had brought in.

Casualties had been very high, and continued so. Losses in North-west Europe look trivial as a proportion of the whole force involved, including a vast preponderant tail which rarely heard a shot fired in anger. In this tail were many fit, experienced officers and soldiers who, among other duties, as the campaign wore on and losses mounted, callously passed on to be minced up in the front line mere children, younger even than I was, bewildered, hardly trained at all. In Holland we got a big draft from the King's Liverpool Regiment. They looked mostly like the original Beatles at the very start of their career. I put two of them on a charge for being, not for the first time, asleep on guard. Well I knew the Colonel had at his disposal no punishment worse than these boys' daily lives. But I thought he might give them a lecture, fatherly or wrathful as he thought fit. He asked them their ages. 'Nineteen, sir', 'eighteen'. He dismissed them, and turned to me. 'Weren't you taught never, never to put two young soldiers on guard together?' I replied that we had almost no old soldiers left. 'How old are you?' he asked. 'Twenty, sir,' and I was dismissed too.

Also lurking in that huge tail, though fortunately in lesser numbers, were psychiatrists who frivolously sent back to the front as 'cured' or *malades imaginaires* poor shell-shocked boys who, so far from being cowards, endangered their own lives and everyone else's by their tragic antics in full view of the enemy. My opinion of psychiatry has never recovered. No blimpish colonel of either war would have behaved with such idiotic inhumanity.

In his exciting, thoughtful and informative *Overlord: D-Day and the Battle for Normandy*, Max Hastings reminds us that many infantry battalions suffered more than 100 per cent casualties in that Normandy summer. My own battalion of the Lincolns, to which I was posted from the Royal Warwicks, lost, I think, 170 per cent in the ten months from D-Day till my number came up in the Reichswald. These are typical First World War figures, unrecognised as such because we were relatively so few to begin with. In the first war the Warwicks had an admittedly exceptional 48 battalions on active service; in the second, not much more than a tenth of that.

Looking down on that first day, never have I seen faces more tired and ill, tired from sleepless nights, ill from bad food and fear, haggard and wan, puffed out and inflamed by ferocious mosquito bites. The men were unnaturally quiet, as if they were stunned or had seen ghosts. I don't suppose I looked too good either. Hours tossing about in a sickening dawn swell off Arromanches, followed by a day or two in a transit camp at Bayeux, must have left their mark.

Through this camp the authorities in their wisdom channelled not only reinforcements like us for the front line but bomb-happy officers on their way home. 'It's hell up there,' shrieked one, the wreck of a once impressive major, his hand shaking so much he couldn't water his whisky. 'HELL, I tell you. Run for it! Get out while you can! It's HELL!' We tittered nervously, shaken despite ourselves; and when the next day I looked down on those upturned faces it was not only with pity but with awe and humility. Here was I, woefully inexperienced, with my shreds of military lore, lectures half-forgotten and field training frivolously scamped, supposed to 'lead' men who had endured what had driven other men, supposedly their superiors, mad. They had shaved too; their weapons were clean; their spirit was subdued but not broken. I bowed my head to them, and was also unnaturally quiet. A part of my education was about to begin.

All schools have their particular smell, a whiff of which, carbolic, polish or sweat, will bring back days long past. The smell of Normandy was death. Holidaymakers will know Normandy as a province of fantastic fecundity with tiny fields and lanes, all steeply banked and thick-hedged, rich orchards, old cottages and farm buildings of red brick and timber. You can hardly see ten yards in any direction, which led to many unpleasant surprises from Tigers and 88s invisible yet near enough almost to touch. Thick on the ground everywhere were fat animals, horses, cows, geese, ducks, chickens, pigeons and their blue-smocked peasant proprietors. It isn't military country; let loose a full-blast war in it, and the result is a gigantic abattoir, bodies everywhere, human, animal, theirs, ours, French, no chance to bury them, all stiff and hideously swollen, covered with white dust or mud, faces blown away or dreadfully distorted, crawling with flies, rotting, giving off that terrible sweet-sour stench which, once smelt, is not forgotten.

Add to it the reek of explosives and burning, of cider and Calvados (which the soldiers drank too young, with results sometimes fatal) pouring from shattered vats and stills. Add, in the tormented cities, in Caen, Rouen, and others we saw later, the mephitic stink of sewers blown open to the sky. Memory still unbidden brings back these smells, and we shiver.

What did this school teach? Well, obviously different things to different people. I wrote 25 years ago in the *Daily Telegraph* about some of the things it had taught me. Few will remember that, but I wouldn't care to bore even them twice. Above all I think it imbued us with a deep, abiding and, to others, perhaps disproportionate hatred of disorder, violence and anarchy. The fragility and preciousness of civil society, as also the dire consequences of its collapse, were indelibly impressed on us.

In a way, we all became profoundly conservative, keenly aware of what had been lost, desperately anxious to preserve what remained. Well do I know that most of the soldiers voted Labour in 1945, though there *may* be a distinction to be drawn between the front line, with its awe-inspiring experience of tragedy, and the progressive, argumentative, ABCA-lecture-infesting, barrackroom lawyer types behind it. I don't know. But certainly Labour, with its passion for order, fairness and regulation, offered them no sort of anarchy – on the contrary. Someone described Hitler's Reich as 'systematised anarchy'. It was against that we fought, against a Caliban-like revolt of greed, lust, hatred, envy, cruelty and destructive rage.

It also imbued in us a great love of Europe. Not in all of us, of course – some could hardly wait to get out and stay out – but in many of us, by whom the spectacle of Europe prostrate, degraded, diminished, morally and materially ruined, could not be viewed coldly from outside. It hurt us personally and deeply, as if our own mother were lying there in pain and woe. Of course we didn't fight for the European Parliament as it is, still less for the CAP or Brussels' swarming bureaucrats. Rightly did Charles Moore in the *Daily Telegraph* ridicule politicians' claims that we did. But we did resolve that, so far as lay in our power, it must never happen again, that Europe must be given institutions which would prevent another civil war and guard her against enemies without. What exists now is a mere ghost or parody of what we sought: no one can look on it and think his task well accomplished. But never shall we be untrue to the idea of Europe, nor turn aside from any road, however muddy, twisting and arduous, which seems to lead towards its being made real.

2 June 1984

MARGINAL COMMENT

Harold Nicolson

The last time that I visited Cherbourg I did not arrive in a large liner; I arrived in a very little yawl. It was the second week of August 1939. They did not allow us to tie up in the *Avant-Port*, but obliged us to go through the lock-gates into the Bassin de Commerce, which was heavy with the scent of herrings and the grime of coal. Cherbourg is an ugly town, and we were glad to leave it. Past Cap de la Hague we sailed next morning, past the summer-lit shape of Alderney, and on to Guernsey on what we imagined was a journey to Brest. But mist descended upon us off Brittany and the surly, sullen bell-buoy off Ushant warned us that it would be wiser to turn back to Plymouth. We entered the Pool and tied up beside a little ketch called the *Outward Bound*. There were two boys and a girl on board the ketch, washing their decks gaily and cleaning their brass-work while they sang aloud. I went down to the cabin and turned on the wireless. It told me that Ribbentrop had left for Moscow on an unspecified mission. As I came up again into the sunlight on deck the boys in the neighbouring ketch were still singing as they rubbed their brass-work. I changed into shore clothes and walked sadly, carrying my bag, to the North Road Station. I knew that my sailing days were over, probably for ever. I knew that we were on the eve of a Second German War. And as I sit here, almost five years later, listening to Hitler's meteor bomb roaring across the pleasant countryside of Southern England, it seems strange to me that Cherbourg, which for so long has in my mind been associated with the last week of peace, should now be becoming the symbol and the portent of the last months of war.

23 June 1944

D-DAY

W. Russell Brain

To you, unknown, whom now I shall not know,
I write these words in greeting and farewell;
A wreath to lay upon the quick-turned earth
Which took and holds you in a quiet surprise
Beneath the apple trees of Normandy,
Beneath the apples fallen on the grass
In June's unripeness from the broken boughs.
Hail and farewell to you, but what to her?
What can I twist from sharp and brittle words
To lay upon the marble of her heart?

30 June 1944

LONDON IN 1970

Hamilton Kerr, MP

The Town and Country Planning Bill recently came before the House of Commons for its Second Reading. The Bill and the White Paper outline the short and long term plans for future development. These two documents propose the means for giving a new face to our country; but they cannot decide the physical aspect of our cities 30 years from now. That will depend upon our architects and town planners, and upon public taste.

And so it is pleasant, and perhaps profitable, to exercise one's imagination by asking oneself what type of towns and cities we should like to see as we travelled through this island, say in the year 1970. Let me deal principally with London, and I will say what I would do if I were an arbiter of taste, although I am more than aware that an aspiring Petronius has even fewer friends than a Cromwell or Mussolini.

When Byron's Don Juan was attacked by footpads on Shooters Hill, just as he saw London spread below him for the first time, he must have seen much the same London as Talleyrand noted from his coach window as he came to take up his post of Ambassador after the Revolution of 1830. It was still the London of the eighteenth century and the Regency, a London of red brick and white stucco, of a crowded and thriving business community surrounded by residential areas laid out in parks and squares and terraces, and spreading beyond these the traveller found the rustic delights of Highgate and Hampstead, Kensington and Kew. The Industrial Revolution had not yet concealed the face of London with a mask of smoke, and had not yet launched a tidal wave of mean, dark and hateful buildings over the present East End to engulf the market garden villages of Essex. It was a London whose physical lineaments still expressed its true soul, which was nothing more than the character and genius of our people. It could not boast the fabulous magnificence of Rome, nor tempt the eye with the ambitious architectural perspectives of Paris or St Petersburg. It was homely and yet a capital city, it was ordered and yet not regimented, and it brought the delights of the country, the trees, the grass, the water, into the everyday life of a great community. It is this essential genius of London which, I believe, we must preserve in the coming age, and, while giving it new outward forms, retain its main characteristics. So let us take a brief voyage into the future.

Suppose that we are flying from New York to London some day in May, in the year 1970. The indicator light in the passenger cabin shows that the pilot is about to land at the great terminal airport of Staines. Flying at 500 miles an hour, the journey from New York has taken us about six hours, and the air-conditioned pressure cabin has maintained the temperature of a May morning in the icy altitudes above 30,000 feet. During the voyage we have been served with a delicious hot lunch, and entertained with a cinema film dealing with a romance among the palms of Tahiti. We have rung up a friend who is travelling for a rest cure to New York on the *Queen Mary*, and have been amazed to learn that, as we pass through the calm stratosphere, the liner has been struggling against a 60-mile per hour gale. Now, as we touch ground, we alight at one end of a three-mile runway, so designed that, should the engines of an air-liner cut out when taking off – the moment of supreme danger – it will still be able to land in safety.

Once past the Customs at the airport, we enter a helicopter for our next destination – namely, the roof of Waterloo Station. During the flight of five or six minutes we take the opportunity of examining the suburbs below us. The new schemes have begun to abolish the old ribbon development, and removed in many areas the endless rows of semi-detached houses of varying architectural styles, some half-timbered, some of brick, some of khaki rough-cast, sprawling like a rash over the countryside. Instead, we see long arterial avenues lined with grass and trees, and behind these pleasant groups of brick houses, each with its own garden behind, but arranged in crescents, blocks, or squares, much as you would find in Bath or Bloomsbury, or a New England town. And everywhere you notice trees, for one of the most effective memorials of the Second World War was the planting of a tree for every person killed.

As our helicopter approaches Waterloo, the winding path of the river through London at once catches the eye. Particularly fine is the south bank, where gardens and well-designed industrial buildings have long since replaced the hideous warehouses which disgraced a former day. (For surely the present Battersea Power Station proves that industrial building can achieve a striking beauty.)

Safely landed on the roof of a newly sited Waterloo Station, we take a taxi for our hotel, and travel along the great ring road which connects all the main London stations. As suggested in the present Royal Academy plan, the road is sunk, with all crossings in the form of fly-overs, and our unobstructed passage allows us to travel at 40 miles per hour, so that we can reach any point in London in under a quarter of an hour. And at intervals along the grass banks of this sunk roadway flower all the shrubs of May, lilac, laburnum, may, as well as the pink chestnut.

Now I hope that our traveller on this spring day of May 1970 will be particularly impressed by the excellent design of the buildings lining the ring road. In New York the architects have enjoyed the advantage of building on a foundation of hard rock, and aided by a brilliant atmosphere producing vivid lights and shadows they have been able to achieve an almost Gothic effect with buildings of enormous height. But in London, a foundation of clay coupled with LCC bye-laws has restricted height, and the architects who have attempted functional architecture have, to my mind, produced an effect as dreary and soulless as numbers of market garden boxes piled one on top of the other. In spite of a few noteworthy exceptions such as St James's Underground Station, the general rule has been such buildings as the Dorchester and Grosvenor House, and in Leeds that much publicised block of workers' flats – the latter always personally reminds me of Van Gogh's 'Rond des prisonniers'. But for us in England, eschewing height, I believe that the principle of classic architecture emphasising the horizontal line offers the best solution. It provides us with the possibility of pediments, mouldings and porticoes, and the decorative use of sculpture, whether in groups or friezes. And when the architect uses materials such as Portland stone or good brick, maintains all that is best in our building tradition.

Now let us suppose that we have arrived at our hotel. Unpacking my luggage I discover, to my extreme annoyance, that I have left my evening tie in New York, and as it is just about 6 o'clock I must buy another before the shops close. The hotel porter tells me that the nearest and most convenient shop is in Piccadilly Circus, and there I repair at full speed. I approach the shopping centre by a covered passage, specially reserved for pedestrians, sloping down under the roadway, and find myself in a large and pleasant garden some twenty feet below street level. Above you can see buses and private cars travelling at considerable speed on the roundabout, but here among the grass and plane trees and tulip beds you find nurses sitting beside their perambulators, children driving hoops or watching the sparrows splashing on the fountain's edge, and people taking tea at an open-air café under a large red and white awning. Shoppers continually pass by with paper parcels from the shops which face this garden below street level, which forms a natural meeting place for the neighbourhood, unmolested by street traffic. Similar shopping centres are to be found at many of the big road intersections.

We cannot finish our visit to London without a trip to St Paul's. Already from halfway down Fleet Street we can see its dome rising above Ludgate Hill. And after we have climbed the dome, what a view greets the eye. From the south transept a broad avenue runs down to the river, for is it not right that the Thames, whose waters reflect so many of the famous buildings of England – Windsor Castle, Hampton Court, Lambeth, the Houses of Parliament, the Tower, and Greenwich Hospital – should as well reflect the dome of the great metropolitan church? In the near foreground smoke rises from vessels loading and unloading in the Pool of London, whilst beyond the Isle of Dogs and the great bend in the river the cranes in the West and East India Docks, and the Albert Dock, fret the sky. But the north bank of the river has radically changed its appearance since the extensive damage to Poplar, Canning Town, Silvertown, and West Ham in the blitz of the Second World War. The trees of squares, gardens and open spaces everywhere appear above the rooftops and add their amenities to those of Victoria Park and Hackney Marshes.

And so ends my imaginary picture of London in 1970. I can, perhaps, see some of my readers raise their eyes from the script and sigh 'How much will this all cost?' The Royal Academy Plan envisages all these improvements, but I have never seen an estimate of their cost in round figures. Doubtless the expenditure could be spread over a number of years. The schemes would certainly give employment to many thousands of men for a long period, whilst the income which France gained from the tourist traffic before the war shows that amenities provide a permanent national asset. All I can say is, that the blitz has given us a second chance in our history to rebuild the capital of the British Empire in a manner worthy of its great traditions, and as a fitting memorial to that immortal moment when a few hundred Spitfires and the imperishable soul of a people stood between the world and enslavement.

21 July 1944

THE GERMAN PEOPLE

Gilbert Murray

SIR: Far be it for me to speak ill of the human race; they might not like it, and where should I be then? But I doubt if they have the power of fighting furiously and thinking calmly at the same time. I have noticed that even in the mild heat of a General Election people are not always just to their opponents. And when I read the letters of Lord Vansittart and Mr George Richards, and the speech of the former in the House of Lords, I cannot but recall a remark made as a sort of last moment SOS by the Brains Trust last week. The question was something about German psychology and 'could the Germans ever become' something or other; the answer was that such questions might profitably be addressed to the Brains Trust ten years after the war was over.

Even the members of the Government, being human, seem to go a little wrong in the head. More than a year ago various bodies, in Parliament and out, led largely by Miss Rathbone, were imploring the Government to do something to facilitate the escape of Jews from the most ghastly of all Nazi atrocities and give them asylum in British territory. The Government's answers were not merely sticky and hesitating. They not only pointed out the real difficulties of the undertaking, but some of them added that to rescue any large number of Jews from massacre and bring them to British territory would be dangerous. It might cause Labour troubles! Or again, it might breed anti-semitism! Would it not be more prudent to leave the victims where they were, and content ourselves with hanging the murderers afterwards?

Wars are breeders of lies and delusions. We do not lie like the Nazis, but we deceive ourselves a good deal and indulge in many foolish dreams. Might it not be well to begin by grasping firmly two plain facts:

(i) The Germans will probably start another war if they have the chance; we must see that they do not have the chance.

(ii) We must eventually be reconciled with the Germans. There are seventy million of them in the heart of Europe, and there can be no peace or happiness for anyone while they are still unreconciled enemies.

The two requirements are not impossible to reconcile; but the man who would reconcile them must keep his head. – Yours faithfully, GILBERT MURRAY

21 July 1944

Eleanor F. Rathbone

SIR: Considerations of space prevent my replying to correspondents who have questioned the existence of great numbers – I never suggested that they are a majority – of Germans who detest Hitlerism and all its works, though I believe the evidence to be considerable. Much of it has been summarised by the Free German Movement and also by British writers. So I will only make two general points.

First, all generalisations about national characteristics seem to me unsound to the point of absurdity if they go further than saying that the history of Nation A shows it to contain a larger (or smaller) percentage of persons conspicuously endowed with quality X than Nation B, C or D, &c. Throughout the greater part of the *corpus* of any nation, at least any European white nation, differences in quality are rather individual than national.

Secondly, I suggest that each of us should ask himself or herself what he would have done if, at any time within the last ten years, he had been a German who loathed Hitler's cruelty, mendacity, and preposterous ambitions for German lordship over Europe. Is he quite certain that he would have had the courage and self-confidence necessary to risk torture and death by open protest or resistance? Or would he perhaps have hesitated, hoping for an opportunity of action and planning for it, but assuring himself that 'the time was not yet'; that to act prematurely would be mere suicide and would imperil future action? If he is confident that he would have taken the first course, then he may well 'thank whatever Gods there be for his unconquerable soul'. Many of us do not feel so confident, either of our courage or how we would have judged the situation, and hence we hesitate to condemn. – Yours faithfully, ELEANOR F. RATHBONE

House of Commons   *28 July 1944*

BIRTHRATE AND HOUSEWORK

D.E. Estcourt

Among the modestly well-off before the war a not uncommon establishment was the three- or four-bedroom house with one domestic. This 'general' received about £1 to 25s. a week in wages, and her room and board. For this she usually did most of the housework and most of the routine cooking; she sometimes did part of the washing; she had one half-day a week off and every other Sunday. She was, with good reason, regarded as doing an exacting full-time job for a very modest wage, and a good deal was heard about improving the status and conditions of the domestic servant. If her employers had expected her, in addition to her regular duties, to look after a couple of children, nurse them when ill, do all the shopping, all the household mending and keep the household accounts, she would very rightly have given notice at once.

Yet it is precisely this more-than-full-time job, plus the bearing of children and the maintenance of the necessary social contacts of the family, which the single-handed housewife has to tackle – usually without the 25s. a week wages attached. It can be done, and is done year in and year out; but it commonly means a working day that begins about 7.30 in the morning and ends, with luck, after a bout of mending and a string of odd jobs, about 10 p.m. In short, one woman, with all the routine of a household dependent upon her unaided labours, definitely has too much to do, and it is not surprising that both she and her husband shrink increasingly from the added burden of a large family.

It is almost impossible for any but the super-robust woman to be an efficient housewife and a good mother under such conditions. Children demand and need a lot of time and unhurried attention, especially in their first seven years. They need, for instance, stories told to them by a mother who is not weary and preoccupied and longing to get them off to bed. Juvenile delinquency is frequently associated with overworked mothers. It is not common among the better off. It is useless for critics to protest that the modern woman is getting lazy and pleasure-loving, and that her predecessors did this job for generations. The well-off – even the modestly well-off – never did it, and the poor were in many cases less burdened than the modern housewife. Before the Industrial Revolution and modern transport increased the mobility of our population, communities were far more static and closely knit than they are now, and a woman usually had a mother, unmarried sister or other relative within call to lend a hand.

However, if one grants that the poor and the very robust have always been able to manage this exacting seven-days-a-week drudgery, do we really wish to establish it as the norm? What use to raise the school-leaving age and improve education? The educated woman simply will not accept this kind of life, with no uninterrupted leisure. Do we, instead of extending privilege, want to re-proletarianise the fortunate few who have learned to expect and use a modicum of leisure; who like to have time to enjoy their children, to read, to play the piano, perhaps to paint or write? If not, what is to be done about it? The pool of cheap female labour which made this leisure possible has gone; it should not, and doubtless will not, be revived after the war. Better houses will be a help, and will come in time, but some change will have to be made in our way of life if every wife is not to be reduced to the status of the pre-war domestic servant, and the one-child family to become even more common than it is already.

One possible change is in the direction of more cheap 'outside' services. For instance, to municipal dustmen and visiting window-cleaners one might add a vacuum-cleaning and floor-polishing service which would work through neighbourhoods on a weekly rota system; better and cheaper laundries to eliminate home washing; a babies' sanitary service such as already exists in parts of the United States (it collects the napkins and delivers them washed and boiled and sealed in cellophane); and especially the Neighbourhood Restaurant.

By a Neighbourhood Restaurant I do not mean just a public eating place which 'breaks up family life' (though heaven knows that washing-up is not a notably unifying family ritual). The Neighbourhood Restaurants would have to be not vast impersonal feeding centres, but small, numerous and local, and rather like clubs. Indeed, club amenities would almost certainly form around them in time. The restaurant would be available only to its own group of households, each of which could pay a subscription and have its own 'family table' reserved for the first or second sitting. Only one meal a day – the main meal – would be taken there. Family life could then be genuinely enjoyed at home over the two lighter and less arduous meals of the day. Workers out all day could take their main meal at a works canteen (these should be improved and extended), at a downtown Neighbourhood Restaurant, or in the evening at the home restaurant. The building might be provided by the local authority; the catering contract could be let to a professional restaurateur, perhaps working with a neighbourhood advisory committee.

I shall not, though I could, develop the Neighbourhood Restaurant idea in its technical detail. There are problems, but no greater than many which are solved every day in other spheres. I will add only that some such institution would save immense duplications of labour, time, fuel, food, hot water and nervous energy expended in individual kitchens day after day, year after year; it would make family life something more convivial than a succession of meal-gettings and meal-clearings; it would give parents a chance to enjoy, educate and perhaps increase their families, and to foster some of those leisure activities which most hard-working homes so conspicuously lack today.

There are many possible modifications and extensions of such ideas, but whatever the detailed outcome, some genuinely new thinking is necessary on the domestic set-up. There is not likely to be, as time goes on and education is extended, any improvement in the birthrate if the majority of women on marriage are expected to live a life somewhat more arduous and rather less well paid than that of the pre-war 'general'.

18 August 1944

COUNTRY LIFE: GUNS AND VERMIN

W. Beach Thomas

On the subject of vermin, one of the only places known to me personally where rabbits (almost extinct in many districts) are a worse plague than they ever have been is over a wide space reserved for gunnery practice. Nobody cares to take the risk of flying bullets, and it is extraordinary how crooked some recruits can shoot. There is a suspicion that some of them make stray rabbits their target. It is odd that neither rabbits nor pheasants seem to object to target practice, however loud and long. I have seen pheasants strolling unconcernedly across a range while bullets were whistling over their heads. Incidentally, while watching the advance of the Guards below the Pilkhem Ridge in the last war, a cock pheasant flew over my head into the utter desolation of the battleground; and the tremendous bombardment which opened the Somme battle did not in the least alarm a family of quails that clucked all round me.

1 September 1944

MARGINAL COMMENT

Harold Nicolson

When the Allied armies reached Paris they discovered that the fuel and transport situation was in fact appalling. Electric light was available only in a few Government offices; the underground railway had ceased to function and there were practically no cars or buses; such transport as existed was either what the French call 'hippomobile' or else restricted to bicycles and hand-carts. Even more serious was the lack of household fuel which rendered it difficult for housewives to cook even such rations as they were able to obtain. And few deprivations can be so personally galling as the prolonged and almost total absence of soap. It is true that the centre of Paris has not suffered the same extent of structural damage as has been dealt to London during four and a half years of bombardment. Yet in the industrial areas which surround the capital heavy damage has been done by Allied air-attack, and this has created a housing problem of great complexity. For the moment, owing to transport difficulties, only a few of those who were evacuated from Paris have returned. But already it is practically impossible to find accommodation in the city, and the hope that a large number of flats would become available once the Germans withdrew has proved an illusion. Already the demand is being made that the apartments of the collaborators should be taken from them in the hope of meeting a shortage which is already acute and which may become critical once the evacuees return. Already the provisional authorities are considering the erection of Portal houses in the industrial areas. In such circumstances it is not unreasonable to suppose that the unity which, under the aegis of de Gaulle and the direction of the *Résistance*, was so admirably maintained during the occupation will be preserved unsullied and for ever. It would be impertinent for us to criticise, and unwise for us to exaggerate, the political divergences which are bound to develop. They will not prove either as damaging or as dangerous as they may seem.

The liberation of Italy has created an even wider diversity of thought and feeling. When once General Alexander's armies reach the industrial north this confusion will become even more pronounced. There are few thinking Italians who do not now realise that Mussolini's imperialism was the most dangerous experiment upon which any weak country could have embarked. There are a few unthinking Italians who seek to persuade themselves that by her eleventh-hour conversion Italy has conferred tremendous benefits upon the Allies. Absurd though this contention is, it would be unfair to ignore what Italy has suffered during the past years or to underestimate the very real assistance which has been given us, and is increasingly being given us, by the Italian partisans. The general impression seems to be that Italy has suffered but little from the war and that her cities have been left almost untouched. This is not true. In Florence, for instance, much wanton damage has been caused. When the bridges were blown up a great wail of misery arose from the city, as if, so a correspondent assures me, 'the plague had come again'. The Germans made a great virtue of having spared the Ponte Vecchio. This is how a British officer describes this act of abnegation: 'While it is true that the actual structure of the bridge is intact, all the little shops on it are quite ruined; their front and back walls are caved in, their roofs are lying in heaps of rubble upon the counters; not one of them today is even a habitable shack. What conceivable reason can they have had for this appalling destruction?'

A few days only after that letter was written, the Germans started shelling the city from the northern heights. The Cathedral was struck and one of the side chapels lost its roof; damage was also done to Giotto's tower, the Strozzi Palace and the Loggia dei Lanzi. The only conceivable purpose of such wanton damage was to embitter the relations between the Florentines and the Allied armies; its sole effect was to create against the Germans feelings of loathing which will never die. Our own Tommies, under the arcades of the Uffizi, pumped the water out of the Arno into huge green canvas reservoirs attached to sterilising plant while the citizens of Florence queued up with large brown water-jars upon their shoulders. 'Liberation' assuredly is not always a comfortable process; it does not always bring repose and it is bound to bring dissension; and in the depths of human nature it stirs up the worst as well as the best.

22 September 1944

JAPAN IN DEFEAT

Captain Gerald Hanley

Despite continuous and savage attacks, the Japanese were unable to take Kohima and Imphal. They got half of Kohima, but could get no further. The savagery in their attacks was due partly to their realisation that the campaign was doomed to fail. Their food and ammunition was running low, the monsoon rains were almost due to start, and they wanted to break the resistance of Imphal and Kohima and use them as monsoon quarters before the advance into India. Each of their attacks was broken. Thousands were killed before they could get out of the fighting, but thousands more died of hunger and disease on the road to the Chindwin. They litter the Imphal–Palel–Tamu road in hundreds. When we followed them, the air was filled with the smell of their dead. The sick and wounded were left behind in hundreds and told to pass south as best they could. We saw dead Japs all along the road, some in their stockinged feet, and where the hills were highest and most exhausting, they lay huddled in groups. They carried only a mess-tin, steel helmet and rifle. Some lay as though asleep, while others were twisted and broken by the bombs which had rained down on them.

Tamu was a scene of nightmare, like something from a Hollywood war-film. Five hundred Japs lay dead and dying amidst the wreckage of buildings. Some buildings had been blasted and burnt, and only charred posts stood in the long grass. The stench was unbearable, and in this scene of horror the Jap wounded, starved into a dazed condition and many delirious from malaria, were waiting to die. The pagoda was choked with them, and they lay among heaps of steel helmets, respirators and equipment of all kinds. They had crawled here, in front of the four tall and golden images, to die. Hand grenades littered the altar. In the centre of the temple was a dais, and carved into this was a perfectly symmetrical pattern of the foot of Buddha. It was littered with blood-soaked bandages and Japanese field-postcards.

Some of the Japs were what the troops called 'dehydrated'. When they were given water, it passed straight through their bodies; the cells were quite unable to absorb water any longer, and those in this condition died where they lay. No men in this war can have been reduced to such a terrible condition. Prisoners were taken in batches of twelve and thirty. Half of them died before they could be moved. Those that survived were unable to walk and had to be loaded into trucks where they lay on their faces, oblivious of everything.

I saw two prisoners who were revived with hot tea. They were tiny men with matted hair which stood up like a golliwog's, and as they lay in the morning sun they moved about under the stimulus of the tea, like kittens, weak and blinking. They had to wait before they could eat the biscuits and bully-beef which they plucked at weakly, breathing hard and exhausted with effort. One of them put his head in his hands and cried like a child. He should have committed suicide, and had failed; it was a disgrace for him to be alive. One could only guess what he had been through. These Japs had lived through storms of shells and bombs, and had tottered nearly a hundred miles before they collapsed. They were alive in this valley that stank of death, where their friends lay littered through the jungle and along the road. In the jungle I saw them dead in huge grass huts, wrapped in their blankets, surrounded by heaps of equipment, ammunition, rifles, curled boots with the separate compartment for the big toe, and rain-sodden documents. Down the tracks in the deep jungle remnants of the Jap forces wandered, lost, starving and utterly without hope. Some killed themselves with their own grenades – a different hara-kiri to that of the silk cushions and the blandishments of admiring friends. Here they killed themselves where they stood, lousy, their hair matted, half mad from hunger and explosions, and deserted by their officers. The rain poured down on them for days, and then the sun came out and burned them into collapse. This is the picture of a shattered army – an army that had never known defeat, and had never been trained for the day when the machine of supply broke down. They had fought with almost maniacal ferocity to crack the British defences, and their high morale broke, not only under a rain of steel, but under their own surprise and disappointment.

The wake of their retreat has to be seen to be understood. The chaos is indescribable, not the usual chaos of smashed tanks and abandoned guns – these are all here – but the chaos of utter defeat, for their dead cannot be buried fast enough, they are so numerous. The hygiene squads, whose hideous task is endless, search them out in the jungles and in the bunkers. The road, churned into a river of red and black mud, shows the signs of what the RAF has done in the past months. Trucks lie wrecked and burned out everywhere, with dead Japs lying round them, and others have gone rolling down the steep mountain-side into the ravines. The Japs, when they exulted and went frantic with victory in 1942, laughed at the British retreat through Burma. They have said nothing of their own retreat back from India. There is not much to say. But the survivors will never forget it.

Overhead, as I write, the RAF bombers are flying south. The nightmare for the Japs is not ended. It grows. The bombers will fly back, load up again, and return, while fighters go boring in, spraying cannon-fire into the groups of Japs who move along the Chindwin. These small men with the savage hearts and the hands that can paint exquisite water-colours in the diaries which they leave lying in the red mud have worked havoc for seven years through the East. The quality of their fanaticism cannot be appreciated by those who have not seen them in war. But it is of the kind that breaks into tears when the body can no longer support the weird power that drives it. Their reactions cannot be measured as can those of any other enemy soldier, for where one breaks under shells the Jap will still fight, and where one is arrogant in defeat, the Jap cries like a child. When the Americans put fifteen thousand tons of bombs and shells on to Kwajalein in the Pacific, it was with the experience of Tarawa, where after three thousand tons of explosives the Japs still fought. They have to be blasted into a coma, and then rooted out of their holes. This is being done now all over the East, and will continue until Japan is crushed. The Jap soldier who kills himself with a grenade can go on doing so as far as the Allied soldier is concerned. But this practice is likely to grow less frequent as the war closes in on Japan. There must come a time when a man asks himself if it is worth it, especially when he finds out that he will be treated well as a prisoner.

Some writers have said that Japan will commit mass-suicide, while others have said the country will have no young men left if this state of exaltation reached by the Japanese in defeat is a permanent part of their mental make-up. But nobody is quite sure, and after Japan's treachery and the frenzy of her victory it is doubtful if anybody cares. No Archbishop is likely to cry out against the bombing of Japan when it comes, for it will be difficult to ask mercy for an enemy that shoots airmen unfortunate enough to bale out over its sacred soil, and perpetrates atrocities of revolting perversity in China. It is not so much hate as absolute necessity that demands the breaking up of Japan's military machine.

The legend that Japanese troops are supermen has been exploded long ago, and soldiers who have fought them for two years in the deep jungles of Burma will tell you that the Japs have little or no jungle-craft, but make as much noise as a family of foraging monkeys as they move. The Allied troops in Burma have a very high morale, for they have measured the Japanese and beaten them into a state that can only be appreciated by a look at their line of retreat from India. Fighting in the climate of the Burmese jungle requires tenacity and physical toughness. The heat is intense, and the mosquitoes are voracious and armed with malaria. The troops march in rain, mud and glaring heat, and still must be fit for battle. The strain is the same for the Japanese as for our troops, and as the gun and plane-power increases in the Eastern war, the Jap will find the strain too much.

So as our troops hump their loads and march into Burma after the fleeing Japs, they do so with a high spirit. These men, muddy, their green battle-dress torn and sun-stained, fighting under possibly the worst conditions in the world, have waited a long time for this day. It is not pleasant to march through litters of corpses, but the scene holds a certain message for the soldier, and he understands it.

29 September 1944

MARGINAL COMMENT

Harold Nicolson

As I walked down to Westminster last week, on the morning of the Prime Minister's great speech upon the war situation, I found myself wondering how he would deal with the most delicate problem which confronted him. It is a problem which must always arise on occasions when intense public interest and emotion are concentrated on one single event and when it is difficult, without causing offence, to relate that event to the general proportions of the whole story. Mr Churchill was speaking at a moment when the adventure of Arnhem – perhaps the most daring of all our enterprises – had aroused among his audience deep feelings of anxiety and expectation, of disappointment and pride. He was faced with the difficulty of adjusting a tactical operation, which had become charged with great emotional content, to the general strategical pattern which it was his duty to unfold. To treat the Arnhem landing as a mere episode in our tremendous sweep of victory would have seemed heartless to those who during the preceding week had spent their days and nights in acute personal anxiety; yet to render Arnhem the central or dominant theme of his discourse would have been to distort the focus of the worldwide story which he had to tell. The Prime Minister solved this problem of composition with a tact which comes naturally to a man of his sensitive human sympathy. He detached the emotional from the explanatory, devoting to the men of Arnhem a decorous and moving cenotaph which eased and comforted distress, and thereafter passing onwards to his gigantic narrative, thereby indicating, without stressing, the true proportions of the whole. And even when his long oration had drawn to its triumphant close, that name still echoed, as a bell tolling, in our ears – Arnhem, Arnhem, Arnhem.

6 October 1944

A POINTLESS BATTLE

Sir Brian Horrocks

A BRIDGE TOO FAR. *By Cornelius Ryan. (Hamish Hamilton.)*
This is unquestionably the most brilliant account of a battle which I have ever read. Cornelius Ryan has already written two best sellers – *The Longest Day*, about D-Day, and *The Last Battle*, dealing with the Siege of Berlin, but both pale into insignificance when compared with his description of this magnificent but terrible battle of Arnhem, *A Bridge Too Far*.

What is so tragic is that the Battle of Arnhem need never have been fought, and this emerges clearly in Part One of this book entitled 'The Retreat'. As a result of their complete defeat during the Normandy battles, the German Army was streaming back to the Fatherland in disorder. The problem facing the Allies at this time was how best to take advantage of the chaos in the enemy army. Montgomery in the north demanded an all-out offensive up the coastal plain, by the 2nd British and Canadian armies on a comparatively narrow front; while, at the other end of the line, Patton's 3rd Army was poised for a similar invasion of the Saar. Both of these threats envisaged continuous pressure day and night, so that the enemy would be given no time to regroup and make a stand. In other words, both Montgomery in the north and Patton in the south could have ended the war in 1944 – if allowed to launch deep, powerful thrusts into the heart of Germany. Eisenhower, the Supreme Commander, who had just taken over command of the ground forces from Montgomery, decided mainly for political and logistical reasons to advance on a broad front. After considerable argument, Montgomery was allowed to stage an all-out attack up the coastal plain, and was given more than his fair share of logistical support, much to Patton's fury, whose thrust into the Saar was halted.

30 Corps, which I commanded, was given the leading role in the advance. Having crossed the River Seine, my orders were to breach the German defences on the Somme before they could be properly organised, seize Brussels and Antwerp, also if possible, bounce the crossings over the Rhine and head for the Zyder Zee – so as to cut off the German forces in the west from their main arsenal in the Ruhr. I had six hundred tanks under command, and we were advancing on a fifty-mile front, and covered two hundred and fifty miles in six days. On the 3rd of September we liberated Brussels and the 11th Armoured Division was directed on Antwerp.

On the 4th of September we were ordered to halt our advance as we were out-running our supplies – particularly petrol, which was still being brought up from the beachhead – a turn-round of some six hundred miles for the lorries. This was a tragedy, as the only troops between us and the Rhine, stretched out in a thin line, was one German division, the 719th, composed mainly of elderly gentlemen who hitherto had been guarding the north coast of Holland and had never heard a shot fired in anger, plus one battalion of Dutch SS, and a few Luftwaffe detachments. Had we been allowed to advance we could have brushed this meagre force aside, bounced the crossing over the Rhine, and probably gone right through to the Zyder Zee. A further advance like this would, of course, have entailed a certain risk, but we already had one hundred kilometres of petrol within reach, and another one hundred twenty-four hours away; moreover, we had captured Brussels Airport, so surely additional supplies could have been flown in if we had got into trouble. I have always felt that this was a risk worth taking. It was not taken. And there can be no doubt that the clash of personalities at the top and inter-allied jealousies prevented a cohesive policy being adopted. *The 4th of September, therefore, when our drive north was halted, was the day when the Battle of Arnhem was lost.*

Von Rundstedt, the most experienced and respected commander in the German Army, was reappointed C-in-C west, while Model took over the command of Army Group B. On Hitler's orders, all the military reserves were to be concentrated on halting the Allied advance into Holland. It has always seemed incredible to me that the utterly disorganised German forces were able to recover so quickly. Cornelius Ryan describes this in detail, but from our immediate point of view it was the speed with which

General Student, the German Airborne Commander, managed to collect and rearm his Parachute formations from all over the Reich which altered the military picture. On the 7th of September, when we were allowed to continue our advance, the situation had completely changed. Instead of sweeping forward on a fifty-mile front, we were now fighting again on a frontage of five miles, and it took the Guards Armoured Division four days' hard battling to advance ten miles to the Meuse Escault Canal.

On the 11th of September I received my orders for 'Market Garden' in which 30 Corps was once again to play the leading role. In outline, the plan was for the 2nd British Army to advance approximately seventy miles to seize the Grave–Nijmegen–Arnhem area and then drive on still further northwards to the Zyder Zee in order to cut off all the Germans in the Low Countries from the Fatherland and make an advance into the Ruhr if possible. It was to entail the greatest airborne operation which had ever been carried out, involving much complicated staff work by the Air Force and the Army, both in the United Kingdom and in the occupied area of Europe. It was estimated that the 17th September was the first day on which it could be launched. By then the Germans would have had some fourteen days in which to recover.

I had three main worries. First, to break through the German defences in front of me. This was not so simple as it looked. Reinforcements, mainly of paratroops, were arriving from Germany daily. The country was wooded and rather marshy, which made any outflanking operation impossible. Secondly, even when we broke through, the country did not favour a rapid advance, because it was intersected with water-ways – canals, bridges and three immense rivers. Thirdly, it looked as though we would have to advance on one road only, and in the Corps were twenty thousand vehicles. The ensuing battle to break through the German crust is brilliantly and accurately described by Ryan.

I would like to turn briefly to the operations of the ground troops. The two American Airborne Divisions were composed of some of the best troops I have ever seen. They consisted of the cream of American manhood, and each paratrooper was a killer, prepared to take the initiative on his own, however dangerous the situation might be. Moreover, they were commanded by two quite exceptional men, Jim Gavin, the 82nd, and Maxwell Taylor, the 101st. No other Division could possibly have kept open some twenty-five miles of road which constituted our one vital link with the rear, under constant enemy pressure from both sides.

Without Jim Gavin's 82nd US Airborne, we should never have captured the two great bridges over the River Waal. While the road bridge was being assaulted, and ultimately captured intact by the Grenadier

Guards and the 505 Parachute Regiment, the 504 US Parachute Regiment, supported by the fire of the Irish Guards' tanks, crossed the swift-running, 400-yards-wide Waal River in British assault boats, which they had never seen before, in the face of vicious German rifle, machine-gun and artillery fire from the far bank. This operation, suggested by Gen. Gavin, was the best and most gallant attack I have ever seen carried out in my life. No wonder the leading paratroopers, when they contacted the Guards' tanks, which had captured the road bridges, were furious that we did not push on straight for Arnhem. They felt that they had risked their lives for nothing, but it was impossible, owing to the confusion which existed in Nijmegen, with houses burning and British and US forces all mixed up.

It is invidious to pick out any commander for special mention but the uncrowned hero of Arnhem must surely be Frost and his 2nd Para Battalion who seized and held the north end of the Arnhem bridge without reinforcements and in spite of being continually attacked by ever-increasing numbers of SS troops. They managed to hold it until the 21st, when Frost was badly wounded, with only some one hundred and fifty to two hundred men. This was the one bright spot of the whole battle, because the 10th SS division was forced to cross the Lower Rhine by ferry – a slow, laborious process which enabled us to capture the vital bridges in Nijmegen. As Mr Ryan says, 'The determination of Frost to hold on at all costs, without any hope of relief, forms one of the really great epics of British military history.'

From the 22nd onwards, the final stages of this terrible battle reached their inevitable conclusion. Our progress across the difficult polder land was all too slow. Then, suddenly, Wrottesley's troop of the Household Cavalry managed to slip through the enemy's lines in the morning mist, and made contact with General Sosabowski, the Polish Commander, and from then on we had good wireless contact with the troops on the south bank of the Neder Rhine. In a particularly daring operation, Col. George Taylor, the CO of the 5th DCLI, broke through the German defences and joined up with the Poles. Unfortunately, the DUKVS, filled with stores and ammunition for the airborne troops which formed part of his column, foundered in the thick mud and failed to get across the river.

On the 24th of September I went forward to carry out a personal reconnaissance, and met Sosabowski and George Taylor. I then climbed to the top of Driel Church Tower, from where I was able to study the southern end of the Airborne bridgehead on the far side of the river. The trouble was that the Germans occupied the high ground on either side of this bridgehead, and were able to sweep the river with fire. It was only possible, therefore, to get anything across in darkness, and under concentrations of fire laid on by the complete corps artillery.

On arrival at my HQ at 10 a.m. next morning, the 25th, I found a gloomy gathering awaiting me. The 4th Dorsets had crossed the night before, but all communications with them had now ceased; few assault boats were left, and ammunition was running short. In fact one artillery regiment was down to five rounds per gun. General Browning (we had fought most of the battle together) and I came to the conclusion that there was nothing for it but to withdraw the 1st British Airborne Division over the river. That night, under a cover of the corps artillery, 2,398 gallant troops reached our lines. It was a tragic scene, as the exhausted paratroopers swam, or were ferried, across the river in torrential rain. It seemed that even the gods were weeping at this grievous end to a gallant enterprise.

9 November 1974

MY ARNHEM ORDERS

William Deedes

Like so many famous battles of the past, Arnhem after 40 years has become a rich field for the 'if only' sort of argument. There has been a lot of it about this last week. Most of us who were there at the time have something to plant in that field.

In the last desperate hours on Arnhem bridge a bold plan was concocted somewhere in XXX Corps which, in deplorably unsuitable territory, was striving to link up with the Airborne. It ran like this: might the battle not be turned by securing for a squadron of tanks (with a company of poor bloody infantry riding on the outside of them) a flying start; and then sending them flat out across the crucial gap between leading elements of XXX Corps and Arnhem Bridge?

One of the few bits of bumf I carried out of the war and still possess is the Bridge operation order for that bold stroke. I got a copy as company commander of the PBI who were to ride the tanks.

We have set the map a bit. At this stage of the battle (22 September) both Guards Armoured and 43 (Wessex) Divisions, bearing the brunt of the advance of Gen. Horrocks's XXX Corps, were meeting stiff opposition. On the same day Major-General R.E. Urquhart, commanding 1st Airborne at Arnhem, had got a message through XXX Corps stressing the urgency of relief.

We, the 12th KRRC, a motor battalion in 8th Armoured Brigade, had moved to the battle in the wake of the Guards. We had got a place called Dievoort, famous for fruit farmers but not much else. At 11 a.m. on this grey, chilly day (22 September) our Brigadier, Errol Prior-Palmer (father of the better-known Lucinda), breezed into our battalion headquarters with the plan. Quite often he flew a cavalry pennant from his armoured scout car. This was missing.

A squadron of 13/18th Hussars, one of our three armoured regiments and the one to which my company was attached, would charge up the road and seize Arnhem Bridge. Like all the best soldiers, the Brigadier had the knack of conveying hazardous operations in sanguine terms. The written orders made it look like a piece of cake.

We were to form up at Elst, about 5½ miles from Arnhem, and with luck get our flying start from Eldon further up the road and about two miles from Arnhem. True, there was a large factory flanking the road at Eldon (later found to have been stuffed with Germans); but our operation order read airily: 'Probably 300/500 Germans left in Arnhem and factory. Arnhem town and high ground to be smoked throughout.' When the bombers stopped, three field regiments, one medium regiment and a heavy battery would lay down a barrage.

How could we miss? While I was studying this inviting prospectus Company Sergeant-Major Hooper sidled towards my armoured half-track. I had acquired CSM Hooper, without much opposition from other company commanders, when my own CSM became a casualty in Normandy. He was thought to be an indifferent disciplinarian and was not at all the sort of man to put on Horse Guards for the Queen's Birthday. But his insolent *sang-froid* appealed to me strongly. Whether it was raining rations or rockets or just raining (as it was on this day), CSM Hooper's morose calm reassured.

A successful post-war industrialist owes his life to Hooper. As a junior officer he took out a patrol one night, and did not return. 'Lost his bloody way,' Hooper said unkindly, and mooched off casually into the night with a couple of reluctant riflemen. He found the future pillar of industry badly wounded on the banks of a Dutch canal and returned him without comment.

Now he approached me with the air of one who had already got wind of

Errol Prior-Palmer's slice of cake. 'Bit of a rum do,' he said. It was the nearest he ever got to an expression of alarm.

By then I had reached aerial photographs, vertical and oblique, of our road to Arnhem. The Brigade IO had thoughtfully marked features of interest en route with white crayon. 'At least, for once,' I said, 'we can see where we're going.' Someone observed, unhelpfully, that a photograph of a factory from the air tells you very little about who are inside it.

We examined the order. 'Speed: flat out from the "off".' Cavalryman's touch there. I pointed out that to give us such a start the Household Cavalry armoured cars would secure the start line; no 'off' till they did.

For the rest of that long day we remained under starter's orders. Then: 'No move before first light.' Some of the riflemen used the interval to write letters home. Absurd details preoccupied me. The op. order said we were to leave our own half-track vehicles at Elst station. How were we to get back to them after riding on the tanks into Arnhem? That sort of commuter problem whetted CSM Hooper's appetite. Not a good night.

Had we then known what all the world knows now about the military state of affairs around the Nijmegen–Arnhem road, we could safely have climbed into pyjamas and overslept. It was well into 23 September before the state of battle compelled even the most sanguine to let it be known in the language of those days that 'it simply isn't on'.

Such are the perverse workings of the human mind that the first reaction was not relief but disgruntlement. If you have to spend hours persuading yourself and 160 other people that something *is* on, you do not, at a stroke, accept that it isn't. 'We've been buggered about,' the rifleman said.

Besides, we couldn't see the 'big picture'. News of fighting around us was scanty, from Arnhem bridgehead non-existent. Hooper looked a trifle smug, but it did not enter my head to say: 'It's the end, the end of Market Garden.'

That came home in the next few days when we tried to help 43 Division salvage what was left of 1st Airborne over the slippery and impossibly steep banks of the Neder Rhine. All I remember clearly is that all the time it pissed with rain, as it often does on soldiers in adversity.

So, the military historians now assure us, it was failure; a plan misconceived and botched in execution. A failure, yes; but, I venture to say, not misconceived. To take a chance, to aim to end the European war that autumn was right.

Nine months later I was directing my company in more shameful duties near Hanover, handing over tracts of Germany to Russian soldiers to honour our undertakings made at Yalta, or was it Potsdam? The Rus-

sians had used that winter to advantage, and we live with the consequences now. The riflemen found this a delightful exercise, swapping
their wristwatches for Russian revolvers. CSM Hooper did not shine in a
disciplinary situation like that.

The failure, perhaps I should say our failure, at Arnhem wrote a lot of
European history, none for our comfort. What a pity 'Sqn 13/18 H carring
one Coy 12 KRRC' never made it.

29 September 1984

BOMBER'S LIFE

J.L. Hodson

'Our heavy bombers were out over Germany again last night.' What lies
behind this radio voice? This: Scattered about our English counties are
small communities of men living, in a sense, a monastic life, a life apart
from the rest of us. Whenever I visit them, the men who are bombing
Germany, I am brought up sharply against the difference between the
lives of most of us and their life. For ours can be seen stretching ahead,
and theirs cannot. There are no return tickets to the Third Reich. They
don't speak of this. They may say: 'Smithy went down last night'; or
'George has gone for a Burton. On his thirtieth, too.' Not much more than
that. There are those who are a trifle exalted by the danger, men who've
done their two tours making together 50 or 55 'trips' (that's their word for
it), and come back voluntarily for a third tour; men who think this squadron life is the only life in the RAF worth living; for being grounded or
doing instructing work bores them to hell. There are others, 'civilian-
minded', who hate it but keep on going, who tick off each trip and think:
'One nearer the end.' Whichever sort they are, they go – without fuss,
with a calculated midnight courage.

As with other men in danger, they find alleviations. First, comrade-
ship. Most crews are a band of brothers, sticking together a good deal, not
only in the air but on the ground. There's some cannibalism, of course,
the borrowing of somebody's rear-gunner or Wop (wireless operator) if
yours is sick. But nobody likes it, and a man will fly when perhaps he
shouldn't to keep the crew intact. If a man is sick, and while he is off his

crew 'doesn't come back', he's fed up to the teeth (call it broken-hearted if you like). Second, their technical skill and their faith in their aircraft. It takes the best part of a couple of years nowadays to train the pilot of a Lancaster, otherwise the captain; he'll probably fly Oxfords, Wellingtons, Stirlings on his way to Lancasters. The navigator who gets them there and back, taking the aircraft a thousand miles, maybe, and putting it in a spot in the sky to a minute; the flight engineer, who helps the pilot in take-off and landing, controlling boost, flaps, &c.; the bomb-aimer, Wop, the gunners, mid-upper and rear who are the aircraft's main eyes – all are long and painfully trained technicians.

And the aircraft? The Lancaster is the best heavy bomber in the world, capable of carrying almost double the bomb-load of a Fortress. Its feats in coming back shot-up are sometimes extravagant. They've come back on two engines often enough. There's a tale, perhaps legendary, that one got back from Milan through a valley in the Alps on one! At all events, the crew's affection for their craft can be deep. Aircraft are still flying which have seventy, or even in one or two instances close on a hundred, trips to their credit (although engines will have to be changed, of course, or even parts of wings and tail). One sees them, perhaps, with their score painted near the nose, a yellow bomb for night raids, white for daylights, a parachute for mine-laying, and maybe an ice-cream cornet for Italy! If your kite is B for Baker, or A for Able, or H for Harry, you want no other, want to raid in no other. You feel B for Baker will bring you back.

I talked with a Yorkshire boy of 23 who not long ago flew back his machine alone. An engine caught fire over the Continent, flames licked round the wing, and he ordered the crew to bail out. He stood alone when they had gone, watching the flames, thinking: 'Well, old D for Dog and I have done eighteen trips together – I don't like leaving her.' And, lo! the flames began to die down, and he climbed back into his seat and brought her back. It was his affection for her that saved her. Wing Commander W.L. Brill, DSO, of Narrandera, New South Wales, could tell a tale about aircraft taking punishment. He came home from Brest on three engines, with one elevator shot off and 150 holes in her. Before that he had been hit by 27 incendiaries over Berlin and lost his rudder. Again, over Nuremberg the blowing-up of another aircraft knocked out his port engine and rear turret, and for a while he flew on two engines. Three times a badly damaged aircraft brought him home.

The strategy and tactics of bombing Germany have changed as the war itself has changed. In the beginning the bomber was superior to defences. In those days, too, a single aircraft or two would sometimes cruise over Germany in a wide area, attacking morale, keeping folk in shelters. Then numbers grew, but flak grew also, driving aircraft to a higher level. For a

space the development of defence outpaced, in some respects, the technical skill of bombers. Next came the method of bombing by heavy concentrations. In the 1,000-bomber raid on Cologne the attack was packed into
90 minutes. That was revolutionary. Today it is outmoded. We deliver an
attack now in ten to twenty minutes (it's a long one if it is more than fifteen minutes). In that brief space we destroy a town. The men say: 'We
wrote it off – there's nothing left.' The Pathfinder force lights up the target, marks it accurately by flares, different colours for different spots in
the town, then in comes the bomber force to hit the target swiftly and
fiercely – and withdraw. There can be few, if any, warlike and mechanical
operations carried out today that have as much terrible precision.

The planning is meticulous. The word superb is not much exaggeration. Briefings are in triplicate – one for navigators, one for captains, one
for everybody. On the wall hangs the gigantic map of Europe with a thin
ribbon from base to target passing through the crucial points, A B C D,
&c., between which various stipulated heights will be kept. Not much is
left to the captain's discretion; his route, times, his approach-bearing,
bombing heights – are all fixed. And over the target works the Pathfinder
– a bomber ace who has himself bombed for months or even years – seeing
that the target is accurately marked. If a marking is wrongly placed he
may 'scrub it out' with another colour till, finally satisfied, he orders:
'OK, come in and bomb,' and in they come, timed to the minute, first
wave, second wave, third wave and so on. Efficiency, precision and damage inflicted are greater than ever before.

How does the danger compare – the ordeal? Opinions vary. Some old-
timer bombers think the flak and searchlights of today are not what they
were in 1942, when a belt of searchlights from Emden to Charleroi was
250 miles long and sixty miles wide, and they worked in cones of fifty;
when Berlin had 500 heavy guns in defences stretching 40 miles from the
capital, and Cologne 500 more – both heavy and light. But are there,
indeed, fewer today? May there not be more? There is less enemy territory
to fly over now, you can bail out over France or Belgium with more safety,
the enemy has lost many night-fighter airfields and prediction-stations –
but as he withdraws into his borders his concentration of night-fighters
becomes heavier, and his prediction-instruments are of high skill. It is
not unknown for a searchlight to snap straight on to an aircraft with no
fumbling. What is sure in considering whether the task grows easier or
tougher is that it remains most hazardous and demands the highest skill
and bravery – and that these are devoted to it.

An hour before take-off engines begin to fill the darkness with their
roaring; it is the last testing. Flare-paths are lit, the great hangar's interior
shines a hideous green, here is a red light, yonder a triangle of green. Test-

ing over, the air-crew wait in their hut near-by – a last cigarette or pipe, badinage: 'He said a night-fighter was following them in – turned out to be a star' – 'Did you get your wings in the last war, sir?' – 'He was upside down and nothing on the clock – shaky do'; 'My rear turret must have been wired by the mess-waiter.' At last, aircraft begin to stack up for their take-off. No command is given – their times are fixed, watches already synchronised. The first – a giant post-historic bird – taxies to the runway, a mile or two miles long. From the control hut a green lamp is pointed at her, and the light turned on. Her engines rise to a screaming roar and a spatter of sparks fly from her exhaust. She moves, moves, till, rushing at 120 to 140 miles an hour along that runway she rises, nothing now to us who watch but a white star slowly ascending into the night. As soon as she is airborne another follows her. No command is given – nothing but that silent green beam from a lamp. Thirty are gone in as many minutes. We see them wheeling above, those stars, setting course – and at length the night is empty.

You cannot watch them go unmoved, nor see them return either. Dawn has broken, thin and grey over this bleak countryside, over these Nissen huts, so cold that your sleep has been small, when the first faint roaring comes again and yonder black speck grows into a great Lancaster. Since you saw her last she has been beset by shells, night-fighters have flung their rockets at her in parabola curves, she has been silhouetted over a sheet of cloud that, lit by flares from below, shone like frosted glass; she has narrowly escaped collision, even narrowly escaped a cookie (4,000 lb. bomb) that fell from above, twenty feet ahead of her nose. Yet, incredibly, she is here – here almost to the minute. And behind her come others, until there may be ten or twenty at a time waiting aloft to come back to earth. In the control-tower they are ticked off until only W for William is missing. The little anxiety becomes a great anxiety; and still no news. Meanwhile the crews are gathering in turn round the intelligence officers, drinking their mugs of tea, giving the time of bombing. 'Yes, lots of night-fighters, but none too close' – 'Yes, marking was OK' – 'Did two orbits' – 'I'd say we did a 60 per cent job – cloud made it difficult' – 'Pretty straightforward job tonight.' It goes on for an hour or so. A woman intelligence officer is interrogating, too. The crews drift off. Somebody pauses. 'Any news of W for William yet?' No, no news.

'On his nineteenth, wasn't he?'

'Yes, nineteenth.'

'Coming?'

'No, I'll wait a bit – he was going on leave with me today.'

'So long, then.'

'So long.'

27 October 1944

WHAT THE SOLDIER THINKS

Captain, B.L.A.

Here is how I suggest the soldier of the 2nd Army is facing the world today.

1. He believes we shall lose the peace and precipitate another war in ten or twenty years' time. He believes the Englishman is fundamentally sentimental towards his enemy – he was himself before he saw for himself the horrors perpetrated by the Germans in France, Belgium and Holland. Knowing that his hatred will only endure until he hears the first German baby ask him for chocolate, he wants to be saved from himself by letting Russia occupy the country and direct the peace. He profoundly distrusts what he reads about Germany in the Press, and is convinced that the bankers, bishops and barons will ensure a peace that will make the Third Great War certain.

2. He is deeply distrustful of all civilian authority – parliamentary, municipal and industrial. A large number of men in my unit will not fill up the form for the electoral register. They are not interested in a vote because 'it won't do me any good'. The soldier distrusts the Tories. He distrusts the Socialists now they have become the Tories' bedfellows. He distrusts the reforms that are brought in, either because they are too late or because they were grudgingly introduced under such pressure that he doubts whether they will ever be honourably implemented. For instance, he suspects the White Paper on Social Insurance because of the previous partial rejection of Beveridge. ('There must be a catch in it.') He questions the policy of the Government on the bombed-out (many soldiers have had their families affected and know personally how unsatisfactory the remedial measures often are); and on Italian prisoners of war (quite a big political issue out here, and one, incidentally, that confirms the suspicion that Germany also will get cotton-wool treatment).

He distrusts industrial authority. He is convinced big business is making a nice thing out of the war. He has read some ugly reports of certain English firms charged in America with trading with the enemy. He suspects that the war may be no bad thing for the firm employed on munitions during the war and on the reconstruction after it. He knows that his fortunate comrades in England are often earning as much in a week as he used to earn in a month. He believes the financier was largely the cause of this war and is already thinking of the next.

He has read about the miners on strike and he wants the nationalisation of the mines – and other public services. He wonders how, after five years of war, he will be able to compete with the civilian for skilled jobs. He is earning relatively good money in the Army now, but he expects to earn more in 'civvy street'. Men of twenty-five now earning, perhaps, £250 a year (taking food and clothing into account) wonder whether they will have to return to unskilled jobs that brought them in 30s. a week when they were twenty, before the war.

3. He is frantically tired of the war, but he is willing to do anything to finish it. It makes him angry when he hears that England is beginning to slacken off and think that it is all over bar the fighting. He knew we should be faced with a winter campaign when all the papers were gaily screaming 'over by Christmas'. He does far more than his share; he expects the civilians to do theirs. Too often he has read of safe hotels, black markets, wire-pulling and phoney exemption. In his gloomier moments he wonders how deep the rottenness has got.

4. He distrusts the BBC and the daily Press. Frequently he reads of events in which he has taken part that are wrongly reported. Too many of the things he was told about Europe he has seen for himself were not true. He is right, then, to be distrustful about facts he cannot check.

5. Religion scarcely touches the fringe of his life. Many have kept their faith untarnished, few, I suspect, have newly found it. There is not, I think, any reason to suppose that Army life has either increased or diminished the number of the faithful.

In short, then, the British soldier is fighting for the future of the world and does not believe in that future. He is tough, hard, honest, intelligent, cynical, kind, soft-hearted, sentimental and completely disillusioned. He is fighting not for any ideal – although he hates his enemy and the ways of the enemy – but because he knows that Germany must be utterly defeated before he can get home to his family, his football, his beer and his fireside. He asks a lot of the future, but he doesn't expect to get any of it. He does expect a bit of fun when first he gets back home. And in the next war he expects to be in the Home Guard while his son bears the burden of the day.

That represents within my own narrow experience (may I be forgiven for speaking when others better qualified hold their peace) broadly what the British combatant forces – the salt of the earth – are thinking. It is, perhaps, encouraging that Tommy, 1944, will not be foozled by facile talk of a land fit for heroes. He wants deeds, not words. It is up to the citizens of England to see he is not disappointed.

24 November 1944

A YULETIDE LONG AGO:
How Winston Churchill Spent Christmas with the Besieged Embassy at Athens

---

Osbert Lancaster[1]

The Ambassadress, who was resolute and High, had arranged for Midnight Mass in the drawing-room. That the arrangement had worked was no small tribute to her force of character, for the Embassy was situated in an uncomfortable no-man's-land midway between the eastern perimeter of the British-held city centre and the Communist lines halfway up the Amalias Boulevard, so that when the only Anglican chaplain in Athens had finally been located General Scobie had had to be persuaded to provide an armoured car, which were in short supply, for his transport. Of the sermon, which was seasonable, I can now only recall an inspired reference to the Herald Angels as 'God's Airborne Division', for the preacher had hardly got into his stride when Harold Caccia, next to whom I was sitting, was summoned to Chancery by a whispered message that the signallers on the roof had reported a 'Most Immediate' to be coming through from Downing Street and my attention had started to stray. When some twenty minutes later I slipped away during the last verse of 'Adeste Fideles' and myself went down to Chancery my curiosity was only partially satisfied, for there I found, in addition to Harold, Mr Macmillan, who had crept away rather earlier in the hymn, and John Wyndham, whose staunch Protestant convictions had not allowed him to attend the service at all, both equally bemused by a mysterious communication which by now had been deciphered but hardly interpreted. Briefly it stated that the PM was sending us a most important envoy for whose identity we were referred to Tel. No. XYZ to Caserta. As no telegram had been repeated from Caserta we assumed, correctly, that it was in the possession of General Alexander, already overdue in Athens, who was at that moment stormbound on a destroyer in the Ionian, and so the early hours of Christmas Day passed in fruitless speculation.

---

[1]Osbert Lancaster, prince of cartoonists, served in the Foreign Office during the war; he was attached to HM Embassy, Athens, 1944–46.

When next morning shortly after midday I had returned by devious back-routes to the Embassy, having shared with the war correspondents at the Grande Bretagne a demijohn of retsina upon which, by some undisclosed chicanery, they had managed to lay their hands, I found the General arrived, the mystery solved and an atmosphere of controlled panic. The envoy, as we might have guessed, was Mr Churchill himself, who had already touched down in Naples and was due in Athens within the next few hours; on the problem of how best to cherish, accommodate and, above all, protect him a handful of colonels and brigadiers were already gloomily pondering. The airfield itself was relatively safe, as the scattered guerrillas roaming Mount Hymettus were too few in number and too lightly armed effectively to interfere with its working, but the road to Athens was dominated by the Phix brewery, a Communist strong-hold, and could only be travelled in armoured convoy. The Grande Bretagne was packed not only with HQ Staff but also with members of the Greek government and all the foreign correspondents, which ren-dered the maintenance of adequate security virtually impossible. It was also, as was discovered the next day, mined. The Embassy, full to burst-ing, was protected only by a captain and half a dozen men, and on one side exposed to enthusiastic if inaccurate rifle-fire from Pankrati. Finally it was decided that Mr Macmillan and the CO should go down to the air-port and explain to the PM and his numerous entourage a state of affairs of which our telegrams would seem, perhaps, to have presented an insuf-ficiently discouraging picture.

On their return the party were eagerly questioned as to the frame of mind and intentions of the newcomers and one gave it as his opinion that they had all the air of men to whom a brilliant idea had been vouchsafed after the third glass of port upon which they had immediately decided to act but which they could now no longer very clearly recall. However, here they were and here, somewhere, they had to stay. Finally it was decided to transfer them to the cruiser *Ajax*, lying off Phaleron, to which the pros-pective Regent, Archbishop Damaskinos, would straightway be con-veyed.

After some slight confusion occasioned by His Beatitude's arrival in full canonicals during a fancy-dress party on the lower deck, and when Mr Churchill had been reassured about his visitor's character ('This Archbishop? He is, I suppose, an ambitious, scheming, political prelate?' Quickly, before the Ambassador could come out with an indignant denial, Mr Macmillan, a more seasoned operator, had heartily agreed. 'Good! He will serve our purposes!'), it was decided that a truce must straightway be called and a round-table conference held. Immediately wires buzzed, signals flashed, sinister go-betweens were contacted and a conference laid on for the afternoon of Boxing Day at the Greek Foreign Office.

Despite the truce, firing was still going briskly on when the PM arrived at the Embassy next morning. The change in his appearance since I had last seen him at close quarters some three years previously was marked. His face seemed to have been moulded in lard lightly veined with cochineal and he badly needed a haircut. But the sound of mortaring and rifle-fire, combined with the historic associations of the countryside through which he had just passed, were clearly already having a tonic effect and he was distinguished from all his companions by an obvious and unswerving sense of purpose none the less impressive for being at the moment indeterminate. We were very shortly joined by the French and American Ambassadors, both scared stiff lest their presence should be held in some way to infringe their countries' carefully preserved neutrality, and the head of the Russian military mission, Colonel Popov, an amiable man rather in the style of Colonel Vershinin in *The Three Sisters*, with whom General Alexander immediately entered into close conversation in Russian. Intrigued by the length and earnestness of this exchange I encouraged David Balfour, who was bilingual, to try and discover the subject of the discussion; after a few minutes of successful eavesdropping he came back and reported 'Epaulettes!'

The big conference room at the Foreign Office was cold as charity and illuminated only by hurricane lamps. At the head of the long narrow table sat the representatives of the three allied but neutral powers; at the foot three seats were reserved for the Communist delegation when they should finally have made their way through the lines. Mr Churchill was seated in the centre of one of the long sides with next to him the Archbishop and alongside Messrs Eden and Macmillan, the Ambassador and Generals Scobie and Alexander; opposite was a representative selection of the *politikos kosmos* ranging from the actual Prime Minister, Mr Papandreou, to such veterans as Mr Sophoulis and Mr Maximos and including General Plastiras, fur-coated and fiercely moustached, whom we had recently, and perhaps misguidedly, flown back from exile in France. ('Plashter-arse? Let us hope his feet are not of clay.' They were.)

After the Prime Minister and the Archbishop had both made speeches so long and brilliantly phrased that the interpreter was in a state of near-collapse, there followed an interminable wait for the arrival of the Communist delegates. When finally word came that they were with us, a further prolonged and, to those inside, inexplicable delay ensued before their actual entry. Once seated they were addressed at some length by the Prime Minister, who then announced that all the outsiders would withdraw leaving the Greeks to continue negotiations under the Archbishop's chairmanship. As we all filed out I found myself immediately behind Mr Churchill, who had in front of him Colonel Popov, whom he at once engaged in conversation. 'What's your name, Colonel? Popov? Well, Popov, I saw your master the other day, Popov! Very good friends your master and I, Popov! Don't forget that, POPOV!' Although the gallant Colonel's knowledge of English was, I knew, limited, his expression indicated that the message had got through.

Arrived outside we discovered that the long wait had been caused by the Communists' reluctance to abandon the large selection of weapons with which they came equipped, which had only finally been overcome by the solemn assurance that no guns were carried by anyone around the table and that even General Alexander had abandoned his side-arms. Upon this being explained to the PM, he looked thoughtful and then said to his companion: 'I cannot tell you the feeling of security one enjoys knowing that one is the only armed man in such an assembly as that.' Whereupon he withdrew from the pocket of his RAF great-coat, and quickly replaced, a loaded pistol.

The next day after the great man had made a brisk tour of our outposts in a biting north-east wind and intermittent snow-squalls, and had climbed the Pnyx for an overall picture of the fighting, closely guarded by Lord Moran and Jock Colville and hotly pursued by a posse of apprehensive and soon exhausted detectives, staff officers and field security police, he returned to the Embassy determined to summon a press conference. This fell to my lot to arrange and presented formidable difficulties. The Press, particularly the Americans, were insistent on taking photographs, a privilege which Mr C was very willing to accord them, but, unfortunately, the electric power had long ceased to function and the supply of flash bulbs was exhausted. This meant that in the failing light of a winter's afternoon the only available rendezvous was the Embassy garden into which both Lord Moran and the security officers were extremely reluctant for their charge to enter. This small plot was in fact relatively safe, being surrounded on all sides by a nine-foot wall, but it was only when I had light-heartedly accepted personal responsibility for the PM's safety that I appreciated the snag. To get to it one had to cross a small platform, bridging the area outside the drawing-room, which was not covered by the wall and was wide open to the Communist-held slopes of Pankrati, just across the road. Summoning the photographers, who were already stationed in the garden, I begged them not to rush forward as the PM and the Regent emerged from the drawing-room as the former would then undoubtedly stop dead on the platform in a suitably aggressive pose. Everything happened exactly as I had foreseen; the photographers rushed forward, the Prime Minister stopped dead and a short crack followed by a shower of plaster announced that a bullet had hit the wall two feet above our heads. Then, summoning all my courage, I made what seems to me in retrospect one of my only two direct and effective contributions to the war effort and gave the infuriated Prime Minister a sharp shove in the back precipitating him smartly down the steps into the comparative safety of the garden, leaving the unfortunate Archbishop, a far more massive target, still exposed on the skyline.

When, next morning, Mr Churchill returned to the Embassy to take his leave, and incidentally be shot at once more at far closer range, the fighting was still going on, and was to continue for another couple of weeks. However, his visit had not been in vain. The Greeks of all parties and not least the Communists, had been much gratified by the thought they had brought the great Allied leader all the way to Athens at a moment when the situation on the Western Front was still critical, and his fellow countrymen had been upheld, stimulated and encouraged by his presence among them. Nevertheless, it was with a feeling approaching relief that some of us heard that Santa Claus had at last climbed back into his sleigh and that the reindeer were now safely airborne.

24 December 1965

Part Seven
1945

O, PEACEFUL ENGLAND! Now, where the drone of enemy aircraft menaced the peace of moorland and meadow, quiet reigns once more. The land of Chaucer and Shakespeare is for ever ours. Let us give thanks. But how? By the same thrift and self-denial that helped so greatly to bring Britain through —by saving to beat the Jap and to build a yet finer Britain!

GIVE THANKS BY SAVING

Issued by the National Savings Committee

SOLDIERS AND POLITICIANS

Vernon Bartlett, MP

It is well known that one of the reasons for the existence of cats is to be kicked by husbands who have quarrelled with their wives. The human being, naturally but regrettably, vents his anger on somebody or something not directly the cause of it. Why, then, should we be surprised if bored and embittered men and women in the forces curse the House of Commons and feel better for having done so? In one way the politician should be reassured by the discovery that so many of the curses are directed at him – people in uniform are evidently not so uninterested in politics as they are supposed to be. A few weeks ago I followed an Army truck for ten miles or so along the road from Eindhoven to Louvain. It rained incessantly on the men in the truck. If one could judge by their faces, they alternated between resentful gloom and a slightly artificial joy induced by songs that were excessively bawdy or excessively sentimental. My companion suddenly gave expression to my own vague thoughts by saying: 'I wonder what they really think about war, peace and all that.'

Some of their doubts and fears, suspicions and hopes, have been printed in the columns of this paper, to the alarm and despondency of some of its readers. But why should one expect starry-eyed enthusiasm from men whose lives are so often acutely uncomfortable, deadly boring or grimly frightening? Since war is only a form of politics, the politician must expect to be blamed for the fact that the soldier has things to grouse about. The sergeant-major along the trench or the brass-hat back at the base may be responsible for some particular piece of misery, but those so-and-sos in Westminster and Whitehall are responsible for the major misery – that the soldier is a soldier at all and not a civilian with a family, a job, and a pint of beer waiting for him in the pub at the corner.

It is a tragedy that the House of Commons was already tired and unrepresentative when the war broke out. Elected in 1935 on the basis of a Government pledge to enforce collective security, its reputation had sunk with each attempt by that Government to avoid fulfilling that pledge. The Hoare-Laval Pact, the Spanish Non-Intervention Committee, the surrender of Czechoslovakia to Hitler, were millstones around its neck. Thus weighted, most of its unfortunate members were certain to be submerged by the flood of hostile votes at the forthcoming general election. Many of them, indeed, would not even have troubled to face the electorate.

But in many of the letters printed in *The Spectator* there is an undertone of contempt which cannot entirely be explained away by the soldier's discomforts or the politician's murky past. There is contempt not only for the individual Member of Parliament, which does not greatly matter, but also for Parliament as an institution, which matters a very great deal. The Parliamentary system, it is argued, has not been successful in preventing any kind of freedom from want or from fear. 'It must never be forgotten,' wrote 'Ex-Pilot' in *The Spectator* last week, 'that these young men grew up under the economic depression. If they were not themselves actually turned out of school to go on the dole – and many of them were – they were surrounded through their most impressionable years by families and friends for whom, apparently, the community had no use . . . Can it be wondered that they have no faith in the competence or honesty of government? They contrast the frustrated and meaningless society of their boyhood with the purposeful organisation of totalitarian countries, which at any rate knew where they were going and set some value on their populations.'

Not every young man who makes this contrast stops to reflect how inevitably these totalitarian States were going towards war, and how entirely the value they set on their populations was a military one. The men were to become more efficient and the women were to become more prolific solely in order that cannon-fodder of the best quality should be available in the greatest possible quantity. But reason and reflection play only a small part in politics, and it is quite clear that freedom of speech and freedom of election – the two basic freedoms in any non-totalitarian and non-sheeplike community – have lost their appeal.

And yet – let's face it – there are only two systems of government in the world. There is government by force and government by consent. The former can satisfy only the Führer himself – the other important-looking leaders have to pay by a humiliating sycophancy for their unhealthy and dangerous right to exploit and control their fellow-men. The method of government by consent must be slower and less sensational, for each measure is a compromise. During this war the great reforms that will become necessary after it are drafted, first, as White Papers which are debated and modified, and, second, as Bills which are again debated and modified. The final Act of Parliament may be depressingly, even dangerously, delayed, but it is one which has taken into account minority opinions. It is an example of government by consent.

One wonders for how long the critics of Parliament would be happy without it. They should remember this. Few Members have the time to sit through long debates on subjects about which they have no expert knowledge. They have no time, because they are busy in the Library dealing with their correspondence, the amount and diversity of which is almost unbelievable. And almost every letter deals with some individual case of difficulty or hardship on which advice or help is sought. With a nation mobilised for total war almost every letter affects directly or indirectly one of those men or women in the forces who are so ready to curse Members of Parliament and all their works. Grievances about pay or leave, medal ribbons or polished buttons, will be debated on the floor of the House and reported by the newspapers and the BBC. But the thousands of minor problems and hardships that worry the community are dealt with in endless and unadvertised correspondence with Government Departments. There is no injustice which cannot be brought before a Member of Parliament by anyone from the humblest to the highest citizen; there is no injustice which can safely be made the subject of protest in a dictator State. Even during the gravest crisis of 1940 the safety valve which is provided by Question Time still operated.

Attacks on Parliament come from two sides. Its Members are accused either of being yes men or of criticising and delaying the Government when it should be left to its job of winning the war. The leaders of the second form of attack are seldom consistent, for they are ready enough to complain when the Government offends them and Parliament does not protest. Nothing can be done about them; either the ending of the war will modify their view that Government is above criticism or they will turn openly to Fascism. They will be influential only if they win the support of men in the first category, and they will not do so if these men are given more chance of playing a part in government. 'It is the essence of the political system which we have built up over a great many centuries,' said Lord Cranborne recently, 'that the British are not governed – they govern themselves.' That, unfortunately, is not as true as it should be.

Reforms of our political machinery might help to make it true. All local government elections might be held on the same day throughout the country, so that they would arouse the same sort of interest as is now aroused by a general election (and they play so large a part in government that they certainly merit that interest). The governors of the BBC or other public utility companies might be elected by some form of public ballot and given more power after election. The Parliamentary vote itself might be enhanced in value by some kind of voter's test, based not, of course, on money, but on evidence that one was socially alive. (This last suggestion contains such obvious dangers that I would rather withdraw it than be called upon to defend it.) Candidates might be forbidden to spend a penny in their own constituencies, so that the electorate would learn to pay more attention to their real qualifications.

Any number of such reforms will suggest themselves. But in the last resort the distrust of Parliament is due, I believe, to the fact that opinion has been changed by blitz and mobilisation more rapidly outside the House of Commons than inside it. Too many of the Members are old and tired; too many of the young ones are themselves away in uniform. And in consequence we are in grave danger of neglecting the words of that earlier President Roosevelt, Theodore. 'A great democracy,' he once said, 'must be progressive. Otherwise it will soon cease to be either great or a democracy.'

19 January 1945

COUNTRY LIFE

W. Beach Thomas

When the war is over there is likely, as definite enquiry proves, to be a great excess of men who want to commence farming; to this enormous tally has to be added an army of women with like ambitions. Besides these, dispossessed farmers, who have been turned out by the accidents of war and by the organisers of wartime agriculture, now number a good many thousand, and they appear to be organising themselves into a rebellious group demanding reinstatement. Is there any way of satisfying this unheard-of demand? Experience after the last war, as well as in the annals of husbandry, prove that smallholdings, organised to respond to the demand, are no answer, though the multiplication of small yeoman farmers is a glorious ideal. The smallholder is born, not made. The manufactured smallholder is doomed to failure and disappointment in nine cases out of ten. Perhaps the best chance, for men with engineering ability, is to associate the small farm or holding with machines with which he can do mechanical work for his neighbours. It has already been found in the west of England, if not in the east, that a smallholder can do such work to the double benefit of himself and his neighbours. It is, I think, a general experience, here and overseas, that the secret of success in farming is most often found in engineering skill.

26 January 1945

UNDERGROUND STORY

Alain Verney

Even in 1940, when the Germans were parading along the avenues of Paris, there lingered within French hearts some frail hope, strengthened by the voices and messages of Mr Winston Churchill and General de Gaulle. Then the petty 'Pétainist Press' began to fawn on the Germans and whine and confess to sins, imaginary in the past, at the time all too real. A few dailies tried to outwit the drastic Nazi control: when compelled to publish their news and their news-comments, they mocked them subtly by altering now a word, now a punctuation mark, so that an undercurrent of truth kept running in their very depths, felt everywhere but coming to the surface at rare intervals. Yet the Germans at last understood, and suppressed them. Apart from two or three exclusive literary reviews, disguising the nation's feeling in poetic, surrealist or mythological garb, there remained only the all-potent French Goebbelised Press. It is all but impossible to imagine the plight of such times: your ideals were being basely traduced and sullied and you could not speak; you felt your silence was being mistaken abroad for consent, your helplessness for help to the hated enemy, and all the time you knew that your hatred and your shame were of no avail. This was a living nightmare, dispelled only by night, but renewed every day by the Nazified morning press, a nightmare akin to, but much worse than, the evil conjured by Kafka in *The Castle* and *The Trial*.

Yet something was possible. Unknown to each other, several groups of readers felt the urge of writing and printing secretly, if only to save honour, what no paper would care or dare to print. The aim of the Clandestine Press was moral and spiritual as much as political, and *Défense de la France – D.F.* – expressed at its best what is involved in the words of Pascal, which it chose to inscribe every month on its secretly published double page, *je ne crois que les histoires dont les témoins se font égorger.*

Great difficulties had to be overcome before the first number of *D.F.* could be completed on the symbolic date, July 14th, 1941. The necessary tools had to be secured; a Rotaprint and a typewriter were needed, as the Roneo system would have given poor results. P— somehow got a light Rotaprint (80 kilogrammes) working quickly without requiring too much electricity. The typewriter was provided by two young volunteers, who entered a Nazified Government office; choosing the best they could find, they put it in an old potato sack and triumphantly walked away, without noticing ten yards of black and red ribbons trailing from the bag behind them. The requisite plant once acquired, the next problem was the question of how to use it. A schoolmaster, a doctor, three young women students and a nurse resolved to learn the technique and succeeded after forty hours of earnest efforts, though the professional man who had agreed to teach them had warned them they would need at least five or six months' training.

It became possible to start work as soon as safe premises could be found. But where could an 'underground' newspaper find safe premises in 1941? The romantic obvious answer was – underground. So *D.F.* established its quarters in a dusty room, crammed with torn uncut old theses, in the very heart of the Sorbonne's substructure. It was, as the crow flies, within three minutes' reach of the great university lecturing hall, or rather as a nightbird flies, for none but that would have known its way in the maze of pitch-dark subterranean staircases and passages. But for the *Résistance* no place can be safe for long. When the group had to leave hurriedly, a better printing plant was ordered by means of specially forged official authorisations. The party which was to fetch it had agreed to telephone a message, referring to the new Offset Rotaprint as Simone – and soon it was learnt that 'Simone was staying as a guest in the bathroom of MAD', the well-known professor of Greek at the Ecole des Hautes Etudes.

Later on Simone was transferred to a cork-lined padded room, as it was necessary otherwise to play the piano or the wireless at their loudest to conceal all the sounds of the noisy machine, and the neighbours began to resent dangerously the proximity of such bohemians. It was consequently only prudent to remove the Rotaprint. Like all of us, it was provided with a false identity card and a fictitious story – a *synonomètre Le Verrier* was being consigned by the Faculty of Science to a branch laboratory. It had a strong escort; girls opened the way – girls always open all ways in the *Résistance* – and armed cyclists accompanied the lorry on its journey. The end of Simone, the Rotaprint then serving with the Maquis, was that of the women and the children of Oradour; it was burnt alive in a quarry, when the Germans found it in 1944. It had had its day, and had long been superseded by several three-ton presses.

Past experiences had shown that deserted out-of-the-way hiding-places were the most dangerous in the long run. So the first press was set up in the back room of a large laundry, where its din was covered by that of the washing-machinery. It pleased the old lady who owned the premises, as she felt she had a personal interest in taking revenge on Pétain, whom she could not forgive for being born in the same year as herself. When Darnand's French Gestapo raided the house, whilst everyone was escaping through a hidden door, 'Granny' loudly protested again and again that they could not teach *her* how to recognise 'wicked terrorists' as she always listened to Darnand and Henriot's descriptions of them; her lodgers did not tally with them, they even had good manners! The Milice was at last convinced of her good faith and sheer stupidity.

Another press was put up in a small Parisian factory (at Clichy), 'working for Germany' under the supervision of a few Nazis. The room in which it was locked was next to that of the Germans, so that no suspicion was aroused. However, if they had rushed in unexpectedly, either there would have been time to lower by a crane the enormous box which hung high above the press, and which when lowered concealed it completely, or the well-armed bodyguard would have availed themselves of another advantage the room possessed – its window looked on to a deep canal. Actually the materials were brought in and the papers brought out in the canteen's lorries without being interfered with at any time. At the next stage a printing concern was openly purchased and installed in a three-storeyed house situated within two hundred yards of the notorious Santé, in the cells of which so many Gaullists were starved to death. It was under the unsuspecting eyes of policemen from the Santé that five lorries discharged the heavy apparatus that was needed to supply every region of France with *D.F.*

When Paris rose, part of the group – which had increased every year – insisted on exchanging setting-sticks for tommy-guns, whilst the others prepared in haste the first open number of *D.F.*, then rushed out to shout its too-long-whispered name in the streets, where the fight was raging: the vicious fire of German guns seemed but to serve as a salute announcing to all clandestine journalists the new birth of their papers. For the first time one met the comrades in arms of *Combat-Franc-Tireur, Libération, Front National, L'Humanité, Le Populaire, La France Libre, Le Parisien Libéré, L'Aurore, L'Aube.* Every one of these had passed through similar experiences and different adventures; *D.F.* has been singled out here not so much as a tribute to a recent past but as a typical example of all clandestine papers, which have shared common anxieties, common hardship and common victory.

23 February 1945

TALK AMONG THE FLYING

Nigel Tangye

A DICTIONARY OF RAF SLANG. *By Eric Partridge. (Michael Joseph.)*
The inherent *joie de vivre* that happily infects the RAF is reflected in its
slang, which invariably provides light-hearted expressions for serious
subjects. Who, for instance, can fail to be touched by the expression *gone
for a Burton*, which means that a comrade has been killed? To *go to the
movies* is to go into action; a fight in the air is described as a *party*; and a
pilot who has escaped death by parachuting to earth might be heard telling a friend that he had to *jump out of the window*. Those minutes of
extreme tension when a pilot is trying to identify his target by circling
round in a probably well-defended area are, in RAF slang, employed in
footling around; and when a pilot suffers the anxiety of being lost in fog –
this must be experienced to be appreciated – he thinks of himself as being
tangled in the soup. Perhaps more obviously expressive is the *solid lump of
blitz*, which is what the fighter pilot will refer to when he tells of the
close-flying formation of enemy aircraft he encountered.

The RAF has discarded several normal words as being inadequate in
meaning and has replaced them with short monosyllabic words of considerable power. To take off in a hurry, for instance, is to *scat*; to bomb a
target heavily is to *prang* it; to cancel something is to *scrub* it; to turn
quickly is to *jink*; to be excessively nervous is to *flap*; and can anybody
think of a better name for a jet-propelled aircraft than a *squirt*?

Much of the slang naturally relates to the pursuit of female compan-
ionship, and some of the words are, shall we say, picturesque to say the
least. Having conducted a *skirt patrol* a young officer, if he is lucky, will
have fixed up his *target for tonight*. If the latter is a pretty Waaf he will
refer to her as his *queen*. But normally he is not allowed to take out a non-
commissioned Waaf, so that probably she would be a *ladybird*, or Waaf
officer. Possibly she might even be the *Queen Bee*, or Waaf officer in
charge of the Waaf detachment. She might become his girl-friend, in
which case he will be referring to her as his *bride*, but it is important to
point out that that appellation does not imply sexual intimacy. Out of
hearing of his ladybird he may be heard to remark on her *blackouts*, or
uniform navy-blue winter-weight knickers. If he was *courting his cat* in

the summer season she would be wearing *twilights*, or summer-weight knickers lighter coloured than *blackouts*.

Mr Partridge has collected some seven hundred and fifty slang expressions into his valuable and amusing book; and perhaps it is not without interest to remark that although this reviewer has had over five years in the RAF as flying instructor, staff officer and operational pilot, he is familiar with only two hundred and fifty of them. Only a comparatively small proportion of the expressions in this book have a common use throughout the Service. The remainder are confined to sections each of which is virtually the property of one of the Commands. There is only one complaint to make to Mr Partridge. He habitually talks about a 'plane when he means an aircraft.

23 February 1945

A HIMMLER EPISODE

SIR: On the 12th December, a squad of the Special Branch raided the premises of Freedom Press, with a search warrant issued under Defence Regulation 39A. This warrant authorised them to seize any objects which they had reason to suppose might be evidence to the commission of an attempt to seduce from their duties members of HM Forces. Instead, however, of choosing relevant material the police proceeded to empty the contents from the letter trays straight into sacks, seize invoices and account books which dealt entirely with transactions with bookshops, the office typewriter, the boxes containing stencils of addresses, letter books, and other material without which it is impossible to carry on the legitimate business of such a concern as Freedom Press. No attempt was made to decide whether the material had any bearing on the investigation, and, in spite of protests, it was two months before any of it was returned.

At the same time raids were made on the homes of at least five persons connected with Freedom Press, and in one case on that of a private citizen who had no direct connection with Freedom Press. Personal correspondence, professional notes, literary manuscripts, cheque counterfoils, etc., were all seized, and again the police made no effort to choose papers which might possibly contain relevant evidence. In one case, when the person visited was not at home, the police broke in and departed without leaving any notification of their action. Furthermore, in the Army and Navy, searches were made in the kits of men who had been in correspondence with Freedom Press, and copies of pamphlets, as well as issues of *War Commentary*, *Peace News* and *Now* were seized.

We submit that such actions are prejudicial to the liberty of speech and writing. If they are allowed to pass without protest, they may become precedents for future persecutions of individuals or of organisations devoted to the spreading of opinions disliked by the authorities.

(*Signed*) ALEX COMFORT; T.S. ELIOT; E.M. FORSTER; ETHEL MANNIN; JOHN MIDDLETON MURRY; HERBERT READ; REGINALD REYNOLDS; D.S. SAVAGE; STEPHEN SPENDER; JULIAN SYMONS.

2 March 1945

MARGINAL COMMENT

Harold Nicolson

There are few more interesting studies than the confrontation of contemporary with historical opinion. To what extent, for instance, is our view of the present condition of Europe, or of the character of the Nazi and Soviet systems, likely to be confirmed by those who, more than a hundred years from now, read our diaries and our newspapers? Will our grandchildren regard us as having been a generation obsessed by purely materialistic values, and one which clung pathetically to the fiction of economic man? Will they be astonished that we of 1945 failed to foresee the great surge of prosperity which came over Europe in the '60s and '70s, even as we had no true intimation of the religious revival which, starting from Lithuania, spread east and west between 1980 and 1992? Will they regard us as dense or perverse in having persisted for so long in believing that the age of tranquillity was over, when in fact it was only just about to begin? Will they read with amazement our own estimate of contemporary events and wonder how we could have been so ignorant or ill-informed as to believe that Adolf Hitler, in 1945, still existed, or still exercised control in Germany? Will they laugh aloud when they read our diaries of 1940 and 1941 and find that many perfectly serious men and women were convinced that the invasion of this island was not only possible but imminent? Will they reflect sombrely on the ineptitude of all human prescience when they discover that, three years before the German War ended, we were thinking of a General Election, and that whereas we suffered agonies of apprehension regarding the housing shortage, we never realised that the whole demographic problem of Europe would be radically altered by the Plague of 1951? It may be, of course, that, being unable to foresee the future, we have got the present wholly out of focus. Yet, if we are to judge by previous experience, it is at least probable that we have got the present fairly right.

9 March 1945

MARGINAL COMMENT

Harold Nicolson

We reached Paris at 5.30 in the morning, and as we steamed into the station I could see the Sacré Coeur gleaming dimly under the light of a gibbous moon. A few hours later Paris stretched its great limbs luxuriantly in the warmth of a spring morning; the buds upon the chestnut trees broke their sticky sheaves; the old people crept out to sun themselves upon the benches; the children danced around. Glittering and superb the tremendous perspectives of Paris opened once again before me. That quality in the Parisian air which lends colour to the colourless, giving a touch of Cézanne to every suburban allotment, and a touch of Utrillo to the meanest alley, has prevented Paris from acquiring the untidy drabness of London. The avenues seem wider, cleaner, emptier than ever before; the glass is in the windows; the concierge, with wicker carpet-beater, still bangs the door-mat out into the street. There is scaffolding around the Hôtel Crillon, the Grand Palais is blackened with smoke, the office wing of the Quai d'Orsay shows hollow windows gaping on a void, and one of the two Sphinxes by the Louvre has received a bullet in her heart. At street corners on the Left Bank one can see the vestiges of snipers, and occasionally of shells, upon the plaster of the apartment houses. A few miserable fiacres, disinterred from the days of Félix

Fauré, creep slowly along the streets. But superficially Paris is as resplendent as ever; luxurious and proud she glitters in the sun. And yet almost at once one notices a difference. There is something which is not the same. It is then that one realises that Paris is tired; tired almost to death.

It is difficult for those who have not experienced it to understand the psychological effects of enemy occupation. There was the constant pang of seeing the swastika flying triumphantly from every public building. There was the remorse of those who gave despairing confidence to Marshal Pétain at feeling that they had been tricked into a deed of shame. And there was fear, not for oneself only, but for one's family. 'You who have never lost it,' remarked a Frenchman, 'do not know what liberty really is. If you hear a knock at the door at seven in the morning you will turn over in bed and murmur to yourself, "That must be the milk." When we hear it even today the hair rises upon our heads. "Gestapo" is the word that thumps in our hearts.' This meant no quick heroic death upon the bastions of the Mont Valérien, or in the moat at Vincennes; it meant interrogations under the glare of searchlights, it meant beatings day and night, it meant the refinement of torture. It is not surprising that a people who have suffered from such things should be labouring under acute nervous shock. What is more surprising is the amazing resilience of the French nature. The men and women of my own generation, it is true, appeared aged to me beyond their years. But one afternoon I addressed the students across the river; the hall was packed from roof to corridor; and I realised from the yells with which they greeted me that the pulse of the young generation in France is strong, and firm, and quick. To their hands France can entrust her future with confidence and hope.

16 March 1945

MARGINAL COMMENT

Harold Nicolson

On Wednesday, September 26th, 1827, Goethe and Eckermann drove out for a picnic to the Hottelstedt Ecke, the westerly summit of the Ettersberg. Having admired the view of the Thüringer forest, the

Inselsberg and the distant Hartz, they sat together upon the grass while Goethe's servant Frederick unpacked the hamper which they had brought with them. They had a brace of partridges, some white bread, and an excellent old wine which they drank together from the golden goblet which Goethe extracted from a yellow leather case. 'I have often been in this spot,' said Goethe, 'and of recent years I have felt that this might be the last time I should look down from here upon the kingdoms of the world and their glories; but, see, it has happened once again, and I hope that even this is not the last time that we shall both spend a pleasant day here. In future we must often come up here.' They finished their meal, and thereafter Goethe showed Eckermann the little hunting-lodge where he and Schiller and the Grand Duke had spent such happy hours in their careless youth. 'Come,' he said, 'I shall show you the tree on which fifty years ago we cut our names. But how it has altered and how everything has grown! That must be the tree; you see it is still in fullest vigour: even our names are still to be traced, confused and distorted, scarcely to be recognised.' Such was the beech wood on the Ettersberg more than a hundred years ago. The Olympian old man would come there frequently, recalling his youth, welcoming old age with philosophic calm. 'At seventy-five,' he said, 'one must, of course, think sometimes of death. But this thought never causes me uneasiness. For I am convinced that our spirit is indestructible and that its activity continues from eternity to eternity. It is like the sun, which seems to set only to our earthly eyes, but which in reality never sets, but shines unceasingly.'

The wood in which Goethe walked that afternoon with Eckermann is known as Buchenwald. A spot which has for long been associated with the radiant youth or sunset splendour of the greatest of German poets is now forever identified with the most shameful of all German deeds. The lesson of Goethe and Schiller has in truth become 'confused and distorted, scarcely to be recognised': the roots of the tree on which nearly two centuries ago they carved their initials have drunk the blood of innocents, and the balanced calm which Goethe preached and practised has been degraded into a frenzy which we cannot understand. I see no special usefulness in abandoning ourselves to horror and anger and in calling down the curses of vengeance upon the whole German race. It is wise and necessary to force German citizens to see with their own eyes the cruelties which have been perpetrated in their name. But it is not sufficient for us, who live among gentler people and in a saner world, merely to deplore these outrages; we must seek to understand by what sad processes the soul of a great nation became afflicted with this sickness. We must force ourselves to imagine by what insensible gradations a whole people can lose its liberties, and how, when once these liberties have been surrendered, it becomes impossible for honourable and courageous men to raise a cry of protest when even the slightest remonstrance becomes punishable with torture and death. Only men of deep faith, such as Cardinal Faulhaber and Pastor Niemöller, possess such transcendent courage. More ordinary mortals seek to disclaim responsibility, to feign ignorance, to murmur miserably to themselves, 'But what could we have done?' For when once the conscience of a nation becomes silent it becomes atrophied, and the sense of personal responsibility is merged in the brutal instincts of the herd.

27 April 1945

MORE ON BUCHENWALD
Mavis Tate, MP

Millions of people will in the last few days have seen films of the German internment camps at Buchenwald and Belsen. They will think they have gained some impression of the conditions under which thousands of people died who had committed no crime and faced no trial. After having studied every available photograph and been to all the films on what are now known as the 'horror camps', I can say without any hesitation whatever that they give but a very faint impression of the reality. It is difficult to know why this should be so; probably it is that the films are shown very rapidly and seem almost unreal, and that photographs do not convey the horror of the reality because they are static. Photographs, if they shock one, shock through the eyes; one is not shocked through any other sense. In fact, while it is possible to photograph some of the results of suffering, there are no means by which suffering itself can be photographed.

When I visited Buchenwald, I saw in the first hut I entered – which had been hastily arranged as a temporary hospital by the Americans – human bodies which were reduced to mere skeletons covered with skin. They tried feebly to wave a hand, or perhaps smile (which they could not do because the skin of their faces was so tightly drawn back that a smile was no longer possible), and it was a terrible shock when some of the worst cases tried to tell us what nationality they were. One realised then that, though one had looked at them with pity and dismay, one was still failing to appreciate them as living humanity with feelings and reactions similar to one's own. That was the most appalling and shocking thing.

None of these men had any clothing other than a very short shirt, camp blouse or singlet. Some of them feebly moved aside the quilts that covered them, to show appalling wounds, and one or two were trying to totter around on legs that were literally nothing more than skeleton sticks. There would normally be some embarrassment for a woman in company with several men, or for several men in company with one woman, if suddenly faced with large numbers of semi-nude men. There was no more embarrassment in Buchenwald when faced with these conditions than there would be in passing a heap of dying rabbits, so little did these people give the impression of being ordinary human beings.

As stated in our official report, the prisoners fell into three classes:

1. German-Jews, or Germans who had opposed the Nazi ideology and been denounced as enemies of the State,

2. Intellectuals, Jews and opponents from occupied countries such as Poland, Belgium, Czechoslovakia and France,

3. People conscripted for slave labour in Germany.

There was doubtless also a percentage of normal prison population in these camps.

If you conscript people for slave labour, you presumably wish to keep them under such conditions as will enable them to perform the work for which you have conscripted them – so conditions at Buchenwald are not easy to understand. A very large percentage of the thin and miserable inhabitants of the Buchenwald camp were certainly capable of, and engaged upon, work, either in quarries or in the munition factory which was situated just outside the main gate of the camp. Those so employed were able to earn very small sums of camp money, which could be spent in the rough camp canteen, and also were undoubtedly able to obtain rather more food than the basic ration of a chunk of bread and some watery soup or potato-peelings which constituted the normal daily ration. If they fell sick, then conditions became finally impossible for the maintenance of life or any semblance of health, and as murder was a daily occurrence in the camp on a large scale, it is very difficult to explain why so many were permitted to linger on in the condition of misery and sickness in which we found some of them. All the internees spoken to were unanimous in assuring us that there had been blocks kept for prisoners upon whom experiments in typhus, cholera, &c., were made, and all agreed that 80 people had automatically to be murdered each day at Buchenwald to make way for newcomers.

We were told that there were 800 children in the camp at the time of our visit, and that the camp guards had intended to march many of them away with the 20,000 or so inhabitants whom they did in fact remove. They failed because they were in a hurry, and many of the children hid in holes that internees had dug under hut floors. Some prisoners also had arms, which they had got together piece by piece by stealing a part here and a part there from the munition factory, and these they produced at the last moment to save themselves from removal.

The so-called children in the camp present a tremendous problem. They speak with utter calm of having seen their relations shot or removed to be put into a gas-chamber. They have many of them lived their most formative years knowing only cruelty, squalor and want in its extreme forms, and they give the impression – and none can wonder at it – of callousness and of lack of interest in anything beyond personal preservation. Those who have survived are tough, and will be unlikely to prove a centre of stability or of kindliness wherever they settle. They should be under care and guidance of a high order for a time and not let loose lonely and stateless in a distraught Europe.

Some German civilians from Weimar were visiting the camp when we were there, but one woman only did I see who appeared genuinely upset. When I said to her, 'Well, you have behaved in a wonderful way under Hitler, have you not?' she burst into tears and said, 'I am ashamed of being a German.' The citizens of Weimar in the main looked anything but cowed. They have never been bombed – their land has been cultivated to the last inch with the help of slave labour, and they look well-fed, truculent and aggressive. I repeatedly said to my fellow delegates that I was deeply shocked by the faces of many of the German women in Weimar. They were cruel and hard beyond belief, and I had seen none like them anywhere – until I looked at the photographs of the women guards of Belsen camp. The Hun ambition may be foiled, but the Hun spirit still lives.

A careful record of daily deaths was kept by the Nazis (which throws a curious sidelight on their mentality) showing that over 17,000 people died at this camp between January 1st, 1945, and the day (April 11th, 1945) when the Americans overran it. One possible explanation of Nazi inconsistency in keeping the sick alive is that the congestion in the camp was such that any proper feeding, any form of hospital arrangements, or any form of reasonable accommodation, became too much for the authorities to deal with. The only other apparent explanation is that it gave the Nazi officials some form of satisfaction to have the power to degrade human beings to this level. Undoubtedly there were large numbers of highly gifted, intelligent doctors, musicians, scientists, etc., in the camps, and to reduce them to a condition in which it was difficult to think of them as human beings at all may have created a sense of superiority in the breasts of the *Herrenvolk*.

Personally I am inclined to think that there is an element of truth in both explanations. It so happened that I was taken over the concentration camp of Oranienburg when I successfully tried to release Frau Seger and her baby from Dachau in 1934. Oranienburg was a very small camp compared with Buchenwald, and at that time it housed only Jews and political prisoners. Torture-chambers and punishment-rooms were undoubtedly established there. Sleeping conditions were much as at Buchenwald, except that each man had a two-foot palliasse on his wooden shelf, and a soup-plate and spoon for his own personal use suspended at the foot of his palliasse. Though living conditions were palatial compared with Buchenwald it is nevertheless possible to imagine how, with eleven years of successive and sustained brutality and increasing callousness towards fellow-beings, and under the difficult conditions created by war, a camp such as Oranienburg could in time deteriorate into Buchenwald on a small scale.

I have returned from Germany firmly convinced that the mere establishment of democratic government for such a people will not solve the problem. There is indubitably a deep streak of evil and sadism in the German race, such as one ought not to expect to find in a people who for generations have paid lip-service to Western culture and civilisation. There has been in Germany open laudation of, and admiration for, the abnormal and the brutal, and an open worship of force as such. This can never be eradicated from them, or indeed from others of the human race, unless they are genuinely imbued with reverence for the individual, respect for women as mothers and guardians of life, veneration for the family ideal and for normal kindly behaviour. In fact, until they follow the law and the teaching given to this world two thousand years ago, no political system, however carefully devised, will cure the ills of Germany. Only with extreme firmness shall we eradicate the beast from the German heart.   *4 May 1945*

THE INTRUDING FATHER

H. Crichton-Miller

SIR: Many plans are being made for the return of our men from the Front. There is one point of view that seems to have been overlooked. It is that of the Toddler. Thousands of boys and girls under five in this country have never seen their father, or at best, have forgotten him entirely. The home-coming, however much it may be regarded as a solution of domestic problems, presents difficulties of a very special nature.

We assume the child has been taught that 'Daddy is fighting the naughty Germans,' and has often been encouraged to kiss his photograph. So far so good. But what happens next? A telegram arrives, and the mother reacts with grief or joy, according to the nature of the message. Hurried arrangements are made for relative or friend to take over, and it is carefully explained to the child that 'Mother has to go to see – or meet – Daddy.' This is the first tactical error. The father is associated by the child with abandonment by mother, and for this may never be forgiven. Such a situation can bring permanent ill-results in its train.

In time, the parents come back, and the father bursts in on a bewildered child, who is glad to see his mother, but reviews the intruding stranger without enthusiasm. This is the second tactical error. The father should come back alone, and the mother stay away, at least for a few days, to allow him to establish a positive relationship of fearless affection, while the magnetic, material field is out of action. The sense of monopolising the father, even for so short a time, goes a long way to tempering the child's urge to possess the mother.

The next mistake is made when the child finds his cot is placed in another room – or it isn't. Either solution is unfortunate, however inevitable in present circumstances. Sooner or later, a child must leave his mother's bedroom. The occasion should not be made to appear as an eviction by the father. Without meaning any harm, the most devoted mothers have already done much mischief by allowing the father to come back as an intruder. – I am, yours faithfully, H. CRICHTON-MILLER

The Athenaeum.   *18 May 1945*

DEATH AND LOVE

F. Tennyson Jesse

How many of us, I wonder, have thought about the feelings of the man who, in cold blood and in perfect health and before he has started to fight, writes a letter which he hopes will never be read – that letter which is to be given to his wife, his mother or his sweetheart only if he is killed? It must be a strange sensation sitting in some barracks, somewhere in England, to try to put the best of yourself into a letter that, with your whole heart, you hope will be wasted. A young man who had just finished his training in July, 1940, was amongst the many thousands who wrote such a letter and, alas, his had to be delivered, although, with the confidence of youth, he thought he never could be killed. He wrote the letter to his wife and she received it in an English village while he lay dead in Burma. These are a few of the things he said, and he said them beautifully because it was impossible for him to write bad English:

'I am writing this because I want you to know what my feelings are at this time. If I survive, you will never read it; you will only read it if I am killed. I want you to know what I felt before I died. I have wanted you to know it for a long while, and I have not been able to tell you. I could not talk about these things during the short but wonderful times we have had together; to do so would have been to bring down upon us with crushing awareness that dreadful shadow which we have so miraculously dispelled. And after that first visit of 48 hours, when I came to you in Suffolk in September, I have not dared to speak again about what might happen to us. Our emotions were so harried then that I could never go through such torture with you again. But I do want to say certain things, though I find it very difficult to write them: my life is so unreal and my surroundings seem so extraordinary, even after ten months, that I cannot fix my coherent thoughts for very long. They are all inside me, but it is hard to bring them out. I do not want to die with them inside me.

'I should hate this to be cold and perfect prose. I want it to be wild and passionate. I don't want to sit and think about the sentences. But the fact of my sitting here, writing a letter for you to read after my death, while my companion stifles my thoughts with his snores, is so extraordinary that heaven only knows how this will turn out. Pleasant, good-natured fool – if he were to wake up and read this he would think me crazy.

'My darling, when the war started we told each other, although at the time we were torn with the most fearful distress, that we both believed we should pull through safely. Now the situation has become far worse, worse than anyone thought possible, but I still believe it. Yes, truly. It is a wonderful thing to believe. If, years from now, I read this letter myself before I tear it up, I shall smile as I come to that, and congratulate myself on being a good prophet. But if you read it – oh, my poor darling, how you will weep over it. Dear, dear child, I cannot imagine it. I think I shall live. I do not know why I think so: S—— F——, whom I sometimes talked to about these things, was convinced that he would be killed. Strange if just the opposite should happen. One night I said to him, when we were both a bit tight: "I don't care what they do to me. They can tear me to pieces, they can kill me now or next year, but so long as I die to stop them taking England, then I am satisfied." He told me afterwards that what I said made him incredibly happy. I had never said it to anyone before, but I said it with terrific vehemence, and I meant it. I had known it all along. I had known it ever since I joined the army.

'Now that kind of talk is all very well for a man who has no real bonds on this earth. There are millions of them, and I've no doubt that they feel the same as I do. But my bonds with you are the strongest that a man can know. I meant it when I said that I would rather sever my bonds with you, lose all our love, all our life that has been so perfect, plunge myself into a darkness of which I know nothing, since I believe in no life after death – rather lose everything than see England defeated. Can you understand this? Do you think I love England more than I love you? You must never think that. I love nothing more than you. How can I possibly compare the two? I joined this war to fight for both of you; my life depends equally on the survival of England and the survival of our love. When I try to separate the two, I find I cannot do it. There is nothing heroic about wishing to die for one's country: every volunteer in the forces is prepared to do it. That is what goes to make victory, and if I can be an infinitesimal part of that victory, then that is enough. Oh my beloved, how impossible it is to write of such things. I only know that if in dying I can help England to win, then I shall die.

'But what about you? I should leave you behind. That is the dreadful part of it: that is what has sometimes made me long to be rid of it all and leave the war to others and fly with you out of reach of all this horror. But that is impossible. The thought of leaving you behind tortures me: and here am I volunteering to die! It is all so unreal. Can you see now how difficult it is for me to sort out my thoughts and write about dying, when all the time sorrow is plucking at my heart as I think of you reading this: reading that I who love you so completely have left you with these thoughts in my head, and have left you with the full knowledge that all your life your arms will be outstretched towards me, and your dear heart weighed down by an inescapable misery. By all that we love, why should I be called upon to do such things? I worship you with all my body and soul; but I have given my body and soul to the cause of England, and if England wants them she must take them. You both possess me; England has claimed me, and if she should give me back to you it will be because she knows that one so precious and dear as yourself cannot be allowed to suffer for the rest of your life.

'What makes all this torturing thought so futile is that if I am killed I shall never know whether England was victorious or not. Or shall I? I *shall* know it for this reason: that I do not believe England can ever be beaten. This is perhaps my clearest belief of all: clearer than belief in my own life, clearer than belief in the ultimate security of ourselves. England will not lose. You may know, my darling, when you read what I am writing, that this was the last thought that came to me before I died; and that with it came some comfort in the fact that England's victory would bring some measure of safety and perhaps, in the end, of happiness for you. I do not believe in God, but I believe unshakably in the triumph of good against evil. I do not pray to God: I pray to the goodness of the earth and the goodness that is the rock of civilisation and the foundation of all that is worth calling progress. These things can never be overthrown. England is the rock of civilisation; and upon that rock is founded the great love that lies between us two. If the rock is swept away from beneath us, what hope is there for us? There is none: and therefore I will fight and die that the rock may stand firm.

'You may say that if I die there is no hope for us in any case. True. But there is hope for you. You must not feel, dear beloved, that I am all that matters in the world. You will, I truly believe, find other sources of happiness. That is what I am fighting for: to make a world from which evil will be banished and in which real joy will be possible. Joy for you, you, you. I *know* that happiness will be possible, no matter what agony you may have to suffer in finding it.

'I know that England will win. The possibility of our losing is something which I have refused to let myself think about, because it creates the hardest problem of all. If this struggle is to be lost, then every true patriot knows that he would rather die on the field than witness the results of defeat. But how can I say that? How can I say that I would rather leave you defenceless in a cruel and hostile world than face the bitterness of that world beside you? I cannot say it; but, when you read this, you will know that I died with the belief of our victory strong in my heart, and that I am now beyond the reach of defeat. And you may know this too: that if I die and we are beaten, and if you see no prospect or possibility of happiness anywhere and if you decide then that you must take your life, then you need never ask yourself if I would have condemned you for it. Because that is what I should have done had I lived to see us brought to defeat; I truly believe I should have killed you and killed myself. There would have been no hope for us: nothing but ruin and tragedy, and black, endless despair. The rock that upheld our love would have vanished for ever.

'But all this will never happen, because England will win. I may die, but England will win. And what does my death matter, if there is a corner in the world in which you may discover happiness and know the meaning of beauty? There will be such a corner; wars are not fought for nothing; I know it, and that is why I beg you to carry on.'

Thus wrote this young soldier five years ago in a barracks in England. Thus wrote many thousands of men but few, if any, more beautifully. The Japanese pounded the position of him and his men with mortar fire and he ordered the men to the slit trenches. Not till it was over did they find that the heart that had beaten both for his wife and for England had been pierced by Japanese metal. His men grieved for him, for they loved him. We who are left remember the Battle of Britain and those first blitzes and how we also felt, quite illogically, that England could not be beaten. And as long as she breeds men of this sort she never will be.

1 June 1945

WHEN PEACE BROKE OUT

William Deedes

There is a certain difficulty about celebrating the 40th anniversary of VE-Day which may well have entered sensitive minds in Whitehall and accounted for the first, fitting reluctance to do much about it. For those under 40 the anniversary arouses no memories and (unless bereaved by the war) little feeling. Most of those now old enough to have been involved at the time know in their hearts that the celebrations cannot echo their innermost feelings at the time. So the performance is addressed to a non-audience, is a ritual rather than a remembrance. But controversialists will have a ball.

I have no difficulty in recalling my innermost feelings when the end came. On the night of 4 May we had just finished dinner with the 13th/ 18th Hussars, an armoured regiment to which my rifle company was attached. At nine o'clock a message came to us from Commander 30 Corps (General Sir Brian Horrocks). It ran like this:

> Germans surrendered unconditionally at 1820 hours(.)
> Hostilities on all Second Army front will cease at 0800 hours
> tomorrow 5 May 45(.) NO repeat NO advance beyond present
> front line without orders from me(.)

There was a supply of Krug non-vintage in the Mess and this was opened. My first thought was: well, this at least will ditch Operation 'Curling' in which most of us were due to play a part at 0730 next morning. I have kept a copy of that, the last operation order we received, signed by one A.K. Howell (Capt.) for the Brigade Major of 129 Inf. Bde. It was never fulfilled, and just as well. It had a hazardous air about it.

Even that thought and the Krug did not lift my spirits very high. This today must seem absurd, attributable to depressive tendencies. No, it was not singular. I take a sentence from a short history written soon afterwards of 8th Armoured Brigade, which had gone in on D-Day and stopped on the night of 4 May 1945. Its commander was Brigadier Errol Prior-Palmer, Lucinda's father.

> Rejoicing there was, but this sudden break in the tension reacting upon men, far more tired than they were prepared to admit, had a quietening effect.

That is well put and easily understood. Depression is sometimes the companion of exhaustion. There were other considerations. We had suffered casualties only days before, when the battle was ending. What a pity, I thought, this surrender didn't come a little sooner; what a difference it would have made to those families.

I also felt dimly aware, with recollections of keeping a company together in England, how much the perils of battle impose their own disciplines. I tried not to think about the likely state of the men's billets next morning, danger departed. They would be unimaginable. We would be back to those awful days off the battlefield, when the Adjutant would call me in for a little talk with the Colonel. 'Bill, I have to tell you that I am not at all happy about the way things are going in your company.'

We'd be back to all that. Worse, military discipline would have to be restored amid a colossal shambles. We had laid waste a great part of the neighbourhood. Hundreds of thousands of displaced persons were drifting around. All the railways were cut and canals filled with bridge wreckage. All important roads were cratered.

A great many Germans were starving, and the famine was aggravated by the disappearance of officials who had been prominent Nazis. It is hard to convey at this distance what that part of Germany looked like in the early summer. A whole country had been battered to a stop. The Germans immediately around us now had lain in the path of our advancing army, of which we were leading elements, so the damage was freshest and the agony deepest just where we were.

I thought we had made a mess until I entered Hanover a day or so later and saw what 84th US Inf. Div., with Allied air forces and supporting arms, had done. I foresaw, as we sat at dinner, an early O-group next day, replacing 'Curling', at which these matters would be brought to our notice and unpleasant duties apportioned. The riflemen would be browned off. This particular appreciation turned out to be too sanguine by half.

Two of the duties which immediately came my way were to take charge of a PoW camp for 6,000 Germans, which included 400 officers and 1,600 NCOs, and tightly to guard a local depot storing a brand of powerful alcohol which had been used for flying bombs. None of the PoWs got out, but some of the displaced persons got into the fuel depot and took one for the road, with lethal consequences.

There were certain other disciplinary problems which, even on this night of unconditional surrender, loomed in the gloomy subconscious – looting and fraternisation. In the advance so far we had made pretty free use of German private property and had not been discouraged from doing so. If you took shelter in a deserted house, found wine in the cellar and poultry in the orchard, you did not consult brigade headquarters about the proper thing to do.

But now, with this ceasefire, the Germans were entirely at our mercy. General Horrocks, the Corps commander, took a severe line on looting; Montgomery, the Army commander, felt a degree less strongly about it. There was unanimity, however, about 'fraternisation'. It was frowned upon. In part, fraternisation was a euphemism for fornication. Plenty of young German women were ready to offer themselves to soldiers – and did – in return for a small portion of the day's ample army ration, still more for a dip in the American food pack. In part also it related to a fear on high of ambush; a notion that soldiers might be lured into German houses by vengeful people and done in.

Most of the nightmares which flickered through my mind above the fumes of Krug on the night of 4 May came to life sooner or later, but the ambush theory did not, in my experience. Precious few Germans, in reality, had any physical resources left for trickery. On arrival in Hanover we found that a lot of them stayed in bed all day. You can live longer on starvation rations if you do not exert yourself.

To be both honest and selfish, one must enter another depressing consideration which circled my mind – and the minds of many more – on this night and on days that were to follow. This ceasefire threatened not only one's professional occupation but what had become the framework of one's life.

Army life in battle can be dirty and dangerous and uncomfortable, but the system is supportive. The Corps or the Brigade might issue unreasonable orders; but they looked after you, body and soul. The quartermaster saw to the first, the padre to the second. The system had for five years protected us from almost all the irritants and anxieties which bedevil our lives in peacetime.

Furthermore, after five years' soldiering, some of us (even as sons of the Territorial Army) felt more confidence in our military professionalism than in any other prospective occupation. The ceasefire had made us redundant. After a suitable interval we would be demobilised and thrown back onto our own resources.

Not much there for comfort. Happily, on this night of revelry, there did not enter my head the future significance of the Corps commander's final instruction: 'NO repeat NO advance beyond present front line without orders from me.' I did not know then that within a matter of days my company would be assisting in the transfer of part of Germany to soldiers of the Soviet Union.

A symbolic act. We had begun an expensive five years of blood and tears in order to rid Europe of Hitler. We were to finish it by handing some of the spoils to Stalin. Ah, well, mercifully I had not grasped as much on this unusual summer night of 1945. If I had, why then I might have felt very depressed.

27 April 1985

MARGINAL COMMENT

Harold Nicolson

I am glad that I witnessed the night of November 11, 1918, since it is a
rare thing to see a whole city united in unreserved exhilaration. But I am
even more glad to have witnessed in London the nights of May 7 and May
8, 1945. Our achievement this time has been even greater; our opportunity is almost frightening in its immensity. Our sobriety during the celebrations of last week must, I know, be to some extent attributed to
material shortages, but no one who compares the two celebrations of
1918 and 1945 can deny the vast difference between them in public
thought and feeling. To some extent, of course, the exuberance of our
celebration was checked by the knowledge that further Far Eastern strug-
gles were still to come. To some extent also (and this is to our credit) the
blaze of triumph was dimmed by the fog of misery which hangs over
Europe. There are those who contend that, having endured so many disil-
lusions, we have entered the age of universal scepticism; and that we are
suffering today from the penalty of semi-education, namely distrust. It
must be realised also that the sense of unchallengeable power which we
possessed in 1918 has lost something of its old certitude and that we are
fully conscious of the economic and political complexities which lie
ahead. But in the demeanour of the crowds last week there was something more positive than scepticism, something more hopeful than distrust. It was a tone of seriousness under all their gaiety, a note of solem-
nity almost in their delight. Is it too optimistic to suppose that this is due
to a vastly increased sense, in the mind of every citizen, of personal
responsibility? I do not regard this optimism as a pathetic fallacy. It can
be confirmed by comparing the level of public thoughtfulness, or sense,
as manifested in this war and in the last. It is from this comparison that
my optimism is derived.

Let me take one test, or illustration, of the increase in public reason, of
the feeling of individual responsibility, between 1915 and 1940. In the
second year of the last war the public succumbed to a discreditable wave
of spy-mania. In the second year of this war there was scarcely any
witch-hunting at all. Yet in 1940 there existed far more justification for

spy-mania than there ever existed in 1915. The danger of invasion was infinitely more immediate and contiguous; the example of the Fifth Column in occupied Europe was far more disturbing; and the invention of the wireless had rendered secret communications with the enemy a much more feasible practice. Yet this time we behaved with commendable kindness to the alien, even to the enemy alien, in our midst. Such measures as were taken against them in 1940 (and they may have been essential) were governmental and not popular. The public of 1940, unlike the public of 1915, kept its head. Is it mere optimism to conclude that it has, this time, a wiser head?

18 May 1945

NEWS OF THE WEEK

The declaration signed by the military representatives of Russia, Britain, the United States and France at Berlin on Tuesday marks the assumption of supreme authority in Germany by the Allied Powers after the unconditional surrender of the German armed forces. The meeting of the four generals and the decision promptly taken and announced puts an end to many uncertainties, and initiates the new phase of joint control by the conquering Powers over a country which has no recognised or recognisable Government of its own. The declaration will dissipate many doubts and fears. The Control Council now set up will sit in Berlin, and it is far best that it should be so. It is so constituted as to give at the start the best possible opportunity of unified control at the centre based upon joint decisions, and with a view to the application of common principles in the four areas for which Russia, Britain, America and France will be responsible. There has always been some fear lest four somewhat different Germanys should emerge from the differing administrations of four separate Powers. That danger is guarded against by the declaration that the Control Council is to ensure appropriate uniformity of action by the Commanders-in-Chief in their respective zones, and by the decision to appoint a permanent co-ordinating committee composed of representatives of the four Commanders, and a joint control staff. Similarly the area of Greater Berlin will come under an Inter-Allied governing authority. Here is a practical arrangement which starts from exactly the right conception of co-operation and joint responsibility for the whole of Germany, with a programme now taking shape for the apprehension of Nazis, the disarmament and demilitarisation of Germany, and the fixing of political, economic and other conditions to which the defeated nation must conform. It is a great gain to have reached these preliminary agreements (previously explored by the European Advisory Commission) without delays. The application of them will involve many personal contacts and direct associations in day-to-day work which should make for better understanding between Russia and the Western Powers. There is still room for that.

8 June 1945

THE BOMB IN THE YELLOW BOX
Group-Captain Leonard Cheshire, VC

There were two teams out on Tinian, the scientists and the aircrew. The scientists, under the administrative control of Brigadier Farell, were charged with the technical aspects of the problem, while the aircrew, commanded by Colonel Tibbetts, were responsible for delivering the bomb. Both teams were amalgamated into one unit and were given the title of the 509th Bombardment Group, so that together they were much the same as a squadron of the RAF. To the headquarters unit was added a security detachment and a communications flight, both of which carried their own authority and were not liable to jurisdiction from anyone else, no matter where they might be.

The communications flight, with its five C54s and seven crew, plied back and forth between Tinian and Salt Lake City, ferrying equipment or personnel as the need arose. These 'Green Hornets', as the aircraft were called, gave the various staging bays along the route plenty of room for thought. Air Transport Command, which controls all out- and inbound flights, work to a rigid and stereotyped formula. Every aeroplane that lands, unless it carries the President or a five-star general, has to follow the formula, and there are never any exceptions. The Green Hornets, however, carried a slip of paper which allowed them to come and go as they pleased and gave them the right to break all ATC regulations except those that affected aircraft safety. If they wanted to take off ahead of turn or refused to take on passengers when their aeroplane was empty, not even a general could stand in their way.

One day towards the end of July a Green Hornet landed at Honolulu on the way to Tinian carrying nothing but two officers and a peculiar yellow box. It was a very peculiar box; in fact, the only way you could describe it is to say that it was the sort of box that must have something unusual inside it. In point of fact, what it had inside it was the vital part of an atom bomb.

The colonel and the major climbed out on to the tarmac carrying the box, and for the rest of their stay on the island they never let it out of their sight. The steward asked them to check it in the baggage room, and, when they refused, said it was very irregular and that he would have to report it. After lunch, and just as they were waiting to take off, there appeared a group of senior officers who had been stranded through engine failure and who wanted to be taken on in the Green Hornet. The colonel said he was very sorry but it could not be done, which, being contrary to the usual regulations, led to an argument. The senior officers threatened to call in the commanding general and demanded to know what was in the box, pointing out that whatever it was it couldn't be anything as important as they had in their brief-cases. To all of this the colonel quietly produced his slip of paper, saying that the box contained his shaving tackle and that if they didn't choose to believe him he was sorry, but there was nothing else he could tell them. The incident was not forgotten. The next time a Green Hornet landed, the ground crews said, 'We don't know what the hell you're carrying, but the sooner you get off again the better we'll be pleased'; so from then on everything went very smoothly.

The 509th was more or less secluded from the rest of the island. It had its own administrative and living quarters, its own compound, and its own dispersal area on the North Field, all of which were closely guarded. If anyone, whether he belonged to the project or not, had tried to approach one of the aeroplanes or any of the equipment without first identifying himself to the guard, he would probably have been shot. One day a small fishing boat came close inshore immediately opposite the compound. It turned out to be a handful of Japanese fishermen under marine escort who had to collect more bait. None the less, the reception they met from the shore caused them to make for the open sea in no small haste, to the evident astonishment of the marines, who did not know of the compound.

The compound itself was tucked away in a low-lying stretch of the North Shore. It looked across the sound towards the hills of Saipan and opened on to the Navy's anchorage, wherein day and night there plied a seemingly endless stream of ships. The road leading to the living quarters ran past the cemetery of the 1,100 marines who died in the battle for the island almost exactly a year earlier. It was in this compound, with the three barbed-wire-guarded enclosures, that the work of assembling and testing the bomb was carried out. In the third enclosure was the inner sanctum, a Nissen hut, air-conditioned against the damp and the humidity. There, amongst a disorderly mess of equipment and test gear, lay the atom cores before their final assembly into bombs. About them there was nothing special and nothing secretive. Anyone who had access to the hut could inspect them and even handle them, so long as they did not touch them with bare hands. To me the most fantastic spectacle of all, more fantastic even than the explosion at Nagasaki, was when Alvarez walked me across to the box and opened it. After all that I had heard and read during the past few weeks, after the speculation and rumours that had filtered through into print about the atom in the course of the last twenty years, I should have expected to find it, if I ever found it, entrenched behind steel and concrete. I should have expected it to be high on a pedestal or deep in the bowels of the earth; but not just lying casually in a box in an ordinary Nissen hut. Equally, I should not have expected the man who showed it to me to open the box in the course of conversation, and after I had glanced at the contents and looked away again because it did not seem to be anything particularly interesting, to say, 'That is the atom,' as though it were straw or anything else that is normally found in boxes.

None of that did I expect, and yet that is how it happened. The image of that commonplace Nissen hut, just one among a row of others, with its piles of equipment lying so aimlessly and without order, has stayed in my mind more vividly than anything else.

Farther along the road from the compound lay the dispersal area, with the squadron and the aircraft. The aircrews had been more or less handpicked and most of them had had battle experience either in Europe or the Mediterranean. For many months past they had been isolated from the world undergoing an extensive course of training. The problems they had to overcome were twofold: first, to drop the bomb accurately; and, second, to avoid the effects of the explosion. The problem of enemy defences was nil, provided they flew high enough, because the Japanese had nothing to match a B29 at height. The danger of damage from the explosion of the bomb resolved itself purely into the question of being far enough away. According to calculation, the bomb was equivalent to the instantaneous detonation of 20,000 tons of high explosive, so that as long as the aircraft was out of range of the lethal area of the resultant blast it would be perfectly safe. This area the scientists estimated to be approximately four miles. Working to this formula, the squadron devised a simple and effective plan of attack which guaranteed the aircraft's safety.

When a bomb is dropped, it tracks forward, at the speed of the aircraft, as well as downwards, so that the aircraft, provided it does not alter course, will be almost directly overhead when the bomb hits the ground. If, for example, a bomb takes thirty seconds to fall from an aircraft flying at 20,000 feet and at a speed of four miles a minute, it will be dropped two miles short of the target. In the case of the atom, the bomb was to be dropped from 30,000 feet with a time of fall of forty-five seconds and a forward speed of six miles a minute, which meant that it would be released three and three-quarter miles short of the target. As soon as it was clear, the aeroplane was to turn as rapidly as possible on to a reciprocal course and fly off at a speed of seven miles a minute. Since the crews needed twenty seconds to turn the aeroplane on to the reciprocal, they had twenty-five seconds' flying time left to make good their escape, which gave them another three and a quarter miles. Thus, at the moment of impact they would be seven miles away and well clear of danger.

This manoeuvre was practised by the crews for weeks on end, and there was no doubt that they could follow the routine as well as they could the path to the cookhouse. There was equally no doubt that, so long as the weather was clear and they could see the target, they could guarantee delivering the bomb within two hundred yards of the aiming point.

In addition to their training in the United States, the squadron started trying out their tactics on the Japanese mainland, dropping single large-calibre bombs. The object in this was partly to test out their bombing accuracy and partly to give the crews battle experience in the Pacific. These single and two-plane raids, carried out in clear weather during the daylight, proved conclusively not only that the squadron's standard of bombing was high, but also that the Japanese had nothing to offer in the way of defence. Furthermore, they gave the ground crews the chance to acclimatise themselves and their equipment, and to make certain that nothing would go wrong on the day itself.

The work of the ground crews has faded deep into the background of the bomb itself, and no one has troubled to tell their story. And yet their story is a good one. It is a story which, although without glamour and no doubt similar to many others across the battlefields of the world, played a crucial part in the story of the atom, for had the aircraft at Hiroshima or Nagasaki developed engine trouble, the clear weather which lasted only so short a time would have been wasted. So far as the world is concerned, those two aircraft took off, dropped their bombs and returned to base without developing engine failure, in which there is nothing unusual. What the world does not know, however, is that in all the attacks that the squadron carried out, involving over one thousand operational flying hours, not a single aeroplane ever failed to complete its mission because of mechanical failure. That this record was achieved in the hot, humid Pacific climate is a remarkable tribute to the teamwork and energy of the 509th ground crews.

As the days went by and passed into August there grew a noticeable air of tension. Zero hour, which had originally been set for the second week, was brought forward to August 8, and then to the fifth and finally to the third. The work in the compound went on later in the evenings and more and more conferences were called. By the evening of August 2 the bomb was assembled and ready for the squadron, but there was other work that still needed to be done. It was not enough to drop the bomb; the explosion had to be measured and readings taken. To do this required recorders and the recorders had to be built; they had to be checked, too, because they were unique instruments and no one was quite certain how they would work.

At the same time, the crews chosen for the attack were briefed and re-briefed to make sure they knew the routine. A few changes were made in the plan, and a special camera was flown in from America. This camera was a fastex, capable of taking 1,600 shots a minute, and its purpose was to measure the size of the flame at the instant of explosion. A suggestion was made that a B29 be filled with movie cameras and experienced opera-tors in order to accompany and film the attack, but the idea was dis-carded. Why I do not know since there was no tactical reason against it.

As August 3 passed with a typhoon covering the targets, more and more interest was taken in the weather office. The weather over Japan is worse even than Europe. The climate is humid with frequent cloud cover. In the month of August there are on average only seven clear days, and the difficulty of making an accurate forecast from so great a range makes it almost impossible to know all the seven days sufficiently far in advance to make use of them. The reports said that the typhoon was beginning to clear the area, and, since a period of fine weather usually fol-lows in the wake of a typhoon, it looked as though the fifth or the sixth might be the day.

In readiness against the event, the aircraft and equipment were given their final check. The attack was to be delivered by three crews, one to drop the bomb and the other two to make visual observations and secure technical recordings. Penney and I would have liked to have gone, but the Americans preferred that we stayed behind, so we relegated ourselves to the role of onlookers. The lead aircraft was to go in on the bombing run at 30,000 feet, with number two a mile or so behind at approximately the same height. Number three, which carried the two 16 mm. cameras, was to break formation on the final turn in to the target, circle around for five minutes, and then follow in the wake of the others. This manoeuvre was designed to position the aircraft some twenty miles away, and heading towards the target, at the time of the explosion, so that the camera operators in the nose would have the best possible chance of taking their shots.

For defence the formation relied upon speed and height. The only guns they carried were two in the tail; the rest had been taken out in the interests of speed.

On the afternoon of August 4 the weather office reported the weather clear for the following day, and a zero hour was given for 9.15 a.m., August 5. And the project had reached its conclusion.

Of the flight to Hiroshima that morning, and the second one to Nagasaki on August 9, there is not much to tell, because the tale was finished when the aeroplane and the bomb left the runway. From that moment the issue was no longer in doubt. There might be some mechanical failure to prevent the bomb exploding or the aeroplane might have to return to base. But in either case there was another to follow and behind that another still. It was not a battle between two strong enemies, but the destruction of the impotent by the invincible.

To those who dropped the atom bomb the one reality was the war – the most terrible war the world has yet known. In their minds only two questions mattered. Would the bomb end the war? Would it cost fewer lives than the one alternative, an all-out invasion of Japan? Undeniably the answer to both questions was yes; and, therefore, undeniably the bomb was right.

Today the emphasis has shifted. It is the dead of Hiroshima and Nagasaki, not the suffering that the world was spared nor even the tyranny and evil with which it was threatened, who have become the one lasting reality, and it is in their light that the bomb is now judged.

Which of these two views, one may ask, is right?

In my opinion neither. If twenty years ago we were right to have used the bomb to end the war, we were not right in the particular way in which we used it. The honour of the cause for which we were fighting demanded that we should give the enemy at least one chance to think twice – by dropping the bomb offshore or something of that sort. Because we did not give them that chance, both our own honour and the justice of our cause have been degraded in the eyes of the world.

If today we are right in giving priority of remembrance to those whom the bomb destroyed, we are wrong in judging its use in isolation from the threat which called it into being. Whether we like it or not, the bomb is a reality of modern life; it is an expression not just of our present scientific age, but of a rapidly integrating world which increasingly thinks and acts in terms of total involvement. The evil is not so much in the bomb itself, which by virtue of its deterrent power can also be an instrument of great good, but in the hearts of men, who if deprived of one weapon will soon enough find another. Our rôle, it seems to me, is to prove by our actions that we have the good of all men at heart, not just our own.

6 August 1965

Part Eight
Profiles

WINSTON CHURCHILL: THREE SCORE AND TEN

James Bridie

If Mr Churchill had not existed it would have been necessary to invent him; but who, in the whole catalogue of ingenious storytellers, could have done the job? A publisher or an impresario of films would have had a bad time in searching for the right man. Homer had qualifications. He could have conveyed the 'earthiness' of his hero. But he was hardly an expert on the twentieth century. The Elizabethans would have got it all wrong, for, strangely enough, Mr Churchill is very little an Elizabethan. The anonymous author of *The Book of Kings* is a little too oriental, and any kind of Saga would have been terrible. Probably a committee of Scotsmen, writing on a scenario by Homer, could have made something of it. My suggestions would be Blind Harry, William Dunbar, Thomas Urquhart, James Boswell, Tobias Smollett and R.L. Stevenson. Defoe might have been brought in as editor. The Scotsmen could have done conscientious justice to the elements of Hamlet, Ariel and Puck (to say nothing of Falstaff) and would certainly have appreciated the Shorter Catechist. They, of all people, would also have noticed that they had in hand an extremely practical person.

I cannot help feeling that Mr Churchill's English and American fellow-countrymen have missed this practicality. Those of us who have lived through the Churchill Era have been dazzled by what some journalists call a colourful personality. We have been cheered throughout our usually dull and often distressing lives by the flashing across our horizon of this filibustering, buccaneering, slambanging, rhetorical, not ungracious, one-down-and-t'other-come-on, flamboyant, formidable soldier of fortune. Scotsmen alone have long divined something more solid in this Playboy of the two Hemispheres.

It is true that Scottish electors have sometimes rejected him; but electors are peculiar people. A Scottish Saint presided over his birth and a Scottish lady granted him her heart and hand. In the War of 1914–1918, a Scottish Regiment found him acceptable as a commander. Nobody at this time of day will impugn Scottish judgement, and the verdict of that country is undoubtedly favourable. We find him a capable man.

The English are suspicious of genius. From time to time they have given him power; but, until today, there has always been a stout string attached to it, and he has never held for long a position of high influence. He has held these positions long enough to set the mark of good craftsmanship on each of them and he has had little thanks for it. The part he played in Early Closing, Prison Reform and the break-up of the Poor Law was a great one and has almost been forgotten.

He has never been allowed to be Foreign Secretary; and yet the only really great achievements in foreign affairs in the last fifty years have been partly or wholly his work. Two or three pieces of British architecture have stood up to extraordinary stresses. It would not have been surprising if our Palestine troubles had resulted in a new and terrible Islamic Revolt. Expert incendiaries laboured towards this very end. But Palestine was surrounded by well-built Arab States which stood the strain. We have T.E. Lawrence's authority for saying that the onlie begetter of these states was Churchill. I do not know how much he was responsible for the settlement after the South African War; but the sure touches of magnanimity, artistry and common sense are obvious there, and it has been proved a good thing that they are. The same creative hand can be seen in present-day Eire. 'God,' they say, 'made the Irish and they aren't much.' But we have so far got through this war without many lethal manifestations from that quarter. We have Churchill and Michael Collins to thank for this state of matters. And so on. I know little or nothing of such things, but it appears to me that these are instances of statesmanship beside which even the feats of Simon, Hoare, Austen Chamberlain, Henderson and Ramsay MacDonald need not be ashamed to stand. As I say, this side of the man would appeal to my committee of inventors. We could find plenty capable of inventing our hubristic adventurer, but few who could toughen the fabric with foresight and intellectual competence.

Another difficulty is the difficulty of Period. Providence, as it happens, has chosen the correct Period to a hairsbreadth, but no prophet or poet could have placed Mr Churchill so accurately in Time. Mr Churchill himself has been doubtful as to which period he properly belongs. Costume is a pathognomonic symptom of Period, and Mr Churchill has always rebelled against the current fashion. We see him in Central Africa wearing pearl-buttoned boots and, at the White House, in dungarees; and nobody has ever been able to explain or to co-relate with the times his hats. Unless they typify an unheard-of crisis in civilisation, it is difficult to say what his garments typify. They are, however, in some singular way, dandified. Perhaps we should add Sir Max Beerbohm to the committee.

It would not have been so troublesome to invent his heredity. As he must be a world figure, the old aristocracy of England and the new aristocracy of America are quite promising stud farms. A reigning beauty of the one and a mettlesome genius of the other are an ideal mother and father. One of his very juvenile speeches contained something like the following passage:

'As you well know, my father, the late Lord Randolph Churchill, was known as the only Tory Democrat. His motto was ever the People's good. I come, Sir, in no way dissociating myself from the work done by my father. On the contrary, Sir, I come to raise a tattered standard that I found upon a stricken field.'

Both lines of heredity speak in these words. Possibly Herman Melville and Edward Gibbon (in collaboration) could have created Churchill in this dimension.

The Artist, the Original, and the Wit are not beyond the invention of man to compose; and here it might be wise to enlist the services of William Shakespeare, Charles Dickens and Alexandre Dumas, with a few hints from J.B.P. Molière. It would be necessary to construct a great comedy figure. A few sketches by Caran d'Ache would not be amiss. Our septuagenarian leaping up pilots' ladders and waving pith helmets on top of umbrellas, or our adolescent addressing burning words to the Empire promenade could each be a proper subject for the picturesque novelist's art.

In the weeks leading up to the thirtieth of November, many fountain pens and typewriters have been attempting to do justice to this remarkable man. I have hinted that this is beyond the powers of most contemporary talent. The greatest writers of the past must have boggled at him. Their only feeling of relief would have been at the reflection that he had never written any poetry. Even if their massive help was at our disposal, we should have no guarantee that they would succeed. We should have to sit back in our chairs and call to Beethoven to play something for us – a better Eroica, we should hope. It would start with the V motif, which Mr Churchill has chosen for his 'signature theme' and then . . .

1 December 1944

ADMIRAL DÖNITZ:
THE OLD FERRET

Ludovic Kennedy

Dönitz first came to public attention in 1939 when as Admiral commanding U-boats he planned the brilliant operation that resulted in Lieutenant Prien in U.47 penetrating the defences of Scapa Flow and sinking the *Royal Oak*. From that time on, his foxy features were seldom out of the papers; welcoming the victorious U-boat crews as they returned from successful forays in the North Atlantic; inspecting units of the surface fleet after he had relieved Raeder as C-in-C of the Navy in 1943; capitulation at Flensburg at the end of the war after reigning briefly as Hitler's successor; the dock at Nuremberg.

An opportunity to meet this legendary figure came some seven or eight years ago when I paid him two visits, one for a television interview for a documentary about the U-boat war, the other for a feature article for the *Telegraph* colour magazine. He had agreed in advance to participate in the U-boat film (it flattered him to know that his opinions were still sought, and I think he was glad of the fee) but stipulated that he be given prior notice of the questions. There were only two. I forget the second but the first was his opinion of how the war at sea might have gone had Raeder been given the 300 U-boats that he had asked for before the war.

Since his release from Spandau in 1956 the Admiral had been living in a small rather gloomy flat on the ground floor of an ugly house in Aumühle, on the outskirts of Hamburg. This was convenient for meeting former naval comrades and U-boat reunion dinners which he rarely missed.

My first impression of him was how small he was, in repose like a wizened nut, in conversation like a virile old ferret. He was very deaf. He showed us the silver model of a U-boat and said he had many other such mementoes, but the Allies had stripped his house of them at the end of the war and never given them back. I was aware how harshly history had treated him, deservedly or not; both sons killed at sea in the war; ten years in Spandau; his wife and son-in-law both dead.

He picked up a large ledger book and said triumphantly, 'I have written ze answers to your qvestions'. My heart sank. In his own hand he had written some 15 pages, partly in English, partly in German. When the camera crew were ready, I sat down and asked: 'Admiral, what do you think would have happened to the war at sea if you had had the 300 U-boats that were asked for earlier?' He picked up the ledger, looked at the camera with steely eye, and addressed it as though it were the furthest sailor on the longest parade ground in the Third Reich. 'In ze sommair of nineteen-sairty-nine,' he bawled, 'I vos saying to Grossadmiral Raeder...'

We stopped. Dönitz said, 'Not good?' The director said, as directors do, 'Fine, just fine. But if you'd be so kind, a little quieter.' Dönitz shouted, 'Vot you say?' And the director shrieked at him, 'NOT QUITE SO LOUD, ADMIRAL. A LITTLE LESS VOICE.' We started again. For a few seconds the voice might have been a semi-tone lower, then rose to its former crescendo. Clearly this seadog was too old for new tricks, and we let him roar on, long after we had run out of film, knowing that we would not be able to use a foot. Afterwards the Admiral and I were filmed walking in the garden, and in a half-minute of commentary I later paraphrased the essentials of what he had said.

The second visit, for the feature article, was altogether more relaxed. It was about this time that the Ultra secret had just been revealed, so I was the first to inform him of it and ask him if he had ever had an inkling that we were regularly decoding U-boats' signals and dispositions. He avoided the question by saying that he knew there were leaks, they had had several inquiries on the matter, and concluded they were due to treachery. Did he now accept the truth of the matter, I asked? He smiled, as I recall, and said something like 'If you say so.' But I don't think he believed it, even then.

What sort of man was Dönitz? Without doubt one of the half-dozen top war leaders of either side. Like Nelson, he was an inspiration to those who served under him. Otto Kretschmer, one of his top U-boat aces and later a NATO admiral, told me, 'We would have gone anywhere he asked.' It was his leadership that sustained U-boat morale to the bitter end, even when the life expectancy of a boat was only one operational trip, and two out of three boats never came back.

Should he have been convicted of war crimes, and in particular of waging aggressive war? Although he worshipped Hitler the far side of idolatry and sang his praises in many speeches, many Westerners thought the charges against him flimsy in the extreme. The irony was that of the four prosecuting powers at Nuremberg, three – Britain, France and the United States – had themselves declared war on Germany, while in the German attack on the fourth, Russia, Dönitz had played no part. So the charge had to be narrowed to the planning of the naval attack on Norway where Raeder was in overall charge and again Dönitz's part was minimal.

His defence was the well-established one of obeying superior orders. If
he was guilty of aggressive war, he often said afterwards, then those who
planned and executed the Franco-British attack on Egypt in 1956 (among
them Mountbatten) were equally guilty. The American judge Francis
Biddle said that he should have been acquitted, and he received public
and private support from many figures, such as General Weygand, London University's law expert Professor Smith, the military historian General J.F.C. Fuller, and what Dönitz called 'eminent soldiers and sailors,
statesmen, historians and lawyers from many countries, particularly
America and Britain'.

And what was his answer to my question about the 300 U-boats? He
thought carefully, then said, 'I think we would have won the war by
1942.' I thought but didn't say, 'If it hadn't been for Ultra you might have
won it anyway.'

3 January 1981

THE BEST BOOK ON THE GENERAL

Sam White

DE GAULLE. *By Bernard Ledwidge. (Weidenfeld & Nicolson.)*
General de Gaulle became a legendary and historic figure by default.
Even after he launched his famous appeal from London for France to continue the fight it would have been easy for any one of a dozen politicians
or his military superiors to have nudged him aside as the leader of the
Free French. That nobody did so provided him with his second shock, the
first being the defeatism which led to surrender while France's empire
was still intact. It is true, of course, that the prize and the prospects it
carried with it seemed particularly dubious at the time – so dubious perhaps that only a middle-ranking officer (de Gaulle's substantive rank at
the time was that of colonel) whose political experience was restricted to
a few days as a junior minister could have undertaken it. It involved not
only dissidence from a government at home headed by so distinguished a
figure as Marshal Pétain but taking the risk that Britain might seek a
compromise peace such as even some members of the British Government were advocating. However, for Churchill in those grim days even

the defection of a little known Frenchman provided comfort (and propaganda material) out of all proportion to the importance of the defector himself. As the author of this magnificent study of de Gaulle drily puts it: 'Doubtless at that point Churchill expected that bigger French fish would cross the Channel: so did de Gaulle. Neither he nor Churchill could have foreseen how big a fish de Gaulle himself was to prove.'

Having had greatness, or the opportunity of greatness, as it were thrust upon him, de Gaulle proceeded to make the most of it in war and peace. Single-handed he spared France, already sufficiently humiliated, the further humiliation of being ruled by an Anglo-American military government after the expulsion of the Germans, as was Roosevelt's intention right up to D-Day. Furthermore, he secured for France, this time with Churchill's support, the status of a victorious nation sharing with its allies in the occupation of Germany as well as a permanent place on the security council of the United Nations. Again the author's comment is apt: 'By the extraordinary device of making himself a sovereign with retrospective effect to the date of Paul Reynaud's resignation he was able to maintain and impose by degrees the fiction that the real France had never surrendered. He gave France an alibi for her fall ' Against this legend, the full strength of which was only revealed by the reception de Gaulle got in liberated France, Stalin was powerless and all Roosevelt's intrigues to be rid of him came to nothing. The relationship with Churchill was of a different kind if only because Churchill having, in a sense, made de Gaulle found it morally more difficult to unmake him. Nor could he easily accept Roosevelt's contempt for the French which underlay his contempt for de Gaulle. As a result, although they were often on the edge of an open break, both knew when to draw back from it.

Roosevelt understood Churchill's half proprietorial interest in de Gaulle and often baited him on this score. ('What are you going to do with de Gaulle after the war? I suggest you make him Governor of Madagascar.') It is interesting too to recall the various anti-de-Gaulle plots of that time, some of them the work of British Intelligence, as well as the long period – 11 months – during which, on Churchill's orders, he was not allowed to leave Britain. However, this work does not concern itself solely with the wartime years. It is a fullscale biography of de Gaulle, taking in so recent an event as Pompidou's posthumous memoirs concerning the General's enigmatic conduct during the May '68 upheaval. As such, it is by far the best book on de Gaulle so far written on either side of the Channel, sparing us the mysticism of such authors as Malraux and Mauriac and the philistinism of many 'Anglo-saxon' commentators. Sir Bernard Ledwidge, a former British Ambassador who was Minister at the British Embassy in Paris during the Sixties, is clearly well placed to write not only about the past but about the more recent present when Anglo-French interests were at loggerheads and a kind of diplomatic cold war existed between the two countries. He does so with great authority and, while treading warily to spare some Foreign Office corns, he indicates clearly that his views of de Gaulle during that period differed considerably from those of his masters in Whitehall.

Harold Macmillan, for example, had two grievances against de Gaulle after his return to power in 1958. The first was that he did not wreck the Common Market as the Prime Minister's diplomatic advisers predicted he would, and the second was that having refused to wreck it he kept us out of it. This original false reading of de Gaulle's intentions delayed our applications to join by two years, by which time it was too late, for it had given de Gaulle time to bring Adenauer on to his side. The quarrel with Britain was only the first step towards the greater quarrel with the United States aimed at giving France a more independent role in Europe. Hence the creation of an independent atomic deterrent and the withdrawal from NATO. The words he uttered at the time still echo: 'Nobody in the world, in particular nobody in America, can say where, when, how or to what extent American nuclear weapons would be used to defend Europe.' Meanwhile in Algeria, resolutely ignoring the sweeping successes the Army was beginning to have in the field, de Gaulle finally succeeded in his step-by-step approach to Algerian independence. At every stage of that long and agonising process he had to carry public opinion with him while at the same time maintaining his authority over the Army. Nor did the French Left help him. It clearly preferred that de Gaulle should fail rather than succeed in settling the war. De Gaulle has often been blamed for not denouncing the original army mutiny which resulted in his return to power. But why should he have done so when the government of the day not only failed to condemn it but sought to appease it by vesting all its powers, civil and military, in General Salan?

Ledwidge has something fresh and interesting to say on such key de Gaulle mysteries as the notorious 'Vive Québec Libre' speech, the Soames affair and his disappearance act at the height of the May '68 troubles. It seems clear to me that de Gaulle's decline dates not from the May upheavals but precisely from that Quebec speech which provoked dismay among members of his government and led to Giscard's attack on 'the solitary exercise of power'. The unconditional 'oui' was henceforth to become the 'oui mais'. In the Soames affair the Foreign Office decision to make public the text of de Gaulle's proposals for confidential talks with Britain on a future Common Market in which she would be a member very nearly led to Soames's resignation. As Ledwidge comments: 'Such treatment of the text of a confidential diplomatic exchange with a foreign Head of State is perhaps without precedent in British history.' As for his disappearance, there is little doubt that he deliberately misled Pompidou into thinking he was leaving for good, which indicates how unlikely it was that he ever considered seriously doing so. Nevertheless, despite his triumphant return, he felt the need for the kind of personal reassurance that only victory in a referendum could bring him.

He was particularly attracted to this course because if defeated, and it steadily became more and more apparent that he would be, it would provide him with a dignified exit from the scene. There was therefore no drawing back and, instead, an ever stronger commitment to resign if he were beaten. And go he did, in great dignity and into complete retirement. Of the many messages of sympathy he received, the one he prized most was from Lady Churchill. He had been writing to her every year on the anniversary of her husband's death.

18 December 1982

JOSEPH GOEBBELS: CROWING AND ROARING

Hugh Trevor-Roper

THE GOEBBELS DIARIES 1939–41. *Translated and edited by Fred Taylor. (Hamish Hamilton.)*

Whatever their value as evidence, the diaries of Joseph Goebbels are a significant historical document. He intended them to be the basis of an official history written by himself. Luckily, he was denied this opportunity, and the raw material remains raw. Three sections of it have so far been published. This new section – 'the largest portion yet to be printed', we are told, with dubious accuracy – covers parts of the period from 1 January 1939 to 8 July 1941.

All the sections previously published have carried their credentials with them. The publishers of this section are curiously reticent. The German text has not been published. We are not told how that text was acquired, or where it is. There are no acknowledgements, no reference to other sources from which we might deduce the answers to such questions. The editor, who is the translator (a very readable translator) and a novelist, gives nothing away. Perhaps he does not himself know. We get the impression that the publishers do not wish us to know. So let us begin by enquiring. The publishers of hitherto unpublished documents ought to be more open.

Throughout his active life, Goebbels was a compulsive diarist. At first he kept his diaries in long-hand. But in the spring of 1941, when the bombs were falling on Berlin, he began to fear for the safety of these valuable documents and took special precautions. 'I shall put my diaries in the vaults of the Reichsbank,' he wrote on 29 March, 'to protect them from fire and air-raids. They will be safer there.' Three days later it was done: 'I have my diaries, twenty fat volumes, deposited in the underground vault of the Reichsbank,' he wrote. 'They provide a picture of my entire life and our times. If fate allows me a few years for the task, I intend to edit them for the sake of future generations. They may well be of some interest to the world at large.' Later, as his preoccupations grew, he took a further step. Lacking the time to write, and perhaps fearful for the survival of a single text, from 9 July 1941 he dictated his diaries to a short-hand typist. Two copies were typed, of which one was kept in his Ministry, the other, presumably, deposited in the Reichsbank. In the last days of the war, micro-copies were also made on photographic plates and buried in a wood outside Berlin. After the fall of Berlin some of these documents were discovered by the Russians and disappeared into their archives. Others lay abandoned in the rubble and came finally into American hands. The latter included the original typescripts for 1942–43, of which a selection – just as long as this new selection – was published by Louis P. Lochner in 1948, and the manuscript diaries of 1923–24, which were published by the *Institut für Zeitgeschichte* in Munich in 1960. The originals of these are now in the Hoover Institution at Stanford.

Several years later, the Russians began to exploit their hitherto disregarded booty. For some reason best known to themselves, they neither acknowledged their possession of these and such documents nor entrusted them to historians nor allowed them to be published in communist countries. They leaked them furtively through journalists for publication exclusively in the West. In this way, through an East German journalist, a West German publishing house acquired copies both of the handwritten and of the typewritten texts of Goebbels' diaries, extending (with gaps) from 1924 to 1945. From these were published, in 1977, the entries for 1945, of which I edited an English version in 1978. These copies, which have marks of previous Russian ownership, are now in the *Institut für Zeitgeschichte* in Munich.

Such is the general history of the texts, as far as I know it. How does this newly published section of the diaries fit into it? Since the entries end on 8 July 1941, and Goebbels began to dictate his diaries on 9 July

1941, they are clearly the last of the manuscript volumes. These, we happen to know, were in Russian hands in 1945 and copies of them passed through the hands of a German journalist to Messrs Hofmann und Campe, the German publishers, in 1972, and from them to the Institute at Munich. The German copyright was acquired by Messrs Hofmann und Campe, but the foreign rights no doubt remain with the Swiss citizen who had skilfully pre-empted them. Since this edition carries none of the usual courtesies – no acknowledgement to the Institute in Munich, or to any other owner, no reference to any German publisher – we are left with the suspicion that, somewhere along the line, unauthorised copies have been made by persons whom the publishers find it imprudent to name. Perhaps, if it should publish its German text, the excellent Institute at Munich will examine and solve this interesting little problem of *Quellengeschichte*.

However that may be, there is no reason to doubt the genuineness of the document, which, we are told (again with great economy of detail) has been warranted by the Wiener Library. So let us turn to it. How did Dr Goebbels view the progress of Hitler's policy, and Hitler's war, from 1939 to 1941?

In some respects, we shall find ourselves disappointed. The diaries are far from continuous, and some of the gaps are disconcerting. The first dramatic episode in 1939 was Hitler's military occupation of the rump of Czechoslovakia left by Munich. With that act, the whole of the Munich 'settlement' was exposed as an illusion or smoke-screen, and war became virtually certain. Unfortunately (except for one unimportant scrap) there is a gap in the diaries from 5 March to 19 May 1939, so that whole adventure is unrecorded. Another large gap from 31 May to 8 October 1939 swallows up the negotiation of the Nazi-Soviet Pact, the outbreak of war and the Polish campaign. Yet another gap stretches effectively from 13 February to 1 October 1940, thus engulfing the Norwegian campaign, the war in the West, and the Battle of Britain in equal oblivion. In 1941 the whole month of January is missing, but there is a complete run of entries from 1 February to 8 July; so we have the benefit of Goebbels' comments on the Balkan campaign, the flight of Hess, and the invasion of Russia.

These gaps may of course be accidental, though the survival of occasional fragments in what are regularly described as 'books' is odd. We cannot be sure that the Russians may not have excised some parts: the Nazi Soviet Pact is not an episode that they like to remember. However, since the editor does not think it necessary to comment on such details, and we do not know how much of the evidence he has himself seen, we can only speculate. Other gaps, of course, may be due to Goebbels's own reticence. He was, we must remember, a propagandist, and he was not going to record the real *arcana imperii*, even if he knew them. His business was to record the outward triumphs of Nazism – and his own part in bringing them about.

Generally speaking, his task was easy in these years, for they were the years of uninterrupted success. Military victory is its own propaganda, and the Minister has only to crow. He crowed to some tune, and without much reflexion. He crowed too about his own skill in crowing. Again and again he admires his own broadcasts, articles, speeches, directives, and inhales, with articulate complacency, the incense offered to him by his obsequious subordinates. Of course he has some trouble with his competitors round the throne. Ribbentrop is 'an insufferable fellow' whose abusive letters are best left unanswered. Bormann, who worms his way upwards after the flight of Hess, is a sinister and alarming creature, 'neither honest nor clear-minded'. The Italian Foreign Minister, Count Ciano, is a stupid, tactless, mannerless, insolent social climber. The Churches too are a great nuisance – they will have to be dealt with later, after victory – and the generals are hand-in-glove with them. But what are these minor domestic frustrations to one who has regular opportunities of admiring the Führer at close quarters, of being irradiated by his vitality and inspired by his profound ideas? These include vegetarianism ('the coming religion'), 'Jewish Christianity' (to be destroyed), the worthless Poles (to be destroyed too), Frederick the Great ('what a giant! what a universal spirit! But also what a sensitive, artistic soul!'), types of feminine beauty, and the 'huge and swift strides' that we are making towards 'a new classical age'.

For of course the Führer has classical tastes. He is a man 'totally attuned to Antiquity' and hates having to make war on Greece. He loathes the gloom and mysticism of Christianity and its cathedrals, 'cannot relate to the Gothic mind', wants 'clarity, light, beauty', and therefore sees 'the high-point of history in the Augustinian age' ('shome mishtake here', as *Private Eye* would say, but the editor does not notice it). Once victory had been attained, the Führer would take steps to realise his new classical age. Having 'put England to the sword', eliminated Russia and Bolshevism, and thus ensured a permanent German hegemony in Europe and the reign of universal peace, he would 'remain in office for a few years, carry through social reforms and his building projects, and then retire'. But even in his retirement he would not cease to serve humanity. He would be 'a benevolent spirit hovering over the political world', and would write a great work, 'a Bible of National Socialism, so to speak'.

How easy it all seemed in those years, when country after country was collapsing before him! All that remained was for Britain to surrender and be 'put to the sword'. Why did this not happen? Goebbels simply could not understand the blindness, folly, obstinacy, 'impudent arrogance', etc. etc. of Britain. Britain, he insisted, was totally destroyed; its morale, always rotten (he knew this from reading Somerset Maugham) has 'collapsed'; London was in ruins, 'a hell on earth', a scene of 'unimaginable devastation'; why then will 'that creature Churchill' not surrender? Goebbels repeatedly demolishes Churchill. He exposes him as 'impudent and cynical', 'a lying old swine'; he cuts his speeches (those 'rag-bags of illusions') to ribbons; declares that he is universally hated in Britain and only broadcasts to the people because he is afraid to appear in Parliament. He is confident that, by his roaring, he will make him tremble and fall. If Churchill has not fallen by the end of the volume, it is certainly not for lack of roaring. In the end, Goebbels is reduced to revealing that Churchill drinks too much and wears pink silk underwear, and to claiming that his own speeches, even if they have not destroyed the enemy, are 'brilliant' and 'a huge success'.

Meanwhile he has to admit some other deceptions. General Franco, for instance, who had recently been 'firmly ours', has suddenly turned out to be a mere 'jumped-up sergeant-major', 'a vain, brainless peacock', 'a clown, conceited, arrogant and stupid'. Fortunately such men could never last (Franco would last another 35 years). And then there was the 'appalling news' of Hess's flight to Scotland – only seven months after Goebbels had described him as 'a good reliable man: the Führer can rely on him blindly'. Fortunately, the British, having no genius like Goebbels, did not exploit the event as they might have done: 'If I were the English Propaganda Minister, I would know what to do.' He would have published a series of damaging lies and fathered them on Hess. Even as it was, he knew how to make the best of a bad job. His own handling of the embarrassing affair, he recorded, was 'a masterpiece of vision, psychological skill and caution'.

So Goebbels was always right, and as he stowed the 20 manuscript volumes away, he could think only of the glorious future of which he was the prophet and would be the historian. The *Wehrmacht* – helped by a brilliant propaganda trick by himself – was now rolling into Russia: 'the Führer estimates that the operation will take four months. I reckon on fewer. Bolshevism will collapse like a house of cards. We face victories unequalled in human history.' As the Führer said, Germany was bound to win; 'and once we have won, who is going to question our methods?' 'In any case,' added Goebbels, 'we have so much to answer for already that we *must* win . . .' Here at least, and at last, the Propaganda Minister deviated into veracity.

20 November 1982

BOOKS AND WRITERS:
RICHARD HILLARY

Robert Kee

Mr Lovat Dickson's book about Richard Hillary, the young airman-writer who was killed in 1943, is not very interesting.[1] Most of it consists of a more or less straightforward paraphrase of the account Hillary gave of his own life in his one book, *The Last Enemy*. That book, though uneven, was a 'natural', and after it Mr Lovat Dickson's has the flavour of dried egg. Even most of the details of Mr Lovat Dickson's own relationship with Hillary (primarily that of publisher and author, although, being a good publisher, Mr Lovat Dickson was human enough to come under Hillary's personal spell) have been described before. The account, for instance, of the burnt and disfigured Hillary insisting on reading the first chapter of his book aloud in Mr Lovat Dickson's office has appeared verbatim in Mr Eric Linklater's book of essays, *The Art of Adventure*, published in 1947 by Macmillan, who also published *The Last Enemy*, and of which firm Mr Lovat Dickson is a director. A good deal of what is interesting in those letters of Hillary's which Mr Lovat Dickson quotes was quoted by Arthur Koestler in his first-class essay on Hillary in *Horizon*, April, 1943. Only the long extracts from Hillary's letters and diary describing the night-fighter course on which he was killed, which form most of Chapter Eight, are new, and they are interesting because they are written by Richard Hillary. No, in itself, Mr Lovat Dickson's book is not very interesting, but it does serve to spotlight the real question which forms easily in the mind at this distance from Hillary's death, and that is: Was Richard Hillary himself very interesting?

That he was brave, attractive, intelligent, athletic, a promising writer, and, until shot down and burnt in the Battle of Britain, a fine fighter pilot – all this is undeniable. But such a combination of qualities, though rare, is not unique in any generation, and certainly was not in his. He was not all *that* intelligent (there is fumbled thinking and a certain inflexibility of outlook in *The Last Enemy*), not all *that* brilliant as a writer ('The air

---

[1]*Richard Hillary: A Life*. By Lovat Dickson. (Macmillan.)

was like champagne'), and it was possible to be at Oxford with him before the war and take a fairly full part in the life of the University without ever being aware of his personality.

And yet Richard Hillary does occupy a unique position among the many hundreds of young men of promise who died in the last war. Many people will have heard of him who never heard of Sidney Keyes, Alun Lewis or Rollo Woolley, who were all better writers. *The Last Enemy* became an immediate best-seller, and the 'idea' of Richard Hillary began to exercise a strange fascination on the imagination of Englishmen from the humblest reader of *John O'London* to the Editor of *Horizon* himself. In 1947 Eric Linklater compared the effect of his death on England with that of Rupert Brooke in the war before, and wrote that he had become a 'national possession, an exemplar of his age, a symbol of the *reverdissement*.' Mr Lovat Dickson is content to see him as 'symbolising the best that boyhood and manhood can be.'

Koestler, writing a few months after Hillary's death, described the myth that was already growing around him. 'It is easy to foresee that it will wax and expand, until his name has become one of the symbolic names of the war. The growth of a myth cannot be influenced and one should not attempt it. For myths grow like crystals: there is some diffuse emotion latent in the social medium which strives for expression as the molecules in a saturated solution strive to form a coherent pattern, and as soon as a suitable core is found, they group themselves around it and the crystal is formed, the myth is born.' And Koestler proceeded to augment the myth himself by labelling Hillary as 'a crusader without a cross.'

Now how on earth did all this come about? *The Last Enemy* does not now seem a great book. To some it will not even seem an important book, although undoubtedly it was important in the effect it had on its time. The best passages are those of pure *reportage*, although they are not the passages with which Hillary himself was most concerned or even those which gave the book its sensational success. But in these descriptions of flying, of the Battle of Britain, of being shot down, and of the long, long, everyday business of being given a new face to replace his burnt one, there are undoubted signs that Hillary *might* have developed into an important writer. The passages from his later writings quoted by Mr. Lovat Dickson confirm these signs, for they show a distinct development towards maturity. But even so one cannot, if one is being quite unemotional and objective, put it at higher than '*might*'. On the other hand the slightly narcissistic self-dramatisation, the unconscious identification of his own Shrewsbury and Trinity, rowing, Verlaine-reading self with the youth of England, the Byronic egotism, the building-up of one of the characters, who, to an outsider, appears as a noble but rather dull young English gentleman, into a sort of upper-class saint – a lot of this has the hollow sound of false maturity.

The main thread running through *The Last Enemy* is Hillary's attempt to explain the mainspring of his life, to explain why he is throwing himself into the war. The easy, elegantly swashbuckling selfishness comes first. Life is to him just a form of self-expression and he will get out of it what he can in peace or war. ('The war . . . promised a chance of self-realisation that would normally take years to achieve. As a fighter pilot I hoped for a concentration of amusement, fear and exaltation which it would be impossible to achieve in any other form of experience.') Then came the deaths of his companions ('I was the last of the long-haired boys' – as if his particular group of 'long-haired boys' were the only one in the RAF at that time), and he begins to feel that these deaths leave him with some strange responsibility. This responsibility is never really clearly defined, but it merges, after the first stage of his reconstruction in 'the beauty shop' and a harrowing experience in an air-raid, into a feeling that he must live and fight for humanity. And the book ends on a note of humility. ' "Le sentiment d'être tout et l'évidence de n'être rien." That was me.' But it was not the final Richard Hillary any more than any of the others he produced at different moments of his life.

Koestler in his essay examined the motives that made Hillary take the decision to go back to flying – night flying on twin-engined night fighters – with his new face and burnt claw-like hands. He found that none of the possible explanations really fitted. Vanity? ('I wonder . . . whether, as some silly girl said, I am going back purely out of vanity?') Self-destruction? Possible, but Hillary had love to live for at the end of his life. Patriotism? (He hated the cheap phrases. He felt embarrassed when people saw his face and said: 'How you must hate those devils.') Fellowship, with the living and the dead? Something of that, certainly, but he is touched on the raw by reading David Garnett's comment on T.E. Lawrence's going back to the RAF ('One wonders whether his will had not become greater than his intelligence') and applying it to himself.

Koestler saw that there was no real coherence or consistency behind this fantastic decision, and so put him down as the desperate crusader in search of a cross. But even this is going too far, just as it is going too far to say that Hillary longed to know what it was he symbolised, what the myth was that was forming round him.

The truth is probably more simple and less romantic than Koestler made it. Richard Hillary, in spite of his terrible experiences, was still a very young man when he died. And like all young men in their early twenties he was intensely absorbed by his attitude to life and this was constantly changing. He didn't really stand for anything. He was in search of something more personal than a cross. The apparent single-mindedness that runs through *The Last Enemy* even lets him down ('It's no good . . . I just don't believe what I wrote in that book – sometimes I do! I meant it when I wrote it, but now I don't'). And so the strange pattern of his life emerges, a pattern which is indeed no pattern at all but that of youth working itself out in dangerous hideous times.

And why should it be otherwise? Why shouldn't he have been changing, altering his attitude, working out his own particular form of that pattern? This is the thing that youth is for. But a society which makes a practice of killing off its young men of 23 every few years has to salve its conscience in some way, and it does this by pretending that they were whole human beings, and that they stood for something, if only for crusading in search of a cross. This guilt might have attached to any one of thousands of promising, attractive young men who died, and turned them into a symbol of heroism, of mass redemption. Circumstances (a moving book at the right moment, a romantic character, a brave decision) made it attach easily to Richard Hillary. So that, in his case at any rate, the last enemy, which is death, was destroyed after all.

3 November 1950

THE THOUGHTS OF FÜHRER ADOLF
Robert Birley

One of the ablest speeches made by Hitler – and one of the most important by any statesman in this century – was delivered to the Industrie-Klub at Düsseldorf on 27 January 1932. It was by means of this speech that he won over to his side the industrialists of the Ruhr and the Rhineland, and this made his victory a year later possible. I have heard it described by one of the very few present who were not won over by it and he has told me of the extraordinary magnetic, in fact hypnotic, quality of the speech – in its delivery rather than its words, which are quite commonplace – and how difficult it was to resist arguments which one saw through completely as they were presented.

One day in the Control Commission Mess in Düsseldorf I spoke to an elderly man, brought in as an additional waiter, who had been on duty at

the Industrie-Klub on that day. Hitler had been presented on his arrival
with a bouquet of flowers. The old man had been in charge of the cloaks.
'It was a good day for me,' he said. 'The wives of the men inside who were
listening to him wanted to smell the Führer's flowers. I charged them a
mark each.'

No explanation of the phenomenon of Adolf Hitler, the most extraordinary phenomenon of all European history, will serve which does not
account for that astonishing magnetism and for the wives of the industrial magnates smelling the magician's flowers. Certainly Mein Kampf,
now published by Hutchinson in a translation by Ralph Manheim, and
introduced by D.C. Watt, will not do that. This long, turgid, badly
organised book can be considered, however, in two ways, as an historical
force, a book which changed people's minds and so altered the course of
history, or as evidence when one tries to understand the mind and feelings of the writer.

As an historical force it did not amount to much. It was not for some
time a commercial success. People did not become Nazis by reading Mein
Kampf; they bought it – and sometimes read it – because they had already
become Nazis. In 1928 its sales were just over 3,000; in 1932, after the
remarkable Nazi success in the elections of 1930, they rose to 90,000. By
1940 six million copies had been sold. But by that time it was an established practice that every bride and bridegroom were given a copy at their
marriage. Winston Churchill spoke of Mein Kampf as 'a new Koran of
faith and war'. It was not that: it did not inspire Hitler's followers. It was
never more than a symbol.

It may be asked, however, whether it should not have influenced readers outside Germany. Before the Nazi success in 1930 a firm of British
publishers had the chance to publish an unexpurgated translation;
which, not unnaturally, they did not take. The English translation which
came out in 1933 was prudently bowdlerised. A French translation in
1934 was immediately suppressed. Would it have made much difference
if foreign statesmen had been able to read it in full before the Nazis
gained power six years prior to the war? It is very doubtful. However, it is
an interesting speculation whether, if there had been an unexpurgated
translation available in England in 1930, much credence would have
been given to an interview with Hitler in the Times in October of that
year, in which he said that 'He would have nothing to do with pogroms
and that was the first word which had always gone forth from him in tur-
bulent times. . . . They had nothing against decent Jews.'

Almost all the ideas in Mein Kampf were expounded by Hitler in subsequent speeches or conversations, but certainly something is gained by

reading them all together in a very long work, intended to be an autobiography, but actually a kind of cistern into which he poured his ideas, feelings and wishes. Let us take, as evidence to show how his mind worked, the question of the Jewish menace. In this book he never actually advocates the extermination of the whole Jewish people, the 'Final Solution', though he is known to have spoken of this as necessary as early as 1919; but he does say that if only 15,000 Jews had been killed with poison gas in 1914 there would have been no war – and the gas chambers of Auschwitz are foreshadowed.

What is most significant, for the study of Hitler's mind, is the way in which the Jew is found lurking everywhere. He was the nineteenth-century capitalist in England – 'By the 'eighties the basic Jewish tendency of Manchester liberalism had reached, if not passed, its highest point in the monarchy of Austria-Hungary'. He is the capitalist of the twentieth century in America – 'It is Jews who govern the stock exchange prices of the American union'. He was responsible for the use by the French of Senegalese troops in the Rhineland and so 'the vital artery of the German people runs through the hunting ground of African Negro hordes'. Above all, as a Jew Marx and as a Jew [sic] Lenin he was responsible for Communism and Bolshevism and 'in Russian Bolshevism we must see the attempt undertaken by the Jews in the twentieth century to achieve world domination'.

The Jew is the same in all ages. 'His traits of character have remained the same, whether two thousand years ago as a grain dealer in Ostia, speaking Roman, or whether as a flour profiteer of today, jabbering German with a Jewish accent.' He plays a part in all aspects of society. In a strange passage on men's clothes, in which Hitler criticises stove-pipe trousers and shirts buttoned up at the neck, we read, 'If physical beauty were today not forced entirely into the background by our foppish fashions, the seduction of hundreds of thousands of girls by bow-legged Jewish bastards would not be possible.' In what must be the maddest of all apocalyptical outbursts in literature he wrote, 'If with the help of his Marxist creed, the Jew is victorious over the other peoples of the world, his crown will be the funeral wreath of humanity and this planet will, as it did millions of years ago, move through the ether devoid of life.'

How, we may well feel, was it that people failed to recognise the paranoiac? Perhaps the answer is that it seemed so mad that no one could take it seriously. But there is no real excuse for the failure of foreign statesmen to realise at least from *Mein Kampf* that Hitler believed it to be Germany's duty to conquer and colonise Russia and its neighbouring states or that he intended to carry out a merciless revenge on France. 'This people [the French], which is basically becoming more and more negrified, constitutes in its tie with the aims of Jewish world domination an enduring danger for the existence of the white race in Europe.'

The present translation is a competent piece of work and the translator's note at the beginning gives one confidence in the way it was carried out. (It seems a pity, though, that no consideration is given in this note to the word *völkisch*, a most difficult problem for a translator. The footnote on page twelve is hardly adequate. 'Folkish' as a translation surely smacks too much of the country green.) The introduction by Mr D.C. Watt is excellent. English readers of a generation that knows not Hitler will find that it makes all the difference to their understanding of a book which may otherwise seem almost incomprehensible. Perhaps there might have been in it a mention of Father Bernard Stempfle, who had the formidable task of polishing Hitler's style. (He was murdered on 30 June 1934, the 'night of the long knives', probably by Emil Maurice, one of the two men to whom Hitler had dictated the first part of the book in prison.)

There remains the question whether this new translation should have been issued now. The publishers, in a sympathetic note, tell us of the regret of the German authorities. If its reappearance were to make people believe that the book represents the attitude of present-day Germans, it would indeed be unfortunate; but after the recent elections it can hardly do that. After all, Hitler is part of history and as such he cannot be ignored.

One day, not long after the end of the war, Herr Grimme, the last Social Democrat Minister of Education in Prussia before the war and the first in Lower Saxony after it, said to a number of young Germans who had asked him angrily if they could be held responsible for the atrocities of the Nazi regime, 'No, of course not – but you will be next time'. He was speaking to all future generations of all nations. We may hope that knowledge of this book, the most evil ever written, will help to make a 'next time' impossible.

11 October 1969

TO WAR WITH HOXHA

David Smiley

I first met Enver Hoxha in July 1943. At that time I was second in command of the First British Military Mission to be infiltrated into Albania by SOE, led by Major Billy McLean. We were living in a disused mosque in a village when we were warned to expect a visit from the *shtab* – the general staff of the LNÇ or National Movement of Liberation.

The *shtab* arrived escorted by a *çeta* (guerrilla band) of some 30 men and consisted of Enver Hoxha and four other senior members of the staff – all of whom were to be executed by Hoxha in later years. Hoxha was a big, beefy man for an Albanian, and looked rather too well fed and fleshy to be a guerrilla fighter. His handshake was flabby. Recent photographs show him to have lost weight.

He wore an Italian army forage cap with the red star badge, an open shirt, baggy breeches, with stockings and shoes, while round his waist was a thin bandolier containing ammunition for his pistol. Our first meeting was cordial because he had started to receive parachute drops of arms, and the chief reason for his coming was to put in a vast list of requests for more.

At the first meeting McLean tried to impress on him that we came as allies to help the Albanians to drive out the Italian occupiers of their country, and as soldiers we would do all we could to help equip, train and go into action with his partisans. While welcoming material help, although he always complained that there was never enough, Hoxha at subsequent meetings would make long speeches denouncing the Albanians of any party that was opposed to his Communists. He referred to them as Fascists, and would fly into a rage if ever we suggested that they too might be helpful in fighting the Italians. Hoxha never trusted us for contacting these groups.

Although he had quite a sense of humour and could laugh and be cheerful, he had a very hot temper and would quickly start shouting and blustering, saliva oozing from his lips. We normally spoke in French, at which he was fluent, though when he was accompanied by Mehmet Shehu, his military adviser who spoke excellent English, Mehmet would interpret from Albanian.

At first we were not sure what Hoxha's actual position was in the *shtab*, for he was always referred to as Professor Enver Hoxha, because he had taught French in Albania. He did not seem to be a military man like Shehu, who had already fought in the Spanish Civil War. We guessed he was the commissar and later learned that he was the secretary-general to the Albanian Communist Party.

A month later, thanks to our training and equipping the partisans with various weapons that had been dropped to us, Hoxha decided to hold a big parade to celebrate the Inauguration of the 'First Partisan Brigade'. This comprised some 800 men under the command of Mehmet Shehu, and they formed up on a large plain where they stood patiently enduring the political speeches.

Hoxha, like Hitler, was a good rabble-rouser and his speech was interrupted at appropriate moments by cries of the Communist slogans *'Vdejke Fashisinit'* ('Death to Fascism') and *'Liri Popullit'* ('Liberty to the People') accompanied by the clenched fist salute. Hoxha got so carried away that he was frothing at the mouth and went on for so long that I secretly hoped that an Italian bomber would fly over and disperse the parade.

However, when all the speeches were over we repaired to a vast barbecue where sheep were roasted whole on spits by the Vlachs, while raki and wine flowed freely (we suspected all this was paid for by British sovereigns). At this party Hoxha was at his most affable, laughing, singing and joking. We were full of hopes that now the partisan brigade would give a good account of themselves against the Italians. Sadly, we were doomed to disappointment, for the brigade only carried out token actions, or fought when they had to defend themselves against Italian counter-measures. It later transpired that Hoxha and Shehu were conserving the brigade to eliminate their political opponents, and in due course this is what happened.

As the movement grew stronger, so Hoxha got more intolerant with the British mission. It must have been infuriating for him that all the supplies he received came from the British rather than his Russian friends, who sent him no aid whatever.

I used deliberately to bait Hoxha, and he usually rose to my taunts, but my final meeting with him was very stormy as he was furious with me for blowing up a bridge without his permission, and became more so when I replied that I did not consider that it was necessary for the British to take orders from him. We parted on bad terms.

Hoxha had further cause to rant against McLean and myself, for after leaving Albania to report to SOE HQ in London, we were parachuted back to work with the Zoggists and Ballists (nationalists) who were Hoxha's rivals for power and hence his bitter enemies. Finally, he sent a signal through a British Legion officer attached to him, to SOE HQ in Italy, stating that McLean, myself and another officer had been tried in our absence by a military tribunal as agents of reactionaries in London and condemned to death. He had already given orders to the partisans to capture us alive if possible but shoot us if we resisted. SOE reacted strongly and informed Hoxha that unless he withdrew this order he would receive no further supplies. He signalled back that he would comply, but we knew that he never cancelled the order, and his partisans continued to hunt us until we finally left the country.

After the war, when he was President, Hoxha wrote endless memoirs, one of which I have read, entitled *The Anglo-American Threat to Albania*. It is full of so many lies, distortions of fact, misinformation and pure Communist propaganda that it is almost laughable. I appreciated the suggestion made by the *Spectator*'s radio critic Noel Malcolm (30 March) that the BBC, instead of making their own efforts at comedy, should merely relay the English-language broadcasts of Radio Albania.

Hoxha's ruthlessness and cruelty were of the same order as Stalin's. In 1981 even his old comrade Mehmet Shehu did not escape being purged, though he was alleged to have committed suicide. It is widely believed that he was either shot on Hoxha's orders or even shot by Hoxha himself. Hoxha will be remembered, like his idol Stalin, for his bloody crimes, and few tears will be shed at his departure. My only regret is that an assassin's bullet did not end his rule sooner.

20 April 1985

BILLY McLEAN

Patrick Leigh Fermor

Anyone looking him up in a work of reference – 'McLean, Neil Loudon Desmond, DSO; born 1918; Educ. Eton; RMC Sandhurst. Gazetted Royal Scots Greys, 1939 . . . MP (C) Inverness . . . Royal Company of Archers . . . Clubs: White's, Cavalry and Guards, Buck's, Pratt's, Highland, Beefsteak, Shikar . . .' might conclude, and rightly, that the subject was cast in a highly honourable but strictly conventional mould. But soon less predictable hints would appear: 'Married, 1949, to Daşka Maria d. of Dr Ivan Richard Ivanovic, a member of National Assembly of Serbs, Croats and Slovenes, 1918 . . .', and visions of a charming Dalmatian bride – again rightly, for Daşka was known as 'the Pearl of Dubrovnik' – would float across the reader's mind. And, glancing down, what about '. . . the Distinguished Military Medal of Haile Selassie' . . . 'Ethiopia' . . . 'Albania' . . . 'Chinese Turkestan'? The vision becomes less parochial and more complex with every word.

I well remember Bill McLean in autumn 1943, returning to Egypt after being dropped, via Greece, for months in command of the first allied mission to Albania. He arrived with David Smiley, and they immediately became founder-inmates of Dara. (This extraordinary Cairo household of SOE members already consisted of Bill Stanley-Moss, Arnold Breen and me, and the two newcomers were soon followed by Xan Fielding and Rowland St Oswald, and a bit later by Alan Hare. Presided over by the beautiful Sophie Tarnowska, who had escaped from Poland, it was a long-lasting haven after our various descents on the Balkans and it soon became notorious for riotous parties and the eccentric behaviour of the inmates, and, incidentally, a durable bond between them.) The sabres sticking out of the bedrolls the *suffraghis* carried upstairs reminded us that they were still both horsed when the war overtook them in Palestine, McLean in the Greys and Smiley in the Blues, but they had soon abandoned their steeds for parachutes. There were Sudanese weapons as well, and a brace of Abyssinian spears from earlier guerrilla campaigns. For a couple of weeks, struggling with their reports, they wore white Albanian fezzes about the house in lieu of thinking caps. Though they were teased about being handier with the sword than the pen, David, long afterwards, wrote *Albanian Assignment*, a very stirring account which told us all about the adventures and perils and successes of their two extraordinary missions in these ranges, the battles and intrigues and clashes, the emergence of Enver Hoxha, the politics which split the resistance movement and finally put the country into quarantine for 40 years. We learn, too, alas, of similar politics nesting unsuspected in their own HQ in Bari, which made them lucky to get out alive: and, later still, of how post-war plans to rescue Albania were check-mated by the treachery of Philby. I wish Billy had also written his memoirs so that we could learn more of his earlier SOE work in Constantinople, and his share in the Wingate campaign in Ethiopia, where he had led Eritrean, Italian and several Abyssinian irregulars – 'McLean's Foot' – against the Italians near Gondar.

He was 25 when they left those ill-starred Albanian mountains. David Smiley, the best possible source, described Billy at the time: 'a tall, slim, good-looking, blond extrovert with straight fair hair' – he wore it rather long – 'which he had a habit of sweeping back when it fell in his eyes. His charming character seemed languid and nonchalant to the point of idleness, but underneath this façade, he was unusually brave, physically tough and extremely intelligent, with a quick, active and unconventional mind. Great powers of mental and physical endurance equipped him for a guerrilla leader and his natural exuberance and charm made him an ideal companion in hardship and danger. With all the panache attributed in romantic fiction to cavalry officers, he was very attractive to and fond of women, but his attitude seemed to be governed by the principle of safety in numbers.'

This hits him off to a tee. When we all broke up in Cairo, news of Billy, like Waring, would filter back from the Far East from time to time. The post of military adviser to the British Consul in Kashgar was followed, when the war stopped, by mysterious travels in Chinese Turkestan and the Fleming trail across Asia via Sinkiang. China, Persia, and India were his washpot and over the Levant he cast out his shoe. Back in London, in discreet corners of clubland, he would enlarge on Central Asian mores and the various Turkic dialects. When one said, 'Yes, Billy, but what were you *really* up to?', a wide silent smile would bisect his face, anomalously accompanied by an oddly youthful blush.

He was soon happily married to Daşka but far from settled down. Irregular warfare beckoned him, as an observer, to Vietnam and Morocco; then came Parliament, which I can't help feeling he sometimes used, like his clansman and namesake Fitzroy, as a convenience for unorthodox and extra-parliamentary ends: he seemed more active behind the scenes, often with his old Albanian messmate Julian Amery, than in addressing his fellow legislators. There were several causes he had at heart – crucial ones for British interests and for blocking hostile encroachment in remote places – which might have baffled or alarmed his Inverness constituents.

Alongside his flair for guerrilla fighting he had a passion for political complexities, deep-laid schemes and secret enterprises. During his travels in the Levant he had made friends with the Kings of Jordan and Saudi Arabia, and when Nasser landed a force of Egyptians in the North Yemen to unseat the Imam and set up a republic, King Hussein and King Saud, perturbed at the prospect of such a neighbour, asked for his help. He made reconnaissance journeys all over the Yemen desert, sometimes in a jeep or a truck, much of it by camel and, in the mountains, on foot: and the report he took up afterwards saved Britain from following the US in recognising the republic. Next he got in touch with David Smiley, who was moodily shooting grouse in the Lowlands – and, again it is to Smiley's pages (*Arabian Assignment* this time) that we must look for details of the Yemen war. 'As the plane headed south, my thoughts went back to a similar night just 20 years ago, when he and I had sat in an aircraft flying through the darkness about to launch ourselves into a guerrilla war in another unknown country. . . .' Their task was to act as advisers to the Imam, to rally the loyalists round his banner in the Yemen and to lead them in action. There were several years of irregular fighting with Smiley constantly on the spot and McLean flying to and fro between Westminster and those wind-swept bastilles and blazing plains; and when Nasser finally withdrew his forces and the loyalists and republicans reached a compromise peace, much had been achieved. In the Yemen, Billy's name and David's were now deep in myth. Little anyone else knew of these bitter conflicts, least of all his constituents in the heather. . . .

A few weeks ago, beside the fireplace in St James's Street, he looked completely unchanged in all essentials. Like many of his friends, I urged him to put his experiences down on paper, saying that the shades of Buchan and Lawrence would have to look to their laurels. He smiled and said, 'I will, one day.' If only he had!

29 November 1986

MEMORIES OF MONTY

Peter Paterson

There seems always to have been a vogue for the life, career and times of Field-Marshal Montgomery of Alamein, ever since Denis Hamilton first signed him up for *Sunday Times* serialisation twenty-odd years ago and simultaneously invented the Sunday paper review-front. There has also been an occasional vogue for people's experiences of National Service since it, too, came to an end about the same time as the Field-Marshal's ability to sell newspapers was recognised.

Christmas brings the Field-Marshal back to my mind, though not because he ever seemed to lay much stress on it – well, not so far as headquarters staff was concerned. My period of service with him followed his time as post-war Chief of the Imperial General Staff under Clement Attlee and coincided with his translation to a curious post as chief of the military side of the Brussels Treaty, a defensive and, I believe, cultural alliance between Britain, France, Belgium, Holland and Luxembourg. Military headquarters was a château in Fontainebleau – the Château Henri Quatre – but the Field-Marshal preferred to run things from London.

He was therefore provided with a personal aeroplane, an ancient Avro Anson which plied between Northolt and Fontainebleau. At Christmas, if one was fortunate enough to have spent a few days in France, it was used by all ranks to ship cigarettes and whisky back to austerity-ridden Britain. Otherwise, my recollections of life at the Field-Marshal's London base, Dover House in Whitehall – now occupied by the Scottish Office – are of endless games of table tennis occasionally interrupted by a French *capitaine-de-vaisseau* or a Dutch colonel or an English major-general demanding one's valuable shorthand-writing services, either for themselves or for Monty.

Usually the Field-Marshal was uncomfortable dictating his thoughts. One sat in on military conferences to record what everyone said, but his solitary musings on the defence of the West he liked to commit to paper himself, writing often in green ink, and covering sheets of foolscap with his neat, almost schoolboyish hand.

The two things I remember most about Monty were his acquisitiveness and his hypochondria. I have never encountered anyone so terrified of the common cold. At its onset he would sit at the head of the long conference table in his room with a towel over his head and a steaming bowl of Epsom salts beneath his beaky nose.

If that failed to cure it, he would retire to his house in Hampshire, a converted mill where he hoarded such mementoes of his wartime services as his famous headquarters caravans, dispatch riders' motorcycles still packed in grease and clearly never used, and even the surrender documents from the war in Europe. I remember particularly after a visit to the United States, where he told an interviewer that he had just discovered peanut butter and liked it very well, that tons of the stuff started to arrive from various manufacturers. All was stashed away at Isington Mill.

Dover House is reputedly where King Charles I spent his last night before crossing Whitehall to the scaffold, and is supposed to be haunted. I never encountered the ghost, but the place was certainly a prison for the young officers chosen by the Field-Marshal as his aides-de-camp. One poor fellow I remember was called Wickham. He was commissioned into the Warwickshire Regiment, of which the Field-Marshal was Colonel, and was having trouble passing his exams for staff college. Monty brought him to London as an ADC, where he probably imagined he would be able to enjoy the fleshpots. But that wasn't the Field-Marshal's idea, and Wickham had to sit night after night over his books, with the victor of Alamein telephoning from Hampshire every 15 minutes to make sure he was studying.

One evening, Montgomery was changing into his blues when Wickham came galloping into our office with an urgent request for a pair of braces as the Field-Marshal's had broken. A portly old warrant officer immediately removed his army-issue fabric braces and handed them over. The ADC returned with them the next morning: inscribed on them was the legend – 'Thank you for the use of these braces, Montgomery of Alamein'. I began to worry about the Field-Marshal at that point: green ink, writing on braces, holy relics.

Soon afterwards, the Brussels Treaty was superseded by SHAPE – Supreme Headquarters, Allied Powers, Europe – and we moved, lock, stock and barrel, to Paris, Monty having been given the post of DSACEUR, Deputy Supreme Allied Commander, Europe, with Eisenhower as Supreme Commander. Not, I suppose, an arrangement entirely to Montgomery's taste, though I never detected any tension between the affable Ike and the peppery, abrupt Monty during that time. For a National Serviceman, the arrangements were pure Heaven. DSACEUR's staff had a suite of rooms at the old Astoria Hotel in the Champs Elysées, and I was quartered in a *pension* – now, alas, disappeared under a huge block of flats – in the Saint Didier quartier behind the Trocadéro. At the insistence of the French, none of us was permitted to wear military uniform.

Somehow life in Paris left little time for table tennis. At work one saw less and less of the Field-Marshal, who may have regarded his appointment as a prelude to final retirement. Security was tightened up considerably, with everything being ceremonially locked into safes at night – no one seemed to have bothered very much with such palaver at Dover House. To the familiar TOP SECRET we rubber-stamped on documents was added the designation METRIC TOP SECRET, without, to my eye, any significant change in the contents.

What does strike me at this distance was the sheer innocence of the military planners, both in the Brussels Treaty and at SHAPE. No one – not Montgomery or Eisenhower, none of the polyglot hordes of staff officers – ever seemed to conceive Western defence in anything but terms of conventional warfare. It was almost as though the next war was to be a re-run of the last one, with the Russians taking the role of the Germans. There was no talk of nuclear war.

Once my National Service came to an end, I saw the Field-Marshal only once. He was being given the freedom of Hammersmith, and as a local reporter I followed his entourage around the borough. Foolishly, his itinerary included not only a stage appearance at the Odeon on Hammersmith Broadway, but a speech as well, to an audience consisting entirely of children waiting for the next episode in the Saturday morning serial. Monty was clearly nonplussed by their refusal to listen to him on the subject of discipline and responsibility. I rejoiced, as a civilian, at the children's perfectly healthy disrespect, causing me to reflect on a remark attributed to Liddell-Hart – we don't have military dictatorships in Britain because no one of any intelligence is allowed to advance beyond the rank of captain in the British Army.

17 December 1983

JOURNALIST-DICTATOR

Owen Chadwick

MUSSOLINI. *By Denis Mack Smith. (Weidenfeld & Nicolson.)*
This is certainly a brilliant life of Mussolini. It is of the man, not of his time; it is Mussolini, not Mussolini's Italy; and men are not quite intelligible except within their time. But Denis Mack Smith has written elsewhere on several aspects of Fascist Italy. So this life is a portrait of a person, what he did, what was the gossip about him, how he managed and by whom he was managed. The result leaves little virtue in Mussolini. If the reader begins by thinking that Mussolini must have been a man of character in doing what he did for the Italians, at least during his middle years as dictator, that hesitantly friendly opinion will hardly survive the evidence set forth in this book. The piling up of information is so devastating that it amounts almost to the destruction of a personality.

What is more, the portrayal takes on the proportions of an epic tragedy. Here, according to Mack Smith, was a worthless man who found himself by accident at the head of a party and then, by the weakness of politicians, at the head of government. Once in power, and once in control of the Press, the only instrument of state which he understood, he found the way to be a people's idol, and achieved the pinnacle of a nation's admiration as the saviour of his country. To remain perched on the pinnacle he had two absolute disqualifications. First, he must push Italy for-

ward towards risks and gambles and aggressive noises for which neither
the Italian economy nor the Italian tradition could possibly be sufficient.
Secondly, the worthlessness of his character meant that the policy was
never a real policy, but only words for popular consumption. And so he
fell into the clutches of Adolf Hitler, maundered away his last months
near Lake Garda like Napoleon boring his visitors on St Helena, and
when he was murdered was the most hated Italian of the centuries. So
this is the tragedy of a nasty young man who in strange circumstances
became the hero of a nation, could not sustain the role, damaged his
country irretrievably, and at last made the mob, jeering at his body hung
upside down in the square at Milan, almost forgivable.

But the biographer is far too subtle and sensitive to make his portrait
unrelieved. The Mussolini of this book is a man, too combative no doubt,
but with courage. He had a natural resilience which continually sustained his faith after disasters. He was more shrewd than intelligent, but
in politics shrewdness and sense of timing are gifts far more useful than
theoretical analysis. He was a very private person, friendless apart from
his women, and hardly even knew the names of men close about him; but
he could charm visitors, and was full of vitality, and entertained with his
readings and memory like a man who often reads articles in the *Encyclo-
paedia*. For part of the time he refused to take his stipend, and gave away
money to charities. He loved fresh air, and riding, and jogging, and
health. The Press were allowed to take pictures of a half naked dictator
keeping fit.

He failed, according to this portrait, because he cared only for façade.
This was government of the media, by the media, and for the media.
Instead of a philosopher-king, Italy had a journalist-dictator. The one
place where he had proved himself was in the editor's chair of a series of
newspapers. In that light he saw all government. He asked not whether
policies were good but whether they made headlines. He therefore
thought that journalists make the best ministers in a cabinet. His own
first task each day was a prolonged study of yesterday's newspapers, and a
planning of the next day's newspapers, and telephoning editors to
explain what they must do. The head of his private press office saw him
frequently and sometimes appeared at meetings of the cabinet. He once
told an assembly of reporters that they carried a marshal's baton in their
knapsack. For foreign information he relied as much upon private letters
from journalists as upon official letters from ambassadors. He gave
Arnaldo Mussolini, who was a second-rate journalist, a funeral like the
obsequies of some saint or emperor, with crowds kneeling along the railway line as the coffin crossed Northern Italy.

His experience with newspapers left him with a contempt for the human race. He knew that he could say one thing on Tuesday and the opposite on Wednesday, and that few would notice and fewer complain. He underestimated anything that could not be put into a column. If a book was long and boring, like *Mein Kampf*, he knew it to be useless. He preferred to avoid anything, even if it was just, which newspapers would have to print and which would reflect discredit on the regime. Thus he preferred to protect scoundrels if they were Fascist scoundrels. Their iniquities were less important than the damage if they were exposed.

Not slowly he was taken over by the myth which he made. He shut himself up, like a Byzantine in a palace, and surrounded himself only with flatterers. He rid himself of advisers who were independent or critical. Even the ritual of an interview became Byzantine, a running the length of the room to his desk, a running to get out before turning at the door to salute. Interviews ceased to be real exchanges of ideas and became formalities.

But behind the ceremonial mask of this portrait lies someone more sinister. The more civilised of the dictators proves, on inspection by Mack Smith, to be cruel, murderous, protective of murderers, and vindictive. During the last months in the Republic of Salò, while the Allied armies advanced into northern Italy, unofficial Fascist bands murdered ruthlessly and innocent leaders were executed on Mussolini's order. This repellent last phase has sometimes been seen as uncharacteristic of Mussolini, and to be attributed to local domination by SS blackguards. But the Mussolini of Mack Smith's Salò is a natural issue of the early Fascist leader with his pleasure in thugs, and proud exhibitor of castor oil as part of his road to power.

Among the crises of this epic inferno which will particularly interest the reader is the moment of Mussolini's fall after the Allied invasion of Sicily in July 1943. He collapsed like a house of cards, pushed over by a breath. Was that because Fascist power was only a veneer, kept in existence by conjuring tricks? On the two vital days when he had a chance of surviving the challenge, Mussolini behaved so strangely that Mack Smith floats the theory that he wanted to fall. The decisions, perhaps, had become intolerable. He could not resist the Allies yet he could not disengage from the Germans. Ahead he saw no course of action which did not end in a blank wall. Italy had no power left to make war, and yet no power to make peace. Perhaps he had a half-desire to abdicate, and leave the impossible decision to someone else. 'He had once speculated that Julius Caesar knew all about the conspiracy to murder him and subconsciously sought in it a way out of the impasse.'

If this theory has truth – it is put forward only as a might be, but with extraordinary persuasiveness – we suddenly look into a new sort of

Mussolini hardly found elsewhere in this book; troubled behind the façade, putting on the best face, less confident than he looked, and less swollen with bombast. Perhaps this different person was caused only by ill-health, or by drugs, or by the advance of Montgomery. But it may touch also a deeper strand of personality.

There was once a child Mussolini who was punished at a bad boarding school by being put out into the dark courtyard at night, and there prayed in an agony of fear to all the saints. What was it in this man which made Clara Petacci follow to the end, to her own murder, to hang side by side with him, upside down in the square at Milan? She had no need to follow, she had plenty of chances to go away. What was it in him that still captivates the memory of some older Italians, who to this day hardly dare to speak, but remember how before the fatal bondage to Hitler he did some good to Italy, and not only because the trains ran on time? They sensed a discovery of the Italian soul. Old divided Italy was united artificially in the Risorgimento. But still it felt the union to be a patchwork, with all the tensions of provincial loyalties and sundered dialects, so that party strife and class war were mingled with still deeper forces to tear the country apart. The historian may reasonably ask whether Italy felt itself to be truly Italy before 1929.

From this very complex Mussolini we only get faint breaths in this book. I should lay more stress on the Lateran Treaty. Italy could never be Italy until the historic war between Garibaldi and the Pope was laid to rest. The old liberal parties of Italy were committed to an anticlerical policy, less by their desires than by their traditions, less by feeling than by the memory of Mazzini and Cavour. No country governed by that archetypal liberal, Giolitti, could have signed the Lateran Treaty. Mussolini believed himself, and was believed by many Italians to be, the heir of the Risorgimento. Yet he won power, partly by strong arm squads, partly by hitching his star to the cause of fantastic D'Annunzio, but chiefly by realising that the votes which could give him power were the Catholic votes. Therefore he could sign away the Vatican to be an independent State, despite the opposition of King and Fascist squad-leaders and most of the old liberals. The act was as important to the making of modern Italy as Napoleon's reconciliation between the Revolution and the Church was important in the making of modern France. It survived its maker's fall and loss of credit, and was a landmark in the history of Italy.

Of such a heritage, Mack Smith makes an interesting diagnosis about the Sicilian Mafia. The Fascist Press was made to pretend that the Mafia did not exist, its banditry would be discreditable to Italy if disclosed. And yet 'the outward manifestations of the Mafia were dealt with far more effectively by Mussolini than by any liberal government in modern times'. He was able to achieve this because his lack of scruple let him seek allies among criminals in Sicily; because he could imprison without trial, and did not hesitate to throw some 2,000 people into gaol; and still more because he rid himself of elections and juries, and the Mafia flourished especially by threats or bribes among electors or jurymen. But this was an achievement less lasting than the Lateran Treaty because it needed methods intolerable to a civilised government. So the portrait in this book is not all darkness.

But it has to be faced, this was a very absurd man. He had a passion for uniforms, so that ministers needed at least ten different uniforms for different occasions; the preposterous puffing out of his chest and rolling back his lips, like a reach-me-down Tarzan in whom no spectator could believe; the choreography of his assemblies, which he borrowed originally from swashbuckling D'Annunzio, and which was developed into orchestrated cries; the Roman salute, which certainly looked, to those of us who remember seeing it, a very ridiculous mode of greeting; the applause squad, whose job was to go round ensuring that every utterance received an ovation.

This book is not the last word on Mussolini. More archives will be opened and sorted, more witnesses will be found to have recorded, more analysis of foreign relations is already in progress. It is the man and only a part of his time; and therefore there are things in this book which cannot be understood by the reader, and remain a mystery. It is possible that the man-in-his-time is more weighty than the man, and that contemptible clowns are on occasion capable of statesmanlike actions. But whatever reserves we make, this is the most compulsive reading of any book of modern Italian history that I ever remember to have read.

27 February 1982

WAVELL OF CYRENAICA

Peter Fleming

An immense, patient strength – perhaps that is the quality in Lord Wavell which seems, now that he is dead, the most important part of his character. With it went gentleness, and wisdom, and a remarkable humility. His one eye looked quizzically rather than sardonically upon the world, and he retained a certain innocence of spirit, the uprightness – almost – of a small boy who does not yet know that there are alternatives to uprightness. He was shy and reserved, and his reserve was a handicap in public life. He was, for instance, seldom understood and almost always undervalued by Americans, who found it incomprehensible that so legendary a figure should be so little concerned to underwrite the legend with some sort of *panache*; and he could not command that extra impulse of affability or effusiveness which is so useful a lubricant when dealing with Orientals.

Behind his taciturn manner, and the drawl which often held an unnecessary note of diffidence, and that speculative but too easily disinterested eye, there was a vivid apprehension of beauty, a boyish sense of humour and a quiet capacity for enjoying life. Perhaps the nearest approach to self-revelation which he allowed himself was the marginal comments in his anthology, *Other Men's Flowers*; and the man who emerges from these brief but charming asides is very different from the monolithic figure which he was sometimes apt to cut in public. Feeling as well as style came out in some of his orders of the day, and the latent warmth of his personality expressed itself in innumerable unobtrusive acts of kindness. He had, moreover, a sort of sunniness – again somehow recalling, to me at any rate, a little boy – which would break out in off moments. As we all trotted back to breakfast from a long scrambling gallop over the unlovely plains round Delhi, a sound not readily distinguishable from a giggle would emanate from the august figure on the big bay. 'Did I ever tell you,' he would begin, 'about the Russian admiral?' and as he told us the anecdote (which was invariably very funny and revealed him as something of a connoisseur of the ridiculous in human nature), the mask which could look so grim would become full of glee, and one suddenly saw in the bay's rider a sort of eternal youthfulness. He was a very lovable character.

That lift of the heart which his destruction of the Italian armies in the desert gave to the whole Empire is not easy to recapture now; and events soon proved that the battles which he won were not decisive. But that first campaign had about it a style and a mastery which will, I imagine, ensure it an honourable and perhaps a unique place in the annals of modern warfare. It combined the well-timed grace of a drive through the covers with the impudence of a practical joke. It took skill and dash to win it; but – even more – it took immense courage to fight it at all. For when it was launched we did not know as much about the weakness of the huge Italian forces as we soon found out; and Wavell's other commitments in Africa might well have deterred a less tough, aggressive and unimaginative commander from an enterprise of such hazard. Not many men in the war conceived and prepared a project for inflicting major damage on the enemy before it had occurred to Mr Churchill; but the first desert campaign was strategically entirely Wavell's idea.

After that the odds lengthened steadily against him, and his pluck and resource and cunning never again enabled him to convert a predicament into an opportunity. I once asked him, towards the end of the war, if he believed that the diversion of German forces to deal with our intervention in Greece had imposed on Hitler's first headlong drive into Russia the small margin of delay which in the event meant that winter caught the Germans just outside Moscow and enabled the Russians to halt their advance. It was a perfectly arguable theory and has since, I believe, been confirmed from German sources; and it was a theory which, since it showed in so favourable a light the long-term results of a quixotic but disastrous adventure, might have been expected to commend itself to the man who had been responsible for the military, though not the political, side of the affair. Wavell's reply was characteristic: 'I've often wondered about that,' he said. 'I imagine Greece did upset the German programme to a certain extent; these diversions always do. But I don't see how anyone can tell at this stage how much effect it really had. We shall know one day, I expect.' He was extraordinarily fair-minded I doubt if anyone ever knew him to claim even indirectly any credit for himself, except in some trivial context and by way of a joke.

In the British Army the men who hold high command at the outbreak of war, as Wavell did, are seldom responsible for innovations which contribute materially to the final victory. Wavell's shrewd and questing mind evolved one idea which, personified first by a single staff officer of his own choosing, was gradually built up into an off-shoot of the General Staff which, though it always remained numerically small, made in the end a vital and wholly disproportionate contribution to the defeat of Germany. Though the idea behind it is as old as warfare itself, the aims and methods of this curious sideshow are not yet in the 'it can now be revealed' category, and it can only be said that Wavell's imagination forged a weapon for which the British showed a perhaps rather unexpected aptitude, and which is unlikely to be left in the armoury when they go to war again.

At cricket the batsman who goes in first faces fresh bowlers and a new ball; but the bat and the pads with which he is equipped are not inferior to those with which his successors confront the terrors he has diminished. This is one of the fairly numerous respects in which war differs from cricket; and everybody knows that, first against the Italians, then against the Germans, and finally against the Japanese, Wavell bore the

initial brunt with resources which were derisory compared with those
deployed later in the long innings. What few, perhaps, realise is the enormously greater personal strain imposed on a theatre-commander in his
day-to-day life if the theatre is ill-found. The machinery of high command is almost as indispensable to the commander as his box of tricks is
to the conjurer; but unlike the box of tricks it is not something he can
carry about with him. He needs an efficient secretarial staff, a long-
distance telephone equipped with a 'scrambler', established channels for
liaison with his allies, an air-conditioned office if he is in the tropics, a
private aeroplane wherever he may be, and many other things. These are
his tools, these enable him to function and prevent the heavy strain upon
him from being increased by petty delays and frustrations.

Both in the Middle and the Far East Wavell started without them. One
day in 1942 I found myself in a Blenheim bomber, with no guns and no
wireless, manned by an Australian crew on their first operational flight,
flying over Central Burma; the only other non-Japanese aircraft in Burma
at that time was a Moth, based on Lashio and used for dropping mail to
Army Headquarters at Nagungo. With me in the tail of the Blenheim – a
rather gnomelike figure wrapped against the cold in an old blanket – was
General Alexander; and somewhere forward, sitting I think on the co-
pilot's knee, was Wavell. It occurred to me at the time (though perhaps to
neither of my distinguished fellow-passengers) that the unruffled exercise of supreme command under these conditions required a certain
resilience of spirit.

But of course that was what they both had – Wavell less obviously but
not less certainly than Alex. It was that quality, allied to a sort of simple
faith and a sense of duty which was so innate that it could not be said
to ride him, which sustained Wavell in the moments of defeat and the
periods of frustration. When he accepted the Viceroyalty I believe it was
the wrench, the almost physical wrench, of leaving the Service to which
he had given his life that prompted the only reservation in his mind. He
had been overseas for four years already, under continuous strain; and I
doubt if he had taken a week's leave in the time. The task in India was not
really in his line, and he knew it would be a thankless one; but his great,
patient strength was needed and he gave it ungrudgingly.

I doubt if history will much alter the current impression that as a Vice-
roy he was less than great; and history, thanks to his reticence, is unlikely
to record in full the shabby circumstances of his recall. But history will
not overlook his claims as a soldier, and in the memories of his countrymen the impression of his selfless and resourceful integrity will shine for
ever alongside the bright battle honours that he won for us in a dark
hour; while to those who knew him he will always be most dear.

26 May 1950

ORDE WINGATE:
VEX NOT HIS GHOST

Strix (Peter Fleming)

If Orde Wingate had been hanged for murder, and if Mr Leonard Mosley had written a play about him, the Lord Chamberlain would not have granted the play a licence on the grounds that it would be liable to cause pain to Wingate's family. But it is a book, and not a play, that Mr Mosley has written, so he is at liberty to say what he likes about a dead man. Judging by the first instalment of his work, which is being serialised in the *Sunday Express*, he intends to make full use of his freedom.

The blurbs with which the Beaverbrook press heralded the publication of extracts from Mr Mosley's book were sensationally worded and implied that Wingate was, among other things, a traitor. Mr Mosley began his reply to a letter of protest from the Wingate family by suggesting that they 'should surely have waited to read my book before deciding that it "traduces" the memory of their distinguished relative.' It is perhaps academic, in this sort of context, to ask whether it is a decent or even a permissible thing to write a book about a man who was killed at the age of forty-one eleven years ago without consulting his family (who have, incidentally, entrusted to Mr Christopher Sykes the task of writing a definitive biography); but it is certainly a fact that neither Mr Mosley nor the *Sunday Express* would have dared to publish what they have published about Wingate if he had been alive, because if they had he would have obtained, without difficulty, very substantial damages for libel. If you don't traduce a man's memory by suggesting that he was a traitor, how on earth do you traduce it?

'I knew Orde Wingate too well,' Mr Mosley wrote in the *Sunday Express*, 'to sully his name with any falsehood or exaggeration or deviation from the strictest fact.' One gains the impression from the first instalment of his book that it is the shabbiest innuendo rather than the strictest fact from which Mr Mosley is determined not to deviate; but perhaps subsequent extracts will make a less disagreeable impression. He is, however, guilty of one thumping inaccuracy on a point which would seem basic to an appreciation of Wingate's character and achievements. The passage reads as follows:

'Those who know the secrets of his mind and heart [among whom the writer did not apparently think Wingate's widow worth including] know that he died an unhappy and frustrated man.'

This simply is not true. I cannot claim, as Mr Mosley does on what I fancy are somewhat slender grounds, to have known Wingate very well; but I saw a good deal of him between 1942 and 1944, and the only occasion on which he did *not* appear unhappy and frustrated was just before he died.

The advanced headquarters of the 3rd Indian Division were then at Imphal (the rather silly 'cover' designation of 3 Ind. Div. had been given to Wingate's force, which consisted entirely of British, Gurkha and West African troops, with a few Burma Rifles and a handful of Chinese). I spent two days and nights there about a week before Wingate was killed. I was in a rather torpid state, having descended in a glider in some quite irrelevant part of Burma on the first night of the operations, and having had in consequence a long walk home; but I retain a vivid memory of a Wingate very different from the wry, brooding, thwarted figure, with head lowered like a buffalo about to charge, whom I had seen tramping the unappreciative corridors of GHQ in Delhi, or threading the steep, tortuous and disillusioning *hutungs* of Chungking.

His head was still lowered – partly, I always imagined, to conceal the broad scar left on his throat by the attempt at suicide in Cairo; but his face (hawk-like, strong and heraldic in a primitive sort of way, like the face of some legendary bird carved on the prow of a war-canoe) was relaxed and alight. One can hardly say of so astringent a character that he was gay; but he gave the impression of a serenity laced with inner excitement, and he talked freely, with the amplitude of an undergraduate and the learning of a very unusual don, on wide and speculative themes which had nothing to do with the campaign he was directing.

This was then going well. The airborne *coup de main*, brilliant in conception but very hazardous in execution, had succeeded. Calvert's 77 Brigade, who had carried it out, were in the process of establishing at 'White City' a stronghold which embodied and vindicated Wingate's theories about the possibilities of supplying isolated but aggressive land forces by air; these theories, which now seem elementary, were then regarded by many as chimerical and far-fetched. 16 Brigade, under Bernard Fergusson, was – even if legend is true and its commander had to report his location as 'three miles south of the second U in UNSURVEYED' – making steady progress. And 111 Brigade (Lentaigne's) was doing well too. Wingate was playing, and winning, a game for which he had invented the rules, fashioned the pieces and ruled out, on an intractable chunk of enemy-occupied Asia, the far from rigid board. It is small won-

der that, in mid-March of 1944, he gave the impression of having fulfilled himself, of being happy.

The point about Wingate was that he was a very great fighting commander. His posthumous news value (out of which Mr Mosley is certain, and
the Sunday Express likely, to make money) lies in less essential attributes.
Some of them are attributes often associated with greatness. Wingate
was eccentric, outspoken, intolerant, autocratic. His powers of endurance were based on will-power rather than physique. He was scruffy. He
sometimes showed off. He made enemies galore, and never bothered
about making friends. Everything he did he did against the grain, insisting that he knew best and eventually getting his way. He was a fanatical
Zionist and allowed himself (deliberately, not in innocence) to be so compromised in Palestine that he could never have served there again. He
riled almost all his superiors (Churchill, Wavell and Mountbatten were
among the few exceptions), and he often bullied his subordinates. He was
not only a perfectionist (which many good and bad commanders are), but
an artist. He was not only moody, but capable of despair. He was a difficult man.

But he did great deeds, and inspired others to do them too. Mr Mosley
clearly does not share the malice which motivated Mr Aldington's nasty
book about T.E. Lawrence, and goes out of his way to express reverence
for the memory of a man, some aspects of whose life have supplied him
with the raw material for a stunt. But I do not think it is honourable to
denigrate a man, who served his country with distinction, only a decade
after his death. In fact – not to put too fine a point upon it – I think it is a
dirty trick.

18 March 1955

Index